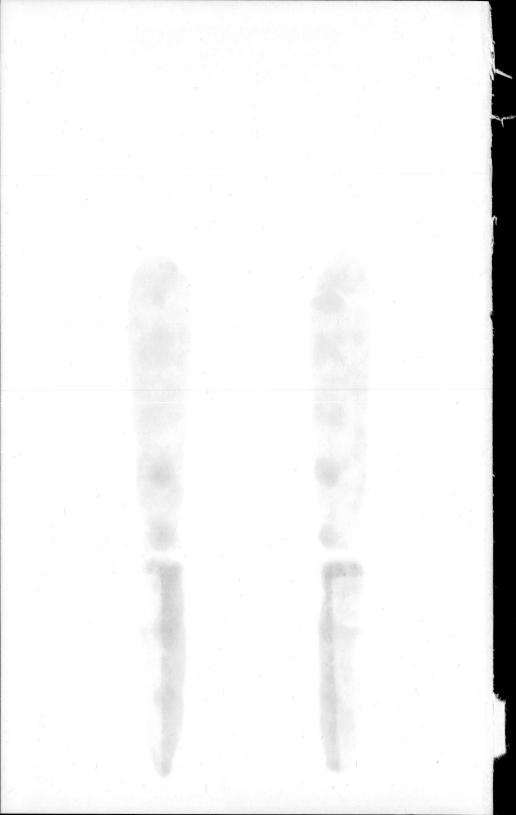

A Diary in America

Captain Frederick Marryat

A Diary in America

With Remarks on Its Institutions

by FREDERICK MARRYAT

EDITED, WITH NOTES

AND AN INTRODUCTION,

BY SYDNEY JACKMAN

GREENWOOD PRESS, PUBLISHERS
WESTPORT, CONNECTICUT

Library of Congress Cataloging in Publication Data

Marryat, Frederick, 1792–1848.
  A diary in America.

    First published in 1839.
    Reprint of the ed. published by Knopf, New York.
    Bibliography: p.
    1. United States—Description and travel—1783–
1848. 2. United States—Social life and customs—
1783–1865. 3. Canada—Description and travel—
1763–1867. I. Jackman, Sydney Wayne, 1925–
ed. II. Title.
  [E165.M373 1973]   917.3'04'5   73–10737
  ISBN 0-8371-7028-1

Originally published in 1962 by Alfred A. Knopf, New York

Reprinted with the permission of Alfred A. Knopf, Inc.

Reprinted in 1973 by Greenwood Press,
a division of Williamhouse-Regency Inc.

Library of Congress Catalogue Card Number 73-10737

ISBN 0-8371-7028-1

Printed in the United States of America

To Paul and Rachel Mellon

Contents

PART II · REMARKS ON ITS INSTITUTIONS

INTRODUCTION

Frederick Marryat in America

According to Samuel Johnson, the traveller "ought to regulate imagination by reality, and instead of thinking how things may be, to see them as they are." In the nineteenth century the European traveller to the New World found that much that he had read and imagined did not exist in actuality. Only one thing was certain: that the American republic with its democratic principles was certainly vastly different from the European monarchies with their aristocratic traditions.

On the third of April 1837 Frederick Marryat boarded the *Quebec* at Portsmouth, England and set sail for New York. To his British contemporaries, Marryat was a popular author of novels and tales of the sea. His books were also widely read—generally in pirated editions —in the United States, and he was heralded on his arrival as a public figure.

Frederick Marryat was almost the beau-ideal Englishman of his time, a combination of such diverse traits as obstinacy, generosity, courage, sensitivity, snobbery, and frankness. He was a rigid Tory who saw in the Reform Bill of 1832 the end of "all that was aristocratical and elegant," but he was not so overwhelmed by his conservatism as to be incapable of protesting against a tradition which he thought unworthy. For example, he wrote against the time-honored use of impressment as a means of recruiting seamen even though the "brass hats" of the day still supported it. One "brass hat" was to have his revenge: William Henry, Duke of Clarence, former Lord High Admiral, never forgave Marryat's opposition, and during his reign as King William IV, he denied Marryat a knighthood.

Marryat was born in 1792, the second son of Joseph and Charlotte Marryat. His mother was a Bostonian, the daughter of Frederic Geyer, a loyalist who lost much of his wealth through his support of the British Crown. Joseph Marryat was a very rich and important man, a senior partner in Marryat, Kaye, Price, and Company, a colonial agent for the islands of Grenada and Trinidad, and a member of Parliament. As a boy, Frederick Marryat was sent to several private schools, where he distinguished himself by his wild and capricious behavior. He was not much of a student, and his fondness for pranks did not endear him to his teachers. His dislike of school was such that he several times attempted, unsuccessfully, to run away. Finally his father, seeing that there was nothing for it but to allow the boy to have his way, obtained a naval appointment for him.

The navy has never been a service for the weak, least of all the nineteenth-century British navy. Perhaps the best description of the service at that time is to be found in Marryat's own works, and in none better than in his first book, *The Naval Officer.* Marryat was appointed to the *Imperieuse*, commanded by the brilliant and erratic Thomas Cochrane, who in the Napoleonic Wars specialized in daring escapades, beginning with the capture, against great odds, of the Spanish frigate *El Gamo.* With his own vessel of fourteen guns and fifty-four men he seized the larger ship, taking 263 prisoners with a loss of only three of his own men. In equally gallant style he later captured the *Minerva* and brought her into Plymouth. These and similar actions gave Cochrane a prodigious reputation for courage and boldness. Under such a captain, with his own youth and vigor, and with a great desire to succeed, Marryat felt that he could not fail. He joined the *Imperieuse* in 1806, and in the following three years under Cochrane had adventures enough for a lifetime. The prolongation of the Napoleonic Wars meant that there were enemy ships to be attacked, batteries to be engaged, and prizes to be won. During these three years his service was chiefly in the Mediterranean, and he continued there for some time, even after Cochrane had left command of the ship. But none of his subsequent captains had quite the glamour of the first.

In 1812 he applied for a commission. He was accepted, with the rank of lieutenant, and was now eligible to command a ship. Henceforth, his career would depend upon survival, good service, and luck.

During the War of 1812 Marryat was assigned to the North American Station where he served under the command of John Taylor in the *Espeigle* and under Lord George Stuart in the *Newcastle*. He participated in the patrols off the eastern coast of the United States. His humdrum activities at this time were a contrast to the adventures under Cochrane. In February 1815 he returned to England on sick leave, and in June he was appointed a commander.

With the conclusion of the War of 1812 and the Napoleonic Wars, life in the services became less exciting and more complicated. Posts were few and promotions were slow. The admiralty placed many officers on half pay and greatly reduced the number of personnel. Marryat himself was without a command for five years. During his enforced idleness he used his father's wealth to the fullest, travelling on the Continent and permitting himself the indulgence of his own personal interests. It was during this period, in the year 1819, that he married Catherine, the daughter of Sir Stephen Shairp. Frederick and Catherine Marryat were to have eleven children, of whom seven were to survive infancy.

It was also during this period that Marryat undertook to improve a particular aspect of naval life: in 1817 he published his *Code of Signals*. Before the introduction of this code, communications between ships were exceedingly difficult. Sir Home Popham had made some improvements, and his system had been used by Nelson at Trafalgar, but the limitation and complexity of Popham's *Telegraphic Signals* made the transmission and reception of messages a difficult affair. Marryat's method was not a semaphore system but an arrangement of flags and pennants set in a series of definite patterns. By means of a jack over a numerical flag, the particular section of the code to be used could be indicated and a set of specific messages relayed. The patterns were simple, readily learned, and relatively inexpensive to install. Marryat's *Code* became very popular and was required for every vessel registered at Lloyd's. Versions in the languages of all European powers soon appeared as well. His ingenuity was given high praise and his name became known throughout the entire maritime world.

In 1820 he was recalled to duty, given command of H.M.S. *Beaver*, and ordered to service off the coast of Africa. In March 1821 he arrived at St. Helena, where Napoleon was then imprisoned. The two men never met; however, some few weeks later, on the morning after the Emperor's death, Marryat, in the company of the governor, Sir Hudson Lowe, and other officers, viewed the body. Marryat made several sketches of the deceased, attended the funeral, completed several more drawings, and then sailed to England with dispatches. He made the return voyage in the *Rosario* and reached Spithead in July. Shortly thereafter he was involved in another notable funeral, that of Caroline of Brunswick, the fantastic and ill-treated wife of George IV. The *Rosario* under Marryat's command was part of the squadron which conveyed the queen's body to Germany. He then returned to serve in the Channel Fleet.

Two years later, in 1823, Marryat took command of H.M.S. *Larne* and was ordered to the East Indies. With the outbreak of the First Burma War in 1824, he joined the great amphibious expedition sent to capture Rangoon. The campaign was successful, the city taken, but the war dragged on. Marryat remained in the theater of operations until late in 1825. For his services he was promoted to the rank of captain and made a Companion of the Bath. He remained in the navy for four more years, his last ship being the *Ariadne,* to which he was appointed in 1829. But his career on the *Ariadne* was not particularly agreeable, and in October 1830 he resigned his command and applied for half pay. He gave as his reason that it was necessary for him to attend to his private estate. He was never again to command a ship.

Though his official career ended at the age of thirty-eight, his real career had only just begun. Before leaving the navy he had already published two novels, *The Naval Officer* (1829) and *The King's Own* (1830), which were immediate successes, and the reception which they received prompted him to begin a new life as a writer. Once out of the navy, he busied himself with his writing, and in 1832 he bought the *Metropolitan Magazine,* assuming the editorship. In this periodical, which catered particularly to readers of nautical literature, he serialized some of his own books, such as *Mr. Midshipman Easy,* and published stories of the same genre by other authors.

Meanwhile he gave some of his time to his recently acquired property at Langham. He enjoyed his role of country gentleman as much as he did his other life as a man about town. In addition, he travelled on the Continent and published accounts of his journeys in his magazine, later employing the material for a book. In 1837 he decided to visit North America to see for himself what the new continent was really like. The numerous accounts of it written by other peripatetic authors varied considerably, ranging from the enthusiastic reports of Fannie Wright, the advocate of women's rights, to Captain Basil Hall's belligerent comments. In fact, each new study of America, instead of clarifying the picture, seemed to confuse it. Marryat gave as his reason for visiting America his desire to see *"what were the effects of a democratic form of government and climate upon a people which, with all its foreign admixture, may be still considered as English."*

He toured the northern part of the United States, travelling as far west as Wisconsin. He also visited the two British colonies of Upper and Lower Canada, so that he could compare the "democratic" citizens in America to the "loyal" subjects of the crown. His tour lasted some eighteen months.

Once back in England he published his *A Diary in America* and then set to work on new novels. These later novels, such as *Poor Jack* (1840), *Joseph Rushbrook* (1842), and *Percival Keene* (1842), were not as successful as his earlier ones, and for a time it seemed as if the popularity he had once known was now forever lost. He acquired a new following, however, by writing books for children. His first, *Masterman Ready* (1841), was in the tradition and style of *Swiss Family Robinson,* and his best work in this genre was the thoroughly delightful *Children of the New Forest.*

Marryat's last years were not easy. Although he had inherited a sizable fortune from his father, and had made considerable sums of money from his writings, his extravagance and general improvidence had kept him poor. He retired to live at Langham and here attempted to farm but with scant success.

His death in 1848 was scarcely noticed. The heroes of the Napoleonic era had given way to the new heroes of the Victorian age. Other authors such as Dickens and Thackeray had achieved the popularity which had once been Marryat's. In the course of time, however, Marryat's writings gained a new public and his works were reissued. Marryat's literary reputation improved, and some of his works have come to be regarded as minor classics. Joseph Conrad wrote of him:

> He is the enslaver of youth, not by the literary artifices of presentation, but by the natural glamour of his own temperament. . . . To the artist his work is interesting as a completely successful expression of an unartistic nature. . . . There is an air of fable about it. Its loss

would be irreparable, like the curtailment of national story or the loss of a historical document. It is the beginning and the embodiment of an inspiring tradition. . . . His adventures are enthralling; the rapidity of his action fascinates, his method is crude, his sentimentality, obviously incidental, is often factitious. His greatness is undeniable.

It is undeniable. . . . He has created a priceless legend. . . . the tradition of the great past he has fixed in his pages will be cherished for ever as the guarantee of the future. He loved his country first, the Service next, the sea perhaps not at all. But the sea loved him without reserve. It gave him his professional distinction and his author's fame—a fame such as not often falls to the lot of the true artist.

Marryat's intention to visit America had been made clear in his *Diary of a Blasé* (1836), which concluded with the following:

Do the faults of this people (to wit, the Swiss) arise from the peculiarity of their constitutions, or from the nature of their government? To ascertain this, one must compare them with those who live under similiar institutions. I must go to America—that's decided.

Although the motive for his voyage was primarily an intellectual one, to make a study of comparative government, and of the effects of democracy on a people, there were also other and more personal reasons behind the trip. The most obvious was simple curiosity; another, the need for new material for his writings, for travel literature was both popular and lucrative. Then, too, he had sold the *Metropolitan Magazine* in October 1836; he had, therefore, no immediate editorial demands. Moreover, possibly he hoped, through a visit to Washington, to be able to influence Congress to enact a good copyright law, the lack of which was robbing Marryat and other English authors of well-earned royalties. Finally, and perhaps this might have been *the* reason, Marryat's domestic life was becoming increasingly

disagreeable. He and his wife were not compatible, and a
trip abroad for an extended period might well be a solution for them both.

Marryat arrived in New York in the late spring of
1837. His first reception was a favorable one, and he was
greeted in the press as "Marryat a Boston Boy," an allusion
to his mother's birthplace and his American connections.
He was well received in New York society, dining with the
best people and capitalizing upon his reputation. He declared that he was here simply as a tourist, but no one
was deceived. Everyone recognized that he had come to
collect copy. In general it may be said that the Americans
were not opposed to authors' writing about them and that
they welcomed comment. But the comment had to be "fair,"
and "fair" comment meant favorable comment.

At the start of his tour he was agreeably impressed by
what he saw of the United States. Philip Hone, sometime
mayor of New York, noted in his journal after meeting
Marryat at dinner that "He seems very pleased with the
little he has seen of this country, and is very desirous to see
more. . . ," and in a letter to his mother in England,
Marryat wrote:

> The more I see of America the more I feel the neces-
> sity of either saying nothing about it, or seeing the
> whole of it properly. Indeed I am now in that situation
> that I cannot do otherwise. It is expected by the Ameri-
> cans, and will also be by the English; and if I do not,
> they will think I shrink from the task because it is too
> difficult, which it really is. All that I have yet read about
> America written by English travellers is absurd, es-
> pecially Miss M[artineau]'s work. The old woman was
> blind as well as deaf. I only mean to publish in the form
> of a diary (but that is the best way); but I will not pub-
> lish until I have seen all, and can be sure I have not
> been led into error like others. It is a wonderful country
> and not understood by the English now; . . . they are
> very much afraid of me here, although they are very
> civil; but I do not wonder at it—they have been treated

with great ingratitude. I at least shall do them justice, without praising them more than they deserve. No traveller has yet examined them with the eye of a philosopher, but with all the prejudices of little minds.

From this letter it is obvious that Marryat, himself that philosopher, felt capable of doing justice to the Americans and of writing the definitive book on the people and their country. To gather his material he toured the country and noted things that interested him and seemed significant. His original intention had been to tour the whole of the United States, but because of the growing tension between the United States and Great Britain arising from the consequences of the rebellion in the Canadas, he was not able to carry out his plans. He never visited the deep south, where he might have found an uncorrupted gentry and a way of life more in harmony with his own. Although he did not travel as extensively as he had hoped, he did manage to cover a good deal of ground. He went from New York to Boston, back to New York, and then

> up the Hudson, crossed to Saratoga, Trenton Falls, Falls of the Mowhawk [*sic*], Oswego River to Lake Ontario; then to Niagara, Buffalo, and Lake Erie—to Detroit; from Detroit to Lake St. Clair, and from Lake Huron to Mackinaw, from Mackinaw took a bark canoe and crossed the Huron, went up the River St. Clair to Sault St. Marie and from thence to Lake Superior . . . then for Canada, passing by Buffalo and Niagara to Toronto . . . from there to Montreal and to New York.

After wintering in New York, with excursions to Philadelphia and Washington, he set out anew, going to Canada, then to Mackinaw, to the Wisconsin territory, from there down the Mississippi to St. Louis, then up the Ohio River to Louisville and Cincinnati. Finally, after a brief stop at Virginia Springs he returned to Cincinnati. The tour concluded with a visit to Lexington, Kentucky which gave him the feeling of having come into contact with the south. He departed from New York at the end of November.

Marryat's fame, his initial enthusiasm, and his discretion made it possible for him to be on cordial terms with his hosts, and he probably would have been able to depart from the country without arousing hostility had he not quite unintentionally fallen afoul of popular opinion. In late 1837 a rebellion had broken out in Upper and Lower Canada—now Ontario and Quebec—and the Americans had been sympathetic to the cause of the insurgents. A group of the latter had fled from Upper Canada and had taken refuge on Navy Island in the Niagara River, where they had set up a revolutionary government. American sympathizers had assisted them and permitted them to use American soil as a supply base. The loyalists of Upper Canada, determined to end the rebellion, and with the active, if not official, support of the governor, Sir Francis Head, crossed the river to the American shore and there destroyed the vessel, the *Caroline,* thus making it impossible for further resistance to continue on Navy Island. The hue and cry which followed this invasion was deafening, and wild stories of massacres and atrocities were published all over the country. The simple destruction of a supply vessel, the *Caroline,* became an international incident. The *Caroline,* so reports had it, was boarded, the American seamen murdered, and the vessel set afire and sent over Niagara Falls. This was not true, but it made a good story. Marryat happened to be visiting Toronto on St. George's Day when a testimonial dinner was given for the "heroes" who had destroyed the *Caroline.* He attended the banquet and proposed a toast "To Captain Drew and his brave comrades, who cut out the *Caroline.*" Reports of this dinner and of Marryat's toast reached the United States, and at once whatever good feelings the Americans had toward the Captain evaporated completely. As the New York *Daily Express* put it:

> This gross insult—for so it must be considered, gratuitously thrown out as it was—to a country whose hospitality has been so freely and universally extended to

him, from whose admiration of his productions he has reaped a harvest of profit and praise, and which has manifested towards him no feelings but those of respect and kindness—must separate the perpetrator, at once and forever, from the esteem and good will of its citizens. They will learn a lesson . . . from those frequent proofs that the favors lavished on English tourists . . . are repaid by the selfish ingrates with abuse, misrepresentation and insult.

Similar remarks, some rather more scurrilous, were printed about him all over the country. His books were burned; so was he—in effigy—and he was threatened with horsewhipping or worse should he dare return.

Even after the event was no longer news, Marryat was pestered with many unpleasant letters, and finally undertook to write a reply. In a letter to the editor of the *Louisville Journal*, he declared that he was not a spy and that he had no intention of writing of the Americans in a way which would hold them up to ridicule. He said that he "came with the best feelings . . . and did anticipate (as he was not unknown) . . . that these feelings would have been reciprocated." He asked only to be allowed to report truthfully the things that he had seen and heard and, further, asked the Americans not to assume an offence against themselves until it was actually given. This caveat did not gain him much, and unpleasant letters continued to plague him.

While the initial rebellions in the Canadas against British authority had been suppressed, the general outlook did not vastly improve. As war fever spread in America, Marryat decided to cut short his trip and return to England. It was his intention, should an Anglo-American war occur, to apply for a naval command. He felt that his general experience, plus the knowledge he had gained of America and the Americans, would be such that the admiralty would welcome his services. Therefore he boarded a packet and was home by the end of the year 1838.

A Diary in America appeared in June 1839. Obviously he had been writing it during his entire stay, for he offered the completed work to an American publisher before he departed from the New World. The book was issued in three volumes, with three supplementary volumes appearing later in the year. It was presented as a diary of his travels, with an appended series of essays or "remarks" on the American scene.

The diary is a travelogue. Marryat was a great stickler for detail in his novels, and he carried this precision into his journal. His keen eye and acute ear made it possible for him to record faithfully much that he saw. Unfortunately, this fidelity was often marred by superficial generalizations based on the flimsiest of evidence. But his descriptions of the country, the people, and the events are both lively and accurate. Consider his picture of the Fourth of July in New York:

> Martial music sounded from a dozen quarters at once; and as you turned your head, you tacked to the first bars of a march from one band, the concluding bars of Yankee Doodle from another. . . . The officers in their regimental dresses and long white feathers, generals and aides-de-camp, colonels, commandants, majors all galloping up and down in front of the line,—white horses and long tails appearing the most fashionable and correct. . . . I recognized many of my literary friends turned into generals, and flourishing their swords instead of their pens. The scene was very animating; the shipping at the wharfs were loaded with star-spangled banners; steamers paddling in every direction, were covered with flags; the whole beautiful Sound was alive with boats and sailing vessels, all flaunting with pennants and streamers.

The 1830's were still much under the influence of the romantic movement and there was great interest in the picturesque; Marryat reflected this interest in his many descriptions of rivers, waterfalls, and lakes. His notes on the Indians demonstrate similar influences. In his diary he devotes nearly ten per cent of the text to comments on Indians, saying nothing very novel, but no book on North America was complete without some remarks on the "red man."

On reading the book casually, the reader may have some difficulty in tracing the itinerary of Marryat's American tour. The published version of the tour has obviously omitted a certain amount of material; for example, early in the diary there is a discussion of Boston, followed by remarks on Passaic Falls in New Jersey, but there is no mention anywhere of the journey from Boston to New Jersey. It would perhaps appear that he moved continually from one place to another, but this is not so. He passed the month of January 1838 in New York, following his trip to Burlington. It is evident, therefore, that the Captain had no intention of presenting a day-to-day account of his trip but rather a free-form journal that drew attention to the events and places that most appealed to him.

The other part of the book, "Remarks on Its Institutions," is a series of interpretive essays on American life. They deal with a variety of topics and are, perhaps, more interesting than the journal itself; here Marryat's literary abilities are allowed a wider scope, and his essays on language, climate, religion, slavery, food, government, and the like demonstrate, as Virginia Woolf has said, that he was a "sound craftsman, not marvellously but sufficiently endowed at his work. . . . that he could use language with the suggestiveness of a poet; . . . [with] that verbal sensibility which at the touch of a congenial thought lets fly a rocket." His world was "drawn vigourously, decisively, from the living face, just as the Captain's pen, we are told, used to dash off caricatures upon a sheet of notepaper."

Because Marryat was the victim of the press, one can scarcely blame him for being censorious when he writes of the newspapers and of their influence in American life. The New York papers—with the exception of the *Herald*— are generally approved, but he finds the provincial papers almost universally bad. The most notable exception, and in his opinion the best paper in the entire country, was the

Louisville Journal. Obviously the editor of this newspaper had not joined in the attacks on Marryat.

When it came to reporting on American political institutions, the ostensible reason for his having made the trip, all of Marryat's latent Toryism came to the fore. He felt that the American government, since the election of Jackson in 1828, had become too democratic and had consequently declined. Little or nothing was left of the aristocratic society which the Federalists had bequeathed the country. Only the mob remained. Andrew Jackson and his friends had "destroyed the moral courage of the American people, and without moral courage what chance is there of any fixed standards of morality?" Courage and industry the Americans had, but these endowments were valueless when associated with bad government. A bad government set the example, and everyone and everything followed its example, with ruin the inevitable result. These strictures on the American government were very much in keeping with Marryat's views before his visit. In 1835 he had written to his friend Lady Blessington, apropos of England:

> Surely we are extremely altered by this Reform. [The liberalizing of the franchise and the alteration of parliamentary representation in the Reform Bill of 1832.] Our House of Lords was the *beau ideal* [Marryat's italics] of all that was aristocratical and elegant. Now we have language that would disgrace the hustings. In the House of Commons it is the same, or even worse. The gentleman's repartee, the quiet sarcasm, the playful hit, where are they? all gone; and, in exchange for them, we have —you lie, and you lie. This is very bad, and it appears to me, strongly smacking of revolution; for if the language of the lower classes is to take the precedence, will not they also do the same?

Marryat was convinced that egalitarianism was evil, that the best government was that of a benevolent aristocracy destined to govern, so that mob rule should not turn liberty into licence. He looked upon society as being not unlike a naval vessel: the officers were the ruling class, the seamen were the people. Each had its station and each had its duties. A mixing or mingling of these elements did not sail the ship better. America's future—political, social, moral—was in grave danger unless a conservative aristocracy were to arise and take power.

Marryat had declared: "All that I have yet read about America written by English travellers is absurd . . ."; consequently much that he wrote was written particularly to refute the statements made by other travellers. Far and away the greatest number of these statements were directed against Harriet Martineau, who shortly before had visited the United States and had published two books on her travels. Harriet Martineau was a bluestocking; she believed in female emancipation; she was deaf, lame, and decidedly not pretty; in short, she was not Marryat's sort of woman. Moreover, her political views were diametrically opposed to his. It is not, perhaps, strange that he criticized her so unmercifully. Not only does he go to some length to demonstrate her lack of perception, but he also accuses her of telling falsehoods. Harriet Martineau certainly made errors of fact and wrote a number of things which hurt the feelings of her hosts, but to say, as Marryat would have us believe, that she was intentionally lying and malicious is unjust.

Marryat himself did not hesitate to quote other authors out of context in order to support his own contentions. Such writers as Basil Hall, the British naval officer who wrote many popular travel books, Thomas Chandler Haliburton, the humorist whose *Sam Slick the Clockmaker* was then very popular, Henry Charles Carey, the Philadelphia publisher and economist, James Fenimore Cooper, Alexis de Tocqueville, and others of less significance are all used to supply material for Marryat's book.

What was the reaction to *A Diary in America* when it appeared in 1839? Americans on the whole were irritated. George Templeton Strong's views might be considered as typical:

Mrs. Trollope can't hold a candle to the captain in fertility of invention. I never read such a farrago of lies.
He don't lie like a gentleman, either (literary lies being
gentlemanly by usage, when genteely done), but ram-
pages in his mendacity like any loafer.

But American criticism did not much concern the jaunty
author. He had expected as much, and the book was not
written for them anyway. Indeed, considering everything,
Marryat was remarkably restrained in his remarks. But the
book's reception in England also was not entirely favorable.
His publishers had paid him £1,600 for the manuscript, but
a large sale did not follow.

The critics on both sides of the Atlantic were mixed in
their opinions. In America, for example, neither *Godey's* nor
the *Ladies Companion* found any merits in the book while,
on the other hand, the *New York Review* said:

> We like the general spirit of the work . . . He is a
> shrewd observer . . . and beneath his jocose and fan-
> tastic style, random and exuberant as it is, you have
> sometimes an almost accidental dash of philosophy, of
> keen observation and just reflection, . . . perhaps the
> greatest merit of the book is that it is very entertain-
> ing, . . . [there are] a great many personal adventures
> related in a jovial and good natured style, and con-
> taining apt and vigorous illustrations of his graver
> matter, . . .

In Ireland the *Dublin Review* was unfavorably impressed
and concluded its general comments with: "There is nothing very remarkable—nothing in short removed from su-
perficiality—in Captain Marryat's . . . essays." The
Edinburgh Review, a Whig organ, was most scathing in its
review—possibly inspired by Harriet Martineau. It irritably
declared that Marryat preferred "invention to description,"
that the work was "poor and tawdry . . . intemperate and
capricious . . . pretensions to philosophical superiority
over former publications on the United States, . . . abso-

lutely ludicrous." The *Quarterly*, that noble trumpet of Toryism, stood loyally by him, declaring the book a captial one;
it found the essays, "which we must recommend to the
deliberate attentions of our readers," perceptive, and cul-
minated its review by stating that Marryat was worthy of
comparison with De Tocqueville.

It is obvious that the book was not the great authoritative work that Marryat had hoped to write. His intention
of ascertaining the effects of a democratic government on
good English stock was never really carried out, nor did he
prove that democracy really weakens the fibre of a society.
And it is to be doubted if he really added much to the cause
of conservatism for which he declared he had written the
book.

In preparing this edition of *A Diary in America with
Remarks on Its Institutions* I have used both the first and
second series. Although the two series were published
some six months apart, they are both portions of the same
work. In the original editions Marryat included many long
quotations from various authors, which often added little
of real value to the text. Some of these quotations I have
shortened considerably and some I have omitted entirely.
Further, there were also a number of speeches by American statesmen, newspaper accounts of events of the time,
and statistical tables which were included by Marryat to
give verisimilitude to his text. Many of these quotations are
available elsewhere, more accurately transcribed, and they
add little that is essential to the meaning of the material;
these have been excluded. From the travel journal itself
almost nothing has been excised except a few of Marryat's
footnotes; some of the "Remarks" have been omitted because
they have little interest to the modern reader. They repeat
in more detail statements and ideas already described; they
consist in a large measure of long quotations from other
authors and present material that has neither great factual
importance nor period charm. I have also omitted a long
section on Canada in the "Remarks" and have excluded, for

obvious reasons, the text of the Constitution. I have re-chaptered the travel journal and given chapter titles; Marryat provided none at all. In addition, I have re-titled some of the "Remarks" to make their context somewhat clearer. Also, Marryat's often inconsistent and sometimes whimsical spelling has, for the most part, been modernized.

In spite of the fact that Marryat's work did not receive the acclaim that he had hoped for it, the book deserves to be rescued from oblivion. Its author's talents and abilities as a writer caused him to rise above his own personal preoccupations and biases to describe the country fairly. His vignettes of the American scene have a vitality which few contemporary authors were able to achieve. He has left us a vivid portrait of a semi-rural America, before the Civil War and the industrial revolution destroyed it— an America that has changed greatly over the years, but which we still recognize today, through Marryat's eyes.

Acknowledgments

IN PREPARING THIS EDITION of Frederick Marryat's *A Diary in America with Remarks on Its Institutions* I should like to express my thanks to the following: to Mr. Oliver Warner for permission to quote from his *Captain Marryat, a Rediscovery* (London: Constable and Co.; 1953); to Mr. Tatton Anfield for providing facilities to do much of the initial editorial work; to Dr. Willard Ireland and his associates of the Provincial Government Library in Victoria, British Columbia; to Miss Alice H. Bonnell of the Columbiana Library of Columbia University, New York; to Mr. P. R. Franton of the British Museum; to Miss Iva Foster and her associates of the Coram Library, Bates College, Lewiston, Maine; to Messrs. Edward C. Smith, Edward R. Scott, David Redding, and David L. Williams for their helpful advice and criticism; to Messrs. Henry Robbins and Patrick Gregory of Alfred A. Knopf, Inc., for their generous assistance and guidance in the preparation of the manuscript as a whole and of the introduction in particular; to Mr. Walter M. Whitehill, Director of the Boston Athenaeum, for his enthusiastic support of the project and for many kindnesses during the preparation of the manuscript; to Miss Judy Hollenbach for clerical assistance. In addition I should like to express very particular thanks to Dr. Ernest P. Muller, without whose assistance I should never have been able to do this edition of Marryat. Dr. Muller interrupted his own work to give me the benefit of his knowledge of Marryat's period whenever I sought him out. Further, Dr. Muller most generously permitted me to use his excellent collection of early nineteenth-century Americana, which was essential for the preparation of the notes.

S. W. J.

Victoria, British Columbia, Canada
Lewiston, Maine

PART ONE

A Diary in America

A KEY TO THE NOTES OF THIS EDITION

* Footnotes by Frederick Marryat in the original edition of *A Diary in America with Remarks on Its Institutions*.

¹ Numbered footnotes are by the present editor.

PART ONE

A Diary in America

A KEY TO THE NOTES OF THIS EDITION

* Footnotes by Frederick Marryat in the original edition of *A Diary in America with Remarks on Its Institutions.*

¹ Numbered footnotes are by the present editor.

Introduction

After many years of travel, during which I had seen men under almost every variety of government, religion, and climate, I looked round to discover if there were not still new combinations under which human nature was to be investigated. I had traversed the old country until satisfied, if not satiated; and I had sailed many a weary thousand miles from west to east, and from north to south, until people, manners, and customs were looked upon by me with indifference.

The press was constantly pouring out works upon the new world, so contradictory to each other, and pronounced so unjust by the Americans, that my curiosity was excited. It appeared strange to me that travellers whose works showed evident marks of talent should view the same people through such very different mediums, and that their gleanings should, generally speaking, be of such meagre materials. Was there so little to be remarked about America, its government, its institutions, and the effect which these had upon the people, that the pages of so many writers upon that country should be filled up with how Americans dined or drank wine, and what description of spoons and forks were used at table? Either the Americans remained purely and unchangedly English, as when they left their fatherland; or the question required more investigation and deeper research than travellers in their hasty movements have been able to bestow upon it. Whether I should be capable of throwing any new light upon the subject, I knew not, but at all events I made up my mind that I would visit the country and judge for myself.

On my first arrival I perceived little difference between the city of New York and one of our principal pro-

vincial towns; and, for its people, not half so much as between the people of Devonshire or Cornwall and those of
Middlesex. I had been two or three weeks in that city, and I
said: There is certainly not much to write about, nor much
more than what has already been so continually repeated.
No wonder that those who preceded me have indulged in
puerilities to swell out their books. But in a short time I
altered my opinion: even at New York, the English appearance of the people gradually wore away; my perception of
character became more keen, my observance consequently
more nice and close, and I found that there was a great deal
to reflect upon and investigate, and that America and the
American people were indeed an enigma; and I was no
longer surprised at the incongruities which were to be de-
tected in those works which had attempted to describe the
country. I do not assert that I shall myself succeed, when
so many have failed, but at any rate, this I am certain of,
my remarks will be based upon a more sure foundation—an
analysis of human nature.

There are many causes why those who have written
upon America have fallen into error: they have represented the Americans as a nation; now they are not yet,
nor will they for many years be, in the true sense of the
word, a nation. They are a mass of many people cemented
together to a certain degree, by a general form of government; but they are in a state of transition, and (what may
at first appear strange) no amalgamation has as yet taken
place: the puritan of the east, the Dutch descent of the
middle states, the cavalier of the south, are nearly as
marked and distinct now as at the first occupation of the
country, softened down indeed, but still distinct. Not only
are the populations of the various states distinct, but even
those of the cities; and it is hardly possible to make a remark which may be considered as general to a country,
where the varieties of soil and of climate are so extensive.
Even on that point upon which you might most safely
venture to generalize, namely, the effect of a democratical
form of government upon the mass, your observations must

be taken with some exceptions, arising from the climate, manners, and customs, and the means of livelihood, so differing in this extended country.

Indeed the habit in which travellers indulge of repeating facts which have taken place, as having taken place in America, has, perhaps unintentionally on their part, very much misled the English reader. It would hardly be considered fair if the wilder parts of Ireland, and the disgraceful acts which are committed there, were represented as characteristic of England, or the British empire; yet between London and Connaught there is less difference than between the most civilized and intellectual portion of America, such as Boston and Philadelphia, and the wild regions and wilder inhabitants of the west of the Mississippi, and Arkansas, where reckless beings compose a scattered population, residing too far for the law to reach, or where, if it could reach, the power of the government would prove much too weak to enforce obedience to it. To do justice to all parties, America should be examined and portrayed piecemeal, every state separately, for every state is different, running down the scale from refinement to a state of barbarism almost unprecedented, but each presenting matter for investigation and research, and curious examples of cause and effect.

Many of those who have preceded me have not been able to devote sufficient time to their object, and therefore have failed. If you have passed through a strange country, totally differing in manners, and customs, and language from your own, you may give your readers some idea of the contrast, and the impressions made upon you by what you saw, even if you have travelled in haste or sojourned there but a few days; but when the similarity in manners, customs, and language is so great that you may imagine yourself to be in your own country, it requires more research, a greater degree of acumen, and a fuller investigation of cause and effect than can be given in a few months of rapid motion. Moreover English travellers have apparently been more active in examining the interior of houses than the

public path from which they should have drawn their conclusions; they have searched with the curiosity of a woman,
instead of examining and surveying with the eye of a
philosopher. Following up this wrong track has been the occasion of much indiscretion and injustice on their parts,
and of justifiably indignant feeling on the part of the
Americans. By many of the writers on America, the little
discrepancies, the mere trifles of custom have been dwelt
upon, with a sarcastic, ill-natured severity to give their
works that semblance of pith, in which, in reality, they
were miserably deficient; and they violated the rights of
hospitality that they might increase their interest as
authors.

The Americans are often themselves the cause of their
being misrepresented; there is no country perhaps in which
the habit of deceiving for amusement, or what is termed
hoaxing, is so common. Indeed this and the hyperbole constitute the major part of American humour. If they have
the slightest suspicion that a foreigner is about to write a
book, nothing appears to give them so much pleasure as to
try to mislead him; this has constantly been practised upon
me, and for all I know, they may in some instances have
been successful; if they have, all I can say of the story is
that *"se non e vero, e si ben trovato,"* that it might have
happened.

When I was at Boston, a gentleman of my acquaintance brought me Miss Martineau's work,[1] and was excessively delighted when he pointed out to me two pages of
fallacies, which he had told her with a grave face, and
which she had duly recorded and printed. This practice,
added to another, that of attempting to conceal (for the

---

[1] Harriet Martineau (1802–76),
English author. A liberal, a utili-
tarian, and a militant abolition-
ist, she was Marryat's bête-noir.
She made a trip to the United
States in 1834 and from her
travels produced two books, *So-
ciety in America* (1837) and
Retrospect of Western Travel
(1838). For the best study of
Harriet Martineau see R. K.
Webb, *Harriet Martineau: a
Radical Victorian* (New York:
Columbia University Press;
1960).

Americans are aware of many of their defects), has been
with me productive of good results: it has led me to much
close investigation, and has made me very cautious in asserting what has not been proved to my own satisfaction to
be worthy of credibility.

Another difficulty and cause of misrepresentation is,
that travellers are not aware of the jealousy existing between the inhabitants of the different states and cities. The
eastern states pronounce the southerners to be choleric,
reckless, regardless of law, and indifferent as to religion;
while the southerners designate the eastern states as a
nursery of over-reaching pedlars, selling clocks and wooden
nutmegs. This running into extremes is produced from the
clashing of their interests as producers and manufacturers.
Again, Boston turns up her erudite nose at New York; Philadelphia, in her pride, looks down upon both New York and
Boston; while New York, chinking her dollars, swears the
Bostonians are a parcel of puritanical prigs, and the Philadelphians a would-be aristocracy. A western man from Kentucky, when at Tremont House in Boston, begged me particularly not to pay attention to what they said of his state in
that quarter. Both a Virginian and Tennessean, when I
was at New York, did the same.

At Boston, I was drinking champagne at a supper.
"Are you drinking champagne?" said a young Bostonian.
"That's New York—take claret; or, if you will drink champagne, pour it into a *green* glass, and they will think it
hock; champagne's not right." How we are to distinguish between right and wrong in this queer world? At New York,
they do drink a great deal of champagne; it is the small beer
of the dinner-table. Champagne becomes associated with
New York, and therefore is not *right*. I will do the New
Yorkers the justice to say that, as far as *drinks* are concerned, they are above prejudice: all's right with them,
provided there is enough of it.

The above remarks will testify that travellers in America have great difficulties to contend with, and that their
channels of information have been chiefly those of the

drawing-room or dinner-table. Had I worked through the same, I should have found them very difficult of access; for the Americans had determined that they would no longer extend their hospitality to those who returned it with ingratitude—nor can they be blamed. Let us reverse the case. Were not the doors of many houses in England shut against an American author when, from his want of knowledge of conventional *usage,* he published what never should have appeared in print? And should another return to England, after his tetchy, absurd remarks upon the English, is there much chance of his receiving a kind welcome? Most assuredly not; both these authors will be received with caution. The Americans, therefore, are not only not to blame, but would prove themselves very deficient in a proper respect for themselves, if they again admitted into their domestic circles those who eventually requited them with abuse.

Admitting this, of course I have no feelings of ill-will towards them for any want of hospitality towards me; on the contrary, I was pleased with the neglect, as it left me free, and unshackled from any real or fancied claims which the Americans might have made upon me on that score. Indeed, I had not been three weeks in the country before I decided upon accepting no more invitations, even charily as they were made. I found that, although invited, my presence was a restraint upon the company; everyone appeared afraid to speak; and when anything ludicrous occurred, the cry would be— "Oh, now, Captain Marryat, don't put that into your book." More than once, when I happened to be in large parties, a question such as follows would be put to me by some "free and enlightened individual": "Now, Captain M., I ask you before this company, and I trust you will give me a categorical answer, Are you or are you not about to write a book upon this country?" I hardly need observe to the English reader that, under such circumstances, the restraint became mutual; I declined all further invitations, and adhered to this determination, as far as I could without cause of offence, during my whole tour through the United States.

But if I admit that, after the usage which they had received, the Americans are justified in not again tendering their hospitality to the English, I cannot, at the same time, but express my opinion as to their conduct towards me personally. They had no right to insult and annoy me in the manner they did, from nearly one end of the Union to the other, either because my predecessors had expressed an unfavourable opinion of them before my arrival or because they expected that I would do the same upon my return to my own country. I remark upon this conduct, not from any feeling of ill-will or desire of retaliation, but to compel the Americans to admit that I am under no obligations to them; that I received from them much more of insult and outrage than of kindness; and, consequently, that the charge of ingratitude cannot be laid to my door, however offensive to them some of the remarks in this work may happen to be.

And here I must observe that the Americans can no longer anticipate lenity from the English traveller, as latterly they have so deeply committed themselves. Once, indeed, they could say: "We admit and are hospitable to the English, who, as soon as they leave our country, turn round, and abuse and revile us. We have our faults, it is true; but such conduct on their part is not kind or generous." But they can say this no longer; they have retaliated, and in *their* attacks they have been regardless of justice. The three last works upon the Americans, written by English authors, were, on the whole, favourable to them; Mr. Power's [2] and Mr. Grund's [3] most decidedly so; and Miss Martineau's,

---

[2] Tyrone Power (1797–1841), Irish actor specializing in comic parts, appeared first in London in 1821 and by 1827 was the leading Irish comedian at Drury Lane. He visited America on tour between 1833 and 1835 and wrote of his experiences and impressions in his book, *Impres-* *sions of America,* which was published in 1836. Power made another tour of the United States but was drowned when his ship, the *President,* was sunk on her way to England.

[3] Marryat is incorrect here. Francis J. Grund (1805–63) was *not* an Englishman but a German

filled as it is with absurdities and fallacies, was *intended,*
at all events, to be favourable.

In opposition to them, we have Mr. Cooper's [4] remarks
upon England, in which my countrymen are certainly not
spared; and, since that publication, we have another of
much greater importance, written by Mr. Carey,[5] of Philadelphia, not, indeed, in a strain of vituperation or ill feeling, but asserting, and no doubt to his own satisfaction and
that of his countrymen, proving, that in every important
point, that is to say, under the heads of "Security of Person
and Property, of Morals, Education, Religion, Industry, Invention, Credit" (and consequently Honesty), America is in
advance of England and every other nation in Europe! The
tables, then, are turned; it is no longer the English but the
Americans who are the assailants; and such being the case,
I beg that it may be remembered that many of the remarks
which will subsequently appear in this work have been
forced from me by the attacks made upon my nation by the
American authors; and that, if I am compelled to draw
comparisons, it is not with the slightest wish to annoy or
humiliate the Americans, but in legitimate and justifiable
defence of my own native land.

America is a wonderful country, endowed by the Om-

---

who resided for many years in
the United States. He wrote *The
Americans in their Moral, Social
and Political Relations,* which
was published in 1837.

[4] James Fenimore Cooper (1789–
1851), the American novelist,
best remembered today for his
Leatherstocking novels. A man
of means, he travelled widely
and wrote of his journeys. Two
of his travel books, *Excursions
in Switzerland* (1836) and *England with Sketches of Society in
the Metropolis* (1837), are cited
by Marryat. For an excellent ex-
position of Cooper's ideas see
Marvin Meyers, *The Jacksonian
Persuasion* (Stanford: Stanford

University Press; 1957), pp.
42–75.

[5] Henry Charles Carey (1793–
1879), an economist and publisher, was a great promoter of
American industrialization, in
his early writings he supported the doctrine of laissez-
faire. He wrote many books and
articles; his *Essay on the Rate of
Wages* (1835) and his *Principles
of Political Economy* (1837)
were used by Marryat. For an account of Carey's ideas, see Joseph Dorfman, *The Economic
Mind in American Civilization,
1606–1865* (New York: Viking
Press; 1946), Vol. II, p. 789 ff.

nipotent with natural advantages which no other can boast
of; and the mind can hardly calculate upon the degree of
perfection and power to which, whether the states are eventually separated or not, it may in the course of two centuries
arrive. At present all is energy and enterprise; everything
is in a state of transition, but of rapid improvement—so
rapid, indeed, that those who would describe America now,
would have to correct all in the short space of ten years; for
ten years in America is almost equal to a century in the old
continent. Now, you may pass through a wild forest, where
the elk browses and the panther howls; in ten years, that
very forest, with its denizens, will, most likely, have disappeared, and in their place you will find towns with thousands of inhabitants; with arts, manufactures, and machinery, all in full activity.

In reviewing America, we must look upon it as showing
the development of the English character under a new aspect, arising from a new state of things. If I were to draw a
comparison between the English and the Americans, I
should say that there is almost as much difference between
the two nations at this present time as there has long been
between the English and the Dutch. The latter are considered by us as phlegmatic and slow; and we may be considered the same, compared with our energetic descendants.
Time to an American is everything, and space he attempts
to reduce to a mere nothing. By the steamboats, railroads,
and the wonderful facilities of water-carriage, a journey
of five hundred miles is as little considered in America
as would be here a journey from London to Brighton. *"Go
ahead"* is the real motto of the country; and every man does
push on, to gain in advance of his neighbour. The American
lives twice as long as others, for he does twice the work
during the time that he lives. He begins life sooner: at fifteen he is considered a man, plunges into the stream of
enterprise, floats and struggles with his fellows. In every
trifle an American shows the value he puts upon time. He
rises early, eats his meals with the rapidity of a wolf, and is
the whole day at his business. If he be a merchant, his

money, whatever it may amount to, is seldom invested; it is all floating—his accumulations remain active; and when he dies, his wealth has to be collected from the four quarters of the globe.

Now, all this energy and activity is of English origin; and were England expanded into America, the same results would be produced. To a certain degree, the English were in former times what the Americans are now; and this it is which has raised our country so high in the scale of nations; but since we have become so closely packed, so crowded, that there is hardly room for the population, our activity has been proportionably cramped and subdued. But, in this vast and favoured country, the very associations and impressions of childhood foster and enlighten the intellect, and precociously rouse the energies. The wide expanse of territory already occupied—the vast and magnificent rivers—the boundless regions yet remaining to be peopled—the rapidity of communication—the dispatch with which everything is effected, are evident almost to the child. To those who have rivers many thousand miles in length, the passage across the Atlantic (of 3,500 miles) appears but a trifle; and the American ladies talk of spending the winter at Paris with as much indifference as one of our landed proprietors would, of going up to London for the season.

We must always bear in mind the peculiar and wonderful advantages of *country* when we examine America and its form of government; for the country has had more to do with upholding this democracy than people might at first imagine. Among the advantages of democracy, the greatest is, perhaps, that *all start fair;* and the boy who holds the traveller's horse, as Van Buren is said to have done, may become the President of the United States. But it is the *country,* and not the government, which has been productive of such rapid strides as have been made by America. Indeed, it is a query whether the form of government would have existed down to this day, had it not been for the advantages derived from the vast extent and boundless resources of the territory in which it was established. Let the American direct his career to any goal he pleases, his energies are unshackled; and, in the race, the best man must win. There is room for all, and millions more. Let him choose his profession—his career is not checked or foiled by the excess of those who have already embarked in it. In every department there is an opening for talent; and for those inclined to work, work is always to be procured. You have no complaint in this country, that every profession is so full that it is impossible to know what to do with your children. There is a vast field, and all may receive the reward due for their labour.

In a country where the ambition and energies of man have been roused to such an extent, the great point is to find out worthy incitements for ambition to feed upon. A virtue directed into a wrong channel may, by circumstances, prove little better than (even if it does not sink down into) actual vice. Hence it is that a democratic form of government is productive of such demoralizing effects. Its rewards are few. Honours of every description, which stir up the soul of man to noble deeds—worthy incitements, they have none. The only compensation they can offer for services is money; and the only distinction—the only means of raising himself above his fellows left to the American—is wealth: consequently, the acquisition of wealth has become the great spring of action. But it is not sought after with the avarice to hoard, but with the ostentation to expend. It is the effect of ambition directed into a wrong channel. Each man would surpass his neighbour; and the only great avenue open to all, and into which thousands may press without much jostling of each other, is that which leads to the shrine of Mammon. It is our nature to attempt to raise ourselves above our fellow-men; it is the mainspring of existence—the incitement to all that is great and virtuous, or great and vicious. In America, but a small portion can raise themselves, or find rewards for superior talent, but wealth is attainable by all; and having no aristocracy, no honours, no distinctions to look forward to, wealth has become the substitute, and, with very few exceptions, every man is great in proportion to his riches. The consequence is that to leave a sum of money when they die is of little importance to the majority of the Americans. Their object is to amass it while young, and obtain the consideration which it gives them during their lifetime.

The society in the United States is that which must naturally be expected in a new country where there are few men of leisure, and the majority are working hard to obtain that wealth which almost alone gives importance under a democratic form of government. You will find intellectual and gentlemanlike people in America, but they are scattered here and there. The circle of society is not complete; wherever you go, you will find an admixture, sudden wealth having admitted those who but a few years back were in humble circumstances; and in the constant state of transition which takes place in this country, it will be half a century, perhaps, before a select circle of society can be collected together in any one city or place. The improvement is rapid, but the vast extent of country which has to be peopled prevents that improvement from being manifest. The stream flows inland, and those who are here today are gone tomorrow, and their places in society filled up by others who ten years back had no prospect of ever being admitted. All is transition, the waves follow one another to the far west, the froth and scum boiling in the advance.

America is, indeed, well worth the study of the philosopher. A vast nation forming, society ever changing, all in motion and activity, nothing complete, the old continent pouring in her surplus to supply the loss of the eastern states, all busy as a hive, full of energy and activity. Every year multitudes swarm off from the east, like bees: not the young only, but the old, quitting the close-built cities, society, and refinement, to settle down in some lone spot in the vast prairies, where the rich soil offers to them the certain prospect of their families and children being one day possessed of competency and wealth.

To write upon America *as a nation* would be absurd,

for nation, properly speaking, it is not; but to consider it in its present chaotic state is well worth the labour. It would not only exhibit to the living a somewhat new picture of the human mind, but, as a curious page in the Philosophy of History, it would hereafter serve as a subject of review for the Americans themselves.

It is not my intention to follow the individualizing plans of the majority of those who have preceded me in this country. I did not sail across the Atlantic to ascertain whether the Americans eat their dinners with two-prong iron or three-prong silver forks, with chopsticks, or their fingers; it is quite sufficient for me to know that they do eat and drink; if they did not, it would be a curious anomaly which I should not pass over. My object was, to examine and ascertain *what were the effects of a democratic form of government and climate upon a people which, with all its foreign admixture, may still be considered as English.*

It is a fact that our virtues and our vices depend more upon circumstances than upon ourselves, and there are no circumstances which operate so powerfully upon us as government and climate. Let it not be supposed that, in the above assertion, I mean to extenuate vice, or imply that we are not free agents. Naturally prone to vices in general, circumstances will render us more prone to one description of vice than to another; but that is no reason why we should not be answerable for it, since it is our duty to guard against the besetting sin. But as an agent in this point, the form of government under which we live is, perhaps, the most powerful in its effects, and thus we constantly hear of vices peculiar to a country, when it ought rather to be said, of vices peculiar to a government.

Never, perhaps, was the foundation of a nation laid under such peculiarly favourable auspices as that of America. The capital they commenced with was industry, activity, and courage. They had, moreover, the advantage of the working of genius and wisdom, and the records of history, as a beacon and a guide; the trial of ages, as to the respective merits of the various governments to which men have submitted; the power to select the merits from the demerits in each; a boundless extent of country, rich in everything that could be of advantage to man; and they were led by those who were really giants in those days, a body of men collected and acting together, forming an aggregate of wisdom and energy such as probably will not for centuries be seen again. Never was there such an opportunity of testing the merits of a republic, of ascertaining if such a form of government could be maintained—in fact, of proving whether an enlightened people could govern themselves. And it must be acknowledged that the work was well begun; Washington, when his career had closed, left the country a pure republic. He did all that man could do. Miss Martineau asserts that "America has solved the great problem, that a republic can exist for fifty years"; but such is not the case. America has proved that, under peculiar advantages, a people can govern themselves for fifty years; but if you put the question to an enlightened American, and ask him, "Were Washington to rise from his grave, would he recognize the present government of America as the one bequeathed to them?" and the American will himself answer in the negative. These fifty years have afforded another proof, were it necessary, how short-sighted and fallible are men—how impossible it is to keep anything in a state of perfection here below. Washington left America as an infant nation, a pure and, I may add, a virtuous republic; but the government of the country has undergone as much change as everything else, and it has now settled down into anything but a pure democracy. Nor could it be otherwise; a republic may be formed and may continue in healthy existence when regulated by a small body of men, but as men increase and multiply so do they deteriorate; the closer they are packed the more vicious they become, and, consequently, the more vicious become their institutions. Washington and his coadjutors had no power to control the nature of man.

It may be inquired by some, what difference there is between a republic and a democracy, as the terms have been, and are often, used indifferently. I know not whether my distinction is right, but I consider that when those possessed of most talent and wisdom are selected to act for the benefit of a people, with full reliance upon their acting for the best, and without any shackle or pledge being enforced, we may consider that form of government as a republic ruled by the most enlightened and capable; but that if, on the contrary, those selected by the people to represent them are not only bound by pledges previous to their election, but ordered by the mass how to vote after their election, then the country is not ruled by the collected wisdom of the people, but by the majority, who are as often wrong as right, and then the governing principle sinks into a democracy, as it now is in America.

It is singular to remark, notwithstanding her monarchical form of government, how much more republican England is in her institutions than America. Ask an American what he considers the necessary qualifications of a President, and, after intellectual qualifications, he will tell you firmness, decision, and undaunted courage; and it is really an enigma to him, although he will not acknowledge it, how the sceptre of a country like England, subject to the monarchical sway which he detests, can be held in the hand of a young female of eighteen years of age.

But upon one point I have made up my mind, which is that, with all its imperfections, democracy is the form of government *best suited to the present condition of America,* in so far as it is the one under which the country has made, and will continue to make, the most rapid advances. That it must eventually be changed is true, but the time of its change must be determined by so many events, hidden in futurity, which may accelerate or retard the convulsion, that it would be presumptuous for anyone to attempt to name a period when the present form of government shall be broken up, and the multitude shall separate and re-embody themselves under new institutions.

In the arrangement of this work, I have considered it advisable to present, first, to the reader those *portions* of my diary which may be interesting, and in which are recorded traits and incidents which will bear strongly upon the commentaries I shall subsequently make upon the institutions of the United States, and the results of those institutions as developed in the American character. Having been preceded by so many writers on America, I must occasionally tread in well-beaten tracts; but, although I shall avoid repetition as much as possible, this will not prevent me from describing what I saw or felt. Different ideas, and different associations of ideas, will strike different travellers, as the same landscape may wear a new appearance, according as it is viewed in the morning, by noon, or at night; the outlines remain the same, but the lights, and shadows, and tints, are reflected from the varying idiosyncrasy of various minds.

My readers will also find many quotations, either embodied in the work or supplied by notes.[6] This I have considered necessary, that my opinions may be corroborated; but these quotations will not be extracted so much from the works of English as from *American* writers. The opinions relative to the United States have been so conflicting in the many works which have been written, that I consider it most important that I should be able to quote American authorities against themselves, and strengthen my opinions and arguments by their own admissions.

[6] As explained in the Editor's Introduction to this edition, most of these long quotations and extracts have been omitted.

CHAPTER I

Departure from England

I like to begin at the beginning; it's a good old fashion, not sufficiently adhered to in these modern times. I recollect a young gentleman who said he was thinking of going to America; on my asking him how he intended to go, he replied: "I don't exactly know; but I think I shall take the fast coach." I wished him a safe passage, and said I was afraid he would find it very dusty. As I could not find the office to book myself by this young gentleman's conveyance, I walked down to St. Katherine's docks, went on board a packet, was shown into a superb cabin, fitted up with bird's-eye maple, mahogany, and looking-glasses, and communicating with certain small cabins, where there was a sleeping berth for each passenger, about as big as that allowed to a pointer in a dog-kennel. I thought that there was more finery than comfort; but it ended in my promising the captain to meet him at Portsmouth. He was to sail from London on the 1st of April, and I did not choose to sail on that day—it was ominous; so I embarked at Portsmouth on the 3rd. It is not my intention to give a description of crossing the Atlantic; but as the reader may be disappointed if I do not tell him how I got over, I shall first inform him that we were thirty-eight in the cabin, and 160 men, women, and children, literally stowed in bulk in the steerage. I shall describe what took place from the time I first went up the side at Spithead, until the ship was underweigh, and then make a very short passage of it.

At 9:30 a.m. — Embarked on board the good ship *Quebec;* and a good ship she proved to be, repeatedly going nine and a-half knots on a bowling, sails lifting. Captain H. quite delighted to see me—all captains of packets are to see passengers: I believed him when he said so.

At 9:50 — Sheriff's officer, as usual, came on board. Observed several of the cabin passengers hasten down below, and one who requested the captain to stow him away. But it was not a pen-and-ink affair; it was a case of burglary. The officer has found his man in the steerage—the handcuffs are on his wrists, and they are rowing him ashore. His wife and two children are on board, her lips quiver as she collects her baggage to follow her husband. One half-hour more, and he would have escaped from justice, and probably have led a better life in a far country, where his crimes were unknown. . . . What cargoes of crime, folly, and recklessness do we yearly ship off to America! America ought to be very much obliged to us.

The women of the steerage are persuading the wife of the burglar not to go on shore; their arguments are strong, but not strong enough against the devoted love of a woman. —"Your husband is certain to be hung; what's the use of following him? Your passage is paid, and you will have no difficulty in supporting your children in America." But she rejects the advice—goes down the side, and presses her children to her breast, as, overcome with the agony of her feelings, she drops into the boat; and, now that she is away from the ship, you hear the sobs, which can no longer be controlled.

10 a.m. — "All hands up anchor."

I was repeating to myself some of the stanzas of Mrs. Norton's [1] "Here's a health to the outward-bound," when I

---

[1] The Honourable Mrs. Caroline Elizabeth Sarah Norton (1808–77), English poetess and novel- ist, was the daughter of Thomas Sheridan and granddaughter of Richard Sheridan, the play-

cast my eyes forward I could not imagine what the seamen were about; they appeared to be *pumping,* instead of heaving, at the windlass. I forced my way through the heterogeneous mixture of human beings, animals, and baggage which crowded the decks, and discovered that they were working a patent windlass, by Dobbinson—a very ingenious and superior invention. The seamen, as usual, lightened their labour with the song and chorus, forbidden by the etiquette of a man-of-war. The one they sung was peculiarly musical, although not refined; and the chorus of "Oh! Sally Brown" was given with great emphasis by the whole crew between every line of the song, sung by an athletic young third mate. I took my seat on the knight-heads—turned my face aft—looked and listened.

"Heave away there, forward."

"Aye, aye, sir."

" 'Sally Brown—oh! my dear Sally.' " (Single voice.)

" 'Oh! Sally Brown.' " (Chorus.)

" 'Sally Brown, of Bubble Al-ley.' " (Single voice.)

" 'Oh! Sal-ly Brown.' " (Chorus.)

"Avast heaving there; send all aft to clear the boat."

"Aye, Aye, sir. Where are we to stow these casks, Mr. Fisher?"

"Stow them! Heaven knows; get them in, at all events."

"Captain H.! Captain H.! there's my piano still on deck; it will be quite spoiled—indeed it will."

"Don't be alarmed, ma'am; as soon as we're underweigh we'll hoist the cow up, and get the piano down."

"What! under the cow?"

"No, ma'am; but the cow's over the hatchway."

"Now, then, my lads, forward to the windlass."

" 'I went to town to get some toddy.' "

---

wright. She was distinguished for her beauty and her wit. After her marriage in 1827 to George Norton, she began her literary career, and her *The Sorrows of Rosalie . . . with Other Poems* was enthusiastically received. She wrote several novels including *Stuart of Dunleath* (1851) and *Lost and Saved* (1863).

" 'Oh! Sally Brown.' "

" 'T'wasn't fit for any body.' "

" 'Oh! Sally Brown.' "—

"Out there, and clear away the jib."

"Aye, aye, sir."

"Mr. Fisher, how much cable is there out?"

"Plenty yet, sir. — Heave away, my lads."

" 'Sally is a bright mulattar.' "

" 'Oh! Sally Brown.' "

" 'Pretty girl, but can't get at her.' "

" 'Oh! ——' "—

"Avast heaving; send the men aft to whip the ladies in. —Now, miss, only sit down and don't be afraid, and you'll be in, in no time. —Whip away, my lads, handsomely; steady her with the guy; lower away. —There, miss, now you are safely *landed.*"

"*Landed* am I? I thought I was *shipped.*"

"Very good, indeed—very good, miss; you'll make an excellent sailor, I see."

"I should make a better sailor's *wife,* I expect, Captain H."

"Excellent! Allow me to hand you aft; you'll excuse me. —Forward now, my men; heave away!"

" 'Seven years I courted Sally.' "

" 'Oh! Sally Brown.' "

" 'Seven more of shilley-shally.' "

" 'Oh! Sally Brown.' "

" 'She won't wed ——' " —

"Avast heaving. Up there, and loose the topsails; stretch along the topsail-sheets. —Upon my soul, half these children will be killed. —Whose child are you?"

"I — don't — know."

"Go and find out, that's a dear. —Let fall; sheet home; belay starboard sheet; clap on the larboard; belay all that. —Now, then, Mr. Fisher."

"Aye, aye, sir. —Heave away, my lads."

" 'She won't wed a Yankee sailor.' "

" 'Oh! Sally Brown.' "

" 'For she's in love with the nigger tailor.' "
" 'Oh! Sally Brown.' " —
"Heave away, my men; heave, and in sight. Hurrah! my lads."
" 'Sally Brown—oh! my dear Sally!' "
" 'Oh! Sally Brown!' "
" 'Sally Brown, of Bubble Alley.' "
" 'Oh! Sally Brown.' "
" 'Sally has a cross old granny.' "
" 'Oh! ——' " —
"Heave and fall—jib-halyards—hoist away."
"Oh! dear—Oh! dear."
"The clumsy brute has half-killed the girl! —Don't cry, my dear."
"Pick up the child, Tom, and shove it out of the way."
"Where shall I put her?"
"Oh, anywhere just now; put her on the turkey-coop."
"Starboard!"
"Starboard it is; steady so." [2]

Thus, with the trifling matter of maiming half-a-dozen children, upsetting two or three women, smashing the lids of a few trunks, and crushing some band-boxes as flat as a muffin, the good ship *Quebec* was at last fairly underweigh, and standing out for St. Helen's.

3 p.m. — Off St. Helen's; ship steady; little wind; water smooth; passengers sure they won't be sick.

3:20 — Apologies from the captain for a cold dinner on this day.

4 o'clock — Dinner over; everybody pulls out a number of "Pickwick"; everybody talks and reads Pickwick;

---

[2] This is one of the many versions of the sea song "Sally Brown." For another version, see Elizabeth B. Greenleaf, *Ballads and Sea Songs of Newfoundland* (Cambridge, Mass.: Harvard University Press; 1933), p. 337. Elizabeth Greenleaf also cites W. Roy Mackenzie, *Ballads and Sea Songs from Nova Scotia* (Cambridge, Mass.: Harvard University Press; 1928) for other versions of this song. Undoubtedly all versions have a common source, and this may well be the poem "Sally in Our Alley," written by the English poet Henry Carey (1693?–1743).

weather getting up squally; passengers not quite so sure they won't be seasick.

Who can tell what the morrow may bring forth? It brought forth a heavy sea, and the passengers were quite sure that they were seasick. Only six out of thirty-eight made their appearance at the breakfast-table; and, for many days afterward, there were Pickwicks in plenty strewed all over the cabin, but passengers were very scarce. But we had more than seasickness to contend with— the influenza broke out and raged. Does not this prove that it is contagious, and not dependant on the atmosphere? It was hard, after having sniffled with it for six weeks on shore, that I should have another month of it on board. But who can control destiny? The ship was like a hospital; an elderly woman was the first victim—then a boy of twelve years of age. Fortunately, there were no more deaths.

But I have said enough of the passage. On the 4th of May, in the year of our Lord, 1837, I found myself walking up Broadway, among the free and enlightened citizens of New York.

CHAPTER II

Arrival in the New World

A visit, to make it agreeable to both parties, should be well timed. My appearance at New York was very much like bursting into a friend's house with a merry face when there is a death in it—with the sudden change from levity to condolence. "Any other time most happy to see you. You find us in a very unfortunate situation."

"Indeed I'm very—very sorry."

Two hundred and sixty houses [1] have already failed,

[1] The famous panic of 1837 came about for a variety of reasons. It resulted in part from the Specie Circular of 1836, which required that all payments for public lands be made in hard money, thus putting a great strain on the banks which were involved in land speculation, and in part from a financial crisis in England which forced English investors in American loans to demand payment. The immediate cause was the collapse of a cotton brokerage in New Orleans which involved other businesses and brought about a panic in the south. Efforts by eastern and northern bankers to halt the crisis were ineffectual and the stock market collapsed. In May 1837 a number of banks suspended payment and the country was plunged into a major depression. Marryat comments that when he arrived 260 businesses had failed. For confirmation of this, see Allan Nevins and Milton Halsey Thomas, editors, *The Diary of George Templeton Strong* (New York: Macmillan; 1952), Vol. I, p. 62, where for the 3rd of May, Strong says that there were "Near two hundred and fifty failures thus far." This is just one day before Marryat actually arrived in New York. On May 5th, the day after Marryat's arrival, Strong notes that on the 4th there had been twenty more failures.

and no one knows where it is to end. Suspicion, fear, and misfortune have taken possession of the city. Had I not been aware of the cause, I should have imagined that the plague was raging, and I had the description of Defoe before me.

Not a smile on one countenance among the crowd who pass and repass; hurried steps, care-worn faces, rapid exchanges of salutation, or hasty communication of anticipated ruin before the sun goes down. Here two or three are gathered on one side, whispering and watching that they are not overheard; there a solitary, with his arms folded and his hat slouched, brooding over departed affluence. Mechanics, thrown out of employment, are pacing up and down with the air of famished wolves. The violent shock has been communicated, like that of electricity, through the country to a distance of hundreds of miles. Canals, railroads, and all public works have been discontinued, and the Irish emigrant leans against his shanty, with his spade idle in his hand, and starves, as his thoughts wander back to his own Emerald Isle.

The Americans delight in the hyperbole; in fact they hardly have a metaphor without it. During this crash, when every day fifteen or twenty merchants' names appeared in the newspapers as bankrupts, one party, not in a very good humour, was hastening down Broadway, when he was run against by another whose temper was equally unamiable. This collision roused the choler of both.

"What the devil do you mean, sir?" cried one. "I've a great mind to knock you into *the middle of next week.*"

This occurring on a Saturday, the wrath of the other was checked by the recollection of how very favourable such a blow would be to his present circumstances.

"Will you! by heavens, then pray do; it's just the thing I want, for how else I am to get over next Monday and the acceptances I must take up, is more than I can tell."

All the banks have stopped payment in specie, and there is not a dollar to be had. I walked down Wall Street and had a convincing proof of the great demand for money, for somebody picked my pocket. The militia are under arms, as riots are expected. The banks in the country and other towns have followed the example of New York, and thus has General Jackson's currency bill been repealed without the aid of Congress. Affairs are now at their worst, and now that such is the case, the New Yorkers appear to recover their spirits. One of the newspapers humorously observes— "All Broadway is like unto a new-made widow, and don't know whether to laugh or cry." There certainly is a very remarkable energy in the American disposition; if they fall, they bound up again. Somebody has observed that the New York merchants are of that *elastic* nature that, when fit for nothing else, they might be converted into *coach springs,* and such really appears to be their character.

Nobody refuses to take the paper of the New York banks, although they virtually have stopped payment—they never refuse anything in New York—but nobody will give specie in change, and great distress is occasioned by this want of a circulating medium. Some of the shopkeepers told me that they had been obliged to turn away a hundred dollars a day, and many a southerner, who has come up with a large supply of southern notes, has found himself a pauper, and has been indebted to a friend for a few dollars in specie to get home again.

The radicals here, for there are radicals, it appears, in a democracy ("in the lowest depth, a lower deep"),[2] are very loud in their complaints. I was watching the swarming multitude in Wall Street this morning, when one of these fellows was declaiming against the banks for stopping specie payments, and "robbing a poor man in such a *w*illanous manner," when one of the merchants, who appeared to know his customer, said to him— "Well, as you say, it is

---

[2] This is a misquotation from John Milton's *Paradise Lost.* See IV, 76.

hard for a poor fellow like you not to be able to get dollars for his notes; hand them out, and I'll give you specie for them myself!" The blackguard had not a cent in his pocket, and walked away looking very foolish. . . .

I was in a store when a thorough-bred democrat walked in: he talked loud, and voluntarily gave it as his opinion that all this distress was the very best thing that could have happened to the country, as America would now keep all the specie and pay her English creditors with bankruptcies. There always appears to me to be a great want of moral principle in all radicals; indeed, the levelling principles of radicalism are adverse to the sacred rights of *meum et tuum.* At Philadelphia the ultra-democrats have held a large public meeting, at which one of the first resolutions brought forward and agreed to was— "That they did not owe one farthing to the English people."

"They may say the times are bad," said a young American to me, "but I think that they are excellent. A twenty-dollar note used to last me but a week, but now it is as good as Fortunatus' purse, which was never empty. I eat my dinner at the hotel, and show them my twenty-dollar note. The landlord turns away from it, as if it were the head of Medusa, and begs that I will pay another time. I buy everything that I want, and I have only to offer my twenty-dollar note in payment, and my credit is unbounded— that is, for any sum under twenty dollars. If they ever do give change again in New York it will make a very unfortunate change in my affairs."

A government circular, enforcing the act of Congress, which obliges all those who have to pay custom-house duties or postage to do so in specie, has created great dissatisfaction, and added much to the distress and difficulty. At the same time that they (the government) refuse to take from their debtors the notes of the banks, upon the ground that they are no longer legal tenders, they compel their creditors to take those very notes—having had a large quantity in their possession at the time that the banks suspended specie payments—an act of despotism which the English government would not venture upon. . . .

The distress for change has produced a curious remedy. Every man is now his own banker. Go to the theatres and places of public amusement, and, instead of change, you receive an I.O.U. from the treasury. At the hotels and oyster-cellars it is the same thing. Call for a glass of brandy and water and the change is fifteen tickets, each "good for one glass of brandy and water." At an oyster shop, eat a plate of oysters, and you have in return seven tickets, good for one plate of oysters each. It is the same every where.— The barbers give you tickets, good for so many shaves; and were there beggars in the streets, I presume they would give you tickets in change, good for so much philanthropy. Dealers, in general, give out their own bank-notes, or as they are called here, *shin-plasters,* which are good for one dollar, and from that down to two and a half cents, all of which are redeemable, and redeemable only upon a general return to cash payment.

Hence arises another variety of exchange in Wall Street.

"Tom, do you want any oysters for lunch today?"

"Yes!"

"Then here's a ticket, and give me two *shaves* in return."

The most prominent causes of this convulsion have already been laid before the English public; but there is one —that of speculating in land—which has not been sufficiently dwelt upon, nor has the importance been given to it which it deserves; as, perhaps, next to the losses occasioned by the great fire,[3] it led, more than any other species of

---

[3] On December 16, 1835, a great fire occurred in New York City and much of the business district in and around Wall Street was totally destroyed. A contemporary newspaper reckoned that some 570 buildings were destroyed and an observer estimated damage at $30,000,000. For a contemporary account, see Bayard Tuckerman, editor, *The Diary of Philip Hone* (New York: Dodd, Mead; 1889), Vol. I, pp. 180–83, 184, 186.

over-speculation and over-trading, to the distress which has ensued. Not but that the event must have taken place in the natural course of things. Cash payments produce sure but small returns; but no commerce can be carried on by this means on any extended scale. Credit, as long as it is good, is so much extra capital, in itself nominal and non-existent, but producing real returns. If anyone will look back upon the commercial history of these last fifty years, he will perceive that the system of credit is always attended with a periodical *blow up;* in England, perhaps, once in twenty years; in America, once in from seven to ten. This arises from there being no safety valve—no check which can be put to it by mutual consent of all parties. One house extends its credit, and for a time, its profits; another follows the example. The facility of credit induces those who obtain it to embark in other speculations, foreign to their business; for credit thus becomes extra capital which they do not know how to employ. Such has been the case in the present instance; but this is no reason for the credit system not being continued. These occasional explosions act as warnings, and, for the time, people are more cautious: they stop for a while to repair damages, and recover from their consternation; and when they go ahead again, it is not quite so fast. The loss is severely felt, because people are not prepared to meet it; but if all the profits of the years of healthy credit were added up, and the balance-sheet struck between that and the loss at the explosion, the advantage gained by the credit system would still be found to be great. The advancement of America depends wholly upon it. It is by credit alone that she has made such rapid strides, and it is by credit alone that she can continue to flourish, at the same time that she enriches those who trade with her. In this latter crisis there was more blame to be attached to the English houses, who *forced* their credit upon the Americans, than to the Americans, who, having such unlimited credit, thought that they might advantageously speculate with the capital of others.

One of the most singular affections of the human

mind is a proneness to excessive speculation; and it may here be noticed that the disease (for such it may be termed) is peculiarly English and American. Men, in their race for gain, appear, like horses that have run away, to have been blinded by the rapidity of their own motion. It almost amounts to an epidemic, and is infectious—the wise and the foolish being equally liable to the disease. We had ample evidence of this in the bubble-manias which took place in England in the years 1825 and 1826. A mania of this kind had infected the people of America for two or three years previous to the crash: it was that of speculating in land; and to show the extent to which it had been carried on, we may take the following examples—

The city of New York, which is built upon a narrow island about ten miles in length, at present covers about three miles of that distance, and has a population of three hundred thousand inhabitants. Building lots were marked out for the other seven miles; and, by calculation, these lots, when built upon, would contain an additional population of one million and three quarters. They were first purchased at from one hundred to one hundred and fifty dollars each, but, as the epidemic raged, they rose to upwards of two thousand dollars. At Brooklyn, on Long Island, opposite to New York, and about half a mile distant from it, lots were marked out to the extent of fourteen miles, which would contain an extra population of one million, and these were as eagerly speculated in.

At Staten Island, at the entrance into the Sound, an estate was purchased by some speculators for ten thousand dollars, was divided into lots and planned as a town to be called New Brighton; and had the whole of the lots been sold at the price which many were, previous to the crash, the original speculators would have realized three million dollars. But the infatuation was not confined to the precincts of New York; everywhere it existed. Government lands, which could only be paid for in specie, were eagerly sought after; plans of new towns were puffed up; drawings made in which every street was laid down and named;

churches, theatres, hospitals, railroad communications, canals, steamboats in the offing, all appeared on paper as if in actual existence, when, in fact, the very site was as yet a forest, with not a log hut within a mile of the pretended city. Lots in these visionary cities were eagerly purchased, increased daily in value, and afforded a fine harvest to those who took advantage of the credulity of others. One man would buy a lot with extensive *water privileges,* and, upon going to examine it, would find those privileges rather too extensive, the whole lot being *under water.* Even after the crisis, there was a man still going about who made a good livelihood by setting up his plan of a city, the lots of which he sold by public auction, on condition of one dollar being paid down to secure the purchase if approved of. The mania had not yet subsided, and many paid down their dollar upon their purchase of a lot. This was all he required. He went to the next town, and sold the same lots over and over again.

To check this madness of speculation was one reason why an act of Congress was passed, obliging all purchasers of government lands to pay in specie. Nevertheless, government received nine or ten millions in specie after the bill passed. Now, when it is considered what a large portion of the capital drawn from England was applied to these wild speculations—sums which, when they were required, could not be realized, as, when the crisis occurred, property thus purchased immediately fell to about one-tenth of what was paid for it—it will be clearly seen that, from this unfortunate mania, a great portion of the present distress must have arisen.

The attempt of General Jackson and his successors, to introduce a specie currency into a country which exists upon credit, was an act of folly, and has ended in complete failure.* A few weeks after he had issued from the mint

---

* One single proof may be given of the ruinous policy of the Jackson administration in temporizing with the credit of the country. To check the export of bullion from our country, the Bank of England had but one remedy, that of rendering money scarce;

a large coinage of gold, there was hardly an eagle to be seen, and the metal might almost as well have remained in the mine from whence it had been extracted.[4] It was still in the country, but had all been absorbed by the agriculturalists; and such will ever be the case in a widely extended agricultural country. The farmers, principally Dutch, live upon a portion of their produce and sell the rest. Formerly they were content with bank bills or Mexican dol-

---

they contracted their issues, and it became so. The consequence was that the price of cotton fell forty dollars per bale. The crop of cotton amounted to 1,600,000 bales, which, at forty dollars per bale, was a loss to the southern planters of $64,000,000.

[4] The policy of restoring gold to circulation was supported by Thomas Hart Benton and Roger Taney, both ardent Jacksonians. Gold was, for many years, undervalued at the ratio of 15 to 1, and consequently no gold eagles, that is, ten-dollar gold pieces, or many other gold coins had been minted since 1805. The majority of the gold coins minted had left the country. Benton and his fellow "hard money" supporters felt that if the gold coins were kept in the country, along with the specie which arrived from foreign trade and the gold found in American mines, they could together provide a satisfactory basis for coinage, and the need for excessive paper money would vanish. In June 1834 a bill was passed by Congress, changing the valuation of gold to the ratio of 16 to 1. The effect for the moment was magical. Gold flowed into the government mints and cheap paper seemed on the way out. In December 1836 Levi Woodbury, the Secretary of the Treasury, reported that more

gold was coined in the previous twelve months than had been coined in the first sixteen years that the mint had existed and more in the period since the value of gold was altered than in the previous thirty-one years. In 1833 there had been $30,000,000 in specie, with $26,000,000 in banks, and in 1836 there was $73,000,000, with $45,000,000 in banks. A. M. Schlesinger, Jr., *The Age of Jackson* (Boston: Little, Brown; 1946), pp. 126–27. However, the hopes for a hard currency were not to prevail. The Specie Circular of 1836 required "that agents for the sale of public lands should take in payment only specie, and no longer receive the notes issued by banks." Banks that were financing western land speculation had to have specie and many did not have the requisite amount to pay for the lands, and land purchases were halted. Further, the collapse of two banks in Ireland and England forced English creditors to call in their loans. Finally, the crop failure of that year forced the importation of foodstuffs which increased the demands for foreign exchange. Davis Rich Dewey, *Financial History of the United States* (New York: Longmans; 1903), pp. 227–30 *passim.*

lars, which they laid by for a rainy day, and they remained locked up for years before they were required. When the gold was issued, it was eagerly collected by these people, as more convenient, and laid by, by the farmers' wives, in the foot of an old worsted stocking, where the major part of it will remain. And thus has the famous gold-currency bill been upset by the hoarding propensities of a parcel of old women.*

---

* A curious proof of this system of hoarding, which immediately took place upon the banks stopping payment, was told me by a gentleman from Baltimore. He went into a store to purchase, as he often had done, a canvass shot-bag, and to his surprise was asked three times the former price for it. Upon his expostulating, the venders told him that the demand for them by the farmers and other people who brought their produce to market, and who used them to put their specie in, was so great that they could hardly supply them.

CHAPTER III

New York City

Fifty years ago, New York was little more than a village; now, it is a fine city with three hundred thousand inhabitants. I have never seen any city so admirably adapted for commerce. It is built upon a narrow island, between Long Island Sound and the Hudson River, Broadway running up it like the vertebrae of some huge animal, and the other streets diverging from it at right angles, like the ribs; each street running to the river, and presenting to the view a forest of masts.

There are some fine buildings in this city, but not many. Astor House, although of simple architecture, is, perhaps, the grandest mass; and next to that is the City Hall, though in architecture very indifferent. In the large room of the latter are some interesting pictures and busts of the Presidents, mayors of the city, and naval and military officers, who have received the thanks of Congress and the freedom of the city. Some are very fair specimens of art; the most spirited is that of Commodore Perry,[1] leaving his sinking vessel, in the combat on the Lakes, to hoist his flag

---

[1] Oliver Hazard Perry (1785–1819), American naval officer who gained fame as a result of his memorable victory at the Battle of Lake Erie on September 10, 1813.

on board of another ship. Decatur's [2] portrait is also very fine. Pity that such a man should have been sacrificed in a foolish duel!

At the corner of many of the squares, or *blocks* of buildings, as they are termed here, is erected a very high mast, with a cap of liberty upon the top. The only idea we have of the cap of liberty is the *bonnet rouge* of the French; but the Americans will not copy the French, although they will the English; so they have a cap of their own, which (begging their pardon), with its gaudy colours and gilding, looks more like a *fool's cap* than anything else.

New York is not equal to London, nor Broadway to Regent Street, although the Americans would compare them. Still, New York is very superior to most of our provincial towns, and to a man who can exist out of London, Broadway will do very well for a lounge—being wide, three miles long, and the upper part composed of very handsome houses; besides which, it may almost challenge Regent Street for pretty faces, except on Sundays.* Many of the shops, or *stores,* as they are here called (for in this land of equality nobody keeps a shop), have already been fitted up with large plate-glass fronts, similar to those in London, and but for the depression which has taken place, many more would have followed the example.

Among the few discrepancies observable between this city and London are the undertakers' *shops.* In England they are all wooden windows below and scutcheons above; planks and shavings within—in fact, mere workshops. Here they are different: they have large glass fronts, like a millinery or cut-glass shop with us, and the shop runs back thirty or forty feet, its sides being filled with coffins stand-

---

[2] Stephen Decatur (1779–1820), American naval officer and hero of the Tripolitanian War. He also served in the War of 1812 and fought in the last engagement of that conflict. His death was the result of a duel which he fought with Commodore James Barron.

* On Sundays the coloured population takes possession of Broadway.

ing on end, mahogany and French polished. Therein you may select as you please, from the seven feet to receive the well-grown adult, to the tiny receptacle of what Burns calls, "Wee unchristened babe." I have, however, never heard of anyone choosing their own coffin; they generally leave it to their relatives to perform that office.

I may here remark that the Americans are sensible enough not to throw away so much money in funerals as we do; still it appears strange to an Englishman to see the open hearse, containing the body, drawn by only one horse, while the carriages which follow are drawn by two; to be sure, the carriages generally contain six individuals, while the hearse is a sulky and carries but one.

The New York tradesmen do all they can, as the English do, to attract the notice of the public by hand-bills, placards, advertisements, etc.; but in one point they have gone ahead of us. Placards, etc., may be read by those who look upward or straight-forward, or to the right or to the left; but there are some people who walk with their eyes to the ground, and consequently see nothing. The New Yorkers have provided for this contingency by having large marble tablets, like horizontal tombstones, let into the flag pavements of the *trottoir* in front of their shops, on which is engraven in duplicate, turning both ways, their names and business; so, whether you walk up or down Broadway, if you cast your eyes downward so as not to see the placards above, you cannot help reading the inscriptions below.

Every traveller who has visited this city has spoken of the numerous fires which take place in it, and the constant running, scampering, hallooing, and trumpeting of the firemen with their engines; but I do not observe that anyone has attempted to investigate the causes which produce, generally speaking, three or four fires in the twenty-four hours. New York has certainly great capabilities, and every chance of improvement as a city; for, about one house in twenty is burnt down every year, and is always rebuilt in a superior manner. But, as to the causes, I have, after minute inquiry, discovered as follows. These fires are occasioned—

1st. By the notorious carelessness of black servants, and the custom of smoking cigars all the day long.

2nd. By the knavery of men without capital, who insure to double and treble the value of their stock, and realize an honest penny by setting fire to their stores. (This is one reason why you can seldom recover from a fire-office without litagation.)

3rd. From the hasty and unsubstantial way in which houses are built up, the rafters and beams often communicating with the flues of the chimneys.

4th. Conflagrations of houses *not* insured, effected by agents employed by the *fire insurance companies,* as a punishment to some and a warning to others, who have neglected to take out policies.

These were gravely stated to me as the causes of so many fires in New York. I cannot vouch for the truth of the last, although I feel bound to mention it. I happen to be lodged opposite to two fire-engine houses, so that I always know when there is a fire. Indeed, so does everybody; for the church nearest to it tolls its bell, and this tolling is repeated by all the others; and as there are more than three hundred churches in New York, if a fire takes place no one can say that he is not aware of it.

The duty of firemen is admirably performed by the young men of the city, who have privileges for a servitude of seven years; but they pay too dearly for their privileges, which are an exemption from militia and jury summons. Many of them are taken off by consumptions, fevers, and severe catarrhs, engendered by the severe trials to which they are exposed: the sudden transitions from extreme heat to extreme cold in winter, being summoned up from a warm bed, when the thermometer is below zero—then exposed to the scorching flames—and afterward (as I have frequently seen them myself), with the water hanging in icicles upon their saturated clothes. To recruit themselves after their fatigue and exhaustion, they are compelled to drink, and thus it is no wonder that their constitutions are undermined. It is, nevertheless, a favourite service, as the young men have an opportunity of showing courage and determination, which raises them high in the opinion of their brother citizens.

I made a purchase at a store; an intelligent-looking little boy brought it home for me. As he walked by my side, he amused me very much by putting the following questions:

"Pray, Captain, has Mr. Easy [3] left the king of England's service?"

"I think he has," replied I. "If you recollect, he married and went on shore."

"Have you seen Mr. Japhet lately?" was the next query.

"Not very lately," replied I. "The last time I saw him was at the publisher's."

The little fellow went away, perfectly satisfied that they were both alive and well.

---

[3] Easy and Japhet were characters in novels written by Marryat. Easy is the hero of *Mr. Midshipman Easy*, one of Marryat's most popular books; Japhet is the hero of *Japhet in Search of a Father*.

CHAPTER IV

Excursion up the Hudson River

The dogs are all tied up, and the mosquitoes have broke loose—it is high time to leave New York.

The American steamboats have been often described. When I first saw one of the largest sweep round the battery, with her two decks, the upper one screened with snow-white awnings—the gay dresses of the ladies—the variety of colours—it reminded me of a floating garden, and I fancied that Isola Bella, on the Lake of Como, had got underweigh, and made the first steam voyage to America.

The Hudson is a noble stream, flowing rapidly through its bold and deep bed. Already it has many associations connected with it—a great many for the time which has elapsed since Henrick Hudson first explored it. Where is the race of red men who hunted on its banks, or fished and paddled their canoes in its stream? They have disappeared from the earth, and scarce a vestige remains of them, except in history. No portion of this world was ever intended to remain for ages untenanted. Beasts of prey and noxious reptiles are permitted to exist in the wild and uninhabited regions until they are swept away by the broad stream of civilization, which, as it pours along, drives them from hold to hold, until they finally disappear. So it is with the more savage nations: they are but *tenants at will*, and never were

40

intended to remain longer than till the time when civilization, with the gospel, arts, and sciences, in her train, should appear, and claim as her own that portion of the universe which they occupy.

About thirty miles from New York is Tarrytown, the abode of Washington Irving, who has here embosomed himself in his own region of romance; for Sleepy Hollow lies behind his domicile. Nearly opposite to it is the sight of a mournful reality—the spot where poor Major André was hung up as a spy.

You pass the State Prison, built on a spot which still retains its Indian name—Sing Sing—rather an odd name for a prison, where people are condemned to perpetual silence. It is a fine building of white marble, like a palace —very appropriate for that portion of the *sovereign* people, who may qualify themselves for a residence in it.

I had a genuine Yankee story from one of the party on deck. I was inquiring if the Hudson was frozen up or not during the winter? This led to a conversation as to the severity of the winter, when one man, by way of proving how cold it was, said— "Why, I had a cow on my lot up the river, and last winter she got in among the ice, and was carried down three miles before we could get her out again. The consequence has been that she has milked nothing but *ice-creams* ever since."

When you have ascended about fifty miles, the bed of the river becomes contracted and deeper, and it pours its waters rapidly through the high lands on each side, having at some distant time forced its passage through a chain of rocky mountains. It was quite dark long before we arrived at West Point, which I had embarked to visit. A storm hung over us, and as we passed through the broad masses piled up on each side of the river, at one moment illuminated by the lightning as it burst from the opaque clouds, and the next towering in sullen gloom, the effect was sublime.

Here I am at West Point.

West Point is famous in the short history of this country. It is the key of the Hudson River. The traitor Arnold had agreed to deliver it up to the English, and it was on his return from arranging the terms with Arnold that André was captured and hung.

At present, a military college is established here, which turns out about forty officers every year. Although they receive commissions in any regiment of the American army when there may be vacancies, they are all educated as engineers. The democrats have made several attempts to break up this establishment, as savouring too much of *monarchy,* but hitherto have been unsuccessful. It would be a pity if they did succeed, for such has been the demand lately for engineers to superintend railroads and canals, that a large portion of them have resigned their commissions, and found employment in the different states. This consideration alone is quite sufficient to warrant the keeping up of the college, for civil engineers are a *sine qua non* in a country like America, and they are always ready to serve should their military services be required. There was an inspection at the time I was there, and it certainly was highly creditable to the students, as well as to those who superintend the various departments.

When I awoke the next morning, I threw open the blinds of my windows, which looked out upon the river, and really was surprised and delighted. A more beautiful view I never gazed upon. The Rhine was fresh in my memory; but, although the general features of the two rivers are not dissimilar, there is no one portion of the Rhine which can be compared to the Hudson at West Point. It was what you may imagine the Rhine to have been in the days of Cæsar, when the lofty mountains through which it sweeps were not bared and naked as they now are, but clothed with forests, and rich in all the variety and beauty of undisturbed nature.

There is a sweet little spot not far from the college, where a tomb has been erected in honour of Kosciusko[1]—

---

[1] Thaddeus Kosciusko (1746–1817), Polish soldier and patriot who joined the Americans during the Revolution. In 1778 he was placed in charge of constructing West Point. He re-

it is called Kosciusko's Garden. I often sat there and talked over the events of the war of Independence. Many anecdotes were narrated to me, some of them very original. I will mention one or two which have not escaped my memory.

One of the officers who most distinguished himself in the struggle was a General Stark; [2] and the following is the speech he is reported to have made to his men previous to an engagement:

"Now, my men, you see them ere Belgians; every man of them bought by the king of England at 17s. 6d. a head, and I've a notion he paid too dear for them. Now, my men, we either beats them this day, or Molly Starke's a widow, by G—d." He did beat them, and in his despatch to headquarters he wrote— "We've had a dreadful hot day of it, general, and I've lost my horse, saddle and bridle and all."

In those times, losing a *saddle* and *bridle* was as bad as losing a horse.

At the same affair, the captain commanding the outposts was very lame, and he thought proper thus to address his men:

"Now, my lads, you see we're only an outpost, and we are not expected to beat the whole army in face of us. The duty of an outpost, when the enemy comes on, is to go in, *treeing* it, and keeping ourselves not exposed. Now, you

---

turned to his native land in 1786 and opposed the Third and final Partition of the Kingdom of Poland. When a national revolution broke out in 1794 against the countries which had occupied Poland, namely Russia, Prussia, and Austria, he was an active participant and was for a time dictator and commander-in-chief of the revolutionary faction. He was finally defeated and taken prisoner at Maciejowice. Upon his release he retired to Switzerland, where he remained until his death.
[2] John Stark (1728–1822) commanded the New Hampshire Militia during the Revolution. He was the victorious commander at the Battle of Bennington (August 16, 1777), which contributed greatly to General Burgoyne's subsequent defeat at Saratoga.

have my orders; and as I am a *little lame,* I'll go in first, and mind you do your duty and come in after me."

I passed several days at this beautiful spot, which is much visited by the Americans. Some future day, when America shall have become wealthy, and New York the abode of affluence and ease, what taste may not be lavished on the banks of this noble river! and what a lovely retreat will be West Point, if permitted to remain in all its present wildness and grandeur!

I re-embarked at midnight in the steamboat descending from Albany, and which is fitted out as a night boat. When I descended into the cabin, it presented a whimsical sight: two rows of bed-places on each side of the immense cabin, running right fore and aft; three other rows in the centre, each of these five rows having three bed-places, one over the other. There were upwards of five hundred people, lying in every variety of posture, and exhibiting every state and degree of repose—from the loud uneasy snorer lying on his back, to the deep sleeper tranquil as death. I walked up and down, through these long ranges of unconsciousness, thinking how much care was for the time forgotten. But as the air below was oppressive, and the moon was beautiful in the heavens, I went on deck, and watched the swift career of the vessel, which, with a favouring tide, was flying past the shores at the rate of twenty miles an hour—one or two people only, out of so many hundreds on board of her, silently watching over the great principle of locomotion. The moon sank down, and the sun rose and gilded the verdure of the banks and the spires of the city of New York, as I revelled in my own thoughts and enjoyed the luxury of being alone—a double luxury in America, where the people are gregarious, and would think themselves very ill-bred if they allowed you one moment for meditation or self-examination.

CHAPTER V

Visit to New England—Boston

Stepped on board of the Narragansett steam-vessel for Providence. Here is a fair specimen of American travelling—from New York to Providence, by the Long Island Sound, is two hundred miles, and this is accomplished, under usual circumstances, in thirteen hours; from Providence to Boston, forty miles by railroad, in two hours—which makes, from New York to Boston, an average speed of sixteen miles an hour, stoppages included.

I was, I must confess, rather surprised, when in the railroad cars, to find that we were passing through a *churchyard*, with tombstones on both sides of us. In Rhode Island and Massachusetts, where the pilgrim-fathers first landed—the two states that take pride to themselves (and with justice) for superior morality and a strict exercise of religious observances—they look down upon the other states of the Union, especially New York, and cry out: "I thank thee, Lord, that I am not as that publican." Yet here, in Rhode Island, are the sleepers of the railway laid over the sleepers in death; here do they grind down the bones of their ancestors for the sake of gain, and consecrated earth is desecrated by the iron wheels, loaded with Mammon-seeking mortals. And this in the puritanical state of Rhode Island! Would any engineer have ventured to propose such

a line in England? I think not. After all, it is but human nature. I have run over the world a long while, and have always observed that people are very religious so long as religion does not interfere with their pockets; but, with gold
in one hand and godliness in the other, the tangible is always preferred to the immaterial. In America every thing is
sacrificed to time; for time is money. The New Yorkers
would have dashed right through the church itself; but
then, *they* are publicans, and don't *pretend* to be good.

Boston is a fine city, and, as a commercial one, almost
as well situated as New York. It has, however, lost a large
portion of its commerce, which the latter has gradually
wrested from it, and it must eventually lose much more.
The population of Boston is about eighty thousand, and it
has probably more people of leisure in it (that is, out of
business and living on their own means) than even Philadelphia, taking into the estimate the difference between the
populations. They are more learned and scientific here than
at New York, though not more so than at Philadelphia; but
they are more English than in any other city in America.
The Massachusetts people are very fond of comparing their
country with that of England. The scenery is not unlike; but
it is not like England in its high state of cultivation. Stone
walls are bad substitutes for green hedges. Still, there are
some lovely spots in the environs of Boston. Mount Auburn,
laid out as a Père la Chaise, is, in natural beauties, far superior to any other place of the kind. One would almost wish
to be buried there; and the proprietors, anxious to have it
peopled, offer, by their arrangements as to the price of
places of interment, a handsome premium to those who
will soonest die and be buried—which is certainly a consideration.

Fresh Pond is also a very romantic spot. It is a lake
of about two hundred acres, whose water is so pure that
the ice is transparent as glass. Its proprietor clears many
thousand dollars a year by the sale of it. It is cut out in
blocks of three feet square, and supplies most parts of
America down to New Orleans; and every winter latterly

two or three ships have been loaded and sent to Calcutta, by which a very handsome profit has been realized.

Since I have been here, I have made every inquiry relative to the sea-serpent which frequents this coast alone. There are many hundreds of most respectable people, who, on other points, would be considered as incapable of falsehood, who declare they have seen the animals, and vouch for their existence. It is rather singular that in America there is but one copy of Bishop Pontoppidon's [1] work on Norway, and in it the sea-serpent is described, and a rough wood-cut of its appearance given. In all the American newspapers a drawing was given of the animal as described by those who saw it, and it proved to be almost a *facsimile* of the one described by the Bishop in his work.

Now that we are on marine matters, I must notice the prodigious size of the lobsters off Boston coast: they could stow a dozen common English lobsters under their coats of mail. My very much respected friend Sir Isaac Coffin,[2] when he was here, once laid a wager that he would produce a lobster weighing thirty pounds. The bet was accepted, and the admiral despatched people to the proper quarter to procure one; but they were not then in season, and could not be had. The admiral, not liking to lose his money, brought up, instead of the lobster, the affidavits of certain people that they had often seen lobsters of that size and weight. The affidavits of the deponents he submitted to the other party, and pretended that he had won the wager. The case was referred to arbitration, and the admiral was cast with the following pithy reply, *"Depositions are not lobsters."*

---

[1] Erik Pontoppidon (1698–1764), Norwegian cleric and Bishop of Bergen. Among his works was *The Natural History of Norway*, which first appeared in an English translation in London in 1755.

[2] Sir Isaac Coffin (1759–1839), a British naval officer born in Boston. He entered the navy in 1773, was Commissioner of the Navy in Corsica 1795–96, and in Minorca in 1797. He became a Rear Admiral in 1804, retired from active service in 1808, and by virtue of seniority was named a full Admiral in 1814. He had been awarded a baronetcy in 1804 and from 1818 to 1826 was a member of the House of Commons.

Massachusetts is certainly very English in its scenery, and Boston essentially English as a city. The Bostonians assert that they are more English than we are, that is, that they have strictly adhered to the old English customs and manners, as handed down to them previous to the revolution. That of sitting a very long while at their wine after dinner is one which they certainly adhere to, and which, *I* think, would be more honoured in the breach than the observance; but their hospitality is unbounded, and you do, as an Englishman, feel at home with them. I agree with the Bostonians so far, that they certainly appear to have made no change in their manners and customs for these last hundred years. You meet here with frequent specimens of the Old English Gentleman, descendants of the best old English families who settled here long before the revolution, and are now living on their incomes, with a town house and a country seat to retire to during the summer season. The society of Boston is very delightful; it wins upon you every day, and that is the greatest compliment that can be paid to it.

Perhaps of all the Americans the Bostonians are the most sensitive to any illiberal remarks made upon the country, for they consider themselves, and pride themselves, as being peculiarly English; while, on the contrary, the majority of the Americans deny that they are English. There certainly is less intermixture of foreign blood in this city than in any other in America. It will appear strange, but so wedded are they to old customs, even to John Bullism, that it is not more than seven or eight years that French wines have been put on the Boston tables and become in general use in this city.

It is a pity that this feeling towards England is not likely to continue; indeed, even at this moment it is gradually wearing away. Self-interest governs the world. At the declaration of the last war with England, it was the northern states which were so opposed to it and the southern who were in favour of it; but now circumstances have changed; the northern states, since the advance in prosperity and increase of produce in the southern and western states, feel aware that it is only as manufacturing states that they can hold their rank with the others. Their commerce has decreased since the completion of the Erie and Ohio canals, and during the war they discovered the advantage that would accrue to them, as manufacturers, to supply the southern and western markets. The imports of English goods have nearly ruined them. They now manufacture nothing but coarse articles, and as you travel through the eastern countries, you are surprised to witness splendid fabrics commenced but, for want of encouragement, not finished. This has changed the interests of the opponent states. The southern are very anxious to remain at peace with England, that their produce may find a market; while the northern, on the contrary, would readily consent to a war, that they might shut out the English manufactures, and have the supply entirely in their own hands. The eastern states (I particularly refer to Massachusetts, Connecticut, and Rhode Island) offer a proof of what can be effected by economy, prudence, and industry. Except on the borders of the rivers, the lands are generally sterile, and the climate is severe, yet, perhaps, the population is more at its ease than in any other part of the Union; but the produce of the states is not sufficient for the increasing population, or rather what the population would have been had it not migrated every year to the west and south. They set a higher value upon good connections in these poor states than they do in others; and if a daughter is to be married, they will ask what family the suitor is of, and if it bears a good name, they are quite indifferent as to whether he has a cent or not. It is remarkable that if a man has three or four sons in these states, one will be a lawyer, another a medical man, another a clergyman, and one will remain at home to take the property; and thus, out of the proceeds of a farm, perhaps not containing more than fifty acres, all these young men shall be properly educated, and in turn sent forth to the west and south, where they gain an honourable independence, and very often are sent to Congress

as senators and representatives. Industry and frugality are
the only entailed estate bequeathed from father to son. Yet
this state alone manufactures to the value of $86,282,616
in the year. As a general axiom it may fairly be asserted
that the more sterile the soil, the more virtuous, industrious, and frugal are the inhabitants; and it may be added,
that such a country sends out more clever and intelligent
men than one that is nominally more blessed by Providence. The fact is, without frugality and industry the eastern states could not exist; they become virtues of necessity,
and are the basis of others; whilst, where there is abundance, vice springs up and idleness takes deep root.

The population of Massachusetts is by the last returns
701,331 souls. I rather think the proportion of women to
men is very great.

An energetic and enterprising people are anxious for
an investigation into cause and effect, a search into which
is, after all, nothing but curiosity well directed, and the
most curious of all men is the philosopher. Curiosity, therefore, becomes a virtue or a small vice, according to the use
made of it. The Americans are excessively curious, especially the mob: they cannot bear anything like a secret—
that's *unconstitutional.* It may be remembered that the
Catholic convent near Boston, which had existed many
years, was attacked by the mob and pulled down.[3] I was
inquiring into the cause of this outrage in a country where
all forms of religion are tolerated; and an American gentleman told me that, although other reasons had been ad-

---

[3] This is a reference to the destruction of a convent in
Charlestown, Massachusetts, on
August 11, 1834. "A most disgraceful riot also occurred on
the night of Monday, the 11th, at
Charlestown, near Boston. The
populace having been deceived
by ill-designing persons into an
erroneous belief that a young lady
was confined against her will in
the Ursuline Convent, a highly
respectable seminary under the
charge of the Roman Catholics,
made an attack upon the convent, a noble edifice near Charlestown, and the other buildings belonging to the sisterhood, and
burned them to the ground with
all the valuable furniture, desecrated the cemetery, and committed every species of outrage."
Bayard Tuckerman, *The Diary of
Philip Hone,* Vol. 1, pp. 110–11.

duced for it, he fully believed, in his own mind, that the majority of the mob were influenced more by *curiosity* than any other feeling. The convent was sealed to them, and they were determined to know what was in it. "Why, sir," continued he, "I will lay a wager that if the authorities were to nail together a dozen planks, and fix them upon the common, with a caution to the public that they were not to go near or touch them, in twenty-four hours a mob would be raised to pull them down and ascertain what the planks contained." I mention this conversation to show in what manner this American gentleman attempted to palliate one of the grossest outrages ever committed by his countrymen.

CHAPTER VI

New Jersey—Passaic Falls

Crossed over to New Jersey, and took the railroad, to view the falls of the Passaic River, about fifteen miles from New York. This water-power has given birth to Paterson, a town with ten thousand inhabitants, where a variety of manufactures is carried on. A more beautiful wild spot can hardly be conceived; and to a European who has been accustomed to travel far in search of the picturesque, it appears singular that at so short a distance from a large city, he should at once find himself in the midst of such a strange combination of nature and art. Independent of their beauty, they are, perhaps, the most singular falls that are known to exist. The whole country is of trappe formation, and the black rocks rise up strictly vertical. The river, which at the falls is about one hundred and twenty yards wide, pours over a bed of rock between hills covered with chestnut, walnut, pine, and sycamore, all mingled together, and descending to the edge of the bank, their bright and various foliage forming a lovely contrast to the clear rushing water. The bed of black rock over which the river runs is, at the fall, suddenly split in two, vertically, and across the whole width of the river. The fissure is about seventy feet deep and not more than twelve feet wide at any part. Down into this chasm pour the whole water of the river,

escaping from it, at a right angle, into a deep basin, surrounded with perpendicular rocks from eighty to ninety
feet high. You may therefore stand on the opposite side of
the chasm, looking up the river, within a few feet of the
fall, and watch the roaring waters as they precipitate themselves below. In this position, with the swift, clear, but not
deep waters before you, forcing their passage through the
rocky bed, with the waving trees on each side, their
branches feathering to the water's edge, or dipping and rising in the stream, you might imagine yourself far removed
from your fellow-men, and you feel that in such a beauteous
spot you could well turn anchorite, and commune with Nature alone. But turn round with your back to the fall—
look below, and all is changed: art in full activity—millions
of reels whirling in their sockets—the bright polished cyl-
inders incessantly turning, and never tiring. What formerly
was the occupation of thousands of industrious females,
who sat with their distaff at the cottage door, is now effected in a hundredth part of the time, and in every variety,
by those compressed machines which require but the attendance of one child to several hundreds. But machinery
cannot perform everything, and notwithstanding this reduc-
tion of labour, the romantic falls of the Passaic find employment for the industry of thousands.

We walked up the banks of the river above the fall and
met with about twenty or thirty urchins who were bathing
at the mouth of the cut, made for the supply of the water-
power to the manufactories below. The river is the property
of an individual, and is very valuable: he receives six hundred dollars per annum for one square foot of water-power;
ten years hence it will be rented at a much higher price.

We amused ourselves by throwing small pieces of
money into the water, where it was about a fathom deep,
for the boys to dive after; they gained them too easily; we
went to another part in the *cut*, where it was much deeper,
and threw in a dollar. The boys stood naked on the rocks,
like so many cormorants, waiting to dart upon their prey;
when the dollar had had time to sink to the bottom the

word was given—they all dashed down like lightning and disappeared. About a minute elapsed ere there was any sign of their reappearance, when they came up, one by one, breathless and flushed (like racers who had pulled up), and at last the victor appeared with the dollar between his teeth. We left the juvenile *Sam Patches** and returned to the town.

There is no part of the world, perhaps, where you have more difficulty in obtaining permission to be alone, and indulge in a reverie, than in America. The Americans are as gregarious as schoolboys, and think it an incivility to leave you by yourself. Everything is done in crowds, and among a crowd. They even prefer a double bed to a single one, and I have often had the offer to sleep with me made out of real kindness. You must go "east of sunrise" (or west of sunset) if you would have solitude.

I never was in a more meditative humour, more anxious to be left to my own dreamings, than when I ascended the railroad car with my companion to return to Jersey City; we were the only two in that division of the car, and my friend, who understood me, had the complaisance to go fast asleep. I made sure that, for an hour or two, I could indulge in my own castle-buildings, and allow my fleeting thoughts to pass over my brain, like the scud over the moon. At our first stoppage a third party stepped in and seated himself between us. He looked at my companion, who was fast asleep. He turned to me, and I turned away my head. Once more was I standing at the falls of the Passaic; once more were the waters rolling down before me, the trees gracefully waving their boughs to the breeze, and the spray cooling my heated brain; my brain was, like the camera-obscura, filled with the pleasing images, which I

---

* Sam Patch, an American peripatetic, who used to amuse himself and astonish his countrymen by leaping down the different falls in America. He leaped down a portion of the Niagara without injury; but one fine day, having taken a drop too much, he took a leap too much. He went down the Genessee Fall, and since that time he has not been seen or heard of.

watched as they passed before me so vividly portrayed, all
in life and motion, when I was interrupted by—

"I was born in the very heart of Cheshire, sir."

Confound the fellow! The river, falls, foliage, all van-
ished at once; and I found myself sitting in a railroad car
(which I had been unconscious of), with a heavy lump of
humanity by my side. I wished one of the largest Cheshire
cheeses down his throat.

"Indeed!" replied I, not looking at the man.

"Yes, sir—in the very heart of Cheshire."

"Would you had stayed there!" thought I, turning away
to the window without replying.

"Will you oblige me with a pinch of your snuff, sir? I
left my box at New York."

I gave him the box, and, when he had helped himself,
laid it down on the vacant seat opposite to him, that he
might not have to apply again, and fell back and shut
my eyes, as a hint to him that I did not wish to enter into
conversation. A pause ensued, and I had hopes; but they
were delusive.

"I have been eighteen years in this country, sir."

"You appear to be quite *Americanized!*" thought I, but
I made him no answer.

"I went up to Paterson, sir," continued he (now turning
round to me, and speaking in my ear), "thinking that I
could get to Philadelphia by that route, and found that I
had made a mistake; so I have come back. I am *told* there
are some pretty falls there, sir."

"Would you were beneath them!" thought I, but I could
not help laughing at the idea of a man going to Paterson and
returning without seeing the falls! By this time he had
awakened his companion, who, being American himself,
and finding that there was to be no more sleep, took him
up, in the American fashion, and put to him successively
the following questions, all of which were answered without hesitation: "What is your name? where are you from?
where are you going? what is your profession? how many
dollars have you made? have you a wife and children?" All

these being duly responded to, he asked my companion who I might be, and was told that I was an operative artist, and one of the first cotton spinners in the country. This communication procured for me considerable deference from our new acquaintance during the remainder of our journey. He observed in the ear of my companion that he thought I knew a thing or two. In a country like America the utilitarian will always command respect.

CHAPTER VII

An American Festival—The Fourth of July in New York City

The 4th of July, the sixty-first anniversary of American independence!

Pop—pop—bang—pop—pop—bang—bang—bang! Mercy on us! how fortunate it is that anniversaries come only once a year. Well, the Americans may have great reason to be proud of this day, and of the deeds of their forefathers, but why do they get so confoundedly drunk? why, on this day of independence, should they become so *dependent* upon posts and rails for support? The day is at last over; my head aches, but there will be many more aching heads tomorrow morning!

What a combination of vowels and consonants have been put together! what strings of tropes, metaphors, and allegories have been used on this day! what varieties and graduations of eloquence! There are at least fifty thousand cities, towns, villages, and hamlets, spread over the surface of America—in each the Declaration of Independence has been read; in all one, and in some two or three, orations have been delivered, with as much gunpowder in them as in the squibs and crackers. But let me describe what I actually saw.

The commemoration commenced, if the day did not, on the evening of the 3rd, by the municipal police going round and pasting up placards, informing the citizens of New York that all persons letting off fireworks would be taken into custody, which notice was immediately followed up by the little boys proving their independence of the authorities, by letting off squibs, crackers, and bombs—and cannons, made out of shin bones, which flew in the face of every passenger, in the exact ratio that the little boys flew in the face of the authorities. This continued the whole night, and thus was ushered in the great and glorious day, illumined by a bright and glaring sun (as if bespoken on purpose by the mayor and corporation), with the thermometer at 90° in the shade. The first sight which met the eye after sunrise was the precipitate escape, from a city visited with the plague of gunpowder, of respectable or timorous people in coaches, carriages, wagons, and every variety of vehicle. "My kingdom for a horse!" was the general cry of all those' who could not stand fire. In the meanwhile, the whole atmosphere was filled with independence. Such was the quantity of American flags which were hoisted on board of the vessels, hung out of windows, or carried about by little boys, that you saw more stars at noonday than ever could be counted on the brightest night. On each side of the whole length of Broadway were ranged booths and stands, similar to those at an English fair, and on which were displayed small plates of oysters, with a fork stuck in the board opposite to each plate; clams sweltering in the hot sun; pineapples, boiled hams, pies, puddings, barley-sugar, and many other indescribables. But what was most remarkable, Broadway being three miles long, and the booths lining each side of it, in every booth there was a roast pig, large or small, as the centre attraction. Six miles of roast pig! and that in New York City alone; and roast pig in every other city, town, hamlet, and village in the Union. What association can there be between roast pig and independence? Let it not be supposed that there was any deficiency in the very necessary articles of potation on this auspicious day: no! the booths were loaded with porter, ale, cider, mead, brandy, wine, ginger-beer, pop, soda-water, whiskey, rum, punch, gin slings, cocktails, mint juleps, besides many other compounds, to name which nothing but the luxuriance of American-English could invent a word. Certainly the preparations in the refreshment way were most imposing, and gave you some idea of what had to be gone through with on this auspicious day. Martial music sounded from a dozen quarters at once; and as you turned your head, you tacked to the first bars of a march from one band, the concluding bars of Yankee Doodle from another. At last the troops of militia and volunteers, who had been gathering in the park and other squares, made their appearance, well dressed and well equipped, and, in honour of the day, marching as independently as they well could. I did not see them go through many manœuvres, but there was one which they appeared to excel in, and that was grounding arms and eating pies. I found that the current went toward Castle Garden, and away I went with it. There the troops were all collected on the green, shaded by the trees, and the effect was very beautiful. The artillery and infantry were drawn up in a line pointing to the water. The officers in their regimental dresses and long white feathers, generals and aides-de-camp, colonels, commandants, majors, all galloping up and down in front of the line—white horses and long tails appearing the most fashionable and correct. The crowds assembled were, as American crowds usually are, quiet and well behaved. I recognized many of my literary friends turned into generals, and flourishing their swords instead of their pens. The scene was very animating; the shipping at the wharfs were loaded with star-spangled banners; steamers, paddling in every direction, were covered with flags; the whole beautiful Sound was alive with boats and sailing vessels, all flaunting with pennants and streamers. It was, as Ducrow [1] would call it, "A Grand Military and Aquatic Spectacle."

Then the troops marched up into town again, and so did I follow them as I used to do the reviews in England, when a boy. All creation appeared to be independent on this day; some of the horses particularly so, for they would not keep "in no line not no how." Some preferred going sideways like crabs, others went backwards, some would not go at all, others went a great deal too fast, and not a few parted company with their riders, whom they kicked off just to show their independence; but let them go which way they would, they could not avoid the squibs and crackers. And the women were in the same predicament: they might dance right, or dance left, it was only out of the frying-pan into the fire, for it was pop, pop; bang; fiz, pop, bang so that you literally trod upon gunpowder.

When the troops marched up Broadway, louder even than the music were to be heard the screams of delight from the children at the crowded windows on each side. "Ma! ma! there's pa!" "Oh! there's John." "Look at uncle on his big horse."

The troops did not march in very good order, because, independently of their not knowing how, there was a great deal of independence to contend with. At one time an omnibus and four would drive in and cut off the general and his staff from his division; at another, a cart would roll in and insist upon following close upon the band of music; so that it was a mixed procession—generals, omnibus and four, music, cartloads of bricks, troops, omnibus and pair, artillery, hackney-coach, etc. etc. Notwithstanding all this, they at last arrived at the City Hall, when those who were old enough heard the Declaration of Independence read for

---

[1] Andrew Ducrow (1793–1842), son of a Flemish "strong man," was the chief equestrian performer at Astley's in London. He produced extravaganzas with "casts of thousands," and was looked upon by his contemporaries as the Florenz Ziegfeld and Cecil B. De Mille of his day. Among his numerous patrons was King William IV of England.

the sixty-first time; and then it was— "Begone, brave army, and don't kick up a row."

I was invited to dine with the mayor and corporation at the City Hall. We sat down in the Hall of Justice, and certainly, great justice was done to the dinner, which (as the wife says to her husband after a party, where the second course follows the first with unusual celerity) "went off remarkably well." The crackers popped outside, and the champagne popped in. The celerity of the Americans at a public dinner is very commendable; they speak only now and then; and the toasts follow so fast that you have just time to empty your glass before you are requested to fill again. Thus the arranged toasts went off rapidly, and after them, anyone might withdraw. I waited till the thirteenth toast, the last on the paper, to wit, the ladies of America; and, having previously, in a speech from the recorder, bolted Bunker's Hill and New Orleans, I thought I might as well bolt myself, as I wished to see the fireworks, which were to be very splendid.

Unless you are an amateur, there is no occasion to go to the various places of public amusement where the fireworks are let off, for they are sent up everywhere in such quantities that you hardly know which way to turn your eyes. It is, however, advisable to go into some place of safety, for the little boys and the big boys have all got their supply of rockets, which they fire off in the streets—some running horizontally up the pavement, and sticking into the back of a passenger, and others mounting slantingdicularly and Paul-Prying into the bedroom windows on the third floor or attics, just to see how things are going on *there*. Look in any point of the compass, and you will see a shower of rockets in the sky: turn from New York to Jersey City, from Jersey City to Brooklyn, and shower is answered by shower on either side of the water. Hoboken repeats the signal; and thus it is carried on to the east, the west, the north, and the south, from Rhode Island to the Missouri, from the Canada frontier to the Gulf of Mexico. At the various gardens the combinations were very beautiful, and exceeded anything that I had witnessed in London or Paris. What with sea-serpents, giant rockets scaling heaven, Bengal lights, Chinese fires, Italian suns, fairy bowers, crowns of Jupiter, exeranthemums, Tartar temples, Vesta's diadems, magic circles, morning glories, stars of Columbia, and temples of liberty, all America was in a blaze; and, in addition to this mode of manifesting its joy, all America was tipsy.

There is something grand in the idea of a national intoxication. In this world, vices on a grand scale dilate into virtues: he who murders one man is strung up with ignominy; but he who murders twenty thousand has a statue to his memory and is handed down to posterity as a hero. A staggering individual is a laughable and, sometimes, a disgusting spectacle; but the whole of a vast continent reeling, offering a holocaust of its brains for mercies vouchsafed, is an appropriate tribute of gratitude for the rights of equality and the *levelling spirit* of their institutions.

CHAPTER VIII

The Hudson River Valley— Albany and Niskayuna

Once more flying up the noble Hudson. After you have passed West Point, the highlands, through which the river has forced its passage, gradually diminish, and, as the shore becomes level, so does the country become more fertile.

We passed the manor of Albany, as it is called, being a Dutch grant of land, now in the possession of one person, a Mr. Van Rensselaer,[1] and equal to many a German principality, being twenty miles by forty-eight miles square. Mr. Van Rensselaer still retains the old title of patroon. It is generally supposed in England that, in America, all property must be divided between the children at the decease of the parent. This is not the case. The entailing of estates was abolished by an act of Congress in 1788, but a man may will away his property entirely to his eldest son if he pleases. This is, however, seldom done; public opinion is too

---

[1] Stephen Van Rensselaer (1764–1839), the eighth patroon, was a descendant of Kiliaen Van Rensselaer, who had been granted, in 1635, Rensselaerswyck, a vast domain of over one million acres.

strong against it, and the Americans fear public opinion beyond the grave. Indeed, were a man so to act, the other claimants would probably appeal to have the will set aside upon the grounds of lunacy, and the sympathy of an American jury would decree in their favour.

As you ascend to Albany city, the banks of the river are very fertile and beautiful, and the river is spotted with many picturesque little islands. The country seats, which fringe the whole line of shore, are all built in the same, and very bad, style. Every house or tenement, be it a palace or a cottage, has its porticos and pillars—a string of petty Parthenons, which tire you by their uniformity and pretence.

I had intended to stop at Hudson, that I might proceed from thence to New Lebanon, to visit the shaking quakers; but, as I discovered that there was a community of them not five miles from Troy, I, to avoid a fatiguing journey, left Albany, and continued on to that city.

Albany is one of the oldest Dutch settlements, and among its inhabitants are to be found many of the descendants of the Dutch aristocracy. Indeed, it may even now be considered as a Dutch city. It is the capital of the state of New York, with a population of nearly thirty thousand. Its commerce is very extensive, as it is here that the Erie canal communications with the far west, as well as the eastern states, debouch into the Hudson.

We have here a singular proof, not only of the rapidity with which cities rise in America, but also how superior energy will overcome every disadvantage. Little more than twenty years ago, Albany stood by itself, a large and populous city without a rival, but its population was chiefly Dutch. The Yankees from the eastern states came down and settled themselves at Troy, not five miles distant, in opposition to them. It would be supposed that Albany could have crushed this city in its birth, but it could not, and Troy is now a beautiful city, with its mayor, its corporation, and a population of twenty thousand souls, and divides the commerce with Albany, from which most of the eastern trade has been ravished. The inhabitants of Albany are termed Albanians, those of Troy, Trojans! In one feature these cities are very similar, being both crowded with lumber and pretty girls. I went out to see the shakers [2] at Niskayuna. So much has already been said about their tenets that I shall not repeat them, farther than to observe that all their goods are in common, and that, although the sexes mix together, they profess the vows of celibacy and chastity. Their lands are in excellent order, and they are said to be very rich. *

We were admitted into a long room on the ground floor, where the shakers were seated on forms, the men opposite to the women, and apart from each other. The men were in their waistcoats and shirt-sleeves, twiddling their thumbs, and looking awfully puritanical. The women were attired in dresses of very light striped cotton, which hung about them like full dressing-gowns, and concealed all shape and proportions. A plain mob-cap on their heads, and a thick muslin handkerchief in many folds over their shoulders, completed their attire. They each held in their hands a pocket-handkerchief as large as a towel and of almost the same sub-

---

[2] "Shakers" was the popular name of the United Society of Believers in Christ's Second Appearing, founded in England by James and Jane Wardley in 1747. The Wardleys were joined by Ann Lee, better known as "Mother Ann," who, after a vision during imprisonment, claimed to be Jesus Christ in His second appearance on earth. In 1774 Mother Ann and a group of her disciples emigrated to the New World, founding a community at Mount Lebanon near Albany. Other settlements were to be established later in almost every state from Maine to Kentucky. The shakers were normally celibate and lived in communistic communities ruled by faith, honesty, charity, simplic-ity, and hard work. The slogan of these Protestant monastic institutions was: "Hands to work and hearts to God." They shook, or rather danced, in a formalized manner during their services.

* I should be very sorry to take away the character of any community, but, as I was a little sceptical as to the possibility of the vow of chastity being observed under circumstances above alluded to, I made some inquiries, and having met with one who had seceded from the fraternity, I discovered that my opinion of human nature was correct, and the conduct of the shakers not altogether so. I must not enter into details, as they would be unfit for publication.

stance. But the appearance of the women was melancholy and unnatural; I say unnatural, because it required to be accounted for. They had all the advantages of exercise and labour in the open air, good food, and good clothing; they were not overworked, for they are not required to work more than they please; and yet there was something so pallid, so unearthly in their complexions, that it gave you the idea that they had been taken up from their coffins a few hours after their decease; not a hue of health, not a vestige of colour in any cheek or lip; one cadaverous yellow tinge prevailed. And yet there were to be seen many faces very beautiful, as far as regarded outline, but they were the features of the beautiful in death. The men, on the contrary, were ruddy, strong, and vigorous. Why, then, this difference between the sexes, where they each performed the same duties, where none were taxed beyond their strength, and all were well fed and clothed?

After a silence of ten minutes, one of the men of the community, evidently a coarse and illiterate person, rose and addressed a few words to the spectators, requesting them not to laugh at what they saw, but to behave themselves properly, etc., and then he sat down.

One of the leaders then burst out into a hymn, to a jigging sort of tune, and all the others joined chorus. After the hymn was sung they all rose, put away the forms on which they had been seated, and stood in lines, eight in a row, men and women separate, facing each other, and about ten feet apart—the ranks of men being flanked by the boys, and those of the women by the girls. They commenced their dancing by advancing in rows, just about as far as profane people do in *L'été* when they dance quadrilles, and then retreated the same distance, all keeping regular time, and turning back to back after every third advance. The movement was rather quick, and they danced to their own singing, of the following beautiful composition:

> Law, law, de lawdel law,
> Law, law, de law,

Law, law, de lawdel law,
Lawdel, lawdel, law—

keeping time also with the hands as well as feet, the former
raised up to the chest, and hanging down like the forepaws
of a dancing bear. After a quarter of an hour they sat down
again, and the women made use of their large towel
pocket-handkerchiefs to wipe off the perspiration. Another
hymn was sung, and then the same person addressed the
spectators, requesting them not to laugh, and inquiring if
any of them felt a wish to be saved—adding "Not one of
you, I don't think." He looked round at all of us with the
most ineffable contempt, and then sat down, and they sang
another hymn, the burden of which was—

Our souls are saved, and we are free
From vice and all in-i-quity—

which was a very comfortable delusion, at all events.

They then rose again, put away the forms as before,
and danced in another fashion. Instead of *L'été*, it was
Grande Ronde. About ten men and women stood in two
lines in the centre of the room, as a vocal band of music,
while all the others, two and two, women first and men following, promenaded round, with a short quick step, to the
tune chanted in the centre. As they went round and round,
shaking their paws up and down before them, the scene was
very absurd, and I could have laughed had I not felt disgusted at such a degradation of rational and immortal beings. This dance lasted a long while, until the music
turned to croaking, and the perspiration was abundant;
they stopped at last, and then announced that their exercise was finished. I waited a little while after the main body
had dispersed, to speak with one of the elders. "I will be
with you directly," replied he, walking hastily away; but he
never came back.

I never heard the principle upon which they dance.
David danced before the ark; but it is to be presumed that

David danced as well as he sung. At least he thought so; for when his wife Michal laughed at him, he made her conduct a ground of divorce.

Every community which works in common, and is provided for in the mass, must become *rich,* especially when it has no children to maintain. It is like receiving a person's labour in exchange for victuals and clothing only, and this is all I can perceive that can be said in favour of these people. Suffice it to say, I have a very bad opinion of them; and were I disposed to dilate on the subject, I should feel no inclination to treat them with the lenity shown to them by other travellers.

From this mockery, I went to see what had a real tendency to make you feel religious—the Falls of the Mohawk, about three miles from Troy. Picturesque and beautiful as all falling water is, to describe it is extremely difficult, unless, indeed, by a forced simile; the flow of language is too tame for the flow of water; but if the reader can imagine a ledge of black rocks, about sixty or seventy feet high, and that over this ledge was poured simultaneously the milk of some millions of cows, he will then have some idea of the beauty of the *creaming* Falls of the Mohawk, imbedded as they are in their wild and luxuriant scenery.

Close to the Falls, I perceived a few small wooden shealings, appearing, under the majestic trees which overshadowed them, more like dog-kennels than the habitations of men; they were tenanted by Irish emigrants, who had taken work at the new locks forming on the Erie canal. I went up to them. In a tenement about fourteen feet by ten, lived an Irishman, his wife, and family, and seven boys as he called them, young men from twenty to thirty years of age, who boarded with him. There was but one bed, on which slept the man, his wife, and family. Above were some planks, extending half way the length of the shealing, and there slept the seven boys, without any mattress, or even straw, to lie upon. I entered into conversation with them: they complained bitterly of the times, saying that their pay was not 2s. 6d. of our money per day, and that they could not live upon it. This was true, but the distress had been communicated to all parts, and they were fortunate in finding work at all, as most of the public works had been discontinued. I mentioned to them that the price of labour in Ohio, Illinois, and the west was said to be two dollars a day, and asked them why they did not go there? They replied that such was the price quoted, to induce people to go, but that they never could find it when they arrived; that the clearing of new lands was attended with ague and fever; and that if once down with these diseases, there was no one to help them to rise again. I looked for the pig, and there he was, sure enough, under the bed.

CHAPTER IX

The Hudson River Valley—Troy

Troy, like a modern academy, is classical, as well as commercial, having Mount Olympus on one side and Mount Ida in its rear. The panorama from the summit of the latter is splendid. A few years back a portion of Mount Ida made a slip, and the avalanche destroyed several cottages and five or şix individuals. The avalanche took place on a dark night and in a heavy snowstorm. Two brick kilns were lighted at the time, and, as the mountains swept them away, the blaze of the disturbed fires called out the fire engines; otherwise more lives would have been lost. Houses, stables, and sheds were all hurled away together. Horses, children, and women rolled together in confusion. One child had a very strange escape. It had been forced out of its bed, and was found on the top of a huge mass of clay, weighing forty or fifty tons; he was crying, and asking who had put him there. Had all the inhabitants of the cottages been within, at least forty must have perished; but notwithstanding the severity of the weather, the day being Sunday, they had all gone to evening meeting, and thus, being good Christians, they were for once rewarded for it on this side of the grave.

As I surveyed the busy scene below me, the gentleman who accompanied me to the summit of the mountain informed me that forty-three years ago his father was the first settler, and that then there was but his one hut in the place where now stood the splendid town.

But signs of the times were manifest here also. Commerce had stopped for the present, and a long line of canal boats were laid up for want of employment.

I remained two hours perched upon the top of the mountain. I should not have stayed so long, perhaps, had they not brought me a basket of cherries, so that I could gratify more senses than one. I felt becomingly classical whilst sitting on the precise birthplace of Jupiter, attended by Pomona, with Troy at my feet, and Mount Olympus in the distance; but I was obliged to descend to lumber and ginslings, and I set off for Albany, where I had an engagement, having been invited to attend at the examination of the young ladies at the seminary.

Here again is a rivalry between Albany and Troy, each of them glorying in possessing the largest seminary [1] for the education of young ladies, who are sent from every state of the Union, to be finished off at one or the other of them. Here, and indeed in many other establishments, the young ladies upon quitting it have diplomas given to them, if they pass their examinations satisfactorily. . . . Conceive three hundred modern Portias, who regularly take their degrees, and emerge from the portico of the seminary full of algebra, equality, and the theory of the Constitution! The quantity and variety crammed into them is beyond all calculation. The examination takes place yearly, to prove to the parents that the preceptors have done their duty, and is in itself very innocent, as it only causes the young ladies to blush a little.

This afternoon they were examined in algebra, and their performance was very creditable. Under a certain age girls are certainly much quicker than boys, and I presume would retain what they learnt if it were not for their subsequent duties in making puddings and nursing babies.

---

[1] The Albany Female Academy was founded in 1814 and the Troy Female Seminary in 1821.

Yet these are affairs which must be attended to by one sex or the other, and of what use can algebra and other abstruse matters be to a woman in her present state of domestic thraldom?

The theory of the American Constitution was the next subject on which they were examined; by their replies, this appeared to be to them more abstruse than algebra; but the fact is, women are born tories, and admit no other than petticoat government as legitimate.

The next day we again repaired to the hall, and French was the language in which they were to be examined, and the examination afforded us much amusement.

The young ladies sat down in rows on one side of the room. In the centre, towards the end, was an easel, on which was placed a large blackboard on which they worked with chalk the questions in algebra, etc.—a towel hanging to it, that they might wipe out and correct. The French preceptor, an old Emigré Count, sat down with the examiners before the board, the visitors (chiefly composed of anxious papas and mamas) being seated on benches behind them. As it happened, I had taken my seat close to the examining board and at some little distance from the other persons who were deputed or invited to attend. I don't know how I came there. I believe I had come in too late; but there I was, within three feet of every young lady who came up to the board.

"Now, messieurs, have the kindness to ask any question you please," said the old Count. "Mademoiselle, you will have the goodness to step forward." A question was proposed in English, which the young lady had to write down in French. The very first went wrong; I perceived it, and without looking at her, pronounced the right word, so that she could hear it. She caught it, rubbed out the wrong word with the towel, and rectified it. This was carried on through the whole sentence, and then she retreated from the board that her work might be examined. "Very well, very well, indeed, Miss, *c'est parfaitement bien"*; and the young lady sat down blushing. Thus were they all called up, and one after another prompted by me; and the old Count was delighted at the success of his pupils.

Now, what amused me in this was the little bit of human nature: the *tact* displayed by the sex, which appears to be innate, and which never deserts them. Had I prompted a boy, he would most likely have turned his head round toward me, and thus have revealed what I was about; but not one of the whole class was guilty of such indiscretion. They heard me, rubbed out, corrected, waited for the word when they did not know it, but never by any look or sign made it appear that there was any understanding between us. Their eyes were constantly fixed on the board, and they appeared not to know that I was in the room. It was really beautiful. When the examination was over, I received a look from them all, half comic, half serious, which amply repaid me for my assistance.

As young ladies are assembled here from every state of the Union, it was a *fair* criterion of American beauty, and it must be acknowledged that the American women are the *prettiest* in the whole world.

CHAPTER X

The Mohawk Valley— Saratoga Springs and Utica

Saratoga Springs.—Watering places all over the world are much alike: they must be well filled with company, and full of bustle, and then they answer the purpose for which they are intended—a general muster, under the banner of folly, to drive care and common sense out of the field. Like assembly-rooms, unless lighted up and full of people, they look desolate and forlorn; so it was with Saratoga: a beautiful spot, beautiful hotels, and beautiful water; but all these beauties were thrown away, and the water ran away unheeded, because the place was empty. People's pockets were empty, and Saratoga was to let. The consequence was that I remained a week there, and should have remained much longer had I not been warned, by repeated arrivals, that the visitors were increasing, and that I should be no longer alone.

The weariness of solitude, as described by Alexander Selkirk [1] and the Anti-Zimmermanns,[2] can surely not be

---

[1] Alexander Selkirk (1676–1721), the prototype of Robinson Crusoe, was born in Scotland. He joined a privateering expedition under William Dampier in 1703. He later joined Thomas Strad-

equal to the misery of never being alone; of feeling that your thoughts and ideas, rapidly accumulating, are in a state of chaos and confusion, and that you have not a moment to put them into any lucid order; of finding yourself, against your will, continually in society, bandied from one person to the other, to make the same bows, extend the same hand to be grasped, and reply to the same eternal questions; until, like a man borne down by sleep after long vigils, and at each moment roused to reply, you either are not aware of what you do say, or are dead beat into an unmeaning smile. Since I have been in this country, I have suffered this to such a degree as at last to become quite nervous on the subject; and I might reply in the words of the spirit summoned by Lochiel—

Now my weary lips I close,
Leave, oh! leave me to repose.

It would be a strange account, had it been possible to keep one, of the number of introductions which I have had since I came into this country. Mr. A introduced Mr. B and C, Mr. B and C introduce Mr. D, E, F, and G. Messrs. D, E, F, and G introduce Messrs. H, I, J, K, L, M, N, O, and so it goes on, *ad infinitum* during the whole of the day; and this to me who never could remember either a face or a name.

At introduction it is invariably the custom to shake hands; and thus you go on shaking hands here, there, and everywhere, and with everybody; for it is impossible to know who is who, in this land of equality.

ling, but after quarrelling with him was marooned on the uninhabited island of Juan Fernandez in 1704, remaining there until 1709. After his rescue he returned to Great Britain and resumed his life as a sailor.

[2] Johann Georg Zimmermann (1728–95), *philosophe* and physician, was born in Brugg, Switzerland. His contemporary fame rested on his philosophical treatise *Von der Einsamkeit* (On Solitude) and he was the friend of many notables, including Frederick the Great and George III. Anti-Zimmermanns were those who did not appreciate Zimmermann's great praise of a life of solitude.

But one shake of the hand will not do; if twenty times during the same day you meet a person to whom you have been introduced, the hand is everywhere extended with— "Well, Captain, how do you find yourself by this time?" and, in their good-will, when they seize your hand, they follow the apothecary's advice— "When taken, to be well shaken." As for the constant query— "How do you like our country?" —that is natural enough. I should ask the same of an American in England, but to reply to it is not the less tedious. It is all well meant, all kindness, but it really requires fortitude and patience to endure it. Every one throws in his voluntary tribute of compliments and good-will, but the accumulated mass is too great for any one individual to bear. How I long for the ocean prairies or the wild forests. Subsequently, I begged hard to be shut up for six months in the penitentiary at Philadelphia, but Sammy Wood [3] said it was against the regulations. He comforted me with a *tête-à-tête* dinner, which was so agreeable that at the time I quite forgot I wished to be alone.

When I left Saratoga, I found no one, as I thought, in the car, who knew me; and I determined, if possible, they should, in the Indian phrase, *lose my trail.* I arrived at Schenectady, and was put down there. I amused myself until the train started for Utica, which was to be in a few hours, in walking about the engine-house and examining the locomotives, and having satisfied myself, set out for a solitary walk in the country. There was no name on my luggage, and I had not given my name when I took my ticket for the railroad. "At last," said I to myself, "*I am incog.*" I had walked out of the engine-house, looked round the compass, and resolved in which direction I would bend my steps, when a young man came up to me, and very politely taking off his hat, said: "I believe I have the pleasure of speaking to Captain M." Had he known my indignation when he mentioned my name, poor fellow! but there was no

---

[3] Samuel R. Wood was the warden of the Eastern State Penitentiary of Pennsylvania from 1829 to 1835.

help for it, and I replied in the affirmative. After apologizing, he introduced himself, and then requested the liberty of introducing his friend. "Well, if ever," thought I; and, "no never," followed afterward as a matter of course, and as a matter of course his friend was introduced. It reminded me of old times when, midshipmen at balls, we used to introduce each other to ladies we had none of us seen before in our lives. Well, there I was, between two overpowering civilities, but they meant it kindly, and I could not be angry. These were students of Schenectady college; would I like to see it? a beautiful location, not half a mile off. I requested to know if there was anything to be seen there, as I did not like to take a hot walk for nothing, instead of the shady one I had proposed for myself. "Yes, there was Professor Nott" [4]—I had of course heard of Professor Nott— Professor Nott, who governed by moral influence and paternal sway, and who had written so largely on stones and anthracite coal. I had never before heard of moral influence, stones, or anthracite coal. Then there were more professors, and a cabinet of minerals—the last was an inducement, and I went.

I saw Professor Nott, but not the cabinet of minerals, for Professor Savage had the key. With Professor Nott I had rather a hot argument about anthracite coal, and then escaped before he was cool again. The students walked back with me to the hotel and, with many apologies for leaving me, informed me that dinner was ready. I would not tax their politeness any longer, and they departed.

Schenectady College, like most of the buildings in America, was commenced on a grand scale, but has never been finished; the two wings are finished, and the centre is lithographed, which looks very imposing in the plate. There

---

[4] Eliphalet Nott (1773–1866), a Presbyterian clergyman and president of Union College from 1802 to 1866. Nott invented a stove which burned anthracite rather than bituminous coal and which was more efficient than its predecessors since it produced greater heat and less smoke. He also wrote many books and articles on religious and temperance themes.

is a peculiarity in this college: it is called the Botany Bay, from its receiving young men who have been expelled from other colleges, and who are kept in order by moral influence and paternal sway, the only means certainly by which wild young men are to be reclaimed. Seriously speaking, Professor Nott is a very clever man, and I suspect this college will turn out more clever men than any other in the Union. It differs from the other colleges in another point. It upholds no peculiar sect of religion, which almost all the rest do. For instance, Yale, William's Town, and Amherst Colleges are under Presbyterian influence; Washington, Episcopal; Cambridge, in Massachusetts, Unitarian.

There is one disadvantage generally attending railroads. Travellers proceed more rapidly, but they lose all the beauty of the country. Railroads of course run through the most level portions of the states; and the levels, except they happen to be on the banks of a river, are invariably uninteresting. The road from Schenectady to Utica is one of the exceptions to this rule: there is not perhaps a more beautiful variety of scenery to be found anywhere. You run the whole way through the lovely valley of the Mohawk, on the banks of the Mohawk River. It was really delightful, but the motion was so rapid that you lamented passing by so fast. The Utica railroad is one of the best in America; the eighty miles are performed in four hours and a half, stoppages for taking in water, passengers, and refreshments included. The locomotive was of great power, and as it snorted along with a train of carriages of half a mile long in tow, it threw out such showers of fire that we were constantly in danger of conflagration. The weather was too warm to admit of the windows being closed, and the ladies, assisted by the gentlemen, were constantly employed in putting out the sparks which settled on their clothes—the first time I ever heard ladies complain of having too many *sparks* about them. As the evening closed in we were actually whirled along through a stream of fiery threads—a beautiful, although humble imitation of the tail of a comet.

I had not been recognized in the rail car, and I again

flattered myself that I was unknown. I proceeded, on my arrival at Utica, to the hotel, and asking at the bar for a bed, the book was handed to me, and I was requested to write my name. Wherever you stop in America, they generally produce a book and demand your name, not on account of any police regulations, but merely because they will not allow secrets in America, and because they choose to know who you may be. Of course you may frustrate this espionage by putting down any name you please; and I had the pen in my hand, and was just thinking whether I should be Mr. Snooks or Mr. Smith, when I received a slap on the shoulder, accompanied with—"Well, Captain, how are you by this time?" In despair I let the pen drop out of my hand, and instead of my name I left on the book a large blot. It was an old acquaintance from Albany, and before I had been ten minutes in the hotel, I was recognized by at least ten more. The Americans are such locomotives themselves that it is useless to attempt the incognito in any part except the west side of the Mississippi, or the Rocky Mountains. Once known at New York, and you are known everywhere, for in every place you will meet with someone whom you have met walking in Broadway.

A tremendous thunderstorm with torrents of rain prevented my leaving Utica for Trenton Falls until late in the afternoon. The roads, ploughed up by the rain, were anything but democratic; there was no level in them; and we were jolted and shaken like peas in a rattle, until we were silent from absolute suffering.

I rose the next morning at four o'clock. There was a heavy fog in the air, and you could not distinguish more than one hundred yards before you. I followed the path pointed out to me the night before, through a forest of majestic trees, and descending a long flight of steps, found myself below the falls. The scene impressed you with awe— the waters roared through deep chasms, between two walls of rock, one hundred and fifty feet high, perpendicular on each side, and the width between the two varying from forty to fifty feet. The high rocks were of black carbonate of lime in perfectly horizontal strata, so equally divided that they appeared like solid masonry. For fifty or sixty feet above the rushing waters they were smooth and bare; above that line vegetation commenced with small bushes, until you arrived at their summits, which were crowned with splendid forest trees, some of them inclining over the chasm, as if they would peep into the abyss below and witness the wild tumult of the waters.

From the narrowness of the pass, the height of the rocks, and the superadded towering of the trees above, but a small portion of the heavens was to be seen, and this was not blue, but of a misty murky grey. The first sensation was that of dizziness and confusion, from the unusual absence of the sky above and the dashing frantic speed of the angry boiling waters. The rocks on each side have been blasted so as to form a path by which you may walk up to the first fall; but this path was at times very narrow, and you have to cling to the chain which is let into the rock. The heavy storms of the day before had swelled the torrent so that it rose nearly a foot above this path; and before I had proceeded far, I found that the flood swept between my legs with a force which would have taken some people off their feet. The rapids below the falls are much grander than the falls themselves; there was one down in a chasm between two riven rocks which it was painful to look long upon and watch with what a deep plunge—what irresistible force— the waters dashed down and then returned to their own surface, as if struggling and out of breath. As I stood over them in their wild career, listening to their roaring as if in anger, and watching the madness of their speed, I felt a sensation of awe—an inward acknowledgment of the tremendous power of nature; and, after a time, I departed with feelings of gladness to escape from thought which became painful when so near to danger.

I gained the lower falls, which now covered the whole width of the rock, which they seldom do except during the freshets. They were extraordinary from their variety. On the side where I stood poured down a rapid column of water about one-half of the width of the fall; on the other, it was running over a clear thin stream, as gentle and amiable as water could be. That part of the fall reminded me of ladies' hair in flowing ringlets, and the one nearest me of the Lord Chancellor Eldon,[5] in all the pomposity and frowning dignity of his full-bottomed wig. And then I thought of the lion and the lamb, not lying down, but falling down together; and then I thought that I was wet through, which was a fact; so I climbed up a ladder and came to a wooden bridge above the fall, which conveyed me to the other side. The bridge passes over a staircase of little falls, sometimes diagonally, sometimes at right angles with the sites, and is very picturesque. On the other side you climb up a ladder of one hundred feet and arrive at a little building with a portico, where travellers are refreshed. Here you have a view of all the upper falls, but these seem tame after witnessing the savage impetuosity of the rapids below. You ascend another ladder of one hundred feet, and you arrive at a path pointed out to you by the broad chips of the woodman's axe. Follow the chips and you will arrive four or five hundred feet above both the bridge and the level of the upper fall. This scene is splendid. The black perpendicular rocks on the other side; the succession of falls; the rapids roaring below; the forest trees rising to the clouds and spreading with their majestic boughs the vapour ascending from the falling waters; together with the occasional glimpses of the skies here and there—all this induces you to wander with your eyes from one point of view to another, never tiring with its beauty, wildness, and vastness; and, if you do not exclaim with the Mussulman, God is great! you *feel* it through every sense and at every pulsation of the heart.

---

[5] John Scott (1751–1838), first Earl of Eldon, a barrister and member of Parliament, was in the government of William Pitt the Younger. In 1801 he became Lord Chancellor and held this office until 1806. In that year he resigned but returned to office in 1807 and continued as Lord Chancellor until 1827. He was a great legal theorist, and many of his decisions still stand as precedents. In politics he was a high Tory and opposed any sort of reform whatsoever.

The mountain was still above me, and I continued my ascent; but the chips now disappeared, and, like Tom Thumb, I lost my way. I attempted to retreat, but in vain; I was no longer amongst forest trees, but in a maze of young mountain ash, from which I could not extricate myself; so I stood still to think what I should do. I recollected that the usual course of proceeding on such occasions was either to sit down and cry or attempt to get out of your scrape. Tom Thumb did both; but I had no time to indulge in the former luxury, so I pushed and pushed, till I pushed myself out of my scrape, and found myself in a more respectable part of the woods. I then stopped to take breath. I heard a rustling behind me, and made sure it was a panther—it was a beautiful little palm squirrel, who came close to me, as if to say: "Who are you?" I took off my hat and told him my name, when, very contemptuously, as I thought, he turned short round, cocked his tail over his back, and skipped away. "Free, but not enlightened," thought I; "hasn't a soul above nuts." I also beat a retreat, and on my arrival at the hotel, found that, although I had no guides to pay, Nature had made a very considerable levy upon my wardrobe: my boots were bursting, my trousers torn to fragments, and my hat was spoilt; and, moreover, I sat shivering in the garments which remained. So I, in my turn, levied upon a cow that was milking, and having improved her juice very much by the addition of some rum, I sat down under the portico and smoked the cigar of meditation.

The walls of the portico were, as usual, scribbled over by those who would obtain cheap celebrity. I always read these productions; they are pages of human life. The majority of the scribblers leave a name and nothing more; beyond that, some few of their productions are witty, some sententious, mostly gross. My thoughts, as I read over the rubbish, were happily expressed by the following distich which I came to:

> *Les Fenêtres et les Murailles,*
> *Sont le papier des Canailles. . . .*

CHAPTER XI

The Erie Canal

Returning to Utica, I fell in with a horse bridled and saddled, that was taking his way home without his master, every now and then cropping the grass at the roadside, and then walking on in a most independent manner. His master had given him a certificate of leave, by chalking in large letters on his saddle-flaps on each side: *"Let him go."* This was a very primitive proceeding; but I am not quite sure that it could be ventured upon in Yorkshire, or in Virginia either, where they know a good horse, and are particularly careful of it. It is a fact, that wherever they breed horses they invariably learn to steal them.

Set off for Oswego in a canal boat; it was called a packet-boat because it did not carry merchandise, but was a very small affair, about fifty feet long by eight wide. The captain of her was, however, in his own opinion, no small affair; he puffed and swelled until he looked larger than his boat. This personage, as soon as we were underweigh, sat down in the narrow cabin, before a small table; sent for his writing-desk, which was about the size of a street organ, and, like himself, no small affair; ordered a bell to be rung in our ears to summon the passengers; and, then, taking down the names of four or five people, received the enormous sum of ten dollars passage-money. He then locked his desk with a key large enough for a street-door, ordered his steward to remove it, and went on deck to walk just three feet and return again. After all, there is nothing like being a captain.

Although many of the boats are laid up, there is still considerable traffic on this canal. We passed Rome, a village of two thousand inhabitants, at which number it has for many years been nearly stationary. This branch of the canal is, of course, cut through the levels, and we passed through swamps and wild forests; here and there some few acres were cleared, and a log-house was erected, looking very solitary and forlorn, surrounded by the stumps of the trees which had been felled, and which now lay corded up on the banks of the canal, ready to be disposed of. Wild and dreary as the country is, the mass of forest is gradually receding, and occasionally some solitary tree is left standing, throwing out its wide arms, and appearing as if in lamentation at its separation from its companions, with whom for centuries it had been in close fellowship.

Extremes meet: as I looked down from the roof of the boat upon .the giants of the forest, which had for so many centuries reared their heads undisturbed, but now lay prostrate before civilization, the same feelings were conjured up in my mind as when I have, in my wanderings, surveyed such fragments of dismembered empires as the ruins of Carthage or of Rome. There the reign of art was over, and nature had resumed her sway; here nature was deposed, and about to resign her throne to the usurper art. By the by, the mosquitoes of this district have reaped some benefit from the cutting of the canal here. Before these impervious forest retreats were thus pierced, they could not have tasted human blood; for ages it must have been unknown to them, even by tradition; and if they taxed all other boats on the canal as they did ours, *a canal share* with them must be considerably above par, and highly profitable.

At five o'clock we arrived at Syracuse. I do detest these old names vamped up. Why do not the Americans take the

Indian names? They need not be so very scrupulous about it; they have robbed the Indians of everything else.

After you pass Syracuse, the country wears a more populous and inviting appearance. Salina is a village built upon a salt spring, which has the greatest flow of water yet known, and this salt spring is the cause of the improved appearance of the country; the banks of the canal for three miles are lined with buildings for the boiling down of the salt water, which is supplied by a double row of wooden pipes. Boats are constantly employed up and down the canal, transporting wood for the supply of the furnaces. It is calculated that two hundred thousand cord of wood are required every year for the present produce; and as they estimate upon an average about sixty cord of wood per acre in these parts, those salt works are the means of yearly clearing away upwards of three thousand acres of land. Two million of bushels of salt are boiled down every year; it is packed in barrels, and transported by the canals and lakes to Canada, Michigan, Chicago, and the far west. When we reflect upon the number of people employed in the manufactories, and in cutting wood, and making barrels, and engaged on the lakes and canals in transporting the produce so many thousand miles, we must admire the spring to industry which has been created by this little, but bounteous, spring presented by nature.

The first sixty miles of this canal (I get on very slow with my description, but canal travelling is very slow), which is through a flat swampy forest, is without a lock; but after you pass Syracuse, you have to descend by locks to the Oswego River, and the same at every rapid of the river; in all, there is a fall of one hundred and sixty feet. Simple as locks are, I could not help reverting to the wild rapids at Trenton falls, and reflecting upon how the ingenuity of man had so easily been able to overcome and control nature! The locks did not detain us long—they never lose time in America. When the boat had entered the lock, and the gate was closed upon her, the water was let off with a rapidity which considerably affected her level, and her bows pointed downward. I timed one lock with a fall of fifteen feet. From the time the gate was closed behind us until the lower one was opened for our egress was exactly one minute and a quarter; and the boat sank down in the lock so rapidly as to give you the idea that she was scuttled and sinking.

The country round the Oswego is fertile and beautiful, and the river, with its islands, falls, and rapids, very picturesque. At one p.m. we arrived at the town of Oswego, on Lake Ontario; I was pleased with the journey, although, what with ducking to bridges, bites from mosquitoes, and the constant blowing of their unearthly horn with only one note, and which one must have been borrowed from the gamut of the infernal regions, I had had enough of it.

For the first time since my arrival in the country, no one—that is to say, on board the canal-boat—knew who I was. As we tracked above the Oswego River, I fell into conversation with a very agreeable person, who had joined us at Syracuse. We conversed the whole day, and I obtained much valuable information from him about the country; when we parted, he expressed a wish that we should meet again. He gave me his name and address, and when I gave my card in return, he looked at it and then said: "I am most happy to make your acquaintance, sir; but I will confess that had I known with whom I had been conversing, I should not have *spoken so freely* upon certain points connected with the government and institutions of this country." This was American all over; they would conceal the truth, and then blame us because we do not find it out. I met him afterwards, but he never would enter into any detailed conversation with me.

CHAPTER XII

Niagara Falls

NIAGARA FALLS.—Perhaps the wisest, if not the best, description of the Falls of Niagara is in the simple ejaculation of Mrs. Butler,[1] for it is almost useless to attempt to describe when you feel that language fails; but if the falls cannot be described, the ideas which are conjured up in the mind, when we contemplate this wonderful combination of grandeur and beauty, are often worth recording. The lines of Mrs. Sigourney,[2] the American poetess, please me most:

> Flow on for ever, in thy glorious robe
> Of terror and of beauty; God hath set
> His rainbow on thy forehead, and the cloud

[1] Frances Anne Kemble Butler (1809–93), English actress, was the daughter of Charles Kemble. She was one of the "stars" at Covent Garden, and her American tour in 1832 was a great success, leading to her marriage to a Philadelphian, Pierce Butler. She wrote several plays and poems, published her *Journal* (1835), her *Journal of a Residence on a Georgian Plantation* (1863), and also a very interesting series of autobiographical volumes: *Records of a Girlhood* (1878), *Records of Later Life* (1882), and *Further Records* (1891). Marryat refers to her remark on Niagara which appears in her *Journal* (Philadelphia, 1835), p. 218: "I saw Niagara—Oh God! who can describe that sight!!!"

[2] Lydia Sigourney (1791–1865), an American poetess of considerable repute in her own day, and for a time an editor of *Godey's Lady's Book.*

Mantles around thy feet. And he doth give
Thy voice of thunder power to speak of him
Eternally—bidding the lip of man
Keep silence, and upon thy rocky altar pour
Incense of awe-struck praise.

When the Indian first looked upon the falls, he declared them to be the dwelling of the Great Spirit. The
savage could not imagine that the Great Spirit dwelt also in
the leaf which he bruised in his hand; but here it appealed
to his senses in thunder and awful majesty, and he was
compelled to acknowledge it.

The effects which the contemplation of these glorious
waters produce are of course very different, according to
one's temperament and disposition. As I stood on the brink
above the falls, continuing for a considerable time to watch
the great mass of water tumbling, dancing, capering, and
rushing wildly along, as if in a hurry to take the leap and
delighted at it, I could not help wishing that I too had been
made of such stuff as would have enabled me to have
joined it; with it to have rushed innocuously down the
precipice; to have rolled uninjured into the deep unfathom-
able gulf below, or to have gamboled in the atmosphere of
spray, which rose again in a dense cloud from its recesses.
For about half an hour more I continued to watch the rolling waters, and then I felt a slight dizziness and a creeping sensation come over me—that sensation arising from
strong excitement, and the same, probably, that occasions
the bird to fall into the jaws of the snake. This is a feeling
which, if too long indulged in, becomes irresistible, and occasions a craving desire to leap into the flood of rushing
waters. It increased upon me every minute; and, retreating
from the brink, I turned my eyes to the surrounding foliage,
until the effect of the excitement had passed away. I
looked upon the waters a second time, and then my
thoughts were directed into a very different channel. I
wished myself a magician, that I might transport the falls
to Italy, and pour their whole volume of waters into the

crater of Mount Vesuvius; witness the terrible conflict between the contending elements, and create the largest steam-boiler that ever entered into the imagination of man. I have no doubt that the opinion that these falls have receded a distance of seven miles is correct; but what time must have passed before even this tremendous power could have sawed away such a mass of solid rock! Within the memory of man it has receded but a few feet—changed but little. How many thousand years must these waters have been flowing and falling, unvarying in their career, and throwing up their sheets of spray to heaven?

It is impossible for either the eye or the mind to compass the whole mass of falling water; you cannot measure, cannot estimate its enormous volume; and this is the reason, perhaps, why travellers often express themselves disappointed by it. But fix your eye upon one portion—one falling and heaving wave out of the millions, as they turn over the edge of the rocks; watch, I say, this fragment for a few minutes, its regular time-beating motion never varying or changing; pursuing the laws of nature with a regularity never ceasing and never tiring; minute after minute; hour after hour; day after day; year after year—until time recedes into creation; then cast your eyes over the whole multitudinous mass which is, and has been, performing the same and coeval duty, and you feel its vastness! Still the majesty of the whole is far too great for the mind to compass—too stupendous for its limited powers of reception.

Sunday.—I had intended to have passed the whole day at the falls; but an old gentleman, whose acquaintance I had made in the steamboat on Lake Ontario, asked me to go to church; and, as I felt he would be annoyed if I did not, I accompanied him to a presbyterian meeting not far from the falls, which sounded like distant thunder. The sermon was upon temperance—a favourite topic in America; and the minister rather quaintly observed that "alcohol was not sealed by the hand of God." It was astonishing to me that he did not allude to the falls, point out that the seal of God was there, and show how feeble was the voice of man when compared to the thunder of the Almighty so close at hand. But the fact was, he had been accustomed to preach every Sunday with the falls roaring in his ear, and (when the wind was in a certain quarter) with the spray damping the leaves of his sermon; he, therefore, did not feel as we did, and, no doubt, thought his sermon better than that from the God of the elements.

Yes, it is through the elements that the Almighty has ever deigned to commune with man, or to execute his supreme will, whether it has been by the wild waters to destroy an impious race—by the fire hurled upon the doomed cities—by seas divided, that the chosen might pass through them—by the thunders on Sinai's Mount when his laws were given to man—by the pillar of fire or the gushing rock—or by the rushing of mighty winds. And it is still through the elements that the Almighty speaks to man, to warn, to terrify, to chasten; to raise him up to wonder, to praise, and adore. The forked and blinding lightning which, with the rapidity of thought, dissolves the union between the body and the soul; the pealing thunder, announcing that the bolt ·has sped; the fierce tornado, sweeping away everything in its career, like a besom of wrath; the howling storm; the mountain waves; the earth quaking, and yawning wide, in a second overthrowing the work and pride of centuries, and burying thousands in a living tomb; the fierce vomiting of the crater, pouring out its flames of liquid fire, and changing fertility to the arid rock: it is through these that the Deity still speaks to man; yet what can inspire more awe of him, more reverence, and more love, than the contemplation of thy falling waters, great Niagara!

CHAPTER XIII

Buffalo and the New West

Two gentlemen have left their cards, and will be happy to see me on my route; one lives at Batavia, the other at Pekin. I recollect going over the ferry to Brooklyn to visit the commodore at the Navy Yard; I walked to where the omnibus started from, to see if one was going my way. There were but two on the stand: one was bound to *Babylon*, the other to *Jericho*.

Buffalo is one of the wonders of America. It is hardly to be credited that such a beautiful city could have risen up in the wilderness in so short a period. In the year 1814 it was burnt down, being then only a village; only one house was left standing, and now it is a city with twenty-five thousand inhabitants. The Americans are very judicious in planning their new towns; the streets are laid out so wide that there will never be any occasion to pull down to widen and improve, as we do in England. The city of Buffalo is remarkably well built; all the houses in the principal streets are lofty and substantial, and are either of brick or granite. The main street is wider and the stores handsomer than the majority of those in New York. It has five or six very fine churches, a handsome theatre, town-hall, and market, and three or four hotels, one of which is superior to most others in America; and to these we must add a fine stone pier, with a lighthouse, a harbour full of shipping and magnificent steamboats. It is almost incomprehensible that all this should have been accomplished since the year 1814. And what has occasioned this springing up of a city in so short a time as to remind you of Aladdin's magic palace? —the Erie canal, which here joins the Hudson River with the lake, passing through the centre of the most populous and fertile states.

At present, however, the business of Buffalo, as well as of every other city, is nearly at a standstill; the machinery of America is under repair; until that repair is completed, the country will remain paralyzed. America may just now be compared to one of her own steamboats, which, under too high pressure, has burst her boiler. Some of her passengers have (in a commercial point of view) been killed outright, others severely injured, and her progress has for a time been stopped; but she will soon be enabled to go ahead as fast as ever, and will then probably pay a little more attention to her safety-valve.

I went out to the Indian reservation, granted to the remnant of the Seneca tribe of Indians, once a portion of the Mohawks, and all that now remains in the United States of the famed six nations.[1] The chief of them (Red

---

[1] The Confederacy of the Iroquois "came about sometime around the middle of the sixteenth century . . . Ostensibly it was a league of five tribes (the Tuscaroras, driven from the south, joined in later to make the sixth) —Mohawk, Seneca, Oneida, Cayuga and Onondaga. The plan was to renounce warfare as between one another and to present an alliance against a warring world. For two centuries, or until the so-called French and Indian Wars, this Confederacy . . . was completely successful. . . . The Confederacy was a nation which enhanced the liberty and responsibility of its compo-nent parts down even to the minutest member." John Collier, *Indians of the Americas* (New York: Mentor Books; 1947), pp. 118–19. During the long conflicts between the English and the French in North America, the Iroquois had tended generally to support the British. The Indians remained loyal to their British allies during the American Revolution. After the Peace of Paris of 1783 the Iroquois were no longer significant as a force, and many of them retired from American territory and took refuge in Canada. The Senecas, who had been allied with the Iroquois, remained in the United

Jacket [2]), lately dead, might be considered as the last of the Mohicans. I had some conversation with his daughter, who was very busily employed in the ornamenting of a pair of moccasins, and then visited the tomb, or rather the spot, where her father was buried, without name or record. This omission has since been repaired, and a tablet is now raised over his grave. It is creditable to the profession that the "poor player," as Shakespeare hath it, should be the foremost to pay tribute to worth. Cooke,[3] the tragedian, was lying without a stone to mark his resting-place, when Kean [4] came to America, found out the spot, and raised a handsome cenotaph to his memory; and it is to Mr. Placide,[5] one of the very best of American actors, that Red Jacket is indebted for the tablet which has been raised to rescue his narrow home from oblivion.

States and settled on reservations at Alleghany, Cattaraugus, and Tonawanda.

[2] Red Jacket (1758–1830), a Seneca chief who, after the Treaty of Fort Stanwix which ceded the Seneca lands to the United States government, lived peaceably on the reservations granted to his people.

[3] George Frederick Cooke (1756–1811), English actor who began his career about 1776. He gained fame in provincial theatres and finally in 1801 appeared at Covent Garden. He was an excellent performer and seemed to have a great future—before he succumbed to the effects of chronic alcoholism. Cooke came to the United States in 1810 and played in New York, but died within a year. He was buried at St. Paul's Church, New York.

[4] Edmund Kean (1787–1833), English actor, celebrated for his portrayal of Shakespearian characters. He first made his name with his great performance as Shylock at Drury Lane in 1814. He was unrivalled in tragic roles. He visited America in 1820 and again in 1825. It was during his 1820 visit that Kean prompted the removal of Cooke's remains to a more prominent location. His later years were plagued by the effects of excessive drinking and by financial difficulties. Like Cooke, Kean's death was caused by intemperance.

[5] Henry Placide (1799–1870), American actor, was the son of Alexander Placide and brother of the theatrical stars Thomas, Caroline, and Jane Placide. Henry Placide made his début in 1808 and continued to act until 1865. He had a long and varied career with the Park Theatre in New York. His most famous roles were Sir Peter Teazle in *The School for Scandal,* Dogberry in *Much Ado About Nothing,* and Captain Cuttle in *Dombey and Son.*

Red Jacket was a great chief and a great man, but, like most of the Indians, he could not resist the temptations of alcohol, and was during the latter part of his life very intemperate. When Red Jacket was sober he was the proudest chief that ever walked, and never would communicate even with the highest of the American authorities but through his interpreter; but when intoxicated he would speak English and French fluently, and then the proud Indian warrior, the most eloquent of his race, the last chief of the six nations, would demean himself by begging for a sixpence to buy more rum.

I must now revert to the singular causes by which, independent of others, such as locality, etc., Buffalo was so rapidly brought to a state of perfection—not like many other towns which, commencing with wooden houses, gradually superseded them by brick and stone. The person who was the cause of this unusual rise was a Mr. Rathbun,[6] who now lies incarcerated in a gaol of his own building. It was he who built all the hotels, churches, and other public edifices; in fact, every structure worthy of observation in the whole town was projected, contracted for, and executed by Mr. Rathbun. His history is singular. Of quiet, unassuming

---

[6] Benjamin Rathbun (1789–1873), hotel keeper in Buffalo until about 1830, was born in Otsego county and came to Buffalo in 1821. He ran the Eagle Tavern and then entered the building trade. He was responsible for much construction in Buffalo and his plans for the City Exchange were exceedingly ambitious. On August 3, 1836, he and his brother were arrested for forgery. The evidence that he had actually committed forgery was not clear, but it was inferred thàt he had planned the criminal conspiracy; Lyman Rathbun, his brother, and Rathbun Allen and Lyman Hullet, his nephews, had been his agents. At the first trial of Benjamin Rathbun in March 1837, the jury could come to no decision, but at a second trial in September 1838 he was found guilty and sentenced to five years' penal servitude. After he was released he moved to New York and again became a hotel proprietor. He died at Fort Washington and was said to have left an estate of more than $75,000. "Sketch of Joseph Clary," in the "Millard Fillmore Papers," *Publications of the Buffalo Historical Society* (Buffalo: Buffalo Historical Society; 1907), Vol. XI, p. 104. There is no indication given that Marryat is correct as to the ultimate fate of Lyman Rathbun.

manners, Quaker in his dress, moderate in all his expenses (except in charity, wherein, assisted by an amiable wife, he was very liberal), he concealed under this apparent simplicity and goodness a mind capable of the vastest conceptions, united with the greatest powers of execution. He undertook contracts, and embarked in building speculations, to an amount almost incredible. Rathbun undertook everything, and everything undertaken by Rathbun was well done. Not only at Buffalo, but at Niagara and other places, he was engaged in raising vast buildings, when the great crash occurred, and Rathbun, with others, was unable to meet his liabilities. Then, for the first time, it was discovered that for more than five years he had been conniving at a system of forgery, to the amount of two millions of dollars; the forgery consisted in putting to his bills the names of responsible parties as indorsers, that they might be more current. It does not appear that he ever intended to defraud, for he took up all his notes as fast as they became due; and it was this extreme regularity on his part which prevented the discovery of his fraud for so unusually long a period. It is surmised that, had not the general failure taken place, he would have eventually withdrawn all these forged bills from the market, and have paid all his creditors, reserving for himself a handsome fortune. It is a singular event in the annals of forgery that this should have been carried on undiscovered for so unprecedented a time. Mr. Rathbun is to be tried as an accessory, as it was his brother who forged the names. As soon as it was discovered, the latter made his escape, and he is said to have died miserably in a hovel on the confines of Texas.

Embarked on board of the *Sandusky*, for Detroit. As we were steering clear of the pier, a small brig of about two hundred tons burthen was pointed out to me as having been the *flag-ship* of Commodore Barclay, in the action upon Lake Erie. The appearance of Buffalo from the lake is very imposing. Stopped at Dunkirk to put some emigrants on shore. As they were landing, I watched them carefully counting over their little property, from the iron teakettle to

the heavy chest. It was their whole fortune, and invaluable
to them; the nest-egg by which, with industry, their children
were to rise to affluence. They remained on the wharf as we
shoved off, and no wonder that they seemed embarrassed
and at a loss. There was the baby in the cradle, the young
children holding fast to their mother's skirt, while the elder
had seated themselves on a log, and watched the departure
of the steam vessel—the bedding, cooking utensils, etc., all
lying in confusion, and all to be housed before night. Weary
did they look, and weary indeed they were, and most joyful
would they be when they at last should gain their resting-
place. It appears, from the reports sent in, that upwards
of one hundred thousand emigrants pass to the west every
year by the route of the lakes, of which it is estimated that
about thirty thousand are from Europe, the remainder
migrating from the eastern states of the Union.

I may keep a log now.— 5 a.m. — Light breezes and
clear weather, land trending from South to S.S.W. Five sail
in the offing.

At 6, ran into Grand River. Within these last two years,
three towns have sprung up here, containing between them
about three thousand inhabitants.

How little are they aware, in Europe, of the vastness
and extent of commerce carried on in these inland seas,
whose coasts are now lined with flourishing towns and
cities, and whose waters are ploughed by magnificent
steamboats, and hundreds of vessels laden with merchandise. Even the Americans themselves are not fully aware
of the rising importance of these lakes as connected with
the west. Since the completion of the Ohio Canal, which
enters the Lake Erie at Cleveland, that town has risen
almost as rapidly as Buffalo. It is beautifully situated. It is
about six years back that it may be said to have commenced its start, and it now contains more than ten thousand inhabitants. The buildings are upon the same scale
as those of Buffalo, and it is conjectured with good reason
that it will become even a larger city than the other, as the
ice breaks up here, and the navigation is open in the spring,

six weeks sooner than it is at Buffalo, abreast of which town the ice is driven down and collected, previous to its forcing its passage over the falls.

Erie, which was the American naval depot during the war, has a fine bay, but it is now falling into insignificance; it has a population of about one thousand.

Sandusky is a fast-rising town, beautifully situated upon the verge of a small prairie; it is between Sandusky and Huron that the prairie lands commence. The bay of Sandusky is very picturesque, being studded with small verdant islands. On one of these are buried in the same grave all those who fell in the hard-fought battle of the lakes, between Perry and Barclay,[7] both of whom have since followed their companions.

Toledo is the next town of consequence on the lake. It is situated at the mouth of the Miami River; and as a railroad has already been commenced across the isthmus, so as to avoid going round the whole peninsula of Michigan, it is fast rising into importance. Three years ago the land was purchased at a dollar and a half per acre; now, it is selling for building lots at one hundred dollars per foot. They handed me a paper printed in this town called *The Toledo Blade*—a not inappropriate title, though rather a bold one for an editor to write up to, as his writings ought to be very *sharp* and, at the same time, extremely *well-tempered*.

The American government have paid every attention to their inland waters. The harbours, lighthouses, piers, etc., have all been built at the expense of government, and every precaution has been taken to make the navigation of the lakes as sage as possible.

In speaking of the new towns rising so fast in America, I wish the reader to understand that, if he compares them

---

[7] Captain Robert Barclay and Commodore Oliver Hazard Perry were opposing commanders at the Battle of Lake Erie, September 10, 1813. It was during this engagement that Perry stated: "We have met the enemy and they are ours." For a full account of the battle, see C. S. Forester, *The Age of Fighting Sail* (New York: Doubleday; 1956), pp. 173–87.

with the country towns of the same population in England, he will not do them justice. In the smaller towns of England you can procure but little, and you have to send to London for anything good; in the larger towns, such as Norwich, etc., you may procure most things; but, still, luxuries must usually be obtained from the metropolis. But in such places as Buffalo and Cleveland, everything is to be had that you can procure at New York or Boston. In those two towns on Lake Erie are stores better furnished, and handsomer, than any shops at Norwich, in England; and you will find, in either of them, articles for which, at Norwich, you would be obliged to send to London. It is the same thing at almost every town in America with which communication is easy. Would you furnish a house in one of them, you will find every article of furniture—carpets, stoves, grates, marble chimney-pieces, pier glasses, pianos, lamps, candelebra, glass, china, etc., in twice the quantity, and in greater variety, than at any provincial town in England.

This arises from the system of credit extended through every vein and artery of the country, and by which English goods are forced, as if with a force-pump, into every available depot in the Union; and thus, in a town so newly raised that the stumps of the forest-trees are not only still surrounding the houses, but remain standing in the cellars, you will find every luxury that can be required. It may be asked what becomes of all these goods. It must be recollected that hundreds of new houses spring up every year in the towns, and that the surrounding country is populous and wealthy. In the farm-houses—mean-looking and often built of logs—is to be found not only comfort, but very often luxury.

CHAPTER XIV

On the Trail of the Voyageur

The French never have succeeded as colonists, and their want of success can only be ascribed to an amiable want of energy. When located at any spot, if a Frenchman has enough he seeks no more; and, instead of working, as the Englishman or the American does, he will pass his time away, and spend his little surplus in social amusements. The town of Detroit was founded as early as the city of Philadelphia,[1] but, favourably as it is situated, it never until lately rose to anything more than, properly speaking, a large village. There is not a paved street in it, or even a foot-path for a pedestrian. In winter, in rainy weather you are up to your knees in mud; in summer, invisible from dust; indeed, until lately, there was not a practicable road for thirty miles round Detroit. The muddy and impassable state of the streets has given rise to a very curious system of making morning or evening calls. A small one-horse cart is backed against the door of a house; the ladies dressed get into it, and seat themselves upon a buffalo-skin at the bottom of it; they are carried to the residence of the party upon whom they wish to call; the cart is backed in again,

[1] Marryat is wrong here. Philadelphia was founded in 1682 by William Penn and Detroit was founded as Fort Pontchartrain in 1701 by De la Motte Cadillac.

and they are landed dry and clean. An old inhabitant of Detroit complained to me that the people were now getting so proud that many of them refused to visit in that way any longer. But owing to the rise of the other towns on the lake, the great increase of commerce, and Michigan having been admitted as a state into the Union, with Detroit as its capital, a large eastern population has now poured into it, and Detroit will soon present an appearance very different from its present, and become one of the most flourishing cities of America. Within these last six years it has increased its population from two to ten thousand. The climate here is the very best in America, although the state itself is unhealthy. The land near the town is fertile. A railroad from Detroit already extends thirty miles through the state; and now that the work has commenced it will be carried on with the usual energy of the Americans.

Left Detroit in the Michigan steam-vessel for Mackinaw; passed through the Lake St. Clair, and entered Lake Huron; stopped at a solitary wharf to take in wood, and met there with a specimen of American politeness or (if you please) independence in the gentleman who cut down and sold it. Without any assignable motive, he called out to me: "You are a damned fool of an Englishman"; for which I suppose I ought to have been very much obliged to him.

Miss Martineau has not been too lavish in her praises of Mackinaw. It has the appearance of a fairy isle floating on the water, which is so pure and transparent that you may see down to almost any depth; and the air above is as pure as the water, so that you feel invigorated as you breathe it. The first reminiscence brought to my mind after I had landed was the description by Walter Scott of the island and residence of Magnus Troil and his daughters Minna and Brenda, in the novel of *The Pirate*.[2]

---

[2] The description of Shetland in Scott's novel, *The Pirate*, is as follows: "That long, narrow, and irregular island, usually called the mainland of Zetland, because it is by far the largest of that Archipelago, terminates, . . . in a cliff of immense height, entitled Sumburgh-Head, which presents its bare scalp and

The low buildings, long stores, and outhouses, full
of nets, barrels, masts, sails and cordage; the abundance
of fish lying about; the rafters of the houses laden with dried
and smoked meat; and the full and jolly proportions of
most of the inhabitants, who would have rivalled Scott's
worthy in height and obesity, immediately struck my eye;
and I might have imagined myself transported to the
Shetland isle, had it not been for the lodges of the Indians
on the beach, and the Indians themselves either running
about or lying stripped in the porches before the whiskey
stores.

I inquired of one of the islanders, why all the white
residents were generally such large portly men, which they
are at a very early age; he replied: "We have good air, good
water, and what we eat agrees with us." This was very
conclusive.

I inquired of another if people lived to a good old age
in the island; his reply was quite American— "I guess they
do; if people want to die, they can't die here—they're
obliged to go elsewhere."

Wandering among the Indian lodges (wigwam is a
term not used nowadays), I heard a sort of flute played in

naked sides to the weight of a
tremendous surge, forming the
extreme point of the isle to the
south-east. This lofty promontory is constantly exposed to the
current of a strong and furious
tide . . .
"On the land side, the
promontory is covered with short
grass, and slopes steeply down
to the little isthmus, upon which
the sea has encroached in creeks,
which, advancing from either
side of the island, gradually
work their way forward, and
seem as if in a short time they
would form a junction. . . ."
The residence of Magnus
Troil and his daughters Minna
and Brenda is described as fol-

lows: "It was a rude building of
rough stone, with nothing about
it to gratify the eye, or to excite
the imagination; a large old
fashioned narrow house, with a
very steep roof, covered with
flags composed of grey sand-
stone, . . . The windows were
few, very small in size, and dis-
tributed up and down the building with utter contempt of regularity. Against the main structure had rested, in former times,
certain smaller compartments of
the mansion house, . . . But
these had become ruinous . . .
the walls had given way in many
places. . . ." from Walter Scott,
The Pirate (Boston: Dana, Estes;
1893), Vol. I, pp. 1–2.

one of them and I entered. The young Indian who was blowing on it handed it to me. It was an imperfect instrument, something between a flute and a clarinet, but the sound which it gave out was soft and musical. An islander informed me that it was the only sort of musical instrument which the northern tribes possessed, and that it was played upon by the young men only when they were *in love.* I suspected at first that he was bantering me, but I afterwards found that what he said was true. The young Indian must have been very deeply smitten, for he continued to play all day and all night, during the time that I was there.

If music be the food of love, play on.

Started in a birch canoe for Sault Ste. Marie, a small town built under the rapids of that name, which pour out a portion of the waters of Lake Superior. Two American gentlemen, one a member of Congress and the other belonging to the American Fur Company, were of the party. Our crew consisted of five Canadian half-breeds—a mixture between the Indian and the white, which spoils both. It was a lovely morning; not a breath of air stirred the wide expanse of the Huron, as far as the eye could scan; and the canoe, as it floated alongside the landing-place, appeared as if it were poised in the air, so light did it float, and so clear and transparent are these northern waters. We started, and in two hours arrived at Goose Island, unpoetical in its name, but in itself full of beauty. As you stand on the beach you can look down through the water on the shelving bottom, bright with its variety of pebbles, and trace it almost as far off as if it had not been covered with water at all. The island was small, but gay as the gayest of parterres, covered with the sweet wild rose in full bloom (certainly the most fragrant rose in the world), blue campanellos, yellow exeranthemums, and white ox-eyed daisies. Underneath there was a perfect carpet of strawberries, ripe, and inviting you to eat them, which we did, while our Canadian brutes swallowed long strings of raw salt pork. And yet, in two months hence, this lovely little spot will be but one mass of snow—a mound rising above to serve as a guide to the chilled traveller who would find his way over the frozen expanse of the wide Huron lake.

As soon as our Canadians had filled themselves to repletion with raw pork, we continued our route that we might cross the lake and gain the detour, or point which forms the entrance of the river St. Marie, before it was dark. We arrived a little before sunset, when we landed, put up our light boat, and bivouacked for the night. As soon as we put our feet on shore, we were assailed by the mosquitoes in myriads. They congregated from all quarters in such numbers that you could only see as if through a black veil, and you could not speak without having your mouth filled with them. But in ten minutes we had a large fire, made, not of logs or branches, but of a dozen small trees. The wind eddied, and the flame and smoke, as they rose in masses, whirled about the mosquitoes right and left, and in every quarter of the compass, until they were fairly beaten off to a respectable distance. We supped upon lake-trout and fried ham; and rolling ourselves up in our Mackinaw blankets, we were soon fast asleep.

There was no occasion to call us the next morning. The Canadians were still snoring and had let the fires go down. The mosquitoes, taking advantage of this neglect, had forced their way into the tent, and sounded the reveille in our ears with their petty trumpets; following up the summons with the pricking of pins, as the fairies of Queen Mab are reported to have done to lazy housemaids.[3] We kicked up our half-breeds, who gave us our breakfast, stowed away the usual quantity of raw pork, and once more did we float on the water in a piece of birch bark. The heat of the sun was oppressive, and we were broiled; but we dipped our hands in the clear cool stream as we skimmed along, listening to the whistling of the solitary loon as it paddled away from us, or watching the serrated back of the sturgeon as he rolled lazily over and showed above the

---

[3] See Robert Herrick's poem, "The Fairies."

water. Now and then we stopped, and the silence of the desert was broken by the report of our fowling-pieces, and a pigeon or two was added to our larder. At noon a breeze sprung up, and we hoisted our sail, and the Canadians who had paddled dropped asleep as we glided quietly along under the guidance of the "timonier." [4]

After you have passed through the river St. Clair, and entered the Huron lake, the fertility of the country gradually disappears. Here and there indeed, especially on the Canadian side, a spot more rich than the soil in general is shown by the large growth of the timber; but the northern part of the Lake Huron shores is certainly little fit for cultivation. The spruce fir now begins to be plentiful; for, until you come to the upper end of the lake, they are scarce, although very abundant in Upper Canada. The country wears the same appearance all the way up to the Sault Ste. Marie, showing maple and black poplar intermingled with fir, the oak but rarely appearing. The whole lake from Mackinaw to the Detour is studded with islands. A large one at the entrance of the river is called St. Joseph's. The Hudson Bay Company had a station there, which is now abandoned, and the island has been purchased, or granted, to an English officer, who has partly settled it. It is said to be the best land in this region, but still hardly fit for cultivation. It was late before our arrival at the Sault, and we were obliged to have recourse to our paddles, for the wind had died away. As the sun went down, we observed a very curious effect from the refraction of tints, the water changing to a bright violet every time that it was disturbed by the paddles. I have witnessed something like this just after sunset on the Lake of Geneva.

We landed at dusk, much fatigued; but the Aurora Borealis flashed in the heavens, spreading out like a vast plume of ostrich feathers across the sky, every minute changing its beautiful and fanciful forms. Tired as we were, we watched it for hours before we could make up our minds to go to bed.

---

[4] A timonier is a helmsman.

CHAPTER XV

The Upper Michigan Peninsula— Sault Ste. Marie

SAULT STE. MARIE.—Our landlord is a very strange being. It appears that he has been annoyed by some traveller, who has published a work in which he has found fault with the accommodations at Sault Ste. Marie, and spoken very disrespectfully of our host's beds and bed-furniture. I have never read the work, but I am so well aware how frequently travellers fill up their pages with fleas, and "such small gear," that I presume the one in question was short of matter to furnish out his book; yet it was neither just nor liberal on his part to expect at Sault Ste. Marie, where, perhaps, not five travellers arrive in the course of a year, the same accommodations as at New York. The bedsteads certainly were a little ricketty, but everything was very clean and comfortable. The house was not an inn, nor, indeed, did it pretend to be one, but the fare was good and well cooked, and you were waited upon by the host's two pretty modest daughters—not only pretty, but well-informed girls; and considering that this village is the Ultima Thule of this portion of America, I think that a traveller might have been very well content with things as they were. In two instances, I found in the log-houses of this village complete editions of Lord Byron's works.

Sault Ste. Marie contains, perhaps, fifty houses, mostly built of logs, and has a palisade put up to repel any attack of the Indians.

There are two companies of soldiers quartered here. The rapids from which the village takes its name are just above it; they are not strong or dangerous, and the canoes descend them twenty times a day. At the foot of the rapids the men are constantly employed in taking the whitefish in scoop-nets, as they attempt to force their way up into Lake Superior. The majority of the inhabitants here are half-breeds. It is remarkable that the females generally improve, and the males degenerate, from the admixture of blood. Indian wives are here preferred to white, and perhaps with reason—they make the best wives for poor men; they labour hard, never complain, and a day of severe toil is amply recompensed by a smile from their lord and master in the evening. They are always faithful and devoted, and very sparing of their talk, all which qualities are considered as recommendations in this part of the world.

It is remarkable that, although the Americans treat the Negro with contumely, they have a respect for the red Indian: a well-educated half-breed Indian is not debarred from entering into society; indeed, they are generally received with great attention. The daughter of a celebrated Indian chief brings heraldry into the family, for the Indians are as proud of their descent (and with good reason) as we, in Europe, are of ours. The Randolph family in Virginia still boast of their descent from Pocahontas, the heroine of one of the most remarkable romances in real life which was ever heard of.

The whole of this region appears to be incapable of cultivation, and must remain in its present state, perhaps, for centuries to come. The chief produce is from the lakes; trout and whitefish are caught in large quantities, salted down, and sent to the west and south. At Mackinaw alone they cure about two thousand barrels, which sell for ten dollars the barrel; at the Sault, about the same quantity; and on Lake Superior, at the station of the American Fur Company, they have commenced the fishing, to lessen the expenses of the establishment, and they now salt down about four thousand barrels; but this traffic is still in its infancy, and will become more profitable as the west becomes more populous. Be it here observed that, although the Canadians have the same rights and the same capabilities of fishing, I do not believe that one barrel is cured on the Canadian side. As the American fish is prohibited in England, it might really become an article of exportation from the Canadas to a considerable amount.

There is another source of profit, which is the collecting of the maple sugar; and this staple, if I may use the term, is rapidly increasing. At an average, the full-grown maple tree will yield about five pounds of sugar each tapping, and, if carefully treated, will last forty years. All the state of Michigan is supplied from this quarter with this sugar, which is good in quality and refines well. At Mackinaw they receive about three hundred thousand pounds every year. It may be collected in any quantity from their vast wildernesses of forests, and although the notion may appear strange, it is not impossible that one day the northern sugar may supersede that of the tropics. The island of St. Joseph, which I have mentioned, is covered with large maple trees, and they make a great quantity upon that spot alone.

I was amused by a reply given me by an American in office here. I asked how much his office was worth, and his answer was six hundred dollars, besides *stealings*. This was, at all events, frank and honest; in England the word would have been softened down to "perquisites." I afterwards found that it was a common expression in the States to say a place was worth so much besides cheatage.

In all this country, from Mackinaw to the Sault, hay is very scarce; and, during the short summer season, the people go twenty or thirty miles in their canoes to any known patch of prairie or grassland to collect it. Nevertheless, they are very often obliged, during the winter, to feed their cattle upon fish, and strange to say, they acquire a taste for it. You will see the horses and cows disputing for the offal; and our landlord told me that he has often witnessed a particular horse wait very quietly while they were landing the fish from the canoes, watch his opportunity, dart in, steal one, *and run away with it in his mouth.*

A mutiny among our lazzaroni of half-breeds, they refuse to work today, because they are tired, they say, and we are obliged to procure others. Carried our canoe over the portage into the canal, and in five minutes were on the vast inland sea of Lake Superior. The waters of this lake are, if possible, more transparent than those of the Huron, or rather the variety and bright colours of the pebbles and agates which lie at the bottom make them appear so. The appearance of the coast, and the growth of timber, are much the same as on Lake Huron, until you arrive at Gros Cape, a bold promontory, about three hundred feet high. We ascended this cape, to have a full view of the expanse of water; this was a severe task, as it was nearly perpendicular, and we were forced to cling from tree to tree to make the ascent. In addition to this difficulty, we were unremittingly pursued by the mosquitoes, which blinded us so as to impede our progress, being moreover assisted in their malevolent attacks by a sort of sand-fly, that made triangular incisions behind our ears, exactly like a small leech bite, from which the blood trickled down two or three inches as soon as the little wretch let go his hold. This variety of stinging made us almost mad, and we descended quite exhausted, the blood trickling down our faces and necks. We threw off our clothes and plunged into the lake; the water was too cold; the agate at the bottom cut our feet severely, and thus were we phlebotomized from head to foot.

There is a singular geological feature at this cape; you do not perceive it until you have forced your way through a belt of firs, which grow at the bottom and screen it from sight. It is a ravine in which the rocks are pouring down from the top to the bottom, all so equal in size, and so arranged, as to wear the appearance of a cascade of stones; and when half-blinded by the mosquitoes, you look upon them, they appear as if they are actually in motion, and falling down in one continued stream.

We embarked again, and after an hour's paddling landed upon a small island, where was the tomb of an Indian chief or warrior. It was in a beautiful spot, surrounded by the wild rose, blue peas, and campanellas. The kinna-kinnec, or weed which the Indians smoke as tobacco, grew plentifully about it. The mound of earth was surrounded by a low palisade, about four feet wide and seven feet long, and at the head of it was the warrior's pole with eagle feathers, and notches denoting the number of scalps he had taken from the enemy.

The Hudson Bay and American Fur Companies both have stations on Lake Superior on their respective sides of the lake, and the Americans have a small schooner which navigates it. There is one question which the traveller cannot help asking himself as he surveys the vast mass of water, into which so many rivers pour their contributions, which is—in what manner is all this accumulation of water carried off? Except by a very small evaporation in the summer time, and the outlet at Sault Ste. Marie, where the water which escapes is not much more than equal to two or three of the rivers which feed the lake, there is no apparent means by which the water is carried off. The only conclusion that can be arrived at is that when the lake rises above a certain height, as the soil around is sandy and porous, the surplus waters find their way through it; and such I believe to be the case.

We saw no bears. They do not come down to the shores (or travel, as they term it here) until the huckleberries are ripe. We were told that a month later there would be plenty of them. It is an ascertained fact that the bears from this region migrate to the west every autumn, but it is not known when they return. They come down to the eastern shores of the Lakes Superior and Huron, swim the lakes and rivers from island to island, never deviating from their course, till they pass through by Wisconsin to the

Mississippi. Nothing stops them; the sight of a canoe will not prevent their taking the water; and the Indians in the River St. Marie have been known to kill fifteen in one day. It is singular that the bears on the other side of the Mississippi are said to migrate to the east exactly in the contrary direction. Perhaps the Mississippi is their fashionable watering-place.

A gathering storm induced us to return, instead of continuing our progress on the lake. A birch canoe in a gale of wind on Lake Superior would not be a very insurable risk. On our return, we found our half-breeds very penitent, for had we not taken them back, they would have stood a good chance of wintering there. But we had had advice as to the treatment of these lazy gluttonous scoundrels, who swallowed long pieces of raw pork the whole of the day, and towards evening were, from repletion, hanging their heads over the sides of the canoe and quite ill. They had been regaled with pork and whiskey going up; we gave them salt fish and a broomstick by way of variety on their return, and they behaved very well under the latter fare.

We started again down with the stream, and the first night took up our quarters on a prairie spot, where they had been making hay, which was lying in cocks about us. To have a soft bed we carried quantities into our tent, forgetting that we disturbed the mosquitoes who had gone to bed in the hay. We smoked the tent to drive them out again; but in smoking the tent we set fire to the hay, and it ended in a conflagration. We were burnt out, and had to re-pitch our tent.

I was sauntering by the side of the river when I heard a rustling in the grass, and perceived a garter-snake, an elegant and harmless little creature, about a foot and a half long. It had a small toad in its mouth, which it had seized by the head; but it was much too large for the snake to swallow, without leisure and preparation. I was amused at the precaution, I may say invention of the toad, to prevent its being swallowed: it had inflated itself till it was as round as a bladder, and upon this, issue was joined—the snake would not let go, the toad would not be swallowed. I lifted up the snake by the tail and threw them three or four yards into the river. The snake rose to the surface, as majestic as the great sea-serpent in miniature, carrying his head well out of the water, with the toad still in his mouth, reminding me of Cæsar with his Commentaries. He landed close to my feet; I threw him in again, and this time he let go the toad, which remained floating and inanimate on the water; but after a time he discharged his superfluous gas and made for the shore, while the snake, to avoid me, swam away down with the current.

The next morning it blew hard, and as we opened upon Lake Huron, we had to encounter a heavy sea; fortunately, the wind was fair for the island of Mackinaw, or we might have been delayed for some days. As soon as we were in the lake we made sail, having fifty-six miles to run before it was dark. The gale increased, but the canoe flew over the water, skimming it like a sea bird. It was beautiful, but not quite so pleasant, to watch it, as, upon the least carelessness on the part of the helmsman, it would immediately have filled. As it was, we shipped some heavy seas, but the blankets at the bottom, being saturated, gave us the extra ballast which we required. Before we were clear of the islands, we were joined by a whole fleet of Indian canoes, with their dirty blankets spread to the storm, running, as we were, for Mackinaw, being on their return from Maniton Islands, where they had congregated to receive presents from the governor of Upper Canada. Their canoes were, most of them, smaller than ours, which had been built for speed, but they were much higher in the gunnel. It was interesting to behold so many hundreds of beings trusting themselves to such fragile conveyances, in a heavy gale and running sea; but the harder it blew, the faster we went; and at last, much to my satisfaction, we found ourselves in smooth water again, alongside of the landing wharf at Mackinaw. I had some wish to see a fresh-water gale of wind, but in a birch canoe I never wish to try the experiment again.

CHAPTER XVI

The Fur Trappers' Paradise—
Mackinaw and Upper Canada

MACKINAW.—I mentioned that, in my trip to Lake
Superior, I was accompanied by a gentleman attached to the American Fur Company, who have a station
at this island. I was amusing myself in their establishment,
superintending the unpacking and cleaning of about forty
or fifty bales of skins, and during the time collected the
following information. It is an average computation of the
furs obtained every year, and the value of each to the
American Fur Company. The Hudson Bay Company are
supposed to average about the same quantity, or rather
more; and they have a larger proportion of valuable furs,
such as beaver and sable, but they have few deer and no
buffalo. When we consider how sterile and unfit for cultivation are these wild northern regions, it certainly appears
better that they should remain as they are:

Skins		*Average Value*
Deer, four varieties	150,000	45 cents per lb.
Buffalo	35,000	5 dollars per skin.
Elk	200	

Skins		*Average Value*
Beaver	15,000	4½ dollars per lb.
Muskrat	500,000	12 cents per skin.
Otters	5,000	6½ dollars per skin.
	2,500	2 "
Marten or Sable	12,000	2 " or more.
Minx	10,000	
Silver and Black Fox	15	
Crop Fox	100	4 dollars per skin.
Red Fox	3,000	1 "
Gray Fox	1,000	1½ "
Prairie Fox	5,000	½ "
Bears	4,000	4½ "
Lynx	500	2½ "
Wild Cat	2,000	2½ "
Racoon	70,000	½ "
Wolves	12,000	½ "
Wolverines	50	2½ "
Panthers	50	
Badgers	250	¼ "

besides skunks, ground hogs, hares, and many others. These are priced at the lowest; in proportion as the skins are finer, so do they yield a higher profit. The two companies may be said to receive, between them, skins yearly to the amount of from two to three millions of dollars.

Fable appropos to the subject.

A hare and a fox met one day on the vast prairie, and after a long conversation they prepared to start upon their several routes. The hare, pleased with the fox, lamented that they would in all probability separate forever. "No, no," replied the fox, "we shall meet again, never fear." "Where?" inquired his companion. "In the *hatter's shop*, to be sure," rejoined the fox, tripping lightly away.

DETROIT.—There are some pleasant people in this town, and the society is quite equal to that of the eastern cities.

From the constant change and transition which take place in this country, go where you will you are sure to fall in with a certain portion of intelligent, educated people. This is not the case in the remoter portions of the old continent, where everything is settled, and generation succeeds generation, as in some obscure country town. But in America, where all is new, and the country has to be peopled from the other parts, there is a proportion of intelligence and education transplanted with the inferior classes, either from the eastern states or from the old world, in whatever quarter you may happen to find yourself.

Left my friends at Detroit with regret, and returned to Buffalo. There is a marked difference between the behaviour of the lower people of the eastern cities and those whom you fall in with in this town; they are much less civil in their behaviour here; indeed, they appear to think rudeness a proof of independence. I went to the theatre, and the behaviour of the majority of the company just reminded me of the Portsmouth and Plymouth theatres. I had forgotten that Buffalo was a fresh-water seaport town.

Returning to Niagara, I took possession of the roof of the rail-coach, that I might enjoy the prospect. I had not travelled three miles before I perceived a strong smell of burning; at last the pocket of my coat, which was of cotton, burst out into flames, a spark having found its way into it; fortunately (not being insured) there was no property on the premises.

When the celebrated Colonel David Crockett first saw a locomotive, with the train smoking along the railroad, he exclaimed, as it flew past him, "Hell in harness, by the 'tarnal!"

I may, in juxtaposition with this, mention an Indian idea. Nothing surprised the Indians so much at first as the percussion-caps for guns; they thought them the *ne plus ultra* of invention; when, therefore, an Indian was first shown a locomotive, he reflected a little while, and then said: "I see—*percussion.*"

There is a beautiful island dividing the falls of Niagara,

called Goat Island; they have there a bridge across the rapids, so that you can now go over. A mill has already been erected there, which is a great pity; it is a contemptible disfigurement of nature's grandest work.

At the head of the island, which is surrounded by the rapids, exactly where the waters divide to run on each side of it, there is a small triangular portion of still or slack water. I perceived this, and went in to bathe. The line of the current on each side of it is plainly marked, and runs at the speed of nine or ten miles an hour; if you put your hand or foot a little way outside this line, they are immediately borne away by its force; if you went into it yourself, nothing could prevent your going down the falls. As I returned, I observed an ugly snake in my path, and I killed it. An American, who came up, exclaimed: "I reckon that's a *copperhead,* stranger. I never knew that they were in this island." I found out that I had killed a snake quite as venomous, if not more so, than a rattlesnake.

One never tires with these falls; indeed, it takes a week at least to find out all their varieties and beauties. There are some sweet spots on Goat Island, where you can meditate and be alone.

I witnessed, during my short stay here, that indifference to the destruction of life, so very remarkable in this country. The rail-car crushed the head of a child of about seven years old, as it was going into the engine-house; the other children ran to the father, a blacksmith, who was at work at his forge close by, crying out: "Father, Billy killed." The man put down his hammer, walked leisurely to where the boy lay, in a pool of his own blood, took up the body, and returned with it under his arm to his house. In a short time, the hammer rang upon the anvil as before.

The game of nine-pins is a favourite game in America, and very superior to what it is in England. In America, the ground is always covered properly over, and the balls are rolled upon a wooden floor, as correctly levelled as a billiard table. The ladies join in the game, which here becomes an agreeable and not too fatiguing an exercise. I was very fond of frequenting their alleys, not only for the exercise, but because, among the various ways of estimating character, I had made up my mind that there was none more likely to be correct than the estimate formed by the manner in which people roll the balls, especially the ladies. There were some very delightful specimens of American females when I was this time at Niagara. We sauntered about the falls and wood in the day time, or else played at nine-pins; in the evening we looked at the moon, spouted verses, and drank mint juleps. But all that was too pleasant to last long: I felt that I had not come to America to play at nine-pins; so I tore myself away, and within the next twenty-four hours found myself at Toronto, in Upper Canada.

Toronto, which is the present capital and seat of government of Upper Canada, is, from its want of spires and steeples, by no means an imposing town, as you view it on entering the harbour. The harbour itself is landlocked, and when deepened will be very good. A great deal of money has been expended by the English government upon the Canadian provinces, but not very wisely. The Rideau and Welland canals are splendid works; they have nothing to compare with them in the United States; but they are too much in advance of the country, and will be of but little use for a long period, if the provinces do not go ahead faster than they do now. One half the money spent in making good roads through the provinces would have done more good, and would have much increased the value of property. The proposed railroad from Hamilton to Detroit would be of greater importance; and if more money is to be expended on Upper Canada, it cannot be better disposed of than in this undertaking.

The minute you put your foot on shore, you feel that you are no longer in the United States; you are at once struck with the difference between the English and the American population, systems, and ideas. On the other side of the lake you have much more apparent property, but much less real solidity and security. The houses and stores at Toronto are not to be compared with those of the American towns opposite. But the Englishman has built according to his means—the American, according to his expectations. The hotels and inns at Toronto are very bad; at Buffalo they are splendid—for the Englishman travels little; the American is ever on the move. The private houses of Toronto are built, according to the English taste and desire of exclusiveness, away from the road, and are embowered in trees; the American, let his house be ever so large, or his plot of ground however extensive, builds within a few feet of the road, that he may see and know what is going on. You do not perceive the bustle, the energy, and activity at Toronto that you do at Buffalo, nor the profusion of articles in the stores; but it should be remembered that the Americans procure their articles upon credit, whilst at Toronto they proceed more cautiously. The Englishman builds his house and furnishes his store according to his means and fair expectations of being able to meet his acceptances. If an American has money sufficient to build a two-story house, he will raise it up to four stories on speculation. We must not, on one side, be dazzled with the effects of the credit system in America, nor yet be too hasty in condemning it. It certainly is the occasion of much over-speculation; but if the parties who speculate are ruined, provided the money has been laid out, as it usually is in America, upon real property—such as wharfs, houses, etc. —a new country becomes a gainer, as the improvements are made and remain, although they fall into other hands. And it should be farther pointed out that the Americans are justified in their speculations from the fact that property improved rises so fast in value that they are soon able to meet all claims and realize a handsome profit. They speculate on the future; but the future with them is not distant as it is with us, ten years in America being, as I have before observed, equal to a century in Europe; they are therefore warranted in so speculating. The property in Buffalo is now worth one hundred times what it was when the first speculators commenced; for as the country and cities become peopled, and the communication becomes easy, so does the value of everything increase.

Why, then, does not Toronto vie with Buffalo? Because the Canadas cannot obtain the credit which is given to the United States, and of which Buffalo has her portion. America has returns to make to England in her cotton crops; Canada has nothing, for her timber would be nothing, if it were not protected. She cannot, therefore, obtain credit as America does. What, then, do the Canadas require, in order to become prosperous? Capital! . . .

CHAPTER XVII

Plattsburg, the Green Mountains, and the Connecticut Valley

Through Lake Ontario to Montreal, by railroad to Lake Champlain, and then by steamboat to Burlington.

Burlington is a pretty county town on the border of the Lake Champlain; there is a large establishment for the education of boys kept here by the bishop of Vermont,[1] a clever man; it is said to be well conducted, and one of the best in the Union. The bishop's salary, as bishop, is only five hundred dollars; as a preacher of the established church he receives seven hundred; while as a schoolmaster his revenue becomes very handsome. The bishop is just now in bad odour with the *majority*, for having published some very sensible objections to the revivals and Temperance Societies.

PLATTSBURG.[2]—This was the scene of an American

---

[1] John Henry Hopkins (1792–1868) was the first Episcopalian Bishop of Vermont.

[2] The Battle of Plattsburg on Lake Champlain was another defeat for the British in the War of 1812. The battle took place on

September 11, 1814. Captain George Downie, R.N., the British commander, was forced into action before he was ready, by order of General Sir George Prevost, the British commander-in-chief. The Americans under triumph. I was talking with a states' officer, who was present during the whole affair, and was much amused with his description of it. There appeared to be some fatality attending almost all our attacks upon America during the last war; and it should be remarked that whenever the Americans entered upon our territory, they met with similar defeat. Much allowance must of course be made for ignorance of the country, and of the strength and disposition of the enemy's force; but certainly there was no excuse for the indecision shown by the British general, with such a force as he had under his command.

Now that the real facts are known, one hardly knows whether to laugh or feel indignant. The person from whom I had the information is of undoubted respectability. At the time that our general advanced with an army of 7,000 peninsular troops, there were but 1,000 militia at Plattsburg, those ordered out from the interior of the state not having arrived. It is true that there were 2,000 of the Vermont militia at Burlington, opposite to Plattsburg, but when they were sent for, they refused to go there; they were alarmed at the preponderating force of the British, and they stood upon their state rights—i.e., militia raised in a state are not bound to leave it, being raised for the defence of that state alone. The small force at Plattsburg hardly knew whether to retreat or not; they expected large reinforcements under General McComb, but did not know when they would come. At last it was proposed and agreed to that they should spread themselves and keep up an incessant firing, but out of distance, so as to make the British believe they had a much larger force than they really possessed; and on this judicious plan they acted, and succeeded.

Thomas MacDonough won a decisive victory, although the loss of lives on both sides was very great. Because of Downie's defeat the attack plan of Prevost could not be undertaken and the British troops withdrew. See C. S. Forester, *The Age of Fighting Sail,* pp. 233–44, and also Commander E. B. Potter, *The United States and World Sea Power* (Englewood Cliffs, N. J.: Prentice-Hall; 1955), pp. 247–49.

In the meantime, the British general was anxious for the assistance of the squadron on the lakes, under Commodore Downie, and pressed him to the attack of the American squadron then off Plattsburg. Some sharp remarks from the general proved fatal to our cause by water. Downie, stung by his insinuations, rushed inconsiderately into a *close* engagement. Now, Commodore Downie's vessels had all long guns. McDonough's vessels had only carronades. Had, therefore, Downie not thrown away this advantage, by engaging at close quarters, there is fair reason to suppose that the victory would have been ours, as he could have chosen his distance, and the fire of the American vessels would have been comparatively harmless; but he ran down close to McDonough's fleet and engaged them broadside to broadside, and then the carronades of the Americans, being of heavy calibre, threw the advantage on their side. Downie was killed by the wind of a shot a few minutes after the commencement of the action. Still it was the hardest contested action of the war, Pring being well worthy to take Downie's place.

It was impossible to have done more on either side; and the gentleman who gave me this information added that McDonough told him that, so nicely balanced were the chances, he took out his watch just before the British colours were hauled down, and observed: "If they hold out ten minutes more, it will be more than, I am afraid, we can do." As soon as the victory was decided on the part of the Americans, the British general commenced his retreat, and was followed by this handful of militia. In a day or two afterward, General McComb came up, and a large force was poured in from all quarters.

There was something very similar and quite as ridiculous in the affair at Sackett's Harbour.[3] Our forces advanc-

---

[3] For the significance of Sackett's Harbour, see C. S. Forester, *The Age of Fighting Sail*, pp. 156–58. Prevost and Yeo attacked Sackett's Harbour on May 28, 1813, and ought to have been successful but Prevost was unwilling to push the offensive and ordered a retreat when, with a little more ardor, the victory would have been his.

ing would have cut off some hundreds of the American militia, who were *really* retreating, but by a road which led in such a direction as for a time to make the English commandant suppose that they were intending to take him in flank. This made him imagine that they must be advancing in large numbers when, the fact was, they were running away from his superior force. He made a retreat; upon ascertaining which, the Americans turned back and followed him, harassing his rear.

I was told, at Baltimore, that had the English advanced, the American militia were quite ready to run away, not having the idea of opposing themselves to trained soldiers. It really was very absurd; but in many instances during the war, which have come to my knowledge, it was exactly this— "If you don't run, I will; but if you will, I won't!"

The name given by the French to Vermont designates the features of the country, which is composed of small mountains, covered with verdure to their summits; but the land is by no means good.

At the bottoms, on the banks of the rivers, the alluvial soil is rich, and, generally speaking, the land in this state admits of cultivation about half-way up the mountains; after which, it is fit for nothing but sheep-walks, or to grow small timber upon. I have travelled much in the eastern states, and have been surprised to find how very small a portion of all of them is under cultivation, considering how long they have been settled; nor will there be more of the land taken up, I presume, for a long period: that is to say, not until the west is so over-peopled that a reflux is compelled to fall back into the eastern states, and the crowded masses, like the Gulf-stream, find vent to the northward and eastward.

Set off by coach, long before daylight. There is something very gratifying when once you *are up,* in finding yourself up before the sun; you can repeat to yourself: "How doth the little busy bee," with such satisfaction. Some few stars still twinkled in the sky, winking like the eyelids of tired sentinels, but soon they were relieved, one after another, by the light of morning.

It was still dark when we started, and off we went, up hill and down hill—short steep *pitches,* as they term them here—at a furious rate. There was no level ground; it was all undulating, and very trying to the springs. But an American driver stops at nothing; he will flog away with six horses in hand; and it is wonderful how few accidents happen; but it is very fatiguing, and one hundred miles of American travelling by stage is equal to four hundred in England.

There is much amusement to be extracted from the drivers of these stages, if you will take your seat with them on the front, which few Americans do, as they prefer the inside. One of the drivers, soon after we had changed our team, called out to the off-leader, as he flanked her with his whip: "Go along, you *no-tongued* crittur!"

"Why *no-tongued?*" enquired I.

"Well, I reckon she has no tongue, having bitten it off herself, I was going to say—but it wasn't exactly that, neither."

"How was it, then?"

"Well, now, the fact is, that she is awful ugly (ill-tempered); she bites like a badger, and kicks up as high as the church-steeple. She's an almighty crittur to handle. I was trying to hitch her under-jaw like, with the halter, but she worretted so, that I could only hitch her tongue. She ran back, the end of the halter was fast to the ring, and so she left her tongue in the hitch—that a *fact!*"

"I wonder it did not kill her; didn't she bleed very much? How does she contrive to eat her corn?"

"Well, now, she bled pretty considerable—but not to speak of. I did keep her *one day* in the stable, because I thought she might feel *queer;* since that she has worked in the team every day; and she'll eat her peck of corn with any horse in the stable. But her tongue is out, that certain— so *she'll tell no more lies!*"

Not the least doubting my friend's veracity, I nevertheless took an opportunity, when we changed, of ascertaining the fact; and her tongue was *half* of it out, that *is* the fact.

When we stopped, we had to shift the luggage to another coach. The driver, who was a slight man, was, for some time, looking rather puzzled at the trunks which lay on the road and which he had to put on the coach; he tried to lift one of the largest, let it down again, and then beckoned to me—

"I say, Captain, them four large trunks be rather overmuch for me; but I guess you can master them, so just lift them up on the hind board for me."

I complied; and as I had to lift them as high as my head, they required all my strength.

"Thank ye, Captain; don't trouble yourself any more. The rest be all right, and I can manage them myself."

The Americans never refuse to assist each other in such difficulties as this. In a young country they must assist each other, if they wish to be assisted themselves—and there always will be a mutual dependence. If a man is in a *fix* in America, everyone stops to assist him, and expects the same for himself.

Bellows Falls, a beautiful, romantic spot on the Connecticut River, which separates the states of New Hampshire and Vermont. The masses of rocks, through which the river forces its way at the falls, are very grand and imposing; and the surrounding hills, rich with the autumnal tints, rivet the eye. On these masses of rocks are many faces, cut out by the tribe of Pequod Indians, who formerly used to fish in their waters. Being informed that there was to be a militia muster, I resolved to attend it.

The militia service is not in good odour with the Americans just now. Formerly, when they did try to do as well as they could, the scene was absurd enough; but now they do all they can to make it ridiculous. In this muster there were three or four companies, well equipped; but the major part of the men were what they call here *flood-wood,* that is, of all sizes and heights—a term suggested by the pieces of wood borne down by the freshets of the river, and which are of all sorts, sizes, and lengths. But not only were the men of all sorts and sizes, but the uniforms also, some of which were the most extraordinary I ever beheld, and not unlike the calico dresses worn by the tumblers and vaulters at an English fair. As for the exercise, they either did not, or would not, know anything about it; indeed, as they are now mustered but once a year, it cannot be expected that they should; but as they faced every way, and made mistakes on purpose, it is evident, from their consistent pertinacity in being wrong, that they did know something. When they marched off single file, quick time, they were one-half of them dancing in and out of the ranks to the lively tune which was played—the only instance I saw of their keeping time. But the most amusing part of the ceremony was the speech made by the brigade-major, whose patience had certainly been tried, and who wished to impress his countrymen with the importance of the militia. He ordered them to form a hollow square. They formed a circle, proving that if they could not square the circle, at all events they could circle the square, which is coming very near to it. The major found himself, on his white horse, in an arena about as large as that in which Mr. Ducrow performs at Astley's.[4] He then commenced a sort of perambulating equestrian speech, riding round and round the circle, with his cocked hat in his hand. As the arena was large, and he constantly turned his head as he spoke to those nearest to him in the circle, it was only when he came to within a few yards of you that you could distinguish what he was saying; and of course the auditors at the other point were in the same predicament. However, he divided his speech out in portions very equally, and those which came to my share were as follows:

"Yes, gentlemen—the President, Senate, and House of Representatives, and all others . . . you militia, the bones

---

[4] See earlier note on Ducrow, chapter vii, p. 60. Astley's was a fashionable London theatre where equestrian performances were staged.

and muscle of the land, and by whom . . . Eagle of America shall ruffle her wings, will ever dart . . . those days so glorious, when our gallant forefathers . . . terrible effect of the use of ardent spirits, and shewing . . . Temperance societies, the full benefits of which, I am . . . Star-spangled banner, ever victorious, blazing like— . . ."

The last word I heard was *glory*; but his audience being very impatient for their dinner, cried out loudly for it— preferring it to the mouthfuls of eloquence which fell to their share, but did not stay their stomach. Altogether it was a scene of much fun and good-humour.

Stopped at the pretty village, Charlestown, celebrated for the defence it made during the French war. There is here, running by the river side, a turnpike road, which gave great offence to the American citizens of this state: they declared that to pay toll was *monarchical*, as they always assert everything to be which taxes their pockets. So, one fine night, they assembled with a hawser and a team or two of horses, made the hawser fast to the house at the gate, dragged it down to the river, and sent it floating down the stream, with the gate and board of tolls in company with it.

Progressing in the stage, I had a very amusing specimen of the ruling passion of the country—the spirit of barter, which is communicated to the females as well as to the boys. I will stop for a moment, however, to say that I heard of an American who had two sons, and he declared that they were so clever at barter that he locked them both up together in a room, without a cent in their pockets, and that before they had *swopped* for an hour, they had each gained two dollars a piece. But now for my fellow-passengers— both young, both good-looking, and both ladies, and evidently were total strangers to each other. One had a pretty pink silk bonnet, very fine for travelling; the other, an indifferent plush one. The young lady in the plush eyed the pink bonnet for some time: at last Plush observed in a drawling half-indifferent way:

"That's rather a pretty bonnet of yours, miss."

"Why, yes, I calculate it's rather smart," replied Pink.

After a pause and closer survey— "You wouldn't have any objection to part with it, miss?"

"Well, now, I don't know but I might; I have worn it but three days, I reckon."

"Oh, my? I should have reckoned that you carried it longer—perhaps it rained on them three days."

"I've a notion it didn't rain, not one. It's not the only bonnet I have, miss."

"Well now, I should not mind an exchange, and paying you the *balance*."

"That's an awful thing that you have on, miss."

"I rather think not, but that's as may be— Come, miss, what will you take?"

"Why I don't know— What will you give?"

"I reckon you'll know best when you answer my question."

"Well, then, I shouldn't like less than five dollars."

"Five dollars and my bonnet! I reckon two would be nearer the mark—but it's of no consequence."

"None in the least, miss, only I know the value of my bonnet. We'll say no more about it."

"Just so, miss."

A pause and silence for half a minute, when Miss Plush looks out of the window and says, as if talking to herself, "I shouldn't mind giving four dollars, but no more." She then fell back in her seat when Miss Pink put her head out of the window and said: "I shouldn't refuse four dollars after all, if it was offered," and then she fell back to her former position.

"Did you think of taking four dollars, miss?"

"Well! I don't care, I've plenty of bonnets at home."

"Well," replied Plush, taking out her purse and offering her the money.

"What bank is this, miss?"

"Oh, all's right there, Safety Fund, I calculate."

The two ladies exchange bonnets, and Pink pockets the balance.

I may here just as well mention the custom of *whit-*

tling, which is so common in the eastern states. It is a habit, arising from the natural restlessness of the American when he is not employed, of cutting a piece of stick, or anything within their reach. A Yankee shown into a room to await the arrival of another has been known to whittle away nearly the whole of the mantel-piece. Lawyers in court whittle away at the table before them; and judges will cut through their own bench. In some courts, they put sticks before noted whittlers to save the furniture. The Down-Easters, as the Yankees are termed generally, whittle when they are making a bargain, as it fills up the pauses, gives them time for reflection, and moreover, prevents any examination of the countenance—for in bargaining, like in the game of brag, the countenance is carefully watched, as an index to the wishes. I was once witness to a bargain made between two respectable Yankees, who wished to agree about a farm, and in which whittling was resorted to.

They sat down on a log of wood, about three or four feet apart from each other, with their faces turned opposite ways—that is, one had his legs on one side of the log with his face to the east, and the other his legs on the other side with his face to the west. One had a piece of soft wood and was sawing it with his penknife; the other had an unbarked hickory stick which he was peeling for a walking-stick. The reader will perceive a strong analogy between this bargain and that in the stage between the two ladies.

"Well, good morning—and about this farm?"

"I don't know; what will you take?"

"What will you give?"

Silence, and whittle away.

"Well, I should think two thousand dollars, a heap of money for this farm."

"I've a notion it will never go for three thousand, anyhow."

"There's a fine farm, and cheaper, on the north side."

"But where's the sun to ripen the corn?"

"Sun shines on all alike."

"Not exactly through a Vermont hill, I reckon. The

driver offered me as much as I say, if I recollect right."

"Money not always to be depended upon. Money not always forthcoming."

"I reckon I shall make an elegant 'backy stopper of this piece of sycamore."

Silence for a few moments. Knives hard at work.

"I've a notion this is as pretty a hickory stick as ever came out of a wood."

"I shouldn't mind two thousand five hundred dollars, and time given."

"It couldn't be more than six months, then, if it goes at that price."

(Pause.)

"Well, that might suit me."

"What do you say then?"

"Suppose it must be so."

"It's a bargain then (rising up), come, let's liquor on it."

The farmers on the banks of the Connecticut River are the richest in the eastern states. The majestic growth of the timber certified that the soil is generally good, although the crops were off the ground. They grow here a large quantity of what is called the broom corn: the stalk and leaves are similar to the maize or Indian corn, but, instead of the ear, it throws out, at top and on the sides, spiky plumes on which seed is carried. These plumes are cut off, and furnish the brooms and whisks of the country. It is said to be a very profitable crop. At Brattleboro we stopped at an inn kept by one of the state representatives, and, as may be supposed, had very bad fare in consequence, the man being above his business. We changed horses at Bloody Brook, so termed in consequence of a massacre of the settlers by the Indians. But there are twenty Bloody Brooks in America, all records of similar catastrophes.

Whether the blue laws of Connecticut are still in force, I know not, but I could not discover that they had ever been repealed. At present there is no theatre in Connecticut, nor does anybody venture to propose one. The proprietors of one of the equestrian studs made their appearance at the confines of the state, and intimated that they wished to perform, but were given to understand that their horses would be confiscated if they entered the state. The consequence is that Connecticut is the dullest, most disagreeable state in the Union; and, if I am to believe the Americans themselves, so far from the morals of the community being kept uncontaminated by this rigour, the very reverse is the case —especially as respects the college students, who are in the secret practice of more vice than is to be found in any other establishment of the kind in the Union. But even if I had not been so informed by creditable people, I should have decided in my own mind that such was the case. Human nature is everywhere the same. . . .

I do not know anything that disgusts me so much as *cant.* Even now we continually hear, in the American public orations, about the *stern virtues* of the pilgrim fathers. *Stern,* indeed! The fact is, that these pilgrim fathers were fanatics and bigots, without charity or mercy, wanting in the very *essence* of Christianity. Witness their conduct to the Indians when they thirsted for their territory.[5] . . .

---

[5] This is a reference to the behaviour of the New Englanders in the late seventeenth century and specifically to King Philip's War. Actually the war began in part as a result of Indian tribal vengeance and partly because of dissatisfaction on the part of the Indians, resulting from their treatment by the white man. Cotton Mather and his contemporaries saw the war as a conspiracy, long planned by Philip, chief of the Wampanoags, against the peaceable settlers, and they felt that any and all measures were justified in bringing about the downfall of the Indian leader. The war lasted from July 1675 to August 1676 when Philip was killed. During the year some twelve towns were destroyed and many settlers were killed. Numerous Indian prisoners were executed, while others were sold into slavery, among them Philip's son, who was sent to Bermuda. See Douglas Leach, *Flintlock and Tomahawk* (New York: Macmillan; 1958), p. 231.

CHAPTER XVIII

The St. Lawrence Valley

Montreal, next to Quebec, is the oldest-looking and most aristocratic city in all North America. Lofty houses, with narrow streets, prove antiquity. After Quebec and Montreal, New Orleans is said to take the next rank, all three of them having been built by the French. It is pleasant to look upon any structure in this new hemisphere which bears the mark of time upon it. The ruins of Fort Putnam are one of the curiosities of America.[1]

Montreal is all alive—mustering here, drilling there, galloping everywhere; and moreover, Montreal is knee-deep in snow, and the thermometer below zero. Every hour brings fresh intelligence of the movements of the rebels, or patriots [2]—the last term is doubtful, yet it may be correct.

---

[1] Fort Putnam was built at West Point in 1778 by Rufus Putnam (1738–1824), American soldier and surveyor. In the Revolution Putnam's engineering skill was put to use and he was made a brigadier general; after the war he settled in Ohio. In 1837, when Marryat visited it, Fort Putnam was no longer in use.

[2] The rebellion in Canada in 1837 was, in a lesser way, a second American Revolution. The main difference was that in Canada the rebels did not succeed in their aim of gaining independence. In the long run, all of the other dissatisfactions were resolved and Canada gained home rule. The two provinces of Upper and Lower Canada had many grievances; the radicals in both colonies had been thwarted by the actions of the conservatives in the Legislative Councils. Louis Joseph Papineau in Lower

When they first opened the theatre at Botany Bay, Barrington [3] spoke the prologue, which ended with these two lines:

Canada and William Lyon Mackenzie in Upper Canada advocated more political and social democracy. They and their followers in the Legislative Assemblies had introduced many extreme measures which, if approved, would have made Canada more like the United States. The rebellion broke out first in Lower Canada when a riot occurred in Montreal on November 7, 1837. Papineau and his friends left the city shortly thereafter, and the government, thinking that they had gone to raise a rebellion, ordered their arrest. This was followed by the *patriotes'* attempting to halt the government's action to capture the radicals. The armed *patriotes* were successful in preventing the troops from taking Papineau. The rebellion was left without any real organization or competent leadership, for Papineau fled to the United States. The *patriotes* made a stand at St. Charles on November 25, 1837, but here they were defeated. This defeat was followed by a second reverse at St. Eustache, when two thousand loyal troops dispersed the rebels after a bloody battle. From then on it may be said that the rebellion in Lower Canada was at an end.

Equally unprepared were the rebels in Upper Canada; Mackenzie and his fellow insurgents gathered near York and they were soundly defeated on December 7, 1837, when Colonel Fitzgibbon and the loyal militia marched against them. Mackenzie fled to the United States and all was virtually over.

For a more complete account, see A. D. Decelles, *Papineau* (Oxford: Oxford University Press; 1926), William Kilbourn, *The Firebrand: William Lyon Mackenzie and the Rebellion in Upper Canada* (Toronto: Clarke Irwin; 1956), Sydney W. Jackman, *Galloping Head, a Biography of Sir Francis Bond Head* (London: Phoenix House; 1958).

[3] George Barrington (1755–?), pickpocket and author, was sentenced to Botany Bay, Australia, in 1790 after having been sentenced twice before for the same offence. He was released in 1792 and became superintendent of convicts and high constable of Paramatta, New South Wales. He later wrote a number of books on Australian life. He appeared on the stage when the first theatre was opened in Australia in 1792 and wrote the prologue for the first production, a play entitled *The Revenge*. The quotation from the prologue given in Marryat's text does not agree with the version given in Geoffrey C. Ingelton, *True Patriots All or News from Early Australia* (Sydney, Australia: Angus and Robertson; 1952), which reads:
> True patriots all; for be it
>   understood
> We left our country for our
>   country's good.

> True *patriots* we, for be it understood,
> We left our country, for our country's good.

In this view of the case, some of them, it is hoped, will turn out patriots before they die, if they have not been murdered already.

Every hour comes in some poor wretch, who in asking to join the insurgents has been made a beggar, cattle, sheep, and pigs driven away; his fodder, his barns, his horse, and all that he possessed, now reduced to ashes. The cold-blooded, heartless murder of Lieutenant Weir has, however, sufficiently raised the choler of the troops, without any farther enormities on the part of the insurgents being requisite to that end: when an English soldier swears to show no mercy, he generally keeps his word. Of all wars, a civil war is the most cruel, the most unrelenting, and the most exterminating; and deep indeed must be the responsibility of those who, by their words or their actions, have contrived to set countryman against countryman, neighbour against neighbour, and very often brother against brother, and father against child.

On the morning of the [December 13, 1837] the ice on the branch of the Ottawa River, which we had to cross, being considered sufficiently strong to bear the weight of the artillery, the whole force marched out, under the command of Sir John Colborne [4] in person, to reduce the insurgents,

---

[4] John Colborne, first Baron Seaton (1778–1863), British army officer, who served in Egypt, Sicily, and Spain, and commanded the Fifty-second Foot at Waterloo. He was made a major general in 1825 and in the same year became Lieutenant-Governor of Guernsey. In 1830 he was appointed Lieutenant-Governor of Upper Canada where he remained until 1836, being succeeded by Sir Francis Bond Head, and in 1837 was appointed Commander-in-Chief of the British forces in North America. Thus he was the officer commanding the troops which crushed the rebellion in 1837. After Lord Durham's resignation in 1838, Colborne became Governor General of British North America. For his many services he was given a barony in 1839. From 1843 to 1849 he was Governor of the Ionian Islands. In 1860 he was made a Field Marshal.

who had fortified themselves at St. Eustache and St. Benoit, two towns of some magnitude in the district of Bois Brulé. The snow, as I before observed, lay very deep; but by the time we started, the road had been well beaten down by the multitudes which had preceded us.

The effect of the whole line of troops, in their fur caps and great coats, with the trains of artillery, ammunition, and baggage-wagons, as they wound along the snow-white road, was very beautiful. It is astonishing how much more numerous the force, and how much larger the men and horses appeared to be, from the strong contrast of their colours with the wide expanse of snow.

As we passed one of the branches of the Ottawa, one of the ammunition-wagons falling through the ice, the horses were immediately all but choked by the drivers—a precaution which was novel to me, and a singular method of saving their lives, but such was the case: the air within them, rarefied by heat, inflated their bodies like balloons, and they floated high on the water. In this state they were easily disengaged from their traces, and hauled out upon the ice; the cords which had nearly strangled them were then removed, and, in a few minutes, they recovered sufficiently to be led to the shore.

Let it not be supposed that I am about to write a regular despatch. I went out with the troops, but was of about as much use as the fifth wheel of a coach, with the exception that, as I rode one of Sir John Colborne's horses, I was, perhaps, so far supplying the place of a groom who was better employed.

The town of St. Eustache is very prettily situated on the high banks of the river, the most remarkable object being the Catholic church, a very massive building, raised about two hundred yards from the river side, upon a commanding situation. This church the insurgents had turned into a fortress, and perhaps, for a fortress "*d'occasion,*" there never was one so well calculated for a vigorous defence, it being flanked by two long stone-built houses, and protected in the rear by several lines of high and strong palisades, running down into the river. The troops halted about three hundred yards from the town, to reconnoitre; the artillery were drawn up and opened their fire, but chiefly with a view that the enemy, by returning the fire, might demonstrate their force and position. These being ascertained, orders were given by Sir John Colborne, so that in a short time the whole town would be invested by the troops. The insurgents perceiving this, many of them escaped, some through the town, others by the frozen river. Those who crossed on the ice were chased by the volunteer dragoons, and the slipping and tumbling of the pursued and the pursuers afforded as much merriment as interest, so true it is that anything ludicrous will make one laugh, in opposition to the feelings of sympathy, anxiety, and fear. Some of the runaways were cut down, and many more taken prisoners.

As soon as that portion of the troops which had entered the town, and marched up the main street toward the church, arrived within half-musket-shot, they were received with a smart volley, which was fired from the large windows of the church, and which wounded a few of the men. The soldiers were then ordered to make their approaches under cover of the houses; and the artillery being brought up, commenced firing upon the church; but the walls of the building were much too solid for the shot to make any impression, and had the insurgents stood firm, they certainly might have given a great deal of trouble, and probably have occasioned a large loss of men; but they became alarmed, and fired one of the houses which abutted upon and flanked the church—this they did with the view of escaping under cover of the smoke. In a few minutes the church itself was obscured by the volumes of smoke thrown out; and at the same time that the insurgents were escaping, the troops marched up and surrounded the church. The poor wretches attempted to get away, either singly, or by twos and threes; but the moment they appeared a volley was discharged, and they fell. Every attempt was made by the officers to take prisoners, but with indifferent success; indeed, such was the exasperation of the troops at the murder of

Lieutenant Weir, that it was a service of danger to attempt to save the life of one of these poor deluded creatures. The fire from the house soon communicated to the church. Chenier, the leader, with ten others, the remnant of the insurgents who were in the church, rushed out; there was one tremendous volley, and all was over.

By this time many other parts of the town were on fire, and there was every prospect of the whole of it being burnt down, leaving no quarters for the soldiers to protect them during the night. The attention of everybody was therefore turned to prevent the progress of the flames. Some houses were pulled down, so as to cut off the communication with the houses in the centre of the town, and in these houses the troops were billetted off. The insurgents had removed their families, and most of their valuables and furniture, before our arrival; but in one house were the commissariat stores, consisting of the carcasses of all the cattle, sheep, pigs, etc., which they had taken from the loyal farmers; there was a large supply, and the soldiers were soon cooking in all directions. The roll was called, men mustered, and order established.

The night was bitterly cold, the sky was clear, and the moon near to her full; houses were still burning in every direction, but they were as mere satellites to the lofty church, which was now one blaze of fire, and throwing out volumes of smoke, which passed over the face of the bright moon, and gave to her a lurid reddish tinge, as if she too had assisted in these deeds of blood. The distant fires scattered over the whole landscape, which was one snow-wreath; the whirling of the smoke from the houses which were burning close to us, and which, from the melting of the snow, were surrounded by pools of water, reflecting the fierce yellow flames, mingled with the pale beams of the bright moon—this, altogether, presented a beautiful, novel, yet melancholy panorama. I thought it might represent, in miniature, the burning of Moscow.

About midnight, when all was quiet, I walked up to the

church, in company with one of Sir John Colborne's aide-de-camps: the roof had fallen, and the flames had subsided for want of farther aliment. As we passed by a house which had just taken fire we heard a cry, and, on going up, found a poor wounded Canadian, utterly incapable of moving, whom the flames had just reached; in a few minutes he would have been burned alive. We dragged him out and gave him in charge of the soldiers, who carried him to the hospital.

But what was this compared to the scene which presented itself in the church! But a few weeks back crowds were there, kneeling in adoration and prayer; I could fancy the Catholic priests in their splendid stoles, the altar, its candlesticks and ornaments, the solemn music, the incense, and all that, by appealing to the senses, is so favourable to the cause of religion with the ignorant and uneducated; and what did I now behold?—nothing but the bare and blackened walls, the glowing beams and rafters, and the window-frames which the flames still licked and flickered through. The floor had been burnt to cinders, and upon and between the sleepers on which the floor had been laid were scattered the remains of human creatures, injured in various degrees, or destroyed by the fire; some with merely the clothes burnt off, leaving the naked body; some burnt to a deep brown tinge; others so far consumed that the viscera were exposed; while here and there the blackened ribs and vertebra were all that the fierce flames had spared.

Not only inside of the church, but without its walls, was the same revolting spectacle. In the remains of the small building used as a receptacle for the coffins previous to interment were several bodies, heaped one upon another, and still burning, the tressels which had once supported the coffins serving as fuel; and farther off were bodies still unscathed by fire, but frozen hard by the severity of the weather.

I could not help thinking, as I stood contemplating this melancholy scene of destruction, bloodshed, and sacrilege, that if Mr. Hume [5] or Mr. Roebuck [6] had been by my side, they might have repented their inflammatory and liberal opinions, as here they beheld the frightful effects of them.

---

[5] Joseph Hume (1777–1855), radical politician, began his career as an employee of the East India Company, serving in India from 1797 to 1807. In 1812 he was elected to Parliament as a Tory, but he shifted his party and became an extreme radical. He consistently supported the *patriotes* and the liberals in the Canadas and opposed Lord John Russell's "Canada Bill," which suspended the constitution of Lower Canada. He favored all later liberal legislation with respect to British North America.

[6] John Arthur Roebuck (1801–79), English politician, was born in India and educated in Canada. He was a lawyer and a member of Parliament in England. For a time he acted as agent for the House of Assembly of Lower Canada. He was intimately associated with Joseph Hume in his support of a liberal colonial policy. In later life Roebuck became an active supporter of Disraeli.

CHAPTER XIX

Northern New England—Vermont

Crossing the river St. Lawrence at this season of the year is not very pleasant, as you must force your passage through the large masses of ice, and are occasionally fixed among them, so that you are swept down the current along with them. Such was our case for about a quarter of an hour, and, in consequence, we landed about three miles lower down than we had intended. The next day the navigation of the river, such as it was, was stopped, and in eight and forty hours heavy wagons and carts were passing over where we had floated across.

My course lay through what were termed the *excited* districts; I had promised to pass through them, and supply the folks at Montreal with any information I could collect. The weather was bitterly cold, and all communication was carried on by sleighs, a very pleasant mode of travelling when the roads are smooth, but rather fatiguing when they are uneven, as the sleigh then jumps from hill to hill, like an oyster-shell thrown by a boy to skim the surface of the water. To defend myself from the cold, I had put on, over my coat, and under my cloak, a wadded black silk dressing-gown; I thought nothing of it at the time, but I afterward discovered that I was supposed to be one of the rebel priests escaping from justice.

Although still in the English dominions, I had not been over on the opposite side more than a quarter of an hour before I perceived that it would be just as well to hold my tongue; and my adherence to this resolution, together with my supposed canonicals, were the cause of not a word being addressed to me by my fellow-travellers. They presumed that I spoke French only, which they did not, and I listened in silence to all that passed.

It is strange how easily the American people are excited, and when excited, they will hesitate at nothing. The coach (for it was the stagecoach, although represented by an open sleigh) stopped at every town, large or small, everybody eager to tell and receive the news. I always got out to warm myself at the stoves in the bar, and heard all the remarks made upon what I do really believe were the most absurd and extravagant lies ever circulated—lies which the very people who uttered them knew to be such, but which produced the momentary effect intended. They were even put into the newspapers, and circulated everywhere; and when the truth was discovered, they still remained uncontradicted, except by a general remark, that such was the tory version of the matter, and of course was false. The majority of those who travelled with me were Americans who had crossed the St. Lawrence in the same boat, and who must, therefore, have known well the whole circumstances attending the expedition against St. Eustache; but, to my surprise, at every place where we stopped they declared that there had been a battle between the insurgents and the king's troops, in which the insurgents had been victorious; that Sir John Colborne had been compelled to retreat to Montreal; that they had themselves seen the troops come back (which was true), and that Montreal was barricaded (which was also true) to prevent the insurgents from marching in. I never said one word; I listened to the exultations—to the declarations of some that they should go and join the patriots, etc. One man amused me by saying

—"I've a great mind to go, but what I want is a good general to take the command; I want a Julius Cæsar, or a Bonaparte, or a Washington—then I'll go."

I stopped for some hours at St. Alban's. I was recommended to go to an inn, the landlord of which was said not to be of the democratic party, for the other two inns were the resort of the Sympathizers, and in these, consequently, scenes of great excitement took place. The landlord put into my hand a newspaper published that day, containing a series of resolutions, founded upon such falsehoods that I thought it might be advantageous to refute them. I asked the landlord whether I could see the editor of the paper; he replied that the party lived next door; and I requested that he would send for him, telling him that I could give him information relative to the affair of St. Eustache.

I had been shown into a large sitting-room on the ground floor, which I presumed was a private room, when the editor of the newspaper, attracted by the message I had sent him, came in. I then pointed to the resolutions passed at the meeting, and asked him whether he would allow me to answer them in his paper. His reply was, certainly: his paper was open to all.

"Well, then, call in an hour [I said] and I will by that time prove to you that they can only be excused or accounted for by the parties who framed them being totally ignorant of the whole affair."

He went away, but did not return at the time requested. It was not until late in the evening that he came and, avoiding the question of the resolutions, begged that I would give him the information relative to St. Eustache. As I presumed that, like most other editors in the United States, he dared not put in anything which would displease his subscribers, I said no more on that subject, but commenced dictating to him, while he wrote the particulars attending the St. Eustache affair. I was standing by the stove, giving the editor this information, when the door of the room opened, and in walked seven or eight people, who, without speaking, took chairs; in a minute, another party of about the same number was ushered into the room by the landlord, who, I thought, gave me a significant look. I felt surprised at what I thought an intrusion, as I had considered my room to be private; however I appeared to take no notice of it, and continued dictating to the editor. The door opened again and again, and more chairs were brought in for the accommodation of the parties who entered, until at last the room was so full that I had but just room to walk round the stove. Not a person said a word; they listened to what I was dictating to the editor, and I observed that they all looked rather fierce; but whether this was a public meeting, or what was to be the end of it, I had no idea. At last, when I had finished, the editor took up his papers and left the room, in which I suppose there might have been from one hundred to a hundred and fifty persons assembled. As soon as the door closed, one of them struck his thick stick on the floor (they most of them had sticks) and gave a loud "Hem!"

"I believe, sir, that you are Captain M——."

"Yes," replied I, "that is my name."

"We are informed, sir, by the gentleman who has just gone out, that you have asserted that our resolutions of yesterday could only be excused or accounted for from our total ignorance." Here he struck his stick again upon the floor, and paused.

"Oh!" thinks I to myself, "the editor has informed against me!"

"Now, sir," continued the spokesman, "we are come to be enlightened; we wish you to prove to us that we are totally ignorant; you will oblige us by an explanation of your assertion."

He was again silent. (Thinks I to myself, I'm in for it now, and if I get away without a broken head, or something else, I am fortunate; however, here goes.) Whereupon, without troubling the reader with what I did say, I will only observe that I thought the best plan was to gain time by going back as far as I could. I therefore commenced my oration at the period when the Canadas were surrendered to the English; remarking upon the system which had been acted upon by our government from that time up to the present; proving, as well as I could, that the Canadians had nothing to complain of, and that if England had treated her other American colonies as well, there never would have been a Declaration of Independence, etc. Having spoken for about an hour, and observing a little impatience on the part of some of the company, I stopped. Upon which, one rose and said that there were several points not fully explained, referring to them one after another, whereupon the "honourable member rose to explain"—and was again silent. Another then spoke, requesting information as to points not referred to by me. I replied, and fortunately had an opportunity of paying the Americans a just compliment, in gratitude for which their features relaxed considerably. Perceiving this, I ventured to introduce a story or two, which made them laugh. After this, the day was my own; for I consider the Americans, when not excited (which they too often are), as a very good-tempered people; at all events, they won't break your head for making them laugh; at least, such I found was the case. We now entered freely into conversation; some went away, others remained, and the affair ended by many of them shaking hands with me, and our taking a drink at the bar.

I must say that the first appearances of this meeting were not at all pleasant; but I was rightly served for my want of caution in so publicly stating that the free and enlightened citizens of St. Albans were very ignorant, and for opposing public opinion at a time when the greatest excitement prevailed. I have mentioned this circumstance as it throws a great deal of light upon the character of the Yankee or American of the eastern states. They would not suffer opposition to the majority to pass unnoticed (who, in England, would have cared what a stranger may have expressed as his opinion?) but, at the same time, they gave me a patient hearing, to know whether I could show cause for what I said. Had I refused this, I might have been very roughly handled; but as I defended my observations, al-

though they were not complimentary to them, they gave me
fair play. They were evidently much excited when they
came into the room, but they gradually cooled down until
convinced of the truth of my assertions; and then all
animosity was over. The landlord said to me afterward: "I
reckon you got out of that uncommon well, Captain." I perfectly agreed with him, and made a resolution to hold my
tongue until I arrived at New York.

The next day, as I was proceeding on my journey, I
fell in with General Brown,[1] celebrated for running away so
fast at the commencement of the fight at St. Charles. He
had a very fine pair of mustachios. We both warmed our
toes at the same stove in solemn silence.

Sunday, at Burlington.— The young ladies are dressing
up the church with festoons and garlands of evergreens for
the celebration of Christmas, and have pressed me into the
service. Last Sunday I was meditating over the blackened
walls of the church of St. Eustache, and the roasted corpses
lying within its precincts; now I am in another church,
weaving laurel and cypress, in company with some of the
prettiest creatures in creation. As the copy-book says, *variety is charming!*

---

[1] Thomas Brown (1803–88)
was a commander of the *patriotes* at the Battle of St. Charles
on November 25, 1837. Following the rebel defeat at this battle
Brown fled to the United States.
After the amnesty was granted
to the former rebels in 1844, he
returned to Canada.

CHAPTER XX

The Quaker City

Philadelphia is certainly, in appearance, the most wealthy and imposing city in the Union. It is well built, and ornamented with magnificent public edifices of white marble; indeed there is a great show of this material throughout the whole of the town, all the flights of steps to the doors, door-lintels, and window-sills being very generally composed of this material. The exterior of the houses, as well as the side pavement, are kept remarkably clean; and there is no intermixture of commerce, as there is at New York, the bustle of business being confined to the Quays and one or two streets adjoining the river side.

The first idea which strikes you when you arrive at Philadelphia is that it is Sunday: everything is so quiet, and there are so few people stirring; but by the time that you have paraded half a dozen streets, you come to a conclusion that it must be Saturday, as that day is, generally speaking, a washing-day. Philadelphia is so admirably supplied with water from the Schuylkill water-works, that every house has it laid on from the attic to the basement; and all day long they wash windows, door, marble step, and pavements in front of the houses. Indeed, they have so much water that they can afford to be very liberal to passers-by. One minute you have a shower-bath from a Negress, who is throwing water at the windows on the first floor; and the next you have to hop over a stream across the pavement, occasioned by some black fellow who, rather than go for a broom to sweep away any small portion of dust collected before his master's door, brings out the leather hose, attached to the hydrants, as they term them here, and fizzes away with it till the stream has forced the dust into the gutter.

Of course, fire has no chance in this city. Indeed, the two elements appear to have arranged that matter between them; fire has the ascendant in New York while water reigns in Philadelphia. If a fire does break out here, the housekeepers have not the fear of being *burnt* to death before them; for the water is poured on in such torrents that the furniture is washed out of the windows, and all they have to look out for is to escape from being drowned.

The public institutions, such as libraries, museums, and the private cabinets of Philadelphia, are certainly very superior to those of any other city or town in America, Boston not excepted. Everything that is undertaken in this city is well done; no expense is spared, although they are not so rapid in their movements as at New York; indeed the affluence and ease pervading the place, with the general cultivation which invariably attend them, are evident to a stranger.

Philadelphia has claimed for herself the title of the most aristocratic city in the Union. If she refers to the aristocracy of wealth, I think she is justified; but if she would say the aristocracy of family, which is much more thought of by the few who can claim it, she must be content to divide that with Boston, Baltimore, Charleston, and the other cities which can date as far back as herself. One thing is certain, that in no city is there so much fuss made about lineage and descent; in no city are there so many cliques and sets in society, who keep apart from each other; and it is very often difficult to ascertain the grounds of their distinctions. One family will live at No. 1, and another at No. 2 in the same street, both have similar establishments, both keep their carriages, both be well educated, and both may talk of their grandfathers and grandmothers; and yet No. 1 will tell you that No. 2 is nobody, and you must not visit there; and when you inquire why? there is no other answer but that they are not of the right sort. As long as a portion are rich and a portion are poor, there is a line of demarcation easy to be drawn, even in a democracy; but in Philadelphia, where there are so many in affluent circumstances, that line has been effaced, and they now seek an imaginary one, like the equinoctial, which none can be permitted to pass without going through the ceremonies of perfect ablution. This social contest, as may be supposed, is carried on among those who have no real pretensions; but there are many old and well-connected families in Philadelphia, whose claims are universally, although perhaps unwillingly, acknowledged.

I doubt if the claims of Boston to be the most scientific city in the Union can be now established. I met a greater number of scientific men in Philadelphia than I did in Boston; and certainly the public and private collections in the former city are much superior. The collection of shells and minerals belonging to Mr. Lea,[1] who is well known as an author and a naturalist, is certainly the most interesting I saw in the states, and I passed two days in examining it; it must have cost him much trouble and research.

The Girard [2] college, when finished, will be a most splendid building. It is, however, as they have now planned it, incorrect, according to the rules of architecture, in the number of columns on the sides in proportion to those in

---

[1] Isaac Lea (1792–1886), eminent American biologist, was an authority on shellfish.

[2] Stephen Girard (1750–1831) was born in France and emigrated to America before the Revolution, settling first in New York and later in Philadelphia. He became an extremely wealthy merchant and shipowner. In 1826 he made a will leaving $6,000,000 to the city of Philadelphia to provide for the education of poor white orphan boys. This educational foundation later became Girard College.

front. This is a great pity; perhaps the plan will be reconsidered, as there is plenty of time to correct it, as well as money to defray the extra expense.

The water-works at Schuylkill are well worth a visit, not only for their beauty, but their simplicity. The whole of the river Schuylkill is dammed up, and forms a huge water-power, which forces up the supply of water for the use of the city. As I presume that river has a god as well as others, I can imagine his indignation, not only at his waters being diverted from his channel, but at being himself obliged to do all the work for the benefit of his tyrannical masters.

I have said that the museums of Philadelphia are far superior to most in the states; but I may just as well here observe that, as in many other things, a great improvement is necessary before they are such as they ought to be. There is not only in these museums, but in all that I ever entered in the United States, a want of taste and discrimination, of that correct feeling which characterizes the real lovers of science, and knowledge of what is worthy of being collected. They are such collections as would be made by schoolboys and schoolgirls, not those of erudite professors and scientific men. Side by side with the most interesting and valuable specimens, such as the fossil mammoth, etc., you have the greatest puerilities and absurdities in the world—such as a cherrystone formed into a basket, a fragment of the boiler of the *Moselle* steamer, and Heaven knows what besides. Then you invariably have a large collection of daubs, called portraits of eminent personages, one-half of whom a stranger never heard of—but that is national vanity; and lastly, I do not recollect to have seen a museum that had not a considerable portion of its space occupied by most execrable waxwork, in which the sleeping beauty (a sad misnomer) generally figures very conspicuously. In some, they have models of celebrated criminals in the act of committing a murder, with the very hatchet or the very knife; or such trophies as the bonnet worn by Mrs. —— when she was killed by her husband; or the shirt, with the blood of his wife on it, worn by Jack Sprat, or whoever he might be, when he committed the bloody deed. The most favourite subject, after the sleeping beauty in the waxwork, is General Jackson, with the battle of New Orleans in the distance. Now all these things are very well in their places; exhibit waxwork as much as you please—it amuses and interests children; but the present collections in the museums remind you of American society—a chaotic mass, in which you occasionally meet what is valuable and interesting, but of which the larger proportion is pretence.

It was not until I had been some time in Philadelphia that I became convinced how very superior the free coloured people were in intelligence and education to what, from my knowledge of them in our West India islands, I had ever imagined them capable of. Not that I mean to imply that they will ever attain to the same powers of intellect as the white man, for I really believe that the race are not formed for it by the Almighty. I do not mean to say that there *never* will be great men among the African race, but that such instances will always be very *rare*, compared to the numbers produced among the white. But this is certain, that in Philadelphia the free coloured people are a very respectable class, and, in my opinion, quite as intelligent as the more humble of the free whites. I have been quite surprised to see them take out their pencils, write down and calculate with quickness and precision, and in every other point show great intelligence and keenness.

In this city they are both numerous and wealthy. The most extravagant funeral I saw in Philadelphia was that of a black; the coaches were very numerous, as well as the pedestrians, who were all well dressed, and behaving with the utmost decorum. They were preceded by a black clergyman, dressed in his full black silk canonicals. He did look very odd, I must confess.

Singular is the degree of contempt and dislike in which the free blacks are held in all the free states of America. They are deprived of their rights as citizens; and the white pauper, who holds out his hand for charity (and there is no want of beggars in Philadelphia), will turn away from a

Negro, or coloured man, with disdain. It is the same thing in the eastern states, notwithstanding their religious professions. In fact, in the United States, a Negro, from his colour, and I believe his colour alone, is a degraded being. Is not this extraordinary, in a land which professes universal liberty, equality, and the rights of man? In England this is not the case. In private society no one objects to sit in company with a man of colour, provided he has the necessary education and respectability. Nor, indeed, is it the case in the slave states, where I have frequently seen a lady in a public conveyance with her Negress sitting by her, and no objection has been raised by the other parties in the coach; but in the free states a man of colour is not admitted into a stagecoach; and in all other public places, such as theatres, churches, etc., there is always a portion divided off for the Negro population, that they may not be mixed up with the whites. When I first landed at New York, I had a specimen of this feeling. Fastened by a rope yarn to the rudder chains of a vessel next in the tier, at the wharf to which the packet had hauled in, I perceived the body of a black man, turning over and over with the ripple of the waves. I was looking at it when a lad came up; probably his curiosity was excited by my eyes being fixed in that direction. He looked, and perceiving the object, turned away with disdain, saying: "Oh, it's only a nigger.". . .

It will be observed . . . that reference is made to the unjust prejudice against any taint of the African blood. There is an existing proof of the truth of this remark, in the case of one of the most distinguished members of the House of Representatives.[3] This gentleman has some children who are not of pure blood; but, to his honour, he has done his duty by them, he has educated them, and received them

---

[3] Possibly this refers to Richard Mentor Johnson (1780–1850), American statesman, who was born in Kentucky. From 1807 to 1819 he was a member of the House of Representatives, from 1819 to 1829 a member of the Senate, and in 1829 he returned to the House. From 1837–41 he served as Vice-President under Van Buren, being the only Vice-President to be elected to that office by the Senate.

into his house as his acknowledged daughters. What is the consequence? Why, it is considered that by doing so he has outraged society; and whenever they want to raise a cry against him, this is the charge, and very injurious it is to his popularity, "that he has done his duty as a father and a Christian."

"Captain Marryat, we are a very moral people!"

The laws of the state relative to the intermarriage of the whites with the coloured population are also referred to. A case of this kind took place at New York when I was there; and as soon as the ceremony was over, the husband, I believe it was, but either the husband or the wife, was seized by the mob and put under the pump for half an hour. At Boston, similar modes of expressing public opinion have been adopted, notwithstanding that that city is the stronghold of the abolitionists.

It also refers to the white slavery, which was not abolished until the year 1789. Previous to that period, a man who arrived out, from the old continent, and could not pay his passage, was put up to auction for the amount of his debt, and was compelled to serve until he had worked it out with the purchaser. But not only for the debt of passage-money, but for other debts, a white man was put up to auction, and sold to the best bidder. . . .

It is usually considered in this country that by going to America you avoid taxation, but such is not the case. The municipal taxes are not very light. I could not obtain any very satisfactory estimates from the other cities, but I gained thus much from Philadelphia.

The assessments are on property.

City Tax, 70 cents upon 100 dollars valuation.

County Tax, 65 cents upon ditto.

Poor's Rate, 40 cents.

Taxes on Horses, 1 dollar each.

Taxes on Dogs, half a dollar each.

Poll Tax, from a quarter dollar to 4 dollars each person.

It is singular that such a tax as the *poll* tax, that which created the insurrection of Wat Tyler in England, should have forced its way into a democracy. In the collection of their taxes, they are quite as summary as they are in England. . . .

It is a strange fact, and one which must have attracted the reader's notice, that there should be a poor's rate in America, where there is work for everybody; and still stranger that there should be one in the city of Philadelphia, in which, perhaps, there are more beneficent and charitable institutions than in any city in the world of the same population; notwithstanding this, there are many mendicants in the street. All this arises from the advantage taken of an unwise philanthropy in the first place, many people preferring to live upon alms in preference to labour; and next from the state of destitution to which many of the emigrants are reduced after their arrival, and before they can obtain employment. Indeed, not only Philadelphia, but Baltimore and New York, are equally charged for the support of these people—the two first by legal enactment, the latter by voluntary subscription. And it is much to the credit of the inhabitants of all these cities that the charge is paid cheerfully, and that an appeal is never made in vain.

But let the Americans beware: the poor rate is at present trifling—40 cents in 100 dollars, or about 1¾d. in the pound; but they must recollect that they were not more in England about half a century back, and see to what they have risen now! It is the principle which is bad. There are now in Philadelphia more than 1,500 paupers, who live entirely upon the public, but who, if relief had not been continued to them, would, in all probability, by this time, have found their way to where their labour is required. The Philadelphians are proverbially generous and charitable; but they should remember that, in thus yielding to the dictates of their hearts, they are sowing the seeds of what will prove a bitter curse to their posterity.

CHAPTER XXI

The National Capital

W ASHINGTON.—Here are assembled from every state in
the Union what ought to be the collected talent, intelligence, and high principle of a free and enlightened nation. Of talent and intelligence there is a very fair supply,
but principle is not so much in demand; and in everything,
and everywhere, by the demand the supply is always regulated.

Everybody knows that Washington has a Capitol; but
the misfortune is that the Capitol wants a city. There it
stands, reminding you of a general without an army, only
surrounded and followed by a parcel of ragged little dirty
boys; for such is the appearance of the dirty, straggling,
ill-built houses which lie at the foot of it.

Washington, notwithstanding, is an agreeable city,
full of pleasant clever people, who come there to amuse
and be amused; and you observe in the company (although
you occasionally meet some very queer importations from
the western settlements) much more *usage du monde* and
continental ease than in any other parts of the state. A large
portion of those who come up for the meeting of Congress,
as well as of the residents, having travelled, and thereby
gained more respect for other nations, are consequently

not so conceited about their own country as are the majority of the Americans.

If anything were required to make Washington a more
agreeable place than it is at all times, the arrival and subsequent conduct of Mr. Fox [1] as British ambassador would be
sufficient. His marked attention to all the Americans of
respectability; his *empressement* in returning the calls of
English gentlemen who may happen to arrive, his open
house; his munificent allowance, dedicated wholly to the
giving of fêtes and dinner parties as his Sovereign's representative; and, above all, his excessive urbanity, can never
be forgotten by those who have ever visited the Capitol.

The Chamber of the House of Representatives is a fine
room, and taking the average of the orations delivered
there, it possesses this one great merit—*you cannot hear in
it.* Were I to make a comparison between the members of
our House of Commons and those of the House of Representatives, I should say that the latter had certainly great advantages. In the first place, the members of the American
Senate and House of Representatives are paid, not only
their travelling expenses to and fro, but eight dollars a day
during the sitting of Congress. Out of these allowances
many save money, and those who do not are at all events
enabled to bring their families up to Washington for a little
amusement. In the next place, they are so comfortably accommodated in the House, every man having his own well-
stuffed arm-chair, and before him his desk, with his papers
and notes! Then they are supplied with everything, even to
pen-knives with their names engraved on them—each knife
having two pen-blades, one whittling blade, and a fourth to
clean their nails with, showing on the part of the govern-

---

[1] Henry Stephen Fox (1791–
1846), British diplomat, was
educated at Eton and Christ
Church, Oxford. Fox was the
first minister plenipotentiary to
Buenos Aires; in 1832 he moved
to Rio de Janeiro. His next appointment was to Washington,
and he became minister to the
United States in 1835. Fox was
actively involved in the negotiations which led to the signing
of the Webster Ashburton Treaty
in 1841.

ment a paternal regard for their cleanliness as well as convenience. Moreover, they never work at night, and do very little during the day.

It is astonishing how little work they get through in a session at Washington; this is owing to every member thinking himself obliged to make two or three speeches, not for the good of the nation, but for the benefit of his constituents. These speeches are printed and sent to them, to prove that their member makes some noise in the House. The subject upon which he speaks is of little consequence, compared to the sentiments expressed. It must be full of eagles, star-spangled banners, sovereign people, clap-trap, flattery, and humbug. I have said that very little business is done in these houses; but this is caused not only by their long-winded speeches about nothing, but by the fact that both parties (in this respect laudably following the example of the old country) are chiefly occupied, the one with the paramount and vital consideration of keeping in, and the other with that of getting in—thus allowing the business of the nation (which after all is not very important, unless such a trump as the Treasury Bill turns up) to become a very secondary consideration.

And yet there are principle and patriotism among the members of the legislature, and the more to be appreciated from their rarity. Like the seeds of beautiful flowers, which, when cast upon a manure-heap, spring up in greater luxuriance and beauty, and yield a sweeter perfume from the rankness which surrounds them, so do these virtues show with more grace and attractiveness from the hot-bed of corruption in which they have been engendered. But there has been a sad falling-off in America since the last war, which brought in the democratic party with General Jackson. America, if she would wish her present institutions to continue, must avoid war; the best security for her present form of government existing another half century is a state of tranquillity and peace; but of that hereafter. As for the party at present in power, all I can say in its favour is that there are three clever gentlemen in it—Mr. Van Buren,[2] Mr. Poinsett,[3] and Mr. Forsyth.[4] There may be more, but I know so little of them that I must be excused if I do not name them, which otherwise I should have had great pleasure in doing.

Mr. Van Buren is a very gentleman-like, intelligent man, very proud of talking over his visit to England and the English with whom he was acquainted. It is remarkable that, although at the head of the democratic party, Mr. Van Buren has taken a step striking at the very roots of their boasted equality, and one on which General Jackson did not venture—i.e., he has prevented the mobocracy from intruding themselves at his levees. The police are now stationed at the door, to prevent the intrusion of any improper person. A few years ago, a fellow would drive his cart, or hackney coach, up to the door, walk into the saloon in all his dirt, and force his way to the President, that he might shake him by the one hand whilst he flourished his whip in the other. The revolting scenes which took place when refreshments were handed round, the injury done to the furniture, and the disgust of the ladies may be well imagined. Mr. Van

---

[2] Martin Van Buren (1782–1862), eighth President of the United States. An ardent Jacksonian, he served as Senator from New York, Secretary of State, Minister to Great Britain, Vice-President, and President. His Presidency was much troubled by financial disorders resulting from Jackson's monetary policies and by disagreements with England as a result of the *Caroline* and Macleod affairs. In his day Van Buren was considered to be an extremely astute and adroit politician.

[3] Joel Robert Poinsett (1779–1851) was born in South Carolina. He was appointed Consul General to the revolutionary government of Buenos Aires in 1810 and subsequently acted as American representative to the governments of Chile and Peru. From 1821 to 1825 he was a member of the House of Representatives and then became the first American Minister to Mexico. In 1837 he was appointed by Van Buren as Secretary of War.

[4] John Forsyth (1780–1841), American statesman, was born in Virginia and graduated from Princeton in 1799. He was a member of the House of Representatives from 1813 to 1818. In 1819 he was appointed Minister to Spain, but upon his return to the United States he once more entered politics. In 1834 he was appointed Secretary of State and served in that office under Jackson and Van Buren.

Buren deserves great credit for this step, for it was a bold one; but I must not praise him too much, or he may lose his next election.

The best lounge at Washington is the library of the Capitol, but the books are certainly not very well treated. I saw a copy of Audubon's *Ornithology,* and many other valuable works, in a very dilapidated state; but this must be the case when the library is open to all, and there are so many juvenile visitors. Still it is much better than locking it up, for only the bindings to be looked at. It is not a library for show, but for use, and is a great comfort and amusement.

There are three things in great request amongst Americans of all classes—male, I mean—to wit, oysters, spirits, and tobacco. The first and third are not prohibited by act of Congress and may be sold in the Capitol, but spirituous liquors may not. I wondered how the members could get on without them, but upon this point I was soon enlightened. Below the basement of the building is an oyster-shop and refectory. The refectory has been permitted by Congress upon the express stipulation that no spirituous liquors should be sold there, but law-makers are too often law-breakers all over the world. You go there and ask for pale sherry, and they hand you gin; brown sherry, and it is brandy; madeira, whiskey; and thus do these potent, grave, and reverend signors evade their own laws, beneath the very hall wherein they were passed in solemn conclave.

It appears that tobacco is considered very properly as an article of fashion. At a store, close to the hotel, the board outside informs you that among fashionable requisites to be found there are gentlemen's shirts, collars, gloves, silk-handkerchiefs, and the best chewing-tobacco. But not only at Washington, but at other large towns, I have seen at silk-mercers and hosiers this notice stuck up in the window— "*Dulcissimus* chewing-tobacco." So prevalent is the habit of chewing, and so little, from long custom, do the ladies care about it, that I have been told that many young ladies in the south carry, in their work-boxes, etc., pigtail, nicely

ornamented with gold and coloured papers; and when their
swains are at fault, administer to their wants, thus meriting
their affections by such endearing solicitude.

I was rather amused in the Senate at hearing the
claims of parties who had suffered during the last war, and
had hitherto not received any redress, discussed for adjudi-
cation. One man's claim, for instance, was for a cow, value
thirty dollars, eaten up, of course, by the Britishers. It
would naturally be supposed that such claims were unworthy the attention of such a body as the Senate, or, when
brought forward, would have been allowed without comment; but it was not so. The member who saves the public
money always finds favour in the eyes of the people, and
therefore every member tries to save as much as he can,
except when he is himself a party concerned. And there
was as much arguing and objecting, and discussion of the
merits of this man's claim, as there would be in the English
House of Commons at passing the Navy Estimates. Eventually he lost it. The claims of the Fulton family were also
brought forward, when I was present, in the House of Representatives. Fulton was certainly the father of steam-
navigation in America, and to his exertions and intelligence America may consider herself in a great degree
indebted for her present prosperity. It once required six
or seven months to ascend the Mississippi, a passage which
is now performed in fifteen days. Had it not been for Fulton's genius, the west would still have remained a wild
desert, and the now flourishing cotton-growing states
would not yet have yielded the crops which are the staple
of the Union. The claim of his surviving relatives was a
mere nothing in comparison with the debt of gratitude owing to that great man; yet member after member rose to oppose it with all the ingenuity of argument. One asserted that
the merit of the invention did not belong to Fulton; another, that even if it did, his relatives certainly could found
no claim upon it; a third rose and declared that he would
prove that, so far from the government owing money to
Fulton, Fulton was in debt to the government. And thus did

they go on, showing to their constituents how great was their consideration for the public money, and to the world (if another proof were required) how little gratitude is to be found in a democracy. The bill was thrown out, and the race of Fultons left to the chance of starving, for anything that the American nation seemed to care to the contrary. Whitney, the inventor of the gin for clearing the cotton of its seeds (perhaps the next greatest boon ever given to America), was treated in the same way. And yet, on talking over the question, there were few of the members who did not individually acknowledge the justice of their claims, and the duty of the state to attend to them; but the *majority* would not have permitted it, and when they went back to their constituents to be re-elected, it would have been urged against them that they had voted away the public money, and they would have had the difficult task of proving that the interests of the *majority*, and of the majority alone, had regulated their conduct in Congress.

There was one event of exciting interest which occurred during my short stay at Washington, and which engrossed the minds of every individual: the fatal duel between Mr. Graves and Mr. Cilley.[5] Not only the duel itself,

---

[5] Jonathan Cilley (1802–38) was born in New Hampshire and attended Bowdoin College—among his classmates were Hawthorne and Longfellow—graduating in 1825. Cilley was the editor of the *Thomaston Register* in Thomaston, Maine, from 1829 to 1831 and then went into politics, serving first in the state house of representatives and, in 1837, as a member of Congress. Cilley's death was the result of a duel. During a debate on charges made by Mrs. Davis against Senator Ruggles, Cilley made critical remarks about Webb, the editor of the New York *Courier and Enquirer*. Webb took measures to obtain satisfaction, but Cilley refused to fight with Webb and gave as his reasons that Webb was not a gentleman. Further, Cilley felt he was not bound to give an account for his statements as they arose during a debate. William Graves, who had borne Webb's charge, then challenged Cilley himself, and this challenge was accepted. The duel occurred on February 24, 1838, on the Annapolis road near Bladensburg; Cilley was killed on the third shot. Congress took a very dim view of the whole business and declared that Graves ought to be severely censured. The members of the Supreme Court expressed their disapproval of the affair by re-

but what took place after it, was to me, as a stranger, a subject for grave reflection.

Notice of Mr. Cilley's decease having been formally given to the House, it adjourned for a day or two, as a mark of respect, and a day was appointed for the funeral.

The coffin containing the body was brought into the House of Representatives, and there lay in state, as it were. The members of the Senate and the Supreme Court were summoned to attend, whilst an eulogium was passed on the merits and virtues of the deceased by the surviving representative of the state of Maine; the funeral sermon was delivered by one clergyman, and an exhortation by another, after which the coffin was carried out to be placed in the hearse. . . .

The burial-ground being at some distance, carriages were provided for the whole of the company, and the procession even then was more than half a mile long. I walked there to witness the whole proceeding; but when the body had been deposited in the vault, I found, on my return, a vacant seat in one of the carriages, in which were two Americans, who went under the head of "Citizens." They were very much inclined to be communicative. One of them observed of the clergyman, who, in his exhortation, had expressed himself very forcibly against the practice of duelling:

"Well, I reckon that chaplain won't be 'lected next year, and sarve him right too; he did pitch it in rather too strong for the members; that last flourish of his was enough to raise all their danders."

To the other, who was a more staid sort of personage, I put the question, how long did he think this tragical event, and the severe observations on duelling, would stop the practice.

"Well, I reckon three days, or thereabouts," replied the man.

---

fusing to attend Cilley's funeral. For an account of the event, not partial to Cilley to be sure, see Bayard Tuckerman, *The Diary of Philip Hone,* Vol. I, pp. 292–96.

I am afraid that the man is not far out in his calculation. Virginia, Mississippi, Louisiana, and now Congress, as
respects the District of Columbia, in which Washington is
built, have all passed severe laws against the practice of
duelling, which is universal; but they are no more than
dead letters. The spirit of their institutions is adverse to
such laws; and duelling always has been, and always will
be, one of the evils of democracy. I have, I believe, before
observed that in many points a young nation is, in all its
faults, very like to a young individual; and this is one in
which the comparison holds good. But there are other
causes for, and other incentives to this practice, besides the
false idea that it is a proof of courage. Slander and detraction are the inseparable evils of a democracy; and as neither public nor private characters are spared, and the law
is impotent to protect them, men have no other resource
than to defend their reputations with their lives, or to deter
the defamer by the risk which he must incur.

And where political animosities are carried to such a
length as they are in this exciting climate, there is no time
given for coolness and reflection. Indeed, for one American
who would attempt to prevent a duel, there are ten who
would urge the parties on to the conflict. I recollect a gentleman introducing me to the son of another gentleman
who was present. The lad, who was about fourteen, I should
think, shortly after left the room; and then the gentleman
told me, before the boy's father, that the lad was one of the
right sort, having already fought and wounded his man;
and the father smiled complacently at this tribute to the
character of his son. The majority of the editors of the newspapers in America are constantly practising with the pis-
tol, that they may be ready when called upon, and are most
of them very good shots. In fact, they could not well refuse
to fight, being all of them colonels, majors, or generals—
"*tam Marte quam Mercurio.*" But the worst feature in the
American system of duelling is that they do not go out, as
we do in this country, to satisfy honour, but with the determination to kill. Independently of general practice, immedi-

ately after a challenge has been given and received, each party practises as much as he can. . . .

And yet the Americans are continually dinning into my ears—Captain Marryat, we are a very moral people! Again, I repeat, the Americans are the happiest people in the world in their own delusions. If they wish to be a moral people, the government must show them some better example than that of paying those honours to vice and immorality which are only due to honour and to virtue.

CHAPTER XXII

Upper Canada

I have been for some time journeying through the province of Upper Canada,[1] and, on the whole, I consider it the finest portion of all North America. In America every degree of longitude which you proceed west is equal to a degree of latitude to the southward in increasing the mildness of the temperature. Upper Canada, which is not so far west as to sever you from the civilized world, has every possible advantage of navigation, and is at the same time, from being nearly surrounded by water, much milder than the American states to the southward of it. Everything grows well and flourishes in Upper Canada, even tobacco, which requires a very warm atmosphere. The land of this province is excellent, but it is a hard land to clear, the timber being very close and of a very large size. A certain proof of the value of the land of Upper Canada, is that there are already so many Americans who have settled there. Most of them had originally migrated to establish themselves in the

---

[1] Upper Canada or Canada West was the name given to the British colony located west of the Ottawa River; Canada was divided into two separate colonies by the Constitutional Act of 1791. What is now the modern province of Quebec was called Lower Canada or Canada East. Upper Canada was settled by English immigrants, United Empire Loyalists, and later by some Americans.

neighbouring state of Michigan; but the greater part of that state is at present so unhealthy from swamps, and the people suffer so much from fever and agues, that the emigrants have fallen back upon Upper Canada, which (a very small portion of it excepted) is the most healthy portion of North America. I have before observed that the Rideau and Welland canals, splendid works as they are, are too much in advance of the country; and had the Government spent one-half the money in opening communications and making good roads, the province would have been much more benefited. In the United States you have a singular proof of the advantages of communication; in the old continent, towns and villages rise up first, and the communications are made afterwards; in the United States, the roads are made first, and when made, towns and villages make their appearance on each side of them, just as the birds drop down for their aliment upon the fresh furrows made across the fallow by the plough.

From Hamilton, on Lake Ontario, to Bradford, the country is very beautifully broken and undulating, occasionally precipitate and hilly. You pass through forests of splendid timber, chiefly fir, but of a size which is surprising. Here are masts for "tall admirals," so lofty that you could not well perceive a squirrel, or even a large animal, if upon one of the topmast boughs. The pine forests are diversified by the oak; you sometimes pass through six or seven miles of the first description of timber, which gradually changes, until you have six or seven miles of forest composed entirely of oak. The road is repairing and leveling, preparatory to its being macadamized—certainly not before it was required, for it is at present execrable throughout the whole province. Every mile or so you descend into a hollow, at the bottom of which is what they term a *mud hole,* that is, a certain quantity of water and mud, which is of a depth unknown, but which you must fathom by passing through it. To give an Englishman an idea of the roads is not easy; I can only [say] that it is very possible for a horse to be drowned in one of the *ruts*, and for a pair of them to disappear, wagon and all, in a mud hole.

At Bradford, on Grand River, are located some remnants of the Mohawk tribe of Indians; they are more than demi-civilized; they till their farms and have plenty of horses and cattle. A smart-looking Indian drove into town, when I was there, in a wagon with a pair of good horses; in the wagon were some daughters of one of their chiefs; they were very richly dressed after their own fashion, their petticoats and leggings being worked with beads to the height of two feet from the bottom, and in very good taste; and they wore beaver hats and feathers of a pattern which used formerly to be much in vogue with the ladies of the seamen at Plymouth and Portsmouth.

From Bradford to London the roads are *comparatively* good; the country rises, and the plain is nearly one hundred feet above the level of the river Thames, a beautifully wide stream, whose two branches join at the site of this town. The land here is considered to be the finest in the whole province, and the country the most healthy.

From London to Chatham the roads are really *awful*. I had the pleasure of tumbling over head and ears into a mud hole, at about twelve o'clock at night; the horses were with difficulty saved, and the wagon remained *fixed* for upwards of three hours, during which we laboured hard, and were refreshed with plentiful showers of rain.

Chatham, on the river Thames, is at present a sad dirty hole but, as the country rises, will be a place of great importance. From Chatham I embarked in the steamboat, and went down the Thames into Lake St. Clair, and from thence to Sandwich, having past through the finest country, the most beautiful land, and about the most infamous roads that are to be met with in all America.

Within these last seven or eight years the lakes have risen; many hypotheses have been offered to account for this change. I do not coincide with any of the opinions which I have heard, yet, at the same time, it is but fair to acknowledge that I can offer none of my own. It is quite a mystery. The consequence of this rising of the waters is that some of the finest farms at the mouth of the river Thames and on Lake St. Clair, occupied by the old Canadian settlers, are, and have been for two or three years, under water. These Canadians have not removed; they are waiting for the water to subside; their houses stand in the lake, the basements being under water, and they occupy the first floors with their families, communicating by boats. As they cannot cultivate their land, they shoot and fish. Several miles on each side of the mouth of the river Thames the water is studded with these houses, which have, as may be supposed, a very forlorn appearance, especially as the top rail of the fences is generally above water, marking out the fields which are now tenanted by fish instead of cattle.

Went out with a party into the bush, as it is termed, to see some land which had been purchased. Part of the road was up to the saddle-flaps under water, from the rise of the lakes. We soon entered the woods, not so thickly growing but that our horses could pass through them, had it not been for the obstacles below our feet. At every third step a tree lay across the path, forming, by its obstruction to the drainage, a pool of water; but the Canadian horses are so accustomed to this that they very coolly walked over them, although some were two feet in diameter. They never attempted to jump, but deliberately put one foot over and the other—with equal dexterity avoiding the stumps and sunken logs concealed under water. An English horse would have been foundered before he had proceeded fifty yards. Sometimes we would be for miles wading through swamps; at others the land rose, and then it was clear and dry, and we could gallop under the oak trees.

We continued till noon before we could arrive at the land in question, forcing our way through the woods, and guided by the blazing of the trees. *Blazing* is cutting off a portion of the bark of the trees on both sides of the road with an axe, and these marks, which will remain for many years, serve as a guide. If lost in the woods, you have but to look out for a blaze, and by following it you are certain to arrive at some inhabited place. We found the land at last, which was high, dry, and covered with large oak trees. A herd of deer bounded past us as we approached the river, which ran through it; and we could perceive the flocks of wild turkeys at a distance, running almost as fast as the deer. The river was choked by trees which had fallen across its bed, damming up its stream, and spreading it over the land; but the scene was very beautiful and wild, and I could not help fancying what a pretty spot it would one day be, when it should be cleared, and farm-houses built on the banks of the river.

On our way we called upon a man who had been in the bush but a year or so; he had a wife and six children. He was young and healthy, and although he had been used to a life of *literary* idleness, he had made up his mind to the change, and taken up the axe—a thing very few people can do. I never saw a person apparently more cheerful and contented. He had already cleared away about fifteen acres, and had procured a summer crop from off a portion of it the year before, having no other assistance than his two boys, one thirteen and the other fourteen years old, healthy, but not powerfully built lads. When we called upon him, he was busied in burning the felled timber and planting Indian corn. One of his boys was fencing-in the ground. I went with the man into his log-hut, which was large and convenient, and found his wife working at her needle, and three little girls all as busy as bees; the eldest of these girls was not twelve years old, yet she cooked, baked, washed, and, with the assistance of her two little sisters, did all that was required for the household. After a short repose, we went out again into the clearing, when one of my friends asked him how he got on with his axe? "Pretty well," replied he, laughing. "I'll show you." He led us to where a button-wood tree was lying; the trunk was at least ninety feet long, and the diameter where it had been cut through between five and six feet; it was an enormous tree. "And did you cut that down yourself?" enquired my companion, who was an old settler. "Not quite; but I cut through the north half while my two boys cut through the south; we did it between us." This was really astonishing, for if these two lads could cut through half the tree, it is evident that they could have cut it down altogether. We had here a proof of how useful children can be made at an early age.

We promised to call upon him on our return, which we did. We found him sitting with his wife in his log-house; it was five o'clock in the afternoon; he told us "work was over now, and that the children had gone into the bush to play." They had all worked from five o'clock in the morning, and had since learnt their lessons. We heard their laughter ringing in the woods at a distance.

Now this is rather a remarkable instance among settlers, as I shall hereafter explain. Had this man been a bachelor, he would have been, in all probability, a drunkard; but, with his family, he was a happy, contented, and thriving man. We parted with him, and arrived at Windsor, opposite Detroit, very tired, having been, with little exception, fourteen hours in the saddle.

I took cold, and was laid up with a fever. I mention this, not as anything interesting to the reader, but merely to show what you may expect when you travel in these countries. I had been in bed three days, when my landlady came into the room. "Well, Captain, how do you find yourself by this time?" "Oh, I am a little better, thank you," replied I. "Well, I am glad of it, because I want to whitewash your room; for if the coloured man stops to do it tomorrow, he'll be for charging us another quarter of a dollar." "But I am not able to leave my room." "Well, then, I'll speak to him; I dare say he won't mind your being in bed while he whitewashes."

I have often remarked the strange effects of intoxication, and the different manner in which persons are affected with liquor. When I was on the road from London to Chatham, a man who was very much intoxicated got into the wagon and sat beside me. As people in that state generally are, he was excessively familiar, and although jerked off with no small degree of violence, would continue, until we arrived at the inn where we were to sup, to attempt to lay his head upon my shoulder.

As soon as we arrived, supper was announced. At first he refused to take any, but on the artful landlady bawling in his ear that all *gentlemen* supped when they arrived, he hesitated to consider (which certainly was not at all necessary) whether he was not bound to take some. Another very important remark of the hostess, which was that he would have nothing to eat until the next morning, it being then eleven o'clock at night, decided him, and he staggered in, observing: "Nothing to eat till next morning! Well, I never thought of that." He sat down opposite to me, at the same table. It appeared as if his vision *was inverted* by the quantity of liquor which he had taken; everything close to him on the table he considered to be out of his reach, whilst everything at a distance he attempted to lay hold of. He sat up as erect as he could, balancing himself so as not to appear *corned,* and fixing his eyes upon me, said: "Sir, I'll trouble you—for some fried ham." Now the ham was in the dish next to him, and altogether out of my reach; I told him so. "Sir," said he again, "as a gentleman, I ask you to give me some of that fried ham." Amused with the curious demand, I rose from my chair, went round to him and helped him. "Shall I give you a potato?" said I, the potatoes being at my end of the table, and I not wishing to rise again. "No, sir," replied he, "I can help myself to them." He made a dash at them, but did not reach them; then made another, and another, till he lost his balance, and lay down upon his plate; this time he gained the potatoes, helped himself, and commenced eating. After a few minutes he again fixed his eyes upon me. "Sir, I'll trouble you—for the pickles." They were actually under his nose, and I pointed them out to him. "I believe, sir, I asked you for the pickles," repeated he, after a time. "Well, there they are," replied I, wishing to see what he would do. "Sir, are you a gentleman —as a gentleman—I ask you as a gentleman, for them 'ere pickles." It was impossible to resist this appeal, so I rose and helped him. I was now convinced that his vision was somehow or another inverted, and to prove it, when he asked me for the salt, which was within his reach, I removed it farther off. "Thank ye, sir," said he, sprawling over the table after it. The circumstance, absurd as it was, was really a subject for the investigation of Dr. Brewster.[2]

At Windsor, which is directly opposite to Detroit, where the river is about half a mile across, are stores of English goods, sent there entirely for the supply of the Americans, by smugglers. There is also a row of tailor shops, for cloth is a very dear article in America and costs nearly double the price it does in the English provinces. The Americans go over there and are measured for a suit of clothes which, when ready, they put on and cross back to Detroit with their old clothes in a bundle. The smuggling is already very extensive and will, of course, increase as the western country becomes more populous.

Near Windsor and Sandwich are several villages of free blacks, probably the major portion of them having been assisted in their escape by the abolitionists. They are not very good neighbours from their propensity to thieving, which either is innate or, as Miss Martineau would have it, is the effect of slavery. I shall not dispute that point; but it is certain that they are most inveterately hostile to the Americans, and will fight to the last, from the dread of being again subjected to their former masters. They are an excellent frontier population; and in the last troubles they proved how valuable they would become, in case their services were more seriously required.

---

[2] David Brewster (1781–1868) was a Scottish natural philosopher. He began his career as a minister, abandoned the clerical profession, and assumed the editorship of the *Edinburgh Magazine*, a scientific journal. In 1831 he organized the British Association for the Advancement of Science, and for this and his scientific work—he was known for his researches in the field of optics—he was awarded a knighthood. In 1860 he was made Vice-Chancellor of Edinburgh University.

CHAPTER XXIII

The Way West— Wisconsin Territory

Once more on board of the *Michigan*, one of the best vessels on Lake Erie; as usual, full of emigrants, chiefly Irish. It is impossible not to feel compassion for these poor people, wearied as they are with confinement and suffering, and yet they do compose occasionally about as laughable a group as can well be conceived. In the first place, they bring out with them, from Ireland, articles which no other people would consider worth the carriage. I saw one Irish woman who had five old tin tea-pots; there was but one spout among the whole, and I believe not one bottom really sound and good. And then their costumes, more particularly the fitting out of the children, who are not troubled with any extra supply of clothes at any time! I have witnessed the seat of an old pair of corduroy trousers transformed into a sort of bonnet for a laughing fair-haired girl. But what amused me more was the very reverse of this arrangement: a boy's father had just put a patch upon the hinder part of his son's trousers, and cloth not being at hand, he had, as an expedient for stopping the gap, inserted a piece of an old straw bonnet; in so doing he had not taken the precaution to put the smooth side of the plait inwards, and, in consequence, young Teddy when he first sat down felt rather uncomfortable. "What's the matter wid ye, Teddy; what makes ye wriggle about in that way? Sit aisy, man; sure enough, havn't ye a straw-bottomed chair to sit down upon all the rest of your journey, which is more than your father ever had before you?" And then their turning in for the night! A single bed will contain one adult and four little ones at one end, and another adult and two half-grown at the other. But they are all packed away so snug and close, and not one venturing to move, there appears to be room for all.

We stopped half an hour at Mackinaw to take in wood, and then started for Green Bay, in the Wisconsin territory. Green Bay is a military station; it is a pretty little place, with soil as rich as garden mould. The Fox River debouches here, but the navigation is checked a few miles above the town by the rapids, which have been dammed up into a water-power; yet there is no doubt that as soon as the whole of the Wisconsin lands are offered for sale by the American government, the river will be made navigable up to its meeting with the Wisconsin, which falls into the Mississippi. There is only a portage of a mile and a half between the two, through which a canal will be cut and then there will be another junction between the lakes and the far west. It was my original intention to have taken the usual route by Chicago and Galena to St. Louis, but I fell in with Major F——, with whom I had been previously acquainted, who informed me that he was about to send a detachment of troops from Green Bay to Fort Winnebago, across Wisconsin territory. As this afforded me an opportunity of seeing the country, which seldom occurs, I availed myself of an offer to join the party. The detachment consisted of about one hundred recruits, nearly the whole of them Canada patriots, as they are usually called, who, having failed in taking the provinces from John Bull, were fain to accept the shilling from uncle Sam.

Major F—— accompanied us to pay the troops at the

fort, and we therefore had five wagons with us, loaded with a considerable quantity of bread and pork, and not quite so large a portion of specie, the latter not having as yet become plentiful again in the United States. We set off, and marched fifteen miles in about half a day, passing through the settlement Des Peres, which is situated at the rapids of the Fox River. Formerly they were called the Rapids des Peres, from a Jesuit college which had been established there by the French. Our course lay along the banks of the Fox River, a beautiful swift stream pouring down between high ridges, covered with fine oak timber.

The American government have disposed of all the land on the banks of this river and the Lake Winnebago, and consequently it is well settled; but the Winnebago territory in Wisconsin, lately purchased of the Winnebago Indians and comprising all the prairie land and rich mineral country from Galena to Mineral Point, is not yet offered for sale; when it is, it will be eagerly purchased, and the American government, as it only paid the Indians at the rate of one cent and a fraction per acre, will make an enormous profit by the speculation. Well may the Indians be said, like Esau, to part with their birthright for a mess of pottage; but, in truth, they are *compelled* to sell—the purchase-money being a mere subterfuge, by which it may *appear* as if their lands were not wrested from them, although, in fact, it is.

On the second day we continued our march along the banks of the Fox River, which, as we advanced, continued to be well settled, and would have been more so, if some of the best land had not fallen, as usual, into the hands of speculators, who, aware of its value, hold out that they may obtain a high price for it. The country through which we passed was undulating, consisting of a succession of ridges, covered with oaks of a large size, but not growing close as in a forest; you could gallop your horse through any part of it. The tracks of deer were frequent, but we saw but one herd of fifteen, and that was at a distance. We now left the banks of the river, and cut across the country to Fond du Lac, at the bottom of Lake Winnebago, of which we had

had already an occasional glimpse through the openings of the forest. The deer were too wild to allow of our getting near them; so I was obliged to content myself with shooting wood pigeons, which were very plentiful.

On the night of the third day we encamped upon a very high ridge, as usual studded with oak trees. The term used here to distinguish this variety of timber land from the impervious woods is *oak openings.* I never saw a more beautiful view than that which was afforded us from our encampment. From the high ground upon which our tents were pitched, we looked down to the left, upon a prairie flat and level as a billiard-table, extending, as far as the eye could scan, one rich surface of unrivalled green. To the right the prairie gradually changed to oak openings, and then to a thick forest, the topmost boughs and heads of which were level with our tents. Beyond them was the whole broad expanse of the Winnebago lake, smooth and reflecting like a mirror the brilliant tints of the setting sun, which disappeared, leaving a portion of his glory behind him; while the moon in her ascent, with the dark portion of her disk as clearly defined as that which was lighted, gradually increased in brilliancy, and the stars twinkled in the clear sky. We watched the features of the landscape gradually fading from our sight, until nothing was left but broad masses partially lighted up by the young moon.

Nor was the foreground less picturesque: the spreading oaks, the tents of the soldiers, the wagons drawn up with the horses tethered, all lighted up by the blaze of our large fires. Now, when I say our large fires, I mean the *large* fires of *America* consisting of three or four oak trees, containing a load of wood each, besides many large boughs and branches, altogether forming a fire some twenty or thirty feet long, with flames flickering up twice as high as one's head. At a certain distance from this blazing pile you may perceive what in another situation would be considered as a large coffee-pot (before this huge fire it makes a very diminutive appearance). It is placed over some embers drawn out from the mass, which would have soon burnt up coffee-pot and coffee all together; and at a still more respectful distance you may perceive small rods, not above four or five feet long, bifurcated at the smaller end, and fixed by the larger in the ground, so as to hang towards the huge fire, at an angle of forty degrees, like so many tiny fishing-rods. These rods have at their bifurcated ends a piece of pork or ham, or of bread, or perhaps of venison, for we bought some, not having shot any; they are all private property, as each party cooks for himself. Seeing these rods at some distance, you might almost imagine that they were the fishing-rods of little imps bobbing for salamanders in the fiery furnace.

In the meantime, while the meat is cooking and the coffee is boiling, the brandy and whiskey are severely taxed, as we lie upon our cloaks and buffalo skins at the front of our tents. There certainly is a charm in this wild sort of life, which wins upon people the more they practise it; nor can it be wondered at: our wants are in reality so few and so easily satisfied, without the restraint of form and ceremony. . . .

On the fourth day we descended, crossed the wide prairie, and arrived at the Fond du Lac, where we again fell in with the Fox River, which runs through the Winnebago lake. The roads through the forests had been very bad, and the men and horses showed signs of fatigue; but we had now passed through all the thickly wooded country, and had entered into the prairie country, extending to Fort Winnebago, and which was beautiful beyond conception. Its features alone can be described; but its effects can only be felt by being seen. The prairies here are not very large, seldom being above six or seven miles in length or breadth; generally speaking, they lie in gentle undulating flats, and the ridges and hills between them are composed of oak openings. To form an idea of these oak openings, imagine an inland country covered with splendid trees, about as thickly planted as in our English parks; in fact, it is English park scenery, nature having here spontaneously produced what it has been the care and labour of centuries in our own country to effect. Sometimes the prairie will rise and extend along the hills and assume an undulating appearance, like the long swell of the ocean; it is then called rolling prairie.

Often, when I looked down upon some fifteen or twenty thousand acres of these prairies, full of rich grass, without one animal, tame or wild, to be seen, I would fancy what thousands of cattle will, in a few years, be luxuriating in those pastures, which, since the herds of buffalo have retreated from them, are now useless, and throwing up each year a fresh crop, to seed and to die unheeded.

On our way we had fallen in with a young Frenchman, who had purchased some land at Fond du Lac, and was proceeding there in company with an American, whom he had hired to settle on it. I now parted company with him; he had gone out with me in my shooting excursions, and talked of nothing but his purchase: it had water; it had a waterfall; it had, in fact, everything that he could desire; but he thought that, after two years, he would go home and get a wife—a Paradise without an Eve would be no Paradise at all.

The price of labour is, as may be supposed, very high in this part of the country. Hiring by the year, you find a man in food, board, and washing, and pay him three hundred dollars per annum (about £70 English).

The last night that we bivouacked out was the only unfortunate one. We had been all comfortably settled for the night, and fast asleep, when a sudden storm came on, accompanied with such torrents of rain as would have washed us out of our tents, if they had not been already blown down by the violence of the gale. Had we had any warning, we should have provided against it; as it was, we made up huge fires, which defied the rain; and thus we remained till daylight, the rain pouring on us, while the heat of the fire drying us almost as fast as we got wet, each man threw up a column of steam from his still saturating and still heated garments. Every night we encamped where there was a run of water and plenty of dead timber for our fires; and thus did we go on, emptying our wagons daily of the bread and pork, and filling up the vacancies left by the removal of the empty casks with the sick and lame, until at last we arrived at Fort Winnebago.

CHAPTER XXIV

Fort Winnebago

We had not to arrive at the fort to receive a welcome, for when we were still distant about seven miles, the officers of the garrison, who had notice of our coming, made their appearance on horseback, bringing a britzka and grey horses for our accommodation. Those who were not on duty (and I was one) accepted the invitation, and we drove in upon a road which, indeed, for the last thirty miles, had been as level as the best in England. The carriage was followed by pointers, hounds, and a variety of dogs, who were off duty like ourselves and who appeared quite as much delighted with their run as we were tired with ours. The medical officer attached to the fort, an old friend and correspondent of Mr. Lea of Philadelphia, received me with all kindness, and immediately installed me into one of the rooms in the hospital.

Fort Winnebago is situated between the Fox and Wisconsin Rivers at the portage, the two rivers being about a mile and a half apart, the Fox River running east, and giving its waters to Lake Michigan at Green Bay, while the Wisconsin turns to the west, and runs into the Mississippi at Prairie du Chien. The fort is merely a square of barracks, connected together with palisades, to protect it from the

Indians; and it is hardly sufficiently strong for even that purpose. It is beautifully situated, and when the country fills up will become a place of importance. Most of the officers are married and live a very quiet, and secluded, but not unpleasant life. I stayed there two days, much pleased with the society and the kindness shown to me; but an opportunity of descending the Wisconsin to Prairie du Chien, in a keel-boat, having presented itself, I availed myself of an invitation to join the party, instead of proceeding by land to Galena, as had been my original intention.

The boat had been towed up the Wisconsin with a cargo of flour for the garrison; and a portion of the officers having been ordered down to Prairie du Chien, they had obtained this large boat to transport themselves, families, furniture, and horses, all at once, down to their destination. The boat was about one hundred and twenty feet long, covered in to the height of six feet above the gunnel, and very much in appearance like the Noah's Ark given to children, excepting that the roof was flat. It was an unwieldy craft, and, to manage it, it required at least twenty-five men with poles and long sweeps; but the army gentlemen had decided that, as we were to go down with the stream, six men with short oars would be sufficient—a very great mistake. In every other respect she was badly found, as we term it at sea, having but one old piece of rope to hang on with, and one axe. Our freight consisted of furniture stowed forward and aft, with a horse and cow. In a cabin in the centre we had a lady and five children, one maid, and two officers. Our crew was composed of six soldiers, a servant, and a French half-breed to pilot us down the river. All Winnebago came out to see us start; and as soon as the rope was cast off, away we went down with the strong current at the rate of five miles an hour. The river passed through forests of oak, the large limbs of which hung from fifteen to twenty feet over the banks on each side; sometimes whole trees lay prostrate in the stream, held by their roots still partially remaining in the ground, while their trunks and branches, offering resistance to the swift current, created a succession of small masses of froth, which floated away on the dark green water.

We had not proceeded far before we found that it was impossible to manage such a large and cumbrous vessel with our few hands; we were almost at the mercy of the current, which appeared to increase in rapidity every minute; however, by exertion and good management, we contrived to keep in the middle of the stream until the wind sprung up and drove us on to the southern bank of the river, and then all was cracking and tearing away of the woodwork, breaking of limbs from the projecting trees, the snapping, cracking, screaming, hallooing, and confusion. As fast as we cleared ourselves of one tree, the current bore us down upon another; as soon as we were clear above water, we were foul and entangled below. It was a pretty general average; but, what was worse than all, a snag had intercepted and unshipped our rudder, and we were floating away from it, as it still remained fixed upon the sunken tree. We had no boat with us, not even a *dug-out* (a canoe made out of the trunk of a tree), so one of the men climbed on shore by the limbs of an oak, and went back to disengage it. He did so, but not being able to resist the force of the stream, down he and the rudder came together—his only chance of salvation being that of our catching him as he came past us. This we fortunately succeeded in affecting; and then hanging on by our old piece of rope to the banks of the river, after an hour's delay we contrived to re-ship our rudder, and proceeded on our voyage, which was a continuation of the same eventful history. Every half hour we found ourselves wedged in between the spreading limbs of the oaks, and were obliged to have recourse to the axe to clear ourselves; and on every occasion we lost a further portion of the framework of our boat, either from the roof, the sides, or by the tearing away of the stancheons themselves.

A little before sunset, we were again swept on to the bank with such force as to draw the pintles of our rudder. This finished us for the day: before it could be replaced, it was time to make fast for the night; so there we lay, holding by our rotten piece of rope, which cracked and strained to such a degree as inclined us to speculate upon where we might find ourselves in the morning. However, we could not help ourselves, so we landed, made a large fire, and cooked our victuals, not, however, venturing to wander away far, on account of the rattlesnakes, which here abounded. Perhaps there is no portion of America in which the rattlesnakes are so large and so numerous as in Wisconsin. There are two varieties: the black rattlesnake, that frequents marshy spots, and renders it rather dangerous to shoot snipes and ducks; and the yellow, which takes up its abode in the rocks and dry places. Dr. F[oote] told me that he had killed, inside of the Fort Winnebago, one of the latter species, between seven and eight feet long. The rattlesnake, although its poison is so fatal, is in fact not a very dangerous animal, and people are seldom bitten by it. This arises from two causes: first, that it invariably gives you notice of its presence by its rattle; and secondly, that it always coils itself up like a watch-spring before it strikes, and then darts forward only about its own length. Where they are common, the people generally carry with them a vial of ammonia, which, if instantly applied to the bite, will at least prevent death. The copperhead is a snake of much more dangerous nature, from its giving no warning and its poison being equally active.

This river has been very appropriately named by the Indians the "Stream of the Thousand Isles," as it is studded with them; indeed, every quarter of a mile you find one or two in its channel. The scenery is fine, as the river runs through high ridges, covered with oak to their summits; sometimes these ridges are backed by higher cliffs and mountains, which half-way up are of a verdant green, and above that present horizontal strata of calcareous rock of rich grey tints, having, at a distance, very much the appearance of the dilapidated castles on the Rhine.

The scenery, though not so grand as the highlands of the Hudson, is more diversified and beautiful. The river was very full, and the current occasionally so rapid, as to leave a foam as it swept by any projecting point. We had, now that the river widened, sand banks to contend with, which required all the exertions of our insufficient crew.

On the second morning, I was very much annoyed at out having left without providing ourselves with a boat, for at the grey of dawn we discovered that some deer had taken the river close to us and were in midstream. Had we had a boat, we might have procured a good supply of venison. We cast off again and resumed our voyage; and without any serious accident we arrived at the shot-tower, where we remained for the night. Finding a shot-tower in such a lone wilderness as this gives you some idea of the enterprise of the Americans; but the Galena, or lead district, commences here, on the south bank of the Wisconsin. The smelting is carried on about twelve miles inland, and the lead is brought here, made into shot, and then sent down the river to the Mississippi, by which, and its tributary streams, it is supplied to all America, west of the Alleghenies. The people were all at work when we arrived. The general distress had even affected the demand for shot, which was now considerably reduced.

On the third day we had the good fortune to have no wind, and consequently made rapid progress, without much further damage. We passed a small settlement called the English prairie—for the prairies were now occasionally mixed up with the mountain scenery. Here there was a smelting-house, and a steam saw-mill.

The *diggings*, as they term the places where the lead is found (for they do not mine, but dig down from the surface), were about sixteen miles distant. We continued our course for about twenty miles lower down, when we wound up our day's work by getting into a more serious *fix* among the trees, and eventually losing our only *axe*, which fell overboard into deep water. All Noah's Ark was in dismay, for we did not know what might happen, or what the next day might bring forth. Fortunately, it was not necessary to cut wood for firing. During the whole of this trip I was much amused with our pilot, who, fully aware of the dangers of the river, was also equally conscious that there were not sufficient means on board to avoid them; when, therefore, we were set upon a sand-bank, or pressed by the wind on the sunken trees, he always whistled: that was all he could do, and in proportion as the danger became more imminent, so did he whistle the louder, until the affair was decided by a bump or a crash, and then he was silent.

On the ensuing day we had nothing but misfortunes. We were continually twisted and twirled about, sometimes with our bows, sometimes with our stern foremost, and as often with our broadside to the stream. We were whirled against one bank, and, as soon as we were clear of that, we were thrown upon the other. Having no axe to cut away, we were obliged to use our hands. Again our rudder was unshipped, and with great difficulty replaced. By this time we had lost nearly the half of the upper works of the boat, one portion after another having been torn off by the limbs of the trees as the impetuous current drove us along. To add to our difficulties, a strong wind rose against the current, and the boat became quite unmanageable. About noon, when we had gained only seven miles, the wind abated, and two Menonnomie Indians, in a *dug-out,* came alongside of us; and as it was doubtful whether we should arrive at the mouth of the river on that night, or be left upon a sand-bank, I got into the canoe with them, to go down to the landing-place, and from thence to cross over to Prairie du Chien, to inform the officers of the garrison of our condition, and obtain assistance. The canoe would exactly hold three and no more; but we paddled swiftly down the stream, and we soon lost sight of the Noah's Ark. Independently of the canoe being so small, she had lost a large portion of her stern, so that at the least ripple of the water she took it in, and threatened us with a swim; and she was so very narrow that the least motion would have destroyed her equilibrium and upset her. One Indian sat in the bow, the other in the stern, whilst I was doubled up in the middle. We had given the Indians some bread and pork, and after paddling about half an hour, they stopped to eat. Now, the Indian at the bow had the pork, while the one at the stern had the bread; any attempt to move, so as to hand the eatables to each other, must have upset us; so this was their plan of communication—the one in the bow cut off a slice of pork, and putting it into the lid of a saucepan which he had with him, and floating it alongside of the canoe, gave it a sufficient momentum to make it swim to the stern, when the other took possession of it. He in the stern then cut off a piece of bread, and sent it back in return by the same conveyance. I had a flask of whiskey, but they would not trust that by the same perilous little conveyance; so I had to lean forward very steadily, and hand it to the foremost, and, when he returned it to me, to lean backwards to give it the other, with whom it remained till we landed, for I could not regain it. After about an hour's more paddling, we arrived safely at the landing-place. I had some trouble to get a horse, and was obliged to go out to the fields where the men were ploughing. In doing so, I passed two or three very large snakes. At last I was mounted somehow, but without stirrups, and set off for Prairie du Chien. After riding about four miles, I had passed the mountain, and I suddenly came upon the prairie (on which were feeding several herd of cattle and horses), with the fort in the distance, and the wide waters of the Upper Mississippi flowing beyond it. I crossed the prairie, found my way into the fort, stated the situation of our party, and requested assistance. This was immediately dispatched, but on their arrival at the landing-place, they found that the keel-boat had arrived at the ferry without further difficulty. Before sunset the carriages returned with the whole party, who were comfortably accommodated in the barracks—a sufficient number of men being left with the boat to bring it round to the Mississippi, a distance of about twelve miles.

CHAPTER XXV

The Frontier—Prairie du Chien

Prairie du Chien is a beautiful meadow, about eight miles long by two broad, situated at the confluence of the Wisconsin and the Mississippi; it is backed with high bluffs, such as I have before described, verdant two thirds of the way up, and crowned with rocky summits. The bluffs, as I must call them, for I know not what other name to give them, rise very abruptly, often in a sugar-loaf form, from the flat lands, and have a very striking appearance; as you look up to them, their peculiar formation and vivid green sides, contrasting with their blue and grey summits, give them the appearance of a succession of ramparts investing the prairie. The fort at the prairie, which is named Fort Crawford, is, like most other American outposts, a mere inclosure, intended to repel the attacks of Indians; but it is large and commodious, and the quarters of the officers are excellent; it is, moreover, built of stone, which is not the case with Fort Winnebago, or Fort Howard at Green Bay. The Upper Mississippi is here a beautiful clear blue stream, intersected with verdant islands, and very different in appearance from the Lower Mississippi, after it has been joined by the Missouri. The opposite shore is composed of high cliffs, covered with timber, which, not only in form, but in tint and colour, remind you very much of Glover's [1] landscapes of the mountainous parts of Scotland and Wales.

I made one or two excursions to examine the ancient mounds which are scattered all over this district, and which have excited much speculation as to their origin, some supposing them to have been fortifications, others the burial-places of the Indians. That they have lately been used by the Indians as burial-places there is no doubt; but I suspect they were not originally raised for that purpose. A Mr. Taylor [2] has written an article in one of the periodicals, stating his opinion that they were the burial-places of chiefs; and to prove it, he asserts that some of them are thrown up in imitation of the figure of the animal which was the heraldic distinction of the chief whose remains they contain, such as the beaver, elk, etc. He has given drawings of some of them. That the Indians have their heraldic distinctions, their *totems*, as they call them, I know to be a fact—as I have seen the fur trader's books, containing the receipts of the chiefs, with their crests drawn by themselves, and very correctly too—but it required more imagination than I possess to make out the form of any animal in the mounds. I should rather suppose the mounds to be the remains of tenements, sometimes fortified, sometimes not, which were formerly built of mud or earth, as is still the custom in the northern portion of the Sioux country. Desertion and time have crumbled them into these mounds, which are generally to be found in a commanding situation, or in a string, as if constructed

---

[1] John Glover (1767–1849), English landscape painter and water-colour artist, was for some years president of the Water Colour Society, exhibiting his works in England and on the Continent. In 1824 he founded the Society of British Artists and exhibited there until he emigrated to Western Australia in 1831.

[2] Stephen Taylor (1805?–77?) wrote "Description of Ancient Remains, Ancient Mounds, and Embankments principally in the Counties of Grant, Iowa, and Richland in Wisconsin Territory," *American Journal of Science and Arts,* Vol. XLIV, pp. 21–40, as quoted in "Captain Marryat in Wisconsin," *Wisconsin Historical Collections* (Madison, Wisconsin: Wisconsin Historical Society; 1898), Vol. XIV.

for mutual defence. On Rock River there is a long line of wall, now below the surface, which extends for a considerable distance, and is supposed to be the remains of a city built by a former race, probably the Mexican, who long since retreated before the northern race of Indians. I cannot recollect the name which has been given to it. I had not time to visit this spot; but an officer showed me some pieces of what they called the brick which composes the wall. Brick it is not—no right angles have been discovered, so far as I could learn; it appears rather as if a wall had been raised of clay, and then exposed to the action of fire, as portions of it are strongly vitrified and others are merely hard clay. But admitting my surmises to be correct, still there is evident proof that this country was formerly peopled by a nation whose habits were very different, and in all appearance more civilized, than those of the races which were found here; and this is all that can be satisfactorily sustained. As, however, it is well substantiated that a race similar to the Mexican formerly existed on these prairie lands, the whole question may perhaps be solved by the following extract from Irving's [3] *Conquest of Florida:*

> The village of Onachili resembles most of the Indian villages of Florida. The natives always endeavoured to build upon high ground, or at least to erect the house of their cacique, or chief, upon an eminence. As the country was very level, and high places seldom to be found, they constructed artificial mounds of earth, capable of containing from two to twenty houses; there resided the chief, his family, and attendants. At the foot of the hill was a square, according to the size of the village, round which were the houses of the leaders and most distinguished inhabitants.

---

[3] Theodore Irving, author of *The Conquest of Florida by Hernan de Soto* (1835), was the nephew of Washington Irving. Theodore Irving was professor of history at Geneva (now Hobart) College from 1836 to 1849 and professor of belles-lettres at the Free Academy of New York from 1849 to 1852. In 1854 he became an Episcopal clergyman.

I consider the Wisconsin territory as the finest portion of North America, not only from its soil, but its climate. The air is pure, and the winters, although severe, are dry and bracing—very different from and more healthy than those of the eastern states. At Prairie du Chien everyone dwelt upon the beauty of the winter; indeed, they appeared to prefer it to the other seasons. The country is, as I have described it in my route from Green Bay, alternate prairie, oak openings, and forest; and the same may be said of the other side of the Mississippi, now distinguished as the district of Ioway. Limestone quarries abound; indeed, the whole of this beautiful and fertile region appears as if nature had so arranged it that man should have all difficulties cleared from before him, and have but little to do but to take possession and enjoy. There is no clearing of timber requisite; on the contrary, you have just as much as you can desire, whether for use or ornament. Prairies of fine rich grass, upon which cattle fatten in three or four months, lay spread in every direction. The soil is so fertile that you have but to turn it up to make it yield grain to any extent; and the climate is healthy, at the same time that there is more than sufficient sun in the summer and autumn to bring every crop to perfection. Land carriage is hardly required from the numerous rivers and streams which pour their waters from every direction into the Upper Mississippi. Add to all this, that the western lands possess an inexhaustible supply of minerals, only a few feet under the surface of their rich soil—a singular and wonderful provision, as, in general, where minerals are found below, the soil above is usually arid and ungrateful. The mineral country is to the south of the Wisconsin River—at least nothing has at present been discovered north of it; but the northern part is still in the possession of the Winnebago Indians, who are waiting for the fulfilment of the treaty before they surrender it, and at present will permit no white settler to enter it. It is said that the other portions of the Wisconsin territory will come into the

market this year; at present, with the exception of the Fox
River and Winnebago Lake settlements, and that of Prairie
du Chien, at the confluence of the two rivers Wisconsin and
Mississippi, there is hardly a log-house in the whole district.
The greatest annoyance at present in this western country
is the quantity and variety of snakes; it is hardly safe to
land upon some parts of the Wisconsin River banks, and
they certainly offer a great impediment to the excursions of
geologist and botanist; you are obliged to look right and left
as you walk, and as for putting your hand into a hole, you
would be almost certain to receive a very unwished-for and
unpleasant shake to welcome you.

I ought here to explain an American law relative to
what is termed squatting, that is, taking possession of land
belonging to government and cultivating it; such was the
custom of the back-woodsmen, and, for want of this law, it
often happened that, after they had cultivated a farm, the
land would be applied for and purchased by some specula-
tor, who would forcibly eject the occupant and take possession of the improved property. A back-woodsman was not
to be trifled with, and the consequences very commonly
were that the new proprietor was found some fine morning
with a rifle-bullet through his head. To prevent this unjust
spoliation on the one part, and summary revenge on the
other, a law has been passed by which any person having
taken possession of land belonging to the states government
shall, as soon as the lands have been surveyed and come
into the market, have the right of purchasing the quarter
section, or one hundred and sixty acres round him. Many
thousands are settled in this way all over the new western
states, and this pre-emption right is one of the few laws in
western America strictly adhered to. A singular proof of this
occurred the other day at Galena. The government had
made regulations with the diggers and smelters on the
government lands for a percentage on the lead raised, as a
government tax; and they erected a large stone building to
warehouse their portion, which was paid in lead. As soon

as the government had finished it, a man stepped forward and proved his right of pre-emption on the land upon which the building was erected, and it was decided against the government, although the land was actually government land.

CHAPTER XXVI

Indian Country

I remained a week at Prairie du Chien, and left my kind entertainers with regret; but an opportunity offering of going up to St. Peters in a steamboat, with General Atkinson,[1] who was on a tour of inspection, I could not neglect so favorable a chance. St. Peters is situated at the confluence of the St. Peters River with the Upper Mississippi, about seven miles below the Falls of St. Anthony, where the river Mississippi becomes no longer navigable; and here, removed many hundred miles from civilization, the Americans have an outpost called Fort Snelling, and the American Fur Company an establishment. The country to the north is occupied by the Chippeway tribe of Indians; that to the east by the Winnebagos, and that to the west by the powerful tribe of Sioux or Dacotahs,[2] who range over the whole prairie territory between the Mississippi and Missouri rivers.

[1] Henry Atkinson (1782–1842), an American army officer, was active in the various military expeditions against the Indians; he had defeated the Winnebegos at Prairie du Chien in 1827.
[2] The term Sioux or Dakota may be used interchangeably to describe the tribe. See John Collier, *Indians of the Americas* (New York: Mentor Books; 1947), p. 135, and also Franz Boas et al., *General Anthropology* (New York: D. C. Heath; 1938), p. 129.

The river here is so constantly divided by numerous islands that its great width is not discernible; it seldom has less than two or three channels, and often more; it courses through a succession of bold bluffs, rising sometimes perpendicularly, and always abruptly from the banks or flat land, occasionally diversified by the prairies, which descend to the edge of the stream. These bluffs are similar to those I have described in the Wisconsin River and Prairie du Chien, but are on a grander scale, and are surmounted by horizontal layers of limestone rock. The islands are all covered with small timber and brushwood, and in the spring, before the leaves have burst out, and the freshets come down, the river rises so as to cover the whole of them, and then you behold the width and magnificence of this vast stream. On the second day we arrived at Lake Pepin, which is little more than an expansion of the river, or rather a portion of it, without islands. On the third we made fast to the wharf, abreast of the American Fur Company's factory, a short distance below the mouth of the river St. Peters. Fort Snelling is about a mile from the factory, and is situated on a steep promontory, in a commanding position; it is built of stone, and may be considered as impregnable to any attempt which the Indians might make, provided that it has a sufficient garrison. Behind it is a splendid prairie, running back for many miles.

The Falls of St. Anthony are not very imposing, although not devoid of beauty. You cannot see the whole of the falls at one view, as they are divided, like those of Niagara, by a large island, about one third of the distance from the eastern shore. The river which, as you ascended, poured through a bed below the strata of calcareous rock, now rises above the limestone formation; and the large masses of this rock, which at the falls have been thrown down in wild confusion over a width of from two hundred to two hundred and fifty yards, have a very picturesque effect. The falls themselves, I do not think, are more than from thirty to thirty-five feet high; but, with rapids above and below them, the descent of the river is said to be more than one hundred feet. Like those of Niagara, these falls have constantly receded, and are still receding.

Here, for the first time, I consider that I have seen the Indians in their primitive state; for till now all that I had fallen in with have been debased by intercourse with the whites and the use of spirituous liquors. The Winnebagos at Prairie du Chien were almost always in a state of intoxication, as were the other tribes at Mackinaw, and on the Lakes. The Winnebagos are considered the dirtiest race of Indians, and with the worst qualities: they were formerly designated by the French, *Puans*, a term sufficiently explanatory. When I was at Prairie du Chien, a circumstance which had occurred there in the previous winter was narrated to me. In many points of manners and customs the red men have a strong analogy with the Jewish tribes: among others, an eye for an eye, and a tooth for a tooth, is most strictly adhered to. If an Indian of one tribe is killed by an Indian of another, the murderer is demanded, and must either be given up, or his life must be taken by his own tribe; if not, a feud between the two nations would be the inevitable result. It appeared that a young Menonnomie, in a drunken fray, had killed a Winnebago, and the culprit was demanded by the head men of the Winnebago tribe. A council was held; and instead of the Menonnomie, the chiefs of the tribe offered them whiskey. The Winnebagos could not resist the temptation; and it was agreed that ten gallons of whiskey should be produced by the Menonnomies, to be drunk by all parties over the grave of the deceased. The squaws of the Menonnomie tribe had to dig the grave, as is the custom—a task of no little labor, as the ground was frozen hard several feet below the surface.

The body was laid in the grave, the mother of the deceased, with the rest of the Winnebago squaws, howling over it and denouncing vengeance against the murderer; but in a short time the whiskey made its appearance, and they all set to drink. In an hour they were all the best friends in the world, and all very drunk. The old squaw mother was hugging the murderer of her son; and it was a scene of intoxication which, in the end, left the majority of the parties assembled, for a time, quite as dead as the man in the grave. Such are the effects of whiskey upon these people, who have been destroyed much more rapidly by spirituous liquors than by all the wars which they have engaged in against the whites.

The Sioux are a large band and are divided into six or seven different tribes; they are said to amount to from 27,000 to 30,000. They are, or have been, constantly at war with the Chippeways to the north of them and with Sacs and Foxes, a small but very warlike band, residing to the south of them abreast of Des Moines River. The Sioux have fixed habitations as well as tents; their tents are large and commodious, made of buffalo skins dressed without the hair, and very often handsomely painted on the outside. I went out about nine miles to visit a Sioux village on the borders of a small lake. Their lodges were built cottage-fashion, of small fir-poles, erected stockadewise, and covered inside and out with bark, the roof also of bark with a hole in the centre for the smoke to escape through. I entered one of these lodges, the interior was surrounded by a continued bed-place round three of the sides, about three feet from the floor, and on the platform was a quantity of buffalo skins and pillows; the fire was in the centre, and their luggage was stowed away under the bed-places. It was very neat and clean; the Sioux generally are—indeed, particularly so, compared with the other tribes of Indians. A missionary resides at this village and has paid great attention to the small band under his care. Their patches of Indian corn were clean and well tilled; and although, from demi-civilization, the people have lost much of their native grandeur, still they are a fine race, and well disposed. But the majority of the Sioux tribe remain in their native state: they are *Horse* Indians, as those who live on the prairies are termed; and although many of them have rifles, the majority still adhere to the use of the bow and arrows, both in their war parties and in the chase of the buffalo.

During the time that I passed here, there were several games of ball played between different bands, and for considerable stakes; one was played on the prairie close to the house of the Indian agent. The Indian game of ball is somewhat similar to the game of golf in Scotland, with this difference, that the sticks used by the Indians have a small network racket at the end, in which they catch the ball and run away with it, as far as they are permitted, towards the goal, before they throw it in that direction. It is one of the most exciting games in the world and requires the greatest activity and address. It is, moreover, rendered celebrated in American history from the circumstance that it was used as a stratagem by the renowned leader of the northern tribes, Pontiac,[3] to surprise in one day all the English forts on and near to the Lakes, a short time after the Canadas had been surrendered to the British. At Mackinaw they succeeded, and put the whole garrison to the sword, as they did at one or two smaller posts; but at Detroit they were foiled by the plan having been revealed by one of the squaws.

Pontiac's plan was as follows. Pretending the greatest good-will and friendship, a game of ball was proposed to be played, on the same day, at all the different outposts, for

[3] Pontiac's conspiracy of 1763 was the most important Indian rebellion after King Philip's War. It was caused by the unwillingness of the English to continue the French policy of annual presents, the rapacity of English traders and trappers, and the fear that traditional Indian hunting grounds would be occupied by settlers. Under the leadership of Pontiac, a chief of the Ottawas, the Indians of the Ohio Valley formed a grand alliance to prevent British expansion westward. The rebellion broke out in May 1763 with the burning of Fort Sandusky; then followed the destruction of all of the western forts except Pittsburgh and Detroit, with the latter under siege for some fifteen months. The entire frontier from Virginia to Niagara was under attack, and numerous settlers and their families were massacred. Of the several colonies involved, only Virginia and Maryland made any real resistance. The revolt was finally crushed by British soldiers and the frontier area pacified by 1767. For the best account of Pontiac's rebellion, see Howard H. Peckham, *Pontiac and the Indian Uprising* (Princeton: Princeton University Press; 1947).

the amusement of the garrisons. The interest taken in the game would, of course, call out a proportion of the officers and men to witness it. The squaws were stationed close to the gates of the fort, with the rifles of the Indians cut short, concealed under their blankets. The ball was, as if by accident, thrown into the fort; the Indians, as usual, were to rush in crowds after it; by this means they were to enter the fort, receiving their rifles from their squaws as they hurried in, and then slaughter the weakened and unprepared garrisons. Fortunately, Detroit, the most important post, and against which Pontiac headed the stratagem in person, was saved by the previous information given by the squaw; not that she had any intention to betray him, but the commanding officer, having employed her to make him several pair of moccasins out of an elk skin, desired her to take the remainder of the skin for the same purpose; this she refused, saying it was of no use, as he would never see it again. This remark excited his suspicions and led to the discovery.

The game played before the fort when I was present lasted nearly two hours, during which I had a good opportunity of estimating the agility of the Indians, who displayed a great deal of mirth and humor at the same time. But the most curious effect produced was by the circumstance that, having divested themselves of all their garments except their middle clothing, they had all of them fastened behind them a horse's tail; and, as they swept by, in their chase of the ball, with their tails streaming to the wind, I really almost made up my mind that such an appendage was rather an improvement to a man's figure than otherwise.

While I was there a band of Sioux from the *Lac qui parle* (so named from a remarkable echo there), distant about two hundred and thirty miles from Fort Snelling, headed by Monsieur Rainville, came down, on a visit to the American Fur Company's factory. Monsieur Rainville (or *de* Rainville, as he told me was his real name) is, he asserts, descended from one of the best families in France, which formerly settled in Canada. He is a half-breed, his father being a Frenchman and his mother a Sioux; his wife is also a Sioux, so that his family are three-quarters red. He had been residing many years with the Sioux tribes, trafficking with them for peltry, and has been very judicious in his treatment of them, not interfering with their pursuits of hunting; he has, moreover, to a certain degree civilized them and obtained great power over them. He has induced the band who reside with him to cultivate a sufficiency of ground for their sustenance, but they still course the prairie on their fiery horses and follow up the chase of the buffalo. They adhere also to their paint, their dresses, and their habits, and all who compose his band are first-rate warriors; but they are all converted to Christianity.

Latterly two missionaries [4] have been sent out to his assistance. The Dacotah language has been reduced to writing, and most of them, if not all, can write and read. I have now in my possession an elementary spelling-book, and Watt's catechism, printed at Boston, in the Sioux tongue, and many letters and notes given to me by the missionaries, written to them by the painted warriors; of course, they do not touch spirituous liquors. The dress of the band which came down with Mr. Rainville was peculiarly martial and elegant. Their hair is divided in long plaits in front, and ornamented with rows of circular silver buckles; the ear is covered with ear-rings up to the top of it, and on the crown of the head they wear the war-eagle's feathers, to which they are entitled by their exploits. The war-eagle is a small one of the genus, but said to be so fierce that it will attack and destroy the largest of his kind; the feathers are black about three inches down from the tips, on each side of the stem, the remainder being white. These feathers are highly valued, as the bird is scarce and difficult to kill. I saw two very fine feathers carried by a Sioux warrior on the point of his spear, and I asked him if

---

[4] The missionaries who made the written version of the Sioux language were Thomas Smith Williamson and Gideon Pond.

he would part with them. He refused, saying that they cost too dear. I asked him how much, and he replied that he had given a very *fine horse* for them. For every scalp taken from the enemy, or grizzly bear killed, an Indian is entitled to wear one feather and no more; and this rule is never deviated from. Were an Indian to put on more feathers than he is entitled to, he would be immediately disgraced. Indeed, you can among this primitive people know all their several merits as warriors. I have now the shield of Yank-ton Sioux, a chief of a tribe near the Missouri. In the centre is a black eagle, which is his *totem*, or heraldic distinction; on each side hang war-eagle's feathers and small locks of human hair, denoting the number of scalps he has taken, and below are smaller feathers, equal to the number of wounds he has received. These warriors of Mr. Rainville's were constantly with me, for they knew that I was an *English* warrior, as they called me, and they are very partial to the English. It was really a pleasing sight, and a subject for meditation, to see one of these fine fellows, dressed in all his wild magnificence, with his buffalo robe on his shoulders and his tomahawk by his side, seated at a table, and writing out for me a Sioux translation of the Psalms of David.

Mr. Rainville's children read and write English, French, and Sioux. They are modest and well behaved, as the Indian women generally are. They had prayers every evening, and I used to attend them. The warriors sat on the floor round the room; the missionary, with Mr. Rainville and his family, in the centre; and they all sang remarkably well. This system with these Indians is, in my opinion, very good. All their fine qualities are retained; and if the system be pursued, I have no doubt but that the sternness and less defensible portions of their characters will be gradually obliterated.

A half-breed, of the name of Jack Fraser,[5] came up

5 Jack Frazer was a half-breed; his mother was a Sioux and his father was French. Frazer was an interpreter for the American authorities and he played a major role in the negotiations

with us in the steamboat. He has been admitted into one of the bands of Sioux who live near the river, and is reckoned one of the bravest of their warriors. I counted twenty-eight notches on the handle of his tomahawk, every one denoting a scalp taken, and when dressed he wears eagle's feathers to that amount. He was a fine intellectual-looking man. I conversed with him through the interpreter, and he told me that the only man that he wished to kill was his *father*. On inquiring why, he replied that his father had broken his word with him; that he had promised to make a *white man* of him (that is, to have educated him, and brought him up in a civilized manner), and that he had left him a Sioux. One could not help admiring the thirst for knowledge and the pride shown by this poor fellow, although mixed up with their inveterate passion for revenge. . . .

The Sioux are said to be very honest, except on the point of stealing horses; but this, it must be recollected, is a part of their system of warfare, and is no more to be considered as stealing than is our taking merchant-vessels on the high seas. Indeed, what are the vast rolling prairies but as the wide ocean, and their armed bands that scour them but men-of-war and privateers, and the horses which they capture but unarmed or defenceless convoys of merchant-vessels? But sometimes they steal when they are not at war, and this is from the force of habit and their irresistible desire to possess a fine horse. Mr. Rainville informed me that three hundred dollars was a very common price for a good horse, and if the animal was very remarkable, swift, and well-trained for buffalo-hunting, they would give any sum (or the equivalent for it) that they could command.

In many customs the Sioux are closely allied to the Jewish nation; indeed, a work has been published in America to prove that the Indians were originally Jews.[6] There is

---

between the government and the Sioux over the surrender of Indian lands in Minnesota.

[6] James Adair (*fl.* 1775), trader and writer on Indians, came to America in 1735 and lived in the

always a separate lodge for the woman to retire to before
and after childbirth, observing a similar purification to that
prescribed by Moses. Although there ever will be, in all societies, instances to the contrary, chastity is honored among
the Sioux. They hold what they term Virgin Feasts, and
when these are held, should any young woman accept the
invitation who has by her misconduct rendered herself unqualified for it, it is the duty of any man who is aware of her
unfitness to go into the circle and lead her out. A circumstance of this kind occurred the other day when the daughter of a celebrated chief gave a Virgin Feast. A young man
of the tribe walked into the circle and led her out; upon
which the chief led his daughter to the lodge of the young
Sioux and told him that he gave her to him for his wife, but
the young man refused to take her, as being unworthy. But
what is more singular (and I have it from authority which
is unquestionable), they also hold Virgin Feasts for the
young men; and should any young man take his seat there
who is unqualified, the woman who is aware of it must lead
him out, although, in so doing, she convicts herself; nevertheless, it is considered a sacred duty, and is done.

The shells found in their western rivers are very interesting. I had promised to procure some for Mr. Lea of Philadelphia, and an old squaw had been dispatched to obtain
them. She brought me a large quantity and then squatted
down by my side. I was seated on the stone steps before the
door, and commenced opening and cleaning them previous
to packing them up. She watched me very attentively for
half an hour, and then got up, and continued, as she walked
away, to chuckle and talk aloud. "Do you know what the
old woman says?" said the old Canadian interpreter to me.

Carolinas and Georgia. Adair put
forth the thesis that the North
American Indians were the Ten
Lost Tribes of Israel, and published his theory in his *History
of the American Indians,* which
appeared in London in 1775.
Aside from his quaint idea on
the origin of the Indians, his
work contained much valuable
material on their language,
habits, and character. Elias
Boudinot (1740–1821) in his
A Star in the West also took
Adair's position as to the origin
of the Indians.

"She says, the man's a fool; he keeps the shells and throws the meat away."

The French Canadians, who are here employed by the Fur Company, are a strange set of people. There is no law here or appeal to law; yet they submit to authority and are managed with very little trouble. They bind themselves for three years, and during that time (little occasional deviations being overlooked) they work diligently and faithfully— ready at all seasons and all hours, and never complaining, although the work is often extremely hard. Occasionally they return to Canada with their earnings, but the major part have connected themselves with Indian women and have numerous families, for children in this fine climate are so numerous that they almost appear to spring from the earth.

While I remained at St. Peters, one or two of the settlers at Red River came down. Red River is a colony established by Lord Selkirk,[7] and at present is said to be composed of a population of four thousand. This settlement, which is four degrees of latitude north of St. Peters, has proved very valuable to the Hudson Bay Company, who are

---

[7] Thomas Douglas, fifth Earl of Selkirk, Baron Daer and Short-cluich (1771–1820), was a promoter of emigration schemes to British North America. In 1803 he sent a number of Highlanders to settle on Prince Edward Island, and following the success of this settlement, he sponsored an unsuccessful community in what is now Ontario. In 1811 Selkirk purchased 116,000 square miles from the Hudson's Bay Company's lands in the Red River Valley, and in 1812 the first parties of immigrants arrived. Adversity and privations nearly caused the total abandonment of the scheme, but with the augmentation of the community by new personnel in 1814 and 1815, the little group managed to keep going. The North West Company, a trading rival of the Hudson's Bay Company, disapproved of the colony because they saw it as an attempt to restrict their trading privileges and also because they feared that the food supply which they normally drew from the area would be diminished. After the arrival of more colonists in 1816 friction increased and there was an armed clash—the Massacre of Seven Oaks—in which twenty settlers were killed. Both sides went to law, Selkirk was actually fined £2,000 by the Canadian courts, but finally, with the union of the Hudson's Bay Company and the North West Company in 1821, the settlement was allowed to remain in the area.

established there—most of their servants remaining at it after their three years' service is completed and those required to be hired in their stead being obtained from the settlement. Formerly they had to send to Montreal for their servants, and those discharged went to Canada and spent their money in the provinces; now that they remain at the settlement, the supplies coming almost wholly from the stores of the Company, the money returns to it, and they procure their servants without trouble. These settlers informed me that provisions were plentiful and cheap, beef being sold at about two pence per lb.; but they complained, and very naturally, that there was no market for their produce, so that if the company did not purchase it, they must consume it how they could; besides that the supply being much greater than the demand, of course favour was shown. This had disgusted many of the settlers, who talked of coming down further south. One of the greatest inducements for remaining at Red River, and which occasioned the population to be so numerous, was the intermixture by marriage with the Indian tribes surrounding them. They do not like to return to Canada with a family of half-breeds, who would not there be looked upon with the same consideration as their parents.

I give the substance of this conversation, without being able to substantiate how far it is true; the parties who gave me the information were certainly to be classed among that portion of the settlers who were discontented.

CHAPTER XXVII

The Wild West—Fort Snelling

Fort Snelling is well built and beautifully situated; as usual I found the officers gentlemanlike, intelligent, and hospitable; and, together with their wives and families, the society was the most agreeable that I became acquainted with in America. They are better supplied here than either at Fort Crawford or Fort Winnebago, having a fine stock of cattle on the prairie and an extensive garden cultivated for the use of the garrison. The principal amusement of the officers is, as may be supposed, the chase; there is no want of game in the season, and they have some very good dogs of every variety. And I here had the pleasure of falling in with Captain Scott, one of the first Nimrods of the United States, and who, perhaps, has seen more of every variety of hunting than any other person. His reputation as a marksman is very great; and there is one feat which he has often performed that appears almost incredible. Two potatoes being thrown up in the air, he will watch his opportunity and pass his rifle ball through them both. I had long conversations with him; and as from his celebrity, he may be accounted a public character. . . .

The band of warriors attached to Monsieur Rainville have set up their war-tent close to the factory, and have entertained us with a variety of dances. Their dresses are very beautiful, and the people, who have been accustomed to witness these exhibitions for years, say that they have never seen anything equal to them before. I was very anxious to obtain one of them, and applied to Mr. Rainville to effect my purpose; but it required all his influence to induce them to part with it, and they had many arguments and debates among themselves before they could make up their minds to consent to do so. I was the more anxious about it as I had seen Mr. Catlin's [1] splendid exhibition, and I knew that he had not one in his possession. The dress in question consisted of a sort of kilt of fine skins, ornamented with beautiful porcupine quill-work and eagle's feathers; garters of animals' tails, worn at their ankles; head-dress of eagle's feathers and ermine's tails, etc. They made little objection to part with any portions of the dress except the kilt; at last they had a meeting of the whole band, as the dress was not the property of any one individual; and I was informed that the warriors would come and have a talk with me.

I received them at the factory's new house, in my room, which was large and held them all. One came and presented me with a pair of garters; another, with a portion of the head-dress; another, with moccasins; at last, the kilt or girdle was handed to me. Mr. Rainville sat by as interpreter. He who had presented me with the kilt or girdle spoke for half a minute, and then stopped while what he said was being interpreted.

"You are an Englishman and a warrior in your own country. You cross the great waters as fast as we can our prairies. We recollect the English, and we like them; they

---

[1] George Catlin (1796–1872), American artist, author, and ethnologist. He lived among the Indians and observed their way of life; the result of his observations is a vast collection of drawings and paintings which portray the fast-disappearing tribal life. In 1840 he went to Europe and exhibited his works, which were received with enthusiasm. In 1841 he published *The Manners, Customs and Conditions of the North American Indians* with some three hundred illustrations. Three years later his *The North American Portfolio* appeared. Many of the original Catlin paintings are in the Smithsonian Institution in Washington.

used us well. The rifles and blankets which they gave us, according to promise, were of good quality; not like the American goods; their rifles are bad, and their blankets are thin. The English keep their word, and they live in our memory."

"Ho!" replied I, which is as much as to say, I understand what you have said, and you may proceed.

"You have asked for the dress which we wear when we dance; we have never parted with one as yet; they belong to the band of warriors; when one who has worn a dress goes to the land of spirits, we hold a council to see who is most worthy to put it on in his place. We value them highly; and we tell you so not to enhance their value, but to prove what we will do for an English warrior."

"Ho!" says I.

"An American, in the fort, has tried hard to obtain this dress from us; he offered us two barrels of flour, and other things. You know that we have no game, and we are hungry; but if he had offered twelve barrels of flour, we would not have parted with them. (This was true.) But our father, Rainville, has spoken; and we have pleasure in giving them to an English warrior. I have spoken."

"Ho!" says I; upon which the Indian took his seat with the others, and it was my turn to speak. I was very near beginning, "Unaccustomed as I am to public speaking," but I knew that such an acknowledgment would, in their estimation, have very much lessened my value as a warrior; for, like the Duke of Wellington, one must be as valuable in the council as in the field, to come up to their notions of excellence. So I rose, and said—

"I receive with great pleasure the dress which you have given me. I know that you do not like to part with it, and that you have refused the American at the fort; and I therefore value it the more. I shall never look upon it, when I am on the other side of the great waters, without thinking of my friends the Sioux; and I will tell my nation that you gave them to me because I was an English warrior, and because you liked the English."

"Ho!" grunted the whole conclave, after this was interpreted.

"I am very glad that you do not forget the English, and that you say they kept their word, and that their rifles and blankets were good. I know that the blankets of the Americans are thin and cold. (I did not think it worth while to say that they were all made in England.) We have buried the hatchet now; but should the tomahawk be raised again between the Americans and the English, you must not take part with the Americans."

"Ho!" said they.

"In the Fur Company's store you will find many things acceptable to you. I leave Mr. Rainville to select for you what you wish; and beg you will receive them in return for the present which you have made me."

"Ho!" said they, and thus ended my first Indian council.

It is remarkable that the Sioux have no expression to signify, "I thank you," although other Indians have. When they receive a present, they always say, *Wash tay:* it is good.

Of all, the tribes I believe the Sioux to be the most inimical to the Americans. They have no hesitation in openly declaring so; and it must be acknowledged that it is not without just grounds. During the time that I was at St. Peters, a council was held at the Indian agent's. It appears that the American government, in its paternal care for the Indians, had decided that at any *strike* taking place between tribes of Indians near to the confines, no war should take place in consequence: that is to say that, should any Indians of one tribe attack or kill any Indians belonging to another, instead of the tribes going to war, they should apply for and receive redress from the American government. Sometime back, a party of Chippeways came down to a trader's house, about half a mile from Fort Snelling. Being almost hereditary enemies of the Sioux, they were fired at, at night, by some of the young men of the Sioux village close by, and two of the Chippeways were wounded. In conformity with the intimation received and the law laid down by the American government and promulgated by the Indian agent, the Chippeways applied for redress. It was granted—four Sioux were taken and shot. This summary justice was expected to produce the best effects, and, had it been followed up, it might have prevented bloodshed; but since the above occurrence, some Chippeways came down and, meeting a party of Sioux, were received kindly into their lodges; they returned this hospitality by treacherously murdering eleven of the Sioux while they were asleep. This time the Sioux brought forward their complaint. "You tell us not to go to war; we will not; you shot four of our people for wounding two Chippeways; now do us justice against the Chippeways, who have murdered eleven of our Sioux." As yet no justice has been done to the Sioux. The fact is that the Chippeways live a long way off; and there are not sufficient men to garrison the fort, still less to send a party out to capture the Chippeways; and the Sioux are, as may well be supposed, indignant at this partial proceeding.

I was at the council, and heard all the speeches made by the Sioux chiefs on the occasion. They were some of them very eloquent and occasionally very severe; and the reply of the Indian agent must have rendered the American government very contemptible in the eyes of the Indians —not that the agent was so much in fault as was the American government, which, by not taking proper measures to put their promises and agreements into force, had left their officer in such a position. First, the Indian agent said that the wounding of the two Chippeways took place close to the fort, and that it was on account of the insult offered to the *American flag* that it was so promptly punished;—a very different explanation and quite at variance with the principle laid down by the American government. The Indians replied; and the agent then said that they had not sufficient troops to defend the fort and, therefore, could not send out a party—an admission very unwise to make, although strictly true. The Indians again replied; and then the agent said, wait a little till we hear from Washington, and then, if you have no redress, you are brave men, you have arms in your hands, and your enemies are before you. This was worse than all, for it implied the inability or the indifference of the American government to do them justice, and told them, after that government had distinctly declared that they should fight no longer but receive redress from it, that they now might do what- the government had forbidden them to do and that they had no other chance of redress. The result of this council was very unsatisfactory. The Indian chiefs declared that they were ashamed to look their people in the face and walked solemnly away.

To make this matter still worse, after I left St. Peters, I read in the St. Louis *Gazette* a report of some Chippeways having come down, and that, in consequence of the advice given by the Indian agent, the Sioux had taken the law into their own hands and murdered some of the Chippeways; and that, although they had never received redress for the murder of their own people, some of the Sioux were again taken and executed.

The arms of the Sioux are the rifle, tomahawk, and bow; they carry spears more for parade than use. Their bows are not more than three feet long, but their execution with them is surprising. A Sioux, when on horseback chasing the buffalo, will drive his arrow, which is about eighteen inches long, with such force that the barb shall appear on the opposite side of the animal. And one of their greatest chiefs, *Wanataw,* has been known to kill two buffaloes with one arrow, it having passed through the first of the animals and mortally wounded the second on the other side of it. I was about two hundred yards from the fort, and asked a Sioux if he could send his arrow into one of the apertures for air, which were near the foundation and about three inches wide. It appeared more like a thread from where we stood. He took his bow, and apparently with a most careless aim he threw the arrow right into it.

The men are tall and straight, and very finely made, with the exception of their arms, which are too small. The arms of the squaws, who do all the labor, are much more muscular. One day, as I was on the prairie, I witnessed the effect of custom upon these people. A Sioux was coming up without perceiving me; his squaw followed very heavily laden, and to assist her he had himself a large package on his shoulder. As soon as they perceived me, he dropped his burden, and it was taken up by the squaw and added to what she had already. If a woman wishes to upbraid another, the severest thing she can say is: "You let your husband carry burthens."

CHAPTER XXVIII

Down the Mississippi

Left St. Peters. Taking the two varieties in the mass, the Indians must be acknowledged the most perfect gentlemen in America, particularly in their deportment. It was with regret that I parted with my friends in the fort, my kind host, Mr. Sibley,[1] and my noble-minded warrior Sioux. I could have remained at St. Peters for a year with pleasure, and could only regret that life was so short and the Mississippi so long.

There is, however, one serious drawback in all America to life in the woods—or life in cities, or every other kind of life—which is the manner, go where you will, in which you are pestered by the mosquitoes. Strangers are not the only sufferers; those who are born and die in the country are equally tormented, and it is slap, slap, slap, all day and all night long, for these animals bite through everything less thick than a buffalo's skin. As we ascended the river they

---

[1] Henry Hastings Sibley (1811–91) entered the service of the American Fur Company in 1829 and soon rose to eminence in the company. He served in Congress as a delegate from both the Minnesota and Wisconsin territories. In 1858 Sibley was elected the first governor of Minnesota. From 1862 to 1865 he was involved with various Indian difficulties but succeeded in negotiating treaties between the Indians and the United States government.

attacked us on the crown of the head—a very unusual thing —and raised swellings as large as pigeon's eggs. I must have immolated at least five hundred of them upon my bump of benevolence. Whatever people may think, I feel that no one can be very imaginative where these animals are so eternally tormenting them. You meditate under the shady boughs of some forest-king (slap knee, slap cheek), and farewell to anything like concentration of thought; you ponder on the sailing moon (slap again, right and left, above, below), always unpleasantly interrupted. It won't do at all: you are teased and phlebotomized out of all poetry and patience.

It is midnight, the darkness is intense, not even a star in the heavens above, and the steamboat appears as if it were gliding through a current of ink, with black masses rising just perceptible on either side of it; no sound except the reiterated note of the "Whip poor Will," answered by the loud coughing of the high-pressure engine. Who, of those in existence fifty years ago, would have contemplated that these vast and still untenanted solitudes would have had their silence invaded by such an unearthly sound? —a sound which ever gives you the idea of vitality. It is this appearance of breathing which makes the high-pressure engine the nearest approach to creation which was ever attained by the ingenuity of man. It appears to have respiration, and that short, quick respiration occasioned by exertion; its internal operations are performed as correctly and as mechanically as are our own; it is as easily put out of order and rendered useless as we are; and, like us, it can only continue its powers of motion by being well supplied with aliment.

Ran up Fever River to Galena, the present emporium of the Mineral Country. There is an unpleasant feeling connected with the name of this river; it is, in fact, one of the American translations. It was originally called Fève, or Bean River, by the French, and this they have construed into Fever. The Mineral district comprehends a tract of country running about one hundred miles north and

south, and fifty miles east and west, from the river Wisconsin to about twenty miles south of Galena. It was purchased by the American government about fifteen years
ago, the northern portion from the Winnebagos and the
southern from the Sac and Fox Indians. The Indians used to
work the diggings to a small extent, bringing the lead which
they obtained to exchange with the traders. As may be supposed, they raised but little, the whole work of digging and
smelting being carried on by the squaws. After the land was
surveyed, a portion of it was sold, but when the minerals
made their appearance, the fact was notified by the sur-
veyors to the government, and the remaining portions were
withdrawn from the market. A licence was granted to
speculators to dig the ore and smelt it, upon condition of
their paying to the government a percentage on the mineral
obtained. Those who found a good vein had permission to
work it for forty yards square, on condition that they carried the ore to a licensed smelter. This occasioned a new
class of people to spring up in this speculative country,
namely, *finders,* who would search all over the country for
what they called a good *prospect,* that is, every appearance
on the surface of a good vein of metal. This when found
they would sell to others, who would turn *diggers;* and as
soon as these finders had spent their money, they would
range over the whole country to find another *prospect* which
they might dispose of. But although it was at first supposed
that the government had retained all the mineral portion
of the district in its own hands, it was soon discovered
that nearly the whole country was one continued lead mine,
and that there was an equal supply of mineral to be obtained from those portions which had been disposed of.
Lead was found not only in the mountains and ravines, but
under the surface of the wide prairies. As the lands sold by
government had not to pay a percentage for the lead raised
from them, those who worked upon the government lands
refused to pay any longer, asserting that it was not *legal.*
The superintendent of government soon found that his office was a sinecure, as all attempt at *coercion* in that half-

civilized country would have been not only useless but dangerous. The government have gone to law with their tenants, but that is of no avail, for a verdict against the latter would not induce them to pay. The cause was not attempted to be tried at Galena, for the government knew what the decision of the jury would have been, but it is contested at Vandalia. It is three years since the mines have paid any percentage, and the government are now advised to sell all their reserved lands and thus get rid of the business. How weak must that government be when it is compelled to submit to such a gross violation of all justice. The quantity of mineral found does not appear to affect the quality of the soil, which is as fine here, if not finer, than in those portions of Wisconsin where the mineral is not so plentiful. The quantity of lead annually smelted is said to amount to from 18,000,000 to 20,000,000 lbs. Galena is a small town, picturesquely situated on the banks of the river, but very dirty.

Ioway,[2] the new district opposite to Wisconsin, on the western banks of the Mississippi, has, in all probability, a large proportion of metal under its surface. When it was in the possession of the Sioux Indians, they used to obtain from it a considerable portion of lead, which they brought down to barter; and I am inclined to think that to the north of the Wisconsin River they will find no want of minerals, even as high up as Lake Superior, where they have already discovered masses of native copper weighing many *tons;* and on the west side of the river, as you proceed south, you arrive at the iron mines, or rather mountains of iron, in the Missouri.

After you proceed south of Prairie du Chien, the features of the Mississippi River gradually change; the bluffs decrease in number and in height, until you descend to

---

[2] Ioway (Iowa) was part of the Missouri territory from 1804 to 1821 and then came under the jurisdiction of the Michigan and Wisconsin territories. It was established as a district in 1832, as a territory in 1838, and was admitted to the union as the state of Iowa in 1846.

Rock Island, below which point they are rarely to be met with. The country on each side now is chiefly composed of variegated rolling prairies, with a less proportion of timber. To describe these prairies would be difficult, that is, to describe the effect of them upon a stranger: I have found myself lost, as it were; and indeed sometimes, although on horseback, have lost myself, having only the sun for my guide. Look round in every quarter of the compass, and there you are as if on the ocean—not a landmark, not a vestige of anything human but yourself. Instead of sky and water, it is one vast field, bounded only by the horizon, its surface gently undulating like the waves of the ocean; and as the wind (which always blows fresh on the prairies) bows down the heads of the high grass, it gives you the idea of a running swell. Every three or four weeks there is a succession of beautiful flowers, giving a variety of tints to the whole map, which die away and are succeeded by others equally beautiful; and in the spring, the strawberries are in such profusion that you have but to sit down wherever you may happen to be and eat as long as you please.

We stopped at Alton, in the state of Missouri,[3] to put on shore three thousand pigs of lead. This town has been rendered notorious by the murder—for murder it was, although it was brought on by his own intemperate conduct —of Mr. Lovejoy,[4] who is now raised to the dignity of a martyr by the abolitionists. Alton is a well-built town, of

---

[3] Marryat is incorrect here. Alton is not in Missouri but in Illinois.
[4] Elijah Parish Lovejoy (1802–37), a graduate of the Princeton Theological Seminary, was the editor of the *St. Louis Observer* where his blunt and outspoken anti-slavery attitude led to attacks on the paper. In 1836 Lovejoy went to Alton and continued his editorials. His press was, in consequence, destroyed by a mob, supposedly from St. Louis. With the support of the Alton citizens he began again and started the *Alton Observer.* This paper was equally outspoken and critical. Two more presses were destroyed; Lovejoy continued his crusade. A third press was delivered to him in November 1837. An armed mob attacked the warehouse where the press was located and in the fracas Lovejoy was shot. For an account by a contemporary, see Edward Beecher, *Narrative of Riots at Alton . . .* (Alton, 1838).

stone, and, from its locality, must increase; it is, however, spoilt by the erection of a penitentiary with huge walls, on a most central and commanding situation. I read a sign put out by a small eating-house, and which was very characteristic of the country—

> Stranger, here's your chicken fixings.

Four miles below Alton, the Missouri joins its waters with the Mississippi; and the change which takes place at the mingling of the two streams is very remarkable—the clear pellucid current of the Upper Mississippi being completely extinguished by the foul mud of the other turbid and impetuous river. It was a great mistake of the first explorers, when they called the western branch, at the meeting of the two rivers, the Missouri, and the eastern the Mississippi; the western branch, or the Missouri, is really the Mississippi, and should have been so designated: it is the longest and farthest navigable of the two branches and therefore is the main river.

The Falls of St. Anthony put an end to the navigation of the eastern branch, or present Upper Missouri, about nine hundred miles above St. Louis, while the western branch, or present Missouri, is navigable above St. Louis for more than one thousand two hundred miles.

The waters of the present Upper Mississippi are clear and beautiful; it is a swift but not an angry stream, full of beauty and freshness, and fertilizing as it sweeps along; while the Missouri is the same impetuous, discolored, devastating current as the Mississippi continues to be after its junction—like it, constantly sweeping down forests of trees in its wild course, overflowing, inundating, and destroying, and exciting awe and fear.

As soon as you arrive at St. Louis, you feel that you are on the great waters of the Mississippi. St. Louis is a well-built town, now containing about twenty thousand inhabitants, and situated on a hill shelving down to the river. The population increases daily; the river abreast of the town is crowded with steamboats, lying in two or three tiers, and ready to start up or down, or to the many tributary navigable rivers which pour their waters into the Mississippi.

In point of heat, St. Louis certainly approaches the nearest to the Black Hole of Calcutta of any city that I have sojourned in. The lower part of the town is badly drained, and very filthy. The flies, on a moderate calculation, are in many parts fifty to the square inch. I wonder that they have not a contagious disease here during the whole summer; it is, however, indebted to heavy rains for its occasional purification. They have not the yellow-fever here; but during the autumn they have one which, under another name, is almost as fatal—the bilious congestive fever. I found sleep almost impossible from the sultriness of the air, and used to remain at the open window for the greater part of the night. I did not expect that the muddy Mississippi would be able to reflect the silver light of the moon; yet it did, and the effect was very beautiful. Truly it may be said of this river, as it is of many ladies, that it is a candle-light beauty. There is another serious evil to which strangers who sojourn here are subject—the violent effects of the waters of the Mississippi upon those who are not used to them. The suburbs of the town are very pretty; and a few miles behind it you are again in a charming prairie country, full of game, large and small. Large and small are only so by comparison. An American was asked what game they had in his district, and his reply was: "Why, we've plenty of *baar* (bear) and deer, but no *large* game to count on."

There is one great luxury in America, which is the quantity of clear pure ice which is to be obtained wherever you are, even in the hottest seasons, and ice-creams are universal and very cheap. I went into an establishment where they vended this and other articles of refreshment, when about a dozen black swarthy fellows, employed at the iron-foundry close at hand, with their dirty shirt-sleeves tucked up, and without their coats and waistcoats, came in, and sitting down, called for ice-creams. Miss Martineau says in her work: "Happy is the country where factory-girls can carry parasols, and pig-drivers wear spectacles." She might have added, and the sons of Vulcan eat ice-creams. I thought at the time what the ladies, who stop in their carriages at Gunter's, would have said had they beheld these Cyclops with their bare sinewy arms, blackened with heat and smoke, refreshing themselves with such luxuries; but it must be remembered that *porter* is much the dearer article. Still, the working classes all over America can command not only all necessary comforts but many luxuries, for labor is dear and they are very well paid. The Americans will point this out and say, behold the effects of our institutions; and they fully believe that such is the case. Government has, however, nothing to do with it; it is the result of circumstances. When two years' exertion will procure a clever mechanic an independence, the effects will be the same, whether they labor under a democratic or a monarchical form of government.

Bear cubs (I mean the black bear) are caught and brought down to the cities on this side of the river, to be fattened for the table. I saw one at Alton about a year old, which the owner told me was to be killed the next day, having been bespoken for the feast of the 4th of July. I have eaten old bear, which I dislike; but they say that the cub is very good. I also saw here a very fine specimen of the grizzly bear (Ursus Herridus of Linnaeus). It was about two years old, and although not so tall, must have weighed quiet as much as a good-sized bullock. Its width of shoulder and apparent strength were enormous, and they have never yet been tamed. Mr. Van Amburgh [5] would be puzzled to handle one of them. The Indians reckon the slaying of one of these animals as a much greater feat than killing a man,

---

[5] Isaac Van Amburgh, "a near sighted lion-tamer" whose menagerie was ultimately acquired by Barnum, was long part of the entertainment world. For the relationship of Barnum and Van Amburgh, see Irving Wallace, *The Fabulous Showman* (New York: Alfred A. Knopf; 1959), pp. 212–13. Van Amburgh had been giving exhibitions of his skill in New York since 1837. See George Odell, *Annals of the New York Stage* (New York: Columbia University Press; 1927–49), Vol. IV, p. 257.

and the proudest ornament they can wear is a necklace of the grizzly bear's claws.

I, for myself, must confess that I had rather be attacked by, and take my chance with, three men than by one of these animals, as they are seldom killed by the first or even the second bullet. It requires numbers to overcome them. The largest lion, or Bengal tiger, would stand but a poor chance if opposed to one of these animals full grown. One of the gentlemen employed by the Fur Company told me that he once saw a grizzly bear attack a bull buffalo, and that, at the first seizure, he tore one of the ribs of the buffalo out of his side, and eventually carried away the whole carcass, without much apparent effort. They are only to be found in the rocky mountains, and valleys between them, when the game is plentiful.

Visited the museum. There were once five large alligators to be seen alive in this museum; but they are now all dead. One demands our sympathy, as there was something Roman in his fate. Unable to support such a life of confinement, and preferring death to the loss of liberty, he committed suicide by throwing himself out of a three-story-high window. He was taken up from the pavement the next morning; the vital spark had fled, as the papers say, and, I believe, his remains were decently interred.

The other four, never having been taught in their youth the hymn, "Birds in their little nests agree," fought so desperately that one by one they all died of their wounds. They were very large, being from seventeen to twenty-one feet long. One, as a memorial, remains preserved in the museum, and to make him look more poetical, he has a stuffed Negro in his mouth.

CHAPTER XXIX

The Ohio Valley—
Louisville and Cincinnati

Thank Heaven I have escaped from St. Louis; during the time that I remained in that city, I was, day and night, so melting away that I expected, like some of the immortal half-breeds of Jupiter, to become a tributary stream to the Mississippi.

As you descend the river, the land through which it flows becomes more level and flat, while the size of the forest trees increases; the log-houses of the squatters, erected on the banks under their trunks, appear, in contrast with their size, more like dog-kennels than the habitations of men. The lianas, or creeping plants, now become plentiful and embrace almost every tree, rising often to the height of fifty or sixty feet, and encircling them with the apparent force of the boa-constrictor. Most of them are poisonous; indeed, it is from these creeping parasites that the Indians, both in North and South America, obtain the most deadly venom. Strange that these plants, in their appearances and their habits so similar to the serpent tribe, should be endowed with the same peculiar attributes, and thus become their parallels in the vegetable kingdom—each carrying sudden death in their respective juices. I hate the Mississippi, and as I look down upon its wild and filthy waters, boiling and eddying, and reflect how uncertain is travelling in this region of high-pressure and disregard of social rights, I cannot help feeling a disgust at the idea of perishing in such a vile sewer, to be buried in mud, and perhaps to be rooted out again by some pig-nosed alligator.

Right glad was I when we turned into the stream of the Ohio, and I found myself on its purer waters. The Ohio is a splendid river, running westward from the chain of Allegheny mountains into the Mississippi, dividing the states of Illinois, Indiana, and Ohio on its northern bank from Kentucky and Virginia on its south, the northern being free and the southern slave states. We stopped at the mouth of the Cumberland River, where we took in passengers. Among others were a slave-dealer and a runaway Negro whom he had captured. He was secured by a heavy chain, and followed his master, who, as soon as he arrived on the upper deck, made him fast with a large padlock to one of the stancheons.

Here he remained, looking wistfully at the northern shore where everyone was free, but occasionally glancing his eye on the southern, which had condemned him to toil for others. I had never seen a slave-dealer, and scrutinized this one severely. His most remarkable feature was his eye; it was large but not projecting, clear as crystal, and eternally in motion. I could not help imagining, as he turned it right and left from one to the other of the passengers, that he was calculating what price he could obtain for them in the market. The Negro had run away about seven months before, and not having a pass, he had been secured in gaol until the return of his master, who had been on a journey with a string of slaves, to the state of Arkansas; he was about to be sold to pay expenses when his master saw the advertisement and claimed him. As may be supposed, a strong feeling exists on the opposite shores of the river as to slavery and freedom. The abolitionists used to assist the slaves to escape and send them off to Canada; even now many do escape; but this has been rendered more difficult by a system which has latterly been put in practice by a set of miscreants living on the free side of the river. These would go to the slave states opposite and persuade the Negroes to run away, promising to conceal them until they could send them off to Canada; for a free state is bound to give up a slave when claimed. Instead of sending them away, they would wait until the reward was offered by the masters for the apprehension of the slaves and then return them, receiving their infamous guerdon. The slaves, aware of this practice, now seldom attempt to escape.

Louisville is the largest city in Kentucky; the country about is very rich, and everything vegetable springs up with a luxuriance which is surprising. It is situated at the falls of the Ohio, which are only navigable during the freshets; there is no river in America which has such a rise and fall as the Ohio, sometimes rising to sixty feet in the spring; but this is very rare, the general average being about forty feet. The French named it La Belle Riviere: it is a very grand stream, running through hills covered with fine timber and underwood, but a very small portion is as yet cleared by the settlers. At the time that I was at Louisville the water was lower than it had been remembered for years, and you could walk for miles over the bed of the river, a calcareous deposit full of interesting fossils; but the mineralogist and geologist have as much to perform in America as the agriculturist.

Arrived at Cincinnati. How rapid has been the advance of this western country. In 1803, deer-skin at the value of forty cents per pound were a legal tender, and if offered instead of money, could not be refused—even by a lawyer. Not fifty years ago, the woods which towered where Cincinnati is now built resounded only to the cry of the wild animals of the forest or the rifle of the Shawnee Indian; now Cincinnati contains a population of forty thousand inhabitants. It is a beautiful, well-built, clean town, reminding you more of Philadelphia than any other city in the Union. Situated on a hill on the banks of the Ohio, it is surrounded by a circular phalanx of other hills, so that look up and down the streets, whichever way you will, your eye reposes upon verdure and forest trees in the distance. The streets have a row of trees on each side, near the curb-stone; and most of the houses have a small frontage, filled with luxuriant flowering shrubs, of which the Althea Frutex is the most abundant. It is, properly speaking, a Yankee city, the majority of its inhabitants coming from the east; but they have intermarried and blended with the Kentuckians of the opposite shore, a circumstance which is advantageous to the character of both.

There are, however, a large number of Dutch and German settlers here; they say ten thousand. They are not much liked by the Americans; but have great influence, as may be conceived when it is stated that, when a motion was brought forward in the Municipal Court for the city regulations to be printed in German as well as English, it was lost by one vote only.

I was told a singular fact, which will prove how rapidly the value of land rises in this country as it becomes peopled. Fifty-six years ago, the major part of the land upon which the city of Cincinnati stands, and which is now worth many millions of dollars, was *swapped* away by the owner of it for a pony!! The man who made this unfortunate bargain is now alive and living in or near Cincinnati.

Cincinnati is the pork-shop of the Union; and in the autumnal and early winter months, the way they kill pigs here is, to use a Yankee phrase, *quite a caution.* Almost all the hogs fed in the oak forests of Ohio, Kentucky, and western Virginia are driven into this city, and some establishments kill as many as fifteen hundred a day; at least so I am told. They are despatched in a way quite surprising, and a pig is killed upon the same principle as a pin is made —by division or, more properly speaking, by combination of labor. The hogs confined in a large pen are driven into a smaller one; one man knocks them on the head with a sledge-hammer and then cuts their throats; two more pull away the carcass, when it is raised by two others, who tumble it into a tub of scalding water. His bristles are removed in about a minute and a half by another party, when the next duty is to fix a stretcher between his legs. It is then hoisted up by two other people, cut open, and disembowelled; and in three minutes and a half from the time that the hog was grunting in his obesity, he has only to get cold before he is again packed up, and reunited in a barrel to travel all over the world. By the by, we laugh at the notion of pork and molasses. In the first place, the American pork is far superior to any that we ever have salted down; and, in the next, it eats uncommonly well with molasses. I have tasted it, and *"it is a fact."* After all, why should we eat currant jelly with venison and not allow the Americans the humble imitation of pork and molasses?

Mrs. Trollope's bazaar [1] raises its head in a very im-

---

[1] This building, an architectural pot-pourri, was quite extraordinary in appearance. It covered "an area of thirty-eight by one hundred feet and varied in height from fifty-two to eighty-five feet. The front facing Third Street was 'taken, in part from the Mosque of St. Athanase, in Egypt,' and was formed of 'three large arabesque windows with arches, supported by four Moorish stone pilasters with capitals.' Above these were 'large and beautifully wrought free stone ornaments,' and still above these was a wall that terminated in 'gothic battlements, each of which supports a stone sphere.' . . . The front facing south toward the Ohio River was, if anything, still more novel in appearance than the front that faced Third Street. Its chief feature was an Egyptian colonnade formed of four massive columns modeled after those 'in the temple of Appollinopolis at Etfou, as exhibited in Denon's Egypt.' The four great columns rose three stories, and their entablature constituted a fourth story. Above this rose a rotunda twenty-four feet in height to its curvilinear roof, and this in turn to be topped by a large Turkish crescent!"—from Donald Smalley, in editor's introduction to Frances Trollope, *Domestic Manners of the Americans* (New York: Alfred A. Knopf; 1949), p. xli.

The interior of this eclectic building was in keeping with the exterior. Mrs. Trollope had come to Cincinnati hoping to recoup her fortunes in business, but her general inexperience, her folly in building the elaborate bazaar, and her inadequate merchandise led to failure. Her effects were taken by the sheriff to satisfy her creditors. The bazaar remained a problem to the local citizens of Cincinnati, for this great white elephant was hopelessly unprofitable; it was to be used for everything from a Presbyterian church to a military hospital.

posing manner: it is composed of many varieties of architecture; but I think the order under which it must be classed is the preposterous. They call it Trollope's folly; and it is remarkable how a shrewd woman like Mrs. Trollope [2] should have committed such an error. A bazaar like an English bazaar is only to be supported in a city which has arrived at the acme of luxury: where there are hundreds of people willing to be employed for a trifle; hundreds who will work at trifles, for want of better employment; and thousands who will spend money on trifles, merely to pass away their time. Now, in America, in the first place, there is no one who makes trifles; no one who will devote their time, as sellers of the articles, unless well compensated; and no one who will be induced, either by fashion or idleness, to give a halfpenny more for a thing than it is worth. In consequence, nothing was sent to Mrs. Trollope's bazaar. She had to furnish it from the shops and had to pay very high salaries to the young women who attended; and the people of Cincinnati, aware that the same articles were to be purchased at the stores for less money, preferred going to the stores. No wonder then that it was a failure; it is now used as a dancing academy and occasionally as an assembly-room.

Whatever the society of Cincinnati may have been at the time that Mrs. Trollope resided there,[3] I cannot pretend to say; probably some change may have taken place in it; but

---

[2] Frances Trollope (1780–1863), English novelist and mother of Anthony Trollope, emigrated to America after her husband had suffered financial reverses. She went to Cincinnati and opened a department store or bazaar, but it was not a success and she decided to return to England. Pressed for money, she undertook to recount her life in the United States, and her *Domestic Manners of the Americans* appeared in England in 1832. It was a huge success with the British, for its author was outrageously frank and opinionated; the book told many home-truths and was recognized as giving a clearer picture of life in the United States than most other similar works. Mrs. Trollope continued to write and gained some contemporary fame as a novelist.

[3] For an account of Mrs. Trollope's experiences in Cincinnati, the best source is her own book. See her *Domestic Manners of the Americans.*

at present it is as good as any in the Union, and infinitely more agreeable than in some other cities, as in it there is a mixture of the southern frankness of character. A lady, who had long resided at Cincinnati, told me that they were not angry with Mrs. Trollope for having described the society which she saw, but for having asserted that that was the best society; and she further remarked— "It is fair to us that it should be understood that when Mrs. Trollope came here, she was quite unknown, except inasmuch as that she was a married woman, travelling without her husband. In a small society, as ours was, it was not surprising, therefore, that we should be cautious about receiving a lady who, in our opinion, was offending against *les bienseances*. Observe, *we do not accuse Mrs. Trollope of any impropriety;* but you must be aware how necessary it is, in this country, to be regardful of appearances, and how afraid everyone is of their neighbor. Mrs. Trollope then took a cottage on the hill, and used to come down to the city to market, and attend to the erection of her bazaar. I have now told you all that we know about her, and the reason why she did not receive those attentions, the omission of which caused her indignation." I think it but fair that the lady's explanation should be given, as Mrs. Trollope is considered to have been very severe and very unjust by the inhabitants of Cincinnati.

The fact is that Mrs. Trollope's representation of the manners and custom of Cincinnati, at the period when she wrote, was probably more correct than the present inhabitants of the city will allow. That it would be a libel upon the Cincinnatians of the present day is certain; whether it was one at the time she wrote, and the city was, comparatively speaking, in its infancy, is quite another affair. However, one thing is certain, which is that the Americans have quite forgiven Mrs. Trollope, and if she were again to cross the water, I think she would be well received. Her book made them laugh, though at their own expense; and the Americans, although appearances are certainly very much against it, are really, at the bottom, a very good-tempered people.

The heat has been this year very remarkable all over the western country, and the drought equally uncommon, the thermometer standing from 100° to 106°, in the shade, everywhere from St. Peters to New Orleans. It is very dangerous to drink iced water, and many have died from yielding to the temptation. One young man came into the bar of the hotel where I resided, drank a glass of water, and fell down dead at the porch. This reminds me of an ingenious plan put in practice by a fellow who had drunk every cent out of his pocket and was as thirsty as ever. The best remedy, in case of a person being taken ill from drinking cold water, is to pour brandy down his throat immediately. Aware of this, the fellow used to go to one of the pumps, pump away, and pretend to drink water in large quantities; he would then fall down by the pump, as if he had been taken suddenly ill; out would run people from every house, with brandy, and pour it down his throat till even he had had enough; he would then pretend gradually to recover, thank them for their kindness, and walk away. When he required another dose, he would perform the same farce at another pûmp; and this he continued to do for some time, before his trick was discovered.

I had two good specimens of democracy during my stay in this city. I sent for a tailor to take my measure for a coat, and he returned, for answer, that such a proceeding was not *republican,* and that I must *go to him.*

A young lady, with whom I was acquainted, was married during the time I was there, and the marriage-party went a short tour. On their return, when but a few miles from the city, they ordered the driver of the carriage to put his horses to, that they might proceed; he replied that he would take them no further. On inquiring the cause of his refusal, he said that he had not been treated as a gentleman; that they had had private meals every day and had not asked him to the table; that they had used him very ill and that he would drive no more. Things appear to be fast verging to the year 1920, or thereabouts, as described by

Theodore Hook.[4] A duchess wishing for a drive, the old mare sends an answer from the stable that "She'll be d——d if she'll go out today."

Left Cincinnati, in a very small steamboat, for Guyandotte, on my way to the Virginia Springs. I have often heard the expression of "Hell afloat" applied to very uncomfortable ships in the service, but this metaphor ought to have been reserved for a small high-pressure steamboat in the summer months in America; the sun darting his fierce rays down upon the roof above you, which is only half-inch plank, and rendering it so hot that you quickly remove your hand if, by chance, you put it there; the deck beneath your feet so heated by the furnaces below that you cannot walk with slippers; you are panting and exhausted between these two fires, without a breath of air to cool your forehead. Go forward, and the chimneys radiate a heat which is even more intolerable. Go—but there is nowhere to go, except overboard, and then you lose your passage. It is, really, a fiery furnace, and, day or night, it is in vain to seek a cool retreat. As we proceeded up the river, things became worse. We had not proceeded more than twenty miles when a larger steamboat, which had started an hour before us, was discovered aground on a bar, which, from the low state of the river, she could not pass. After a parley between the captains, we went alongside and took out all her passengers, amounting to upwards of a hundred, being more than we were on board of our own vessel. But they behaved like pirates and treated us just as if we had been a captured

---

[4] Theodore Edward Hook (1788–1841), humorist, wit, and practical joker, was a popular figure in London society. In 1813 he was appointed to a post in the government of Mauritius, but his incompetence was such that large sums of money were totally unaccounted for. In 1820 he became the editor of *John Bull* and was a violent critic of Queen Caroline and her supporters. From 1822 to 1825 he was imprisoned for debt arising from his losses in Mauritius. He published a number of novels, among them *Maxwell* (1830) and *Gilbert Gurney* (1836), and was for the five years prior to his death editor of *The New Monthly Magazine*.

vessel. Dinner was just ready; they sat down and took possession of it, leaving us to wait till the table was replenished. A young Englishman had just taken his seat by me when a very queer-looking man came up to him and begged that he would give up his place to a *lady.* Aware of the custom of the country, he immediately resigned his seat and went to look for another. When the lady took her seat by me, I involuntarily drew my chair to a more respectful distance, there being something so particularly uninviting in her ladyship's appearance. On our arrival at Maysville, this lady, with her gentleman, told the captain that they were sorry they had not a cent wherewith to defray the expenses of their passage. Their luggage had been landed before this declaration was made, but it was immediately ordered on board again by the captain; and as, of course, they would not part with their goods and chattels, they remained on board of the boat. The captain took them up the river about twenty miles further, and then landed them on the bank, with their luggage, to find their way back to Maysville how they could. This is the usual punishment for such malpractices; but, after all, it is only the punishment of delay, as they would hail the first boat which came down the river, make out a piteous tale of ill-treatment, be received on board, and landed at their destination. . . .

The Ohio River becomes much more rapid as you ascend. Abreast of Guyandotte, where we landed, the current was so strong that it was very difficult for men to wade across it, and the steamboats running against the stream could not gain more than a mile in the course of half an hour.

On board of this steamboat was a Negro woman, very neatly dressed, with a very good-looking Negro child, about nine months old, in her arms. It was of the darkest ebony in color, and its dress rather surprised me. It was a challis frock, of a neat fawn-colored pattern, with fine muslin trousers edged with Valenciennes lace at the bottom; and very pretty did its little tiny black feet look, relieved by these expensive *un*necessaries. I did not inquire who the young gentleman was; but I thought what pleasure the sight of him would have given Miss Martineau, who, as I have before observed, exclaims: "Happy is the country where factory-girls carry parasols, and pig-drivers wear spectacles." How much more happy must be that country where a little black boy, of nine months old, wears Valenciennes lace at the bottom of his trousers! It is, however, a question of figures, and may be solved, not by the rule of three, but by the rule of five, which follows it in the arithmetic-book.

If a pig-driver   : produces so much :: a little black boy
with spectacles   happiness,   Valenciennes lace.

I leave Miss Martineau to make the calculation.

CHAPTER XXX

The Greenbriar Country— The Virginia Springs

There is extreme beauty in the Ohio River. As may be supposed, where the rise and fall are so great the banks are very steep; and, now that the water is low, it appears deeply embedded in the wild forest scenery through which it flows. The whole stream is alive with small fresh-water turtle, who play on the surface of its clear water; while the most beautiful varieties of the butterfly tribe cross over from one side to the other, from the slave states to the free —their liberty, at all events, not being interfered with as, on the free side, it would be thought absurd to catch what would not produce a cent, while, on the slaves', their idleness and their indifference to them are their security.

Set off, one of nine, in a stagecoach, for the Blue Sulphur Springs. The country, which is very picturesque, has been already described. It is one continuation of rising ground, through mountains covered with trees and verdure. Nature is excessively fond of drapery in America: I have never yet fallen in with a naked rock. She clothes everything; and although you may occasionally meet with a slight nudity, it is no more than the exposure of the neck or the

230

bare feet of the mountain-nymph. This ridge of the Alleghenies is very steep; but you have no distinct view as you climb up, not even at the Hawk's Nest, where you merely peep down into the ravine below. You are jammed up in the forests through which you pass nearly the whole of the way; and it was delightful to arrive at any level and fall in with the houses and well-tilled fields of the Virginia farmers, exhibiting every proof of prosperity and ease. The heat was dreadful; two horses fell dead, and I thought that many others would have died, for two of the wheels were defective, and the labor of the poor animals, in dragging us constantly up hill, was most severe.

The indifference of the proprietors of public conveyances in America as to the safety of their passengers can only be accounted for by the extreme indifference of the passengers themselves, and the independent feeling shewn by every class, who, whatever may be their profession, will never acknowledge themselves to be what we term the servants of the public. Here was an instance. The coach we were put into was defective in two of its wheels and could only be repaired at Louisburg, about a hundred miles distant. Instead of sending it on to that town empty, as would have been done by our coach proprietors, and providing another (as they had plenty) for the passengers—instead of this, in order to save the extra trouble and expense, they risked the lives of the passengers on a road with a precipice on one side of it for at least four fifths of the way. One of the wheels would not hold the grease, and we were obliged to stop and pour water on it continually. The box and irons of the other were loose, and before we were half-way it came off, and we were obliged to stop and get out. But the Americans are never at a loss, when they are in a *fix*. The passengers borrowed an axe; in a short time wedges were cut from one of the trees at the roadside, and the wheel was so well repaired that it lasted us the remainder of our journey.

Our road for some time lay through the valley of Kanawha, through which runs the river of that name—a

strong, clear stream. It is hemmed in by mountains on each
side of it; and here, perhaps, is presented the most curious
varieties of mineral produce that ever were combined in one
locality. The river runs over a bed of horizontal calcareous
strata, and by perforating this strata about forty or fifty feet
below the level of the river, you arrive at salt-springs, the
waters of which are pumped up by small steam-engines
and boiled down into salt in buildings erected on the river's
banks. The mountains which hem in the river are one mass
of coal; a gallery is opened at that part of the foot of the
mountain most convenient to the buildings, and the coal is
thrown down by shoots or small railways. Here you have coal
for your fuel; salt water under fresh; and as soon as the
salt is put into the barrels (which are also made from the
mountain timber), the river is all ready to transplant them
down to Ohio. But there is another great curiosity in this
valley: these beds of coal have produced springs, as they
are termed, of carburetted hydrogen gas, which run along
the banks of the river close to the water's edge. The Negroes
take advantage of these springs when they come down at
night to wash clothes; they set fire to the springs, which
yield them sufficient light for their work. The one which I
examined was dry, and the gas bubbled up through the
sand. By kicking the sand about, so as to make communications after I had lighted the gas, I obtained a very large
flame, which I left burning.

The heat, as we ascended, was excessive, and the passengers availed themselves of every spring, with the exception of those just described, that they fell in with on the
route. We drank of every variety of water excepting pure
water—sometimes iron, sometimes sulphur; and, indeed,
every kind of chalybeate, for every rill was impregnated in
some way or another. At last it occurred to me that there
were such things as chemical affinities, and that there was
no saying what changes might take place by the admixture
of such a variety of metals and gasses, so drank no more. I
did not like, however, to interfere with the happiness of

others, so I did not communicate my ideas to my fellow-passengers, who continued drinking during the whole day and, as I afterwards found out, did not sleep very well that night; they were, moreover, very sparing in the use of them the next day.

There are a great variety of springs already discovered on these mountains, and probably there will be a great many more. Already they have the blue, the white, and the red sulphur springs; the sweet and the salt; the warm and the hot, all of which have their several virtues; but the greatest virtue of all these mineral springs is, as in England and everywhere else, that they occasion people to live regularly, to be moderate in the use of wine, and to dwell in a pure and wholesome air. They always remind me of the eastern story of the Dervise, who, being sent for by a king who had injured his health by continual indulgence, gave him a racket-ball, which he informed the king possessed wonderful medicinal virtues; with this ball his majesty was ·to play at racket two or three hours every day with his courtiers. The exercise it induced, which was the only medicinal virtue the ball possessed, restored the king to health. So it is with all watering places; it is not so much the use of the water as the abstinence from what is pernicious, together with exercise and early hours, which effect the majority of cures.

We arrived first at the Blue Sulphur Springs, and I remained there for one day to get rid of the dust of travelling. They have a very excellent hotel there, with a ball-room, which is open till eleven o'clock every night; the scenery is very pretty, and the company was good—as, indeed, is the company at all these springs, for they are too distant and the travelling too expensive for everybody to get there. But the Blue Sulphur are not fashionable, and the consequence was, we were not crowded and were very comfortable. People who cannot get accommodated at the White Sulphur remain here until they can, the distance between those being only twenty-two miles.

The only springs which are fashionable are the White Sulphur, and as these springs are a feature in American society, I shall describe them more particularly.

They are situated in a small valley, many hundred feet above the level of the sea, and are of about fifteen or twenty acres in area, surrounded by small hills, covered with foliage to their summits; at one end of the valley is the hotel, with the large dining-room for all the visitors. Close to the hotel, but in another building, is the ball-room, and a little below the hotel on the other side is the spring itself; but beautiful as is the whole scenery, the great charm of this watering place is the way in which those live who visit it. The rises of the hills which surround the valley are covered with little cottages, log-houses, and other picturesque buildings, sometimes in rows, and ornamented with verandahs, without a second storey above or kitchen below. Some are very elegant and more commodious than the rest, having been built by gentlemen who have the right given to them by the company to whom the springs belong of occupying themselves when there, but not of preventing others from taking possession of them in their absence. The dinners and other meals are, generally speaking, bad, not that there is not a plentiful supply, but that it is so difficult to supply seven hundred people sitting down in one room. In the morning they all turn out from their little burrows, meet in the public walks, and go down to the spring before breakfast; during the forenoon, when it is too warm, they remain at home; after dinner they ride out or day-visit, and then end the day either at the ball-room or in little societies among one another. There is no want of handsome equipages, many four in hand (Virginny long-tails), and every accommodation for these equipages. The crowd is very great, and it is astonishing what inconvenience people will submit to rather than not be accommodated somehow or another. Every cabin is like a rabbit burrow. In the one next to where I was lodged, in a room about fourteen feet square and partitioned off as well as it could be, there slept a gentleman and his wife, his sister and brother, and a female servant. I am not sure that the nigger was not under the bed—at all events, the young sister told me that it was not at all pleasant.

There is a sort of major-domo [1] here who regulates every department: his word is law and his fiat immovable, and he presumes not a little upon his power—a circumstance not to be surprised at, as he is as much courted and is as despotic as all the lady patronesses of Almacks [2] rolled into one. He is called the Metternich [3] of the mountains. No one is allowed accommodation at these springs who is not known and, generally speaking, only those families who travel in their private carriages. It is at this place that you feel how excessively aristocratical and exclusive the Americans would be, and indeed will be, in spite of their institutions. Spa, in its palmiest days, when princes had to sleep in their carriages at the doors of the hotels, was not more in vogue than are these White Sulphur Springs with the *élite* of the United States. And it is here, and here only, in the states, that you do meet with what may be fairly considered as select society, for at Washington there is a great mixture. Of course, all the celebrated belles of the different states are to be met with here, as well as all the large fortunes, nor is there a scarcity of pretty and wealthy widows. The President, Mrs. Caton, the mother of Lady Wellesley, Lady Strafford, and Lady Caermarthen, the daughter of Carrol, of Car-

---

[1] The major-domo was Major Baylin Anderson.

[2] Almacks, a club with assembly rooms, was founded in 1764 by a Scotchman named McCall. The name Almack is an anagram on his name. Initially Almacks was in Pall Mall, but in 1765 it was moved to King Street, St. James's in London. Balls of great exclusiveness were held here under the patronage of the leading ladies of society. Possession of tickets to these balls by various individuals was taken to mean that they had definitely arrived in society. In 1781 Almacks became the property of Mrs. Willis, the neice of McCall, and the club remained in operation until 1890, being very often referred to as Willis's Room through much of the last century.

[3] This is a reference to Prince Metternich (1773–1859), the Austrian Chancellor, who was the dominant political figure in Europe from 1815 to 1848. Apparently Baylin Anderson behaved as despotically in White Sulphur Springs as Metternich supposedly did in Europe.

roltown, one of the real aristocracy of America and a signer of the Declaration of Independence, and all the first old Virginian and Carolina families, many of them descendants of the old cavaliers, were at the springs when I arrived there; and I certainly must say that I never was at any watering-place in England where the company was so good and so select as at the Virginia springs in America.

I passed many pleasant days at this beautiful spot, and was almost as unwilling to leave it as I was to part with the Sioux Indians at St. Peters. Refinement and simplicity are equally charming. I was introduced to a very beautiful girl here, whom I should not have mentioned so particularly had it not been that she was the first and only lady in America that I observed to *whittle.* She was sitting one fine morning on a wooden bench, surrounded by admirers, and as she carved away her seat with her pen-knife, so did she cut deep into the hearts of those who listened to her lively conversation.

There are, as may be supposed, a large number of Negro servants here attending their masters and mistresses. I have often been amused, not only here, but during my residence in Kentucky, at the high-sounding Christian names which have been given to them. "Byron, tell Ada to come here directly." "Now, *Telemachus,* if you can't leave *Calypso* alone, you'll get a taste of the *cow-hide.*"

Among others, attracted to the springs professionally, was a very clever German painter, who, like all Germans, had a very correct ear for music. He had painted a kitchen-dance in Old Virginia, and in the picture he had introduced all the well-known colored people in the place; among the rest were the band of musicians, but I observed that one man was missing. "Why did you not put him in?" inquired I. "Why, sir, I could not put him in; it was impossible; he never *plays in tune.* Why, if I put him in, sir, he would spoil the *harmony* of my whole picture!"

I asked this artist how he got on in America. He replied: "But so-so; the Americans in general do not estimate genius. They come to me and ask what I want for my pictures, and I tell them. Then they say: 'How long did it take you to paint it?' I answer: 'So many days.' Well, then they calculate and say: 'If it took you only so many days, you ask so many dollars a day for your work; you ask a great deal too much; you ought to be content with so much per day, and I will give you that.' So that, thought I, invention and years of study go for nothing with these people. There is only one way to dispose of a picture in America, and that is, to raffle it; the Americans will then run the chance of getting it. If you do not like to part with your pictures in that way, you must paint portraits; people will purchase their own faces all over the world; the worst of it is that, in this country, they will purchase nothing else."

During my stay here, I was told of one of the most remarkable instances that perhaps ever occurred, of the discovery of a fact by the party from whom it was of the utmost importance to conceal it—a very pretty interesting young widow. She had married a promising young man, to whom she was tenderly attached, and who, a few months after the marriage, unfortunately fell in a duel. Aware that the knowledge of the cause of her husband's death would render the blow still more severe to her (the ball having passed through the eye into his brain, and there being no evident gun-shot wound), her relations informed her that he had been thrown from his horse and killed by the fall. She believed them. She was living in the country when, about nine months after her widowhood, her brother rode down to see her, and as soon as he arrived went into his room to shave and dress. The window of his room, which was on the ground-floor, looked out upon the garden, and it being summer time, it was open. He tore off a portion of an old newspaper to wipe his razor. The breeze caught it and carried it away into the garden until it stopped at the feet of his sister, who happened to be walking. Mechanically she took up the fragment, and perceiving her husband's name upon it, she read it. It contained a full account of the duel in which he lost his life! The shock she received was so great that it unsettled her mind for nearly two years. She had but just recovered, and for the first time reappeared in public, when she was pointed out to me.

Returning to Guyandotte, one of the travellers wished to see the view from the Hawk's Nest, or rather wished to be able to say that he had seen it. We passed the spot when it was quite dark, but he persisted in going there, and, to help his vision, borrowed one of the coach-lamps from the driver. He returned, and declared that with the assistance of the lamp he had had a very excellent view, down a precipice of several hundred feet. His bird's-eye view by candle-light must have been very extensive. After all, it is but to be able to say that they had been to such a place, or have seen such a thing, that, more than any real taste for it, induces the majority of the world to incur the trouble and fatigue of travelling.

CHAPTER XXXI

Camp Meeting Near Cincinnati

I was informed that a camp-meeting [1] was to be held about seven miles from Cincinnati, and, anxious to verify the accounts I had heard of them, I availed myself of this opportunity of deciding for myself. We proceeded about five miles on the high road, and then diverged by a cross-road until we arrived at a steep conical hill, crowned with splendid forest trees without underwood, the trees being sufficiently apart to admit of wagons and other vehicles to pass in every direction. The camp was raised upon the summit of this hill, a piece of table-land comprising many acres. About an acre and a half was surrounded on the four sides by cabins built up of rough boards; the whole area in the centre was fitted up with planks, laid about a foot from the ground, as seats. At one end, but not close to the cabins, was a raised stand, which served as a pulpit for the preachers, one of them praying, while five or six others sat down

---

[1] Camp meetings were very much part of frontier life. For an account of them, see R. Carlyle Buley, *The Old Northwest* (Bloomington, Ind.: Indiana University Press; 1951), Vol. II, pp. 454–60; Harvey Wish, *Society and Thought in Early America* (New York: Longmans, Green; 1950), pp. 248–50; Alexis de Tocqueville, *Democracy in America* (New York: Vintage Books; 1954), Vol. II, p. 142; Frances Trollope, *Domestic Manners of the Americans*, pp. 167–75.

behind him on benches. There was ingress to the area by the four corners; the whole of it was shaded by vast forest trees, which ran up to the height of fifty or sixty feet without throwing out a branch; and to the trunks of these trees were fixed lamps in every direction, for the continuance of service by night. Outside the area, which may be designated as the church, were hundreds of tents pitched in every quarter, their snowy whiteness contrasting beautifully with the deep verdure and gloom of the forest. These were the temporary habitations of those who had come many miles to attend the meeting, and who remained there from the commencement until it concluded—usually a period of from ten to twelve days, but often much longer. The tents were furnished with every article necessary for cooking; mattresses to sleep upon, etc.; some of them even had bedsteads and chests of drawers, which had been brought in the wagons in which the people in this country usually travel. At a farther distance were all the wagons and other vehicles which had conveyed the people to the meeting, whilst hundreds of horses were tethered under the trees and plentifully provided with forage. Such were the general outlines of a most interesting and beautiful scene.

Where, indeed, could so magnificent a temple to the Lord be raised as on this lofty hill, crowned as it was with such majestic verdure? Compared with these giants of the forest, the cabins and tents of the multitude appeared as insignificant and contemptible as almost would man himself in the presence of the Deity. Many generations of men must have been mowed down before the arrival of these enormous trees to their present state of maturity; and at the time they sent forth their first shoots, probably were not on the whole of this continent, now teeming with millions, as many white men as are now assembled on this field. I walked about for some time surveying the panorama, when I returned to the area and took my seat upon a bench. In one quarter the coloured population had collected themselves; their tents appeared to be better furnished and better supplied with comforts than most of those belonging to the

whites. I put my head into one of the tents and discovered a
sable damsel lying on a bed and singing hymns in a loud
voice.

The major portion of those not in the area were cooking the dinners. Fires were burning in every direction: pots
boiling, chickens roasting, hams seething; indeed, there appeared to be no want of creature comforts.

But the trumpet sounded, as in days of yore, as a signal that the service was about to recommence, and I went
into the area and took my seat. One of the preachers rose
and gave out a hymn, which was sung by the congregation,
amounting to about seven or eight hundred. After the singing of the hymn was concluded he commenced an ex-
tempore sermon: it was good, sound doctrine, although
Methodism of the mildest tone, and divested of its bitterness of denunciation, as indeed is generally the case with
Methodism in America. I heard nothing which could be offensive to any other sect, or which could be considered
objectionable by the most orthodox, and I began to doubt
whether such scenes as had been described to me did really
take place at these meetings. A prayer followed, and after
about two hours the congregation were dismissed to their
dinners, being first informed that the service would recommence at two o'clock at the sound of the trumpet. In front
of the pulpit there was a space railed off, and strewed with
straw, which I was told was the *anxious seat* and on which
sat those who were touched by their consciences or the dis-
course of the preacher; but, although there were several
sitting on it, I did not perceive any emotion on the part of
the occupants: they were attentive, but nothing more.

When I first examined the area, I saw a very large tent
at one corner of it, probably fifty feet long by twenty wide.
It was open at the end, and, being full of straw, I concluded
it was used as a sleeping-place for those who had not provided themselves with separate accommodation. About an
hour after the service was over, perceiving many people
directing their steps towards it, I followed them. On one side
of the tent were about twenty females, mostly young,

squatted down on the straw; on the other a few men; in
the centre was a long form, against which were some other
men kneeling, with their faces covered with their hands,
as if occupied in prayer. Gradually the numbers increased,
girl after girl dropped down upon the straw on the one side
and men on the other. At last an elderly man gave out a
hymn, which was sung with peculiar energy; then another
knelt down in the centre and commenced a prayer, shutting
his eyes (as I observed most clergymen in the United States
do when they pray) and raising his hands above his head;
then another burst out into a prayer, and another followed
him; then their voices became all confused together; and
then were heard the more silvery tones of woman's supplica-
tion. As the din increased so did their enthusiasm; handker-
chiefs were raised to bright eyes, and sobs were intermingled with prayers and ejaculations. It became a scene of
Babel; more than twenty men and women were crying out at
the highest pitch of their voices and trying apparently to be
heard above the others. Every minute the excitement increased; some wrung their hands and called for mercy;
some tore their hair; boys laid down crying bitterly, with
their heads buried in the straw; there was sobbing almost
to suffocation, and hysterics and deep agony. One young
man clung to the form, crying: "Satan tears at me, but I
would hold fast. Help—help, he drags me down!" It was
a scene of horrible agony and despair; and, when it was at
its height, one of the preachers came in, and raising his
voice high above the tumult, intreated the Lord to receive
into his fold those who now repented and would fain return. Another of the ministers knelt down by some young
men, whose faces were covered up and who appeared to be
almost in a state of frenzy; and putting his hands upon
them, poured forth an energetic prayer, well calculated to
work upon their over-excited feelings. Groans, ejaculations,
broken sobs, frantic motions, and convulsions succeeded;
some fell on their backs with their eyes closed, waving their
hands with a slow motion and crying out— "Glory, glory,
glory!" I quitted the spot and hastened away into the forest,

for the sight was too painful, too melancholy. Its sincerity could not be doubted, but it was the effect of over-excitement, not of sober reasoning. Could such violence of feeling have been produced had each party retired to commune alone?—most surely not. It was a fever created by collision and contact, of the same nature as that which stimulates a mob to deeds of blood and horror.

Gregarious animals are by nature inoffensive. The cruel and the savage live apart and in solitude; but the gregarious, upheld and stimulated by each other, become formidable. So it is with man.

I was told that the scene would be much more interesting and exciting after the lamps were lighted; but I had seen quite enough of it. It was too serious to laugh at, and I felt that it was not for me to condemn. "Cry aloud, and spare not" was the exhortation of the preacher; and certainly, if heaven was only to be taken by storm, he was a proper leader for his congregation.

Whatever may be the opinion of the reader as to the meeting which I have described, it is certain that nothing could be more laudable than the intention by which these meetings were originated. At the first settling of the country the people were widely scattered, and the truths of the Gospel, owing to the scarcity of preachers, but seldom heard. It was to remedy this unavoidable evil that they agreed, like the Christians in earlier times, to collect together from all quarters and pass many days in meditation and prayer, "exhorting one another—comforting one another." Even now it is not uncommon for the settlers in Indiana and Illinois to travel one hundred miles in their wagons to attend one of these meetings—meetings which are now too often sullied by fanaticism on the one hand and, on the other, by the levity and infidelity of those who go not to pray, but to scoff; or to indulge in the licentiousness which, it is said, but too often follows, when night has thrown her veil over the scene.

CHAPTER XXXII

Lexington

Lexington, the capital of the state, is embosomed in the very heart of the vale of Kentucky. This vale was the favorite hunting-ground of the Indians; and a fairer country for the chase could not well be imagined than this rolling, well-wooded, luxuriant valley, extending from hill to hill, from dale to dale, for so many long miles. No wonder that the Indians fought so hard to retain, or the Virginians to acquire it; nor was it until much blood had saturated the ground, many reeking scalps had been torn from the head, and many a mother and her children murdered at their hearths that the contest was relinquished. So severe were the struggles that the ground obtained the name of the "Bloody Ground." But the strife is over; the red man has been exterminated, and peace and plenty now reign over this smiling country. It is indeed a beautiful and bounteous land; on the whole, the most eligible in the Union. The valley is seven hundred and fifty feet above the level of the sea and, therefore, not so subject to fevers as the states of Indiana and Illinois and indeed that portion of its own state which borders on the Mississippi. But all the rest of the Kentucky land is by no means equal in richness of soil to that of this valley. There are about ninety counties in the state, of which about thirty are of rich land; but four of them, namely, Fayette, Bourbon, Scotts, and Woodford, are the finest. The whole of these four counties are held by large proprietors, who graze and breed stock to a very great extent, supplying the whole of the western states with the best description of every kind of cattle. Cattle-shows are held every year, and high prizes awarded to the owners of the finest beasts which are there produced. The state of Kentucky, as well as Virginia, is in fact an agricultural and grazing state; the pasture is very rich, and studded with oak and other timber, as in the manner I have described in Ioway and Wisconsin. The staples of Kentucky are hemp and mules; the latter are in such demand for the south that they can hardly produce them fast enough for the market. The minimum price of a three-year-old mule is about eighty dollars; the maximum usually one hundred and sixty dollars, or thirty-five pounds, but they often fetch much higher prices. I saw a pair in harness, well matched and about seventeen hands high, for which they refused one thousand dollars—upwards of two hundred pounds.

The cattle-show took place when I was at Lexington. That of horned beasts I was too late for; but the second day I went to the exhibition of thoroughbred horses. The premiums were for the best two-year-olds, yearlings, and colts, and many of them were very fine animals. The third day was for the exhibition of mules, which, on account of size there being a great desideratum, are bred only from mares; the full-grown averaged from fifteen to sixteen hands high, but they have often been known to be seventeen hands high. I had seen them quite as large in a nobleman's carriage in the south of Spain; but then they were considered rare, and of great value. After all the other varieties of age had made their appearance, and the judges had given their decision, the mules foaled down this year were to be examined. As they were still sucking, it was necessary that the brood mares should be led into the enclosed paddock, where the animals were inspected, that the foals might be induced to follow; as soon as they were all in the enclosure the mares were sent out, leaving all the foals by themselves. At first they commenced a concert of wailing after their mothers and then turned their lamentations into indignation and revenge upon each other. Such a ridiculous scene of kicking took place as I never before witnessed, about thirty of them being most sedulously engaged in the occupation, all at the same time. I never saw such ill-behaved mules; it was quite impossible for the judges to decide upon the prize, for you could see nothing but heels in the air; it was rap, rap, rap, incessantly against one another's sides, until they were all turned out, and the show was over. I rather think the prize must, in this instance, have been awarded to the one that kicked highest.

The fourth day was for the exhibition of jackasses, of two-year and one-year, and for foals, and jennies also; this sight was to me one of peculiar interest. Accustomed as we are in England to value a jackass at thirty shillings, we look down upon them with contempt; but here the case is reversed: you look up at them with surprise and admiration. Several were shown standing fifteen hands high, with head and ears in proportion; the breed has been obtained from the Maltese jackass, crossed by those of Spain and the south of France. Those imported seldom average more than fourteen hands high; but the Kentuckians, by great attention and care, have raised them up to fifteen hands, and sometimes even to sixteen.

But the price paid for these splendid animals, for such they really were, will prove how much they are in request. Warrior, a jackass of great celebrity, sold for $5,000, upwards of £1,000 sterling. . . . I never felt such respect for donkeys before; but the fact is that mule-breeding is so lucrative, that there is no price which a very large donkey will not command.

I afterwards went to a cattle sale a few miles out of the town. Don Juan, a two-year old bull, Durham breed, fetched $1,075; an imported Durham cow, with her calf, $985. Before I arrived, a bull and cow fetched $1,300 each of them, about £280. The cause of this is that the demand for good stock, now that the western states are filling up, becomes so great that they cannot be produced fast enough. Mr. Clay, who resides near Lexington, is one of the best breeders in the state, which is much indebted to him for the fine stock which he has imported from England. . . .

It must be considered that, although a good Durham cow will not cost more than twenty guineas perhaps in England, the expenses of transport are very great, and they generally stand in, to the importers, about $600, before they arrive at the state of Kentucky. . . .

Lexington is a very pretty town, with very pleasant society, and afforded me great relief after the unpleasant sojourn I had had at Louisville. Conversing one day with Mr. Clay,[1] I had another instance given me of the mischief which the conduct of Miss Martineau has entailed upon all those English who may happen to visit America. Mr. Clay observed that Miss Martineau had remained with him for some time, and that during her stay, she had professed very different or at least more modified opinions on the subject of slavery than those she has expressed in her book—so much so, that one day, having read a letter from Boston cautioning her against being cajoled by the hospitality and pleasant society of the western states, she handed it to him, saying: "They want to make a regular abolitionist of me." "When her work came out," continued Mr. Clay, "although I read but very little of it, I turned to this subject so important with us, and I must say I was a little surprised to

---

[1] Henry Clay (1777–1852), American statesman from Kentucky, was a member of the House of Representatives and later of the Senate. Entering Congress in 1811, he was associated with the "War Hawks," who, through their advocacy, did much to bring on the War of 1812. At the end of the war he was one of the commissioners representing the United States when the Treaty of Ghent was signed. He was appointed Secretary of State in 1825 by John Quincy Adams, and Clay hoped ultimately to succeed Adams to the Presidency. In 1831 he returned to the Senate and remained there until his death. He was an active supporter of the "American System" of protective tariffs and internal improvements. Clay was also known as the "Great Compromiser" for his attempts to resolve the conflicts between the north and the south.

find that she had so changed her opinions." The fact is, Miss Martineau appears to have been what the Kentuckians call, "playing 'possum." I have met with some of the southern ladies whose conversations on slavery are said, or supposed, to have been those printed by Miss Martineau, and they deny that they are correct. That the southern ladies are very apt to express great horror at living too long a time at the plantations, is very certain; not, however, because they expect to be murdered in their beds by the slaves, as they tell their husbands, but because they are anxious to spend more of their time at the cities, where they can enjoy more luxury and amusement than can be procured at the plantations.

Everybody rides in Virginia and Kentucky, master, man, woman, and slave, and they all ride well; it is quite as common to meet a woman on horseback as a man, and it is a pretty sight in their states to walk by the church doors and see them all arrive. The churches have stables, or rather sheds, built close to them, for the accommodation of the cattle.

Elopments in these states are all made on horseback. The goal to be obtained is to cross to the other side of the Ohio. The consequence is that it is a regular steeple-chase, the young couple clearing everything, father and brothers following. Whether it is that, having the choice, the young people are the best mounted, I know not, but the runaways are seldom overtaken. One couple crossed the Ohio when I was at Cincinnati, and had just time to tie the noose before their pursuers arrived.

At Lexington, on Sunday, there is not a carriage or horse to be obtained by a white man for any consideration, they having all been regularly engaged for that day by the Negro slaves, who go out junketting in every direction. Where they get the money I do not know; but certain it is that it is always produced when required. I was waiting at the counter of a sort of pastry-cook's when three Negro lads, about twelve or fourteen years old, came in and, in a most authoritative tone, ordered three glasses of soda-water.

Returned to Louisville.

CHAPTER XXXIII

Envoi

There is one great inconvenience in American travelling, arising from the uncertainty of river navigation. Excepting the Lower Mississippi and the Hudson, and not always the latter, the communication by water is obstructed during a considerable portion of the year—by ice in the winter or a deficiency of water in the dry season. This has been a remarkable season for heat and drought; and thousands of people remain in the states of Ohio, Virginia, and Kentucky who are most anxious to return home. It must be understood that during the unhealthy season in the southern states on the Mississippi, the planters, cotton-growers, slave-holders, store-keepers, and indeed almost every class, excepting the slaves and overseers, migrate to the northward, to escape the yellow fever and spend a portion of their gains in amusement.

They go to Cincinnati and the towns of Ohio, to the Lakes occasionally, but principally to the cities and watering places of Virginia and Kentucky, more especially Louisville, where I now am; and Louisville, being also the sort of general rendezvous for departure south, is now crammed with southern people. The steamboats cannot run, for the river is almost dry; and I (as well as others) have been detained much longer on the banks of the Ohio than was my intention. There is land-carriage certainly, but the heat of the weather is so overpowering that even the southerns dread it; and in consequence of this extreme heat, the sickness in these western states has been much greater than usual. Even Kentucky, especially that part which borders on the Mississippi, which, generally speaking, is healthy, is now suffering under malignant fevers. I may here remark that the two states, Illinois and Indiana, and the western portions of Kentucky and Tennessee are very unhealthy; not a year passes without a great mortality from the bilious congestive fever, a variety of the yellow fever, and the ague—more especially Illinois and Indiana, with the western portion of Ohio, which is equally flat with the other two states. The two states of Indiana and Illinois lie, as it were, at the bottom of the western basin; the soil is wonderfully rich, but the drainage is insufficient, as may be seen from the sluggishness with which these rivers flow. Many and many thousands of poor Irish emigrants, and settlers also, have been struck down by disease, never to rise again, in these rich but unhealthy states, to which, stimulated by the works published by land-speculators, thousands and thousands every year repair and, notwithstanding the annual expenditure of life, rapidly increase the population. I had made up my mind to travel by land-carriage to St. Louis, Missouri, through the states of Indiana and Illinois, but two American gentlemen, who had just arrived by that route, succeeded in dissuading me. They had come over on horseback. They described the disease and mortality as dreadful —that sometimes, when they wished to put up their horses at seven or eight o'clock in the evening, they were compelled to travel on till twelve or one o'clock before they could gain admittance, some portion in every house suffering under the bilious fever, tertian ague, or flux. They described the scene as quite appalling. At some houses there was not one person able to rise and attend upon the others; all were dying or dead; and to increase the misery of their situations, the springs had dried up, and in many places they could not procure water except by sending many miles. A friend of mine, who had been on a mission through the portion of Kentucky and Tennessee bordering on the Mississippi, made a very similar statement. He was not refused to remain where he stopped, but he could procure no assistance, and everywhere ran the risk of contagion. He said that some of the people were obliged to send their Negroes with a wagon upwards of fifteen miles to wash their clothes.

That this has been a very unhealthy season is certain, but still, from all the information I could obtain, there is a great mortality every year in the districts I have pointed out; and such indeed must be the case, from the miasma created every fall of the year in these rich alluvial soils, some portions of which have been worked for fifty years without the assistance of manure, and still yield abundant crops. It will be a long while before the drainage necessary to render them healthy can be accomplished. The sickly appearance of the inhabitants establishes but too well the facts related to me; and yet, strange to say, it would appear to be a provision of Providence that a remarkable fecundity on the part of the women in the more healthy portions of their western states should meet the annual expenditure of life. Three children at a birth are more common here than twins are in England; and they, generally speaking, are all reared up. There have been many instances of even four.

The western valley of America, of which the Mississippi may be considered as the common drain, must, from the surprising depth of the alluvial soil, have been (ages back) wholly under water, and, perhaps, by some convulsion raised up. What insects are we in our own estimation when we meditate upon such stupendous changes.

Since I have been in these states, I have been surprised at the stream of emigration which appears to flow from North Carolina to Indiana, Illinois, and Missouri. Every hour you meet with a caravan of emigrants from that sterile but healthy state. Every night the banks of the Ohio are lighted up with their fires, where they bivouacked previously to crossing the river; but they are not like the poor

German or Irish settlers: they are well prepared and have nothing to do, apparently, but to sit down upon their land. These caravans consist of two or three covered wagons, full of women and children, furniture, and other necessaries, each drawn by a team of horses; brood mares, with foals by their sides, following; half a dozen or more cows, flanked on each side by the men, with their long rifles on their shoulders; sometimes a boy or two, or a half-grown girl on horseback. Occasionally they wear an appearance of more refinement and cultivation, as well as wealth, the principals travelling in a sort of worn-out old carriage, the remains of the competence of former days.

I often surmised, as they travelled cheerfully along, saluting me as they passed by, whether they would not repent their decision, and sigh for their pine barrens and heath, after they had discovered that with fertility they had to encounter such disease and mortality.

I have often heard it asserted by Englishmen that America has no coal. There never was a greater mistake: she has an abundance, and of the very finest that ever was seen. At Wheeling and Pittsburgh, and on all the borders of the Ohio River above Guyandotte, they have an inexhaustible supply, equal to the very best offered to the London market. All the spurs of the Allegheny range appear to be one mass of coal. In the eastern states the coal is of a different quality, although there is some very tolerable. The anthracite is bad, throwing out a strong sulphurous gas. The fact is that wood is at present cheaper than coal, and therefore the latter is not in demand. An American told me one day that a company had been working a coal mine in an eastern state, which proved to be of a very bad quality; they had sent some to an influential person as a present, requesting him to give his opinion of it, as that would be important to them. After a certain time he forwarded to them a certificate couched in such terms as these:

"I do hereby certify that I have tried the coal sent me by the company at ————, and it is my decided opinion, that when the general conflagration of the world shall take place, any man who will take his position on that *coal-mine* will certainly be the *last man* who will be *burnt*."

I had to travel by coach for six days and nights, to arrive at Baltimore. As it may be supposed, I was not a little tired before my journey was half over; I therefore was glad, when the coach stopped for a few hours, to throw off my coat and lie down on a bed. At one town, where I had stopped, I had been reposing more than two hours when my door was opened—but this was too common a circumstance for me to think anything of it; the people would come into my room whether I was in bed or out of bed, dressed or not dressed, and if I expostulated, they would reply: "Never mind, *we* don't care, Captain." On this occasion I called out: "Well, what do you want?"

"Are you Captain M——?" said the person walking up to the bed where I was lying.

"Yes, I am," replied I.

"Well, I reckon I wouldn't allow you to go through our town without seeing you anyhow. Of all the humans, you're the one I most wish to see."

I told him I was highly flattered.

"Well now," said he, giving a jump and coming down right upon the bed in his great coat, "I'll just tell you; I said to the chap at the bar: 'Ain't the Captain in your house?' 'Yes,' says he. 'Then where is he?' says I. 'Oh,' says he, 'he's gone into his own room, and locked himself up; he's a d——d aristocrat, and won't drink at the bar with other gentlemen.' So, thought I, I've read M——'s works, and I'll be swamped if he is an aristocrat, and by the 'tarnal I'll go up and see; so here I am, and you're no aristocrat."

"I should think not," replied I, moving my feet away, which he was half sitting on.

"Oh, don't move; never mind me, Captain, I'm quite comfortable. And how do you find yourself by this time?"

"Very tired indeed," replied I.

"I suspicion as much. Now, d'ye see, I left four or five good fellows down below who wish to see you; I said I'd go up first, and come down to them. The fact is, Captain, we

don't like you should pass through our town without showing you a little American hospitality."

So saying, he slid off the bed and went out of the room.
In a minute he returned, bringing with him four or five
others, all of whom he introduced by name, and reseated
himself on my bed, while the others took chairs.

"Now, gentlemen," said he, "as I was telling the Captain, we wish to show him a little American hospitality;
what shall it be, gentlemen; what d'ye say—a bottle of
Madeira?"

An immediate answer not being returned, he continued:

"Yes, gentlemen, a bottle of Madeira; at my expense,
gentlemen, recollect that; now ring the bell."

"I shall be most happy to take a glass of wine with
you," observed I, "but in my own room the wine must be at
my expense."

"At *your* expense, Captain; well, if it must be, I don't
care; at *your* expense then, Captain, if you say so; only,
you see, we must show you a little American hospitality, as
I said to them all down below; didn't I, gentlemen?"

The wine was ordered, and it ended in my hospitable
friends drinking three bottles; and then they all shook hands
with me, declaring how happy they should be if I came to
the town again, allowed them to show me a little more
American hospitality.

There was something so very ridiculous in this event
that I cannot help narrating it; but let it not be supposed,
for a moment, that I intend it as a sarcasm upon American hospitality in general. There certainly are conditions
usually attached to their hospitality, if you wish to profit by
it to any extent; and one is that you do not venture to find
fault with themselves, their manners, or their institutions.

Note.—That a guest, partaking of their hospitality,
should give his opinions unasked, and find fault, would be
in very bad taste, to say the least of it. But the fault in
America is that you are compelled to give an opinion, and

you cannot escape by a doubtful reply; as the American said to me in Philadelphia: "I wish a *categorical* answer." Thus, should you not agree with them, you are placed upon the horns of a dilemma: either you must affront the company or sacrifice truth.

PART TWO

Remarks on Its Institutions

CHAPTER XXXIV

Language

The Americans boldly assert that they speak better English than we do. . . . What I believe the Americans would imply by the above assertion is that you may travel through all the United States and find less difficulty in understanding or being understood than in some of the counties of England, such as Cornwall, Devonshire, Lancashire, and Suffolk. So far they are correct; but it is remarkable how very debased the language has become in a short period in America. There are few provincial dialects in England much less intelligible than the following. A Yankee girl, who wished to hire herself out, was asked if she had any followers or sweethearts. After a little hesitation, she replied: "Well, now, can't exactly say; I bees a sorter courted and a sorter not; reckon more a sorter yes than a sorter no." In many points the Americans have to a certain degree obtained that equality which they profess; and, as respects their language, it certainly is the case. If their lower classes are more intelligible than ours, it is equally true that the higher classes do not speak the language so purely or so classically as it is spoken among the well-educated English. The peculiar dialect of the English counties is kept up because we are a settled country; the people who are born in a county live in it, and die in it, transmit-

ting their sites of labour or of amusement to their descendants, generation after generation, without change; consequently, the provincialisms of the language become equally
hereditary. Now, in America, they have a dictionary containing many thousands of words, which, with us, are either
obsolete, or are provincialisms, or are words necessarily invented by the Americans. When the people of England emigrated to the states, they came from every county in England, and each county brought its provincialisms with it.
These were admitted into the general stock, and were since
all collected and bound up by one Mr. Webster. With the
exception of a few words coined for local uses (such as
snags and *sawyers,* on the Mississippi) I do not recollect a
word which I have not traced to be either a provincialism of
some English county or else to be obsolete English. There
are a few from the Dutch, such as *stoup,* for the porch of a
door, etc. I was once talking with an American about Webster's dictionary, and he observed: "Well now, sir, I understand it's the only one used in the Court of St. James, by the
king, queen, and princesses, and that by royal order."

The upper class of the Americans do not, however,
speak or pronounce English according to our standard; they
appear to have no exact rule to guide them, probably from
the want of any intimate knowledge of Greek or Latin. You
seldom hear a derivation from the Greek pronounced correctly, the accent being generally laid upon the wrong syl-
lable. In fact, everyone appears to be independent and
pronounces just as he pleases.

But it is not for me to decide the very momentous
question as to which nation speaks the best English. The
Americans generally improve upon the inventions of others;
probably they may have improved upon our language.

I recollect someone observing how very superior the
German language was to the English, from their possessing
so many compound substantives and adjectives; whereupon
his friend replied that it was just as easy for us to possess
them in England if we pleased, and gave as an example an
observation made by his old dame at Eton, who declared

that young Paulet was, without any exception, the most *good-for-nothingest,* the most *provoking-people-est,* and the most *poke-about-every-cornerest* boy she had ever had charge of in her life.

Assuming this principle of improvement to be correct, it must be acknowledged that the Americans have added considerably to our dictionary; but, as I have before observed, this being a point of too much delicacy for me to decide upon, I shall just submit to the reader the occasional variations, or improvements, as they may be, which met my ears during my residence in America, as also the idiomatic peculiarities, and having so done, I must leave him to decide for himself.

I recollect once talking with one of the first men in America, who was narrating to me the advantages which might have accrued to him if he had followed up a certain speculation, when he said: "Sir, if I had done so, I should not only have *doubled* and *trebled,* but I should have *fourbled* and *fivebled* my money."

One of the members of Congress once said: "What the honourable gentleman has just asserted I consider as *catamount* to a denial." (Catamount is the term given to a panther or lynx.)

"I presume," replied his opponent, "that the honourable gentleman means *tantamount.*"

"No, sir, I do not mean *tantamount;* I am not so ignorant of our language not to be aware that *cata*mount and *tant*amount are *an*onymous."

The Americans dwell upon their words when they speak—a custom arising, I presume, from their cautious, calculating habits; and they have always more or less of a nasal twang. I once said to a lady: "Why do you drawl out your words in that way?"

"Well," replied she, "I'd drawl all the way from Maine to Georgia rather than *clip* my words as you English people do."

Many English words are used in a very different sense from that which we attach to them, for instance: a *clever* person in America means an amiable, good-tempered person, and the Americans make the distinction by saying: "I mean English clever."

Our *clever* is represented by the word *smart*.

The verb *to admire* is also used in the east, instead of the verb *to like*.

"Have you ever been at Paris?"

"No, but I should *admire* to go."

A Yankee description of a clever woman:

"Well, now, she'll walk right into you, and talk to you like a book"; or, as I have heard them say: "She'll talk you out of sight."

The word *ugly* is used for cross, ill-tempered. "I did feel so *ugly* when he said that."

Bad is used in an odd sense: it is employed for awkward, uncomfortable, sorry:

"I did feel so *bad* when I read that"—awkward.

"I have felt quite *bad* about it ever since"—uncomfortable.

"She was so *bad*, I thought she would cry"—sorry.

And as *bad* is tantamount to *not good*, I have heard a lady say: "I don't feel *at all good* this morning."

Mean is occasionally used for ashamed.

"I never felt so *mean* in my life."

The word *handsome* is oddly used.

"We reckon this very *handsome* scenery, sir," said an American to me, pointing to the landscape.

"I consider him very truthful," is another expression.

"He stimulates too much."

"He dissipates awfully."

And they are very fond of using the noun as a verb, as—

"I *suspicion* that's a fact."

"I *opinion* quite the contrary."

The word *considerable* is in considerable demand in the United States. In a work in which the letters of the party had been given to the public as specimens of good style and polite literature, it is used as follows:

"My dear sister, I have taken up the pen early this morning, as I intend to write *considerable*."

The word *great* is oddly used for fine, splendid.

"She's the *greatest* gal in the whole Union."

But there is one word which we must surrender up to the Americans as their *very own*, as the children say. I will quote a passage from one of their papers:

"The editor of the *Philadelphia Gazette* is wrong in calling absquatiated a Kentucky *phrase* (he may well say phrase instead of *word*). It may prevail there, but its origin was in South Carolina, where it was a few years since regularly derived from the Latin, as we can prove from undoubted authority. By the way, there is a little *corruption* in the word as the *Gazette* uses it; *absquatalized* is the true reading."

Certainly a word worth quarrelling about!

"Are you cold, miss?" said I to a young lady, who pulled the shawl closer over her shoulders.

"*Some,*" was the reply.

The English *what?* implying that you did not hear what was said to you, is changed in America to the word *how?*

"I reckon," "I calculate," "I guess," are all used as the common English phrase, "I suppose." Each term is said to be peculiar to different states, but I found them used everywhere, one as often as the other. *I opine* is not so common.

A specimen of Yankee dialect and conversation:

"Well now, I'll tell you—you know Marble Head?"

"Guess I do."

"Well, then, you know Sally Hackett."

"No, indeed."

"Not know Sally Hackett? Why, she lives at Marble Head."

"Guess I don't."

"You don't mean to say that?"

"Yes, indeed."

"And you really don't know Sally Hackett?"

"No, indeed."

"I guess you've heard talk of her?"

"No, indeed."

"Well, that's considerable odd. Now, I'll tell you— Ephraim Bagg, he that has the farm three miles from Marble Head—just as—but now, are you sure you don't know Sally Hackett?"

"No, indeed."

"Well, he's a pretty substantial man, and no mistake. He has got a heart as big as an ox, and everything else in proportion, I've a notion. He loves Sal, the worst kind; and if she gets up there, she'll think she has got to Palestine (Paradise); aren't she a screamer? I were thinking of Sal myself, for I feel lonesome, and when I am thrown into my store promiscuous alone, I can tell you I have the blues, the worst kind, no mistake— I can tell you that. I always feel a kind o' queer when I sees Sal, but when I meet any of the other gals I am as calm and cool as the milky way," etc., etc.

The verb "to fix" is universal. It means to do anything.

"Shall I *fix* your coat or your breakfast first?" That is: "Shall I *brush* your coat or *get ready* your breakfast first?"

Right away, for immediately or at once, is very general.

"Shall I fix it *right away?*"—i.e., "Shall I do it immediately?"

In the west, when you stop at an inn, they say—

"What will you have? Brown meal and common doings, or white wheat and chicken *fixings?*"—that is, "Will you have pork and brown bread, or white bread and fried chicken?"

Also, "Will you have a *feed* or a *check?*"—A dinner or a luncheon?

In *full blast*—something in the extreme.

"When she came to meeting, with her yellow hat and feathers, wasn't she in *full blast?*" . . .

There are two syllables—*um, hu*—which are very generally used by the Americans as a sort of reply, intimating that they are attentive and that the party may proceed with his narrative; but, by inflection and intonation, these two syllables are made to express dissent or assent, surprise, disdain, and (like Lord Burleigh's nod in the play [1]) a great deal more. The reason why these two syllables have been selected is that they can be pronounced without the trouble of opening your mouth, and you may be in a state of listlessness and repose while others talk. I myself found them very convenient at times, and gradually got into the habit of using them.

The Americans are very local in their phrases, and borrow their similes very much from the nature of their occupations and pursuits. If you ask a Virginian or Kentuckian where he was born, he will invariably tell you that he was *raised* in such a county—the term applied to horses and, in breeding states, to men also.

When a man is tipsy (spirits being made from grain), they generally say he is *corned*.

In the west, where steam-navigation is so abundant, when they ask you to drink they say: "Stranger, will you take in wood?"—the vessels taking in wood as fuel to keep the steam up, and the person taking in spirits to keep *his* steam up.

The roads in the country being cut through woods, and the stumps of the trees left standing, the carriages are often brought up by them. Hence the expression of: "Well, I am *stumped* this time."

---

[1] Burleigh is a character in Richard Sheridan's play, *The Critic*. The exact reference is as follows:
(*Burleigh comes forward, shakes his head and exits.*)
SNEER: He is very perfect indeed. Now pray what did he mean by that?
PUFF: Why by the shake of the head, he gave you to understand that even though they had more justice in their cause and wisdom in their measures, yet if there was not a greater spirit shown on the part of the people, the country would at last fall a sacrifice to the hostile ambition of the Spanish monarchy.
SNEER: The devil!—did he mean all that by shaking his head?
PUFF: Every word of it. If he shook his head as I taught him.
The Critic, Act III, Scene 1.

I heard a young man, a farmer in Vermont, say, when talking about another having gained the heart of a pretty girl, "Well, how he contrived to *fork* into her young affections, I can't tell; but I've a mind *to put my whole team on,* and see if I can't run him off the road."

The old phrase of "straining at a gnat and swallowing a camel" is, in the eastern states, rendered "straining at a *gate,* and swallowing a *saw-mill.*"

To *strike* means to attack. "The Indians have struck on the frontier";—"A rattlesnake *struck* at me."

To *make tracks*—to walk away. "Well, now, I shall *make tracks*";—from foot-tracks in the snow.

Clear out, quit, and *put*—all mean "be off." "Captain, now, you *hush* or *put*"—that is, "Either hold your tongue or be off." Also, "Will you *shut,* mister?"—i.e., will you shut your mouth?—i.e., hold your tongue?

"Curl up"—to be angry—from the panther and other animals when angry raising their hair. "Rise my dandee up," from the human hair; and a nasty idea. "Wrathy" is another common expression. Also, "Savage as a meat-axe."

Here are two real American words:

"Sloping"—for slinking away.

"Splunging," like a porpoise.

The word "enthusiasm," in the south, is changed to "entuzzy-muzzy."

In the western states, where the racoon is plentiful, they use the abbreviation *'coon* when speaking of people. When at New York, I went into a hair-dresser's shop to have my hair cut; there were two young men from the west— one under the barber's hands, the other standing by him.

"I say," said the one who was having his hair cut, "I hear Captain M—— is in the country."

"Yes," replied the other, "so they say; I should like to see the *'coon.*"

"I'm a *gone 'coon*" implies "I am distressed—*or* ruined —*or* lost." I once asked the origin of this expression and was gravely told as follows:

"There is a Captain Martin Scott in the United States Army who is a remarkable shot with a rifle. He was raised, I believe, in Vermont. His fame was so considerable through the state that even the animals were aware of it. He went out one morning with his rifle, and spying a racoon upon the upper branches of a high tree, brought his gun up to his shoulder; when the racoon perceiving it, raised his paw for a parley. 'I beg your pardon, mister,' said the racoon, very politely, 'but may I ask you if your name is *Scott?* — 'Yes,' replied the captain.—'*Martin* Scott?' continued the racoon—'Yes,' replied the captain.—'*Captain* Martin Scott?' still ⌐ontinued the animal.—'Yes,' replied the captain, 'Captain Martin Scott.'—'Oh! then,' says the animal, 'I may just as well come down, for I'm a *gone 'coon.'* "

But one of the strangest perversions of the meaning of a word which I ever heard of is in Kentucky, where sometimes the word *nasty* is used for *nice.* For instance: at a rustic dance in that state a Kentuckian said to an acquaintance of mine, in reply to his asking the name of a very fine girl, "That's my sister, stranger; and I flatter myself that she shows the *nastiest* ankle in all Kentuck."—*Unde derivatur,* from the constant rifle-practice in that state, a good shot or a pretty shot is termed also a nasty shot, because it would make a *nasty* wound: *ergo,* a nice or pretty ankle becomes a *nasty* one.

The term for all baggage, especially in the south or west, is "plunder." This has been derived from the buccaneers, who for so long a time infested the bayous and creeks near the mouth of the Mississippi, and whose luggage was probably very correctly so designated.

I must not omit a specimen of American criticism.

"Well, Abel, what d'ye think of our native genus, Mister Forrest?"

"Well, I don't go much to theatricals, that's a fact; but I do think *he piled the agony up a little too high* in that last scene."

The gamblers on the Mississippi use a very refined

phrase for "cheating"—"playing the advantages over him."

But, as may be supposed, the principal terms used are those which are borrowed from trade and commerce.

The rest, or remainder, is usually termed the *balance.*

"Put some of those apples into a dish, and the *balance* into the store-room."

When a person has made a mistake, or is out in his calculation, they say: "You missed a figure that time."

In a skirmish in the last war, the fire from the British was very severe, and the men in the American ranks were falling fast, when one of the soldiers stepped up to the commanding officer and said: "Colonel, don't you think that we might compromise this affair?" "Well, I reckon I should have no objection to *submit it to arbitration* myself," replied the Colonel.

Even the thieves must be commercial in their ideas. One rogue, meeting another, asked him what he had done that morning. "Not much," was the reply, "I've only *realized* this umbrella."

This reminds me of a conversation between a man and his wife, which was overheard by the party who repeated it to me. It appears that the lady was economically inclined, and in cutting out some shirts for her husband, resolved that they should not descend much lower than his hips, as thereby so much linen would be saved. The husband expostulated, but in vain. She pointed out to him that it would improve his figure and make his nether garments set much better—in a word, that long shirt-tails were quite unnecessary; and she wound up her arguments by observing that linen was a very expensive article and that she could not see what on earth was the reason that people should stuff so much *capital* into their pantaloons.

There is sometimes in the American metaphors an energy which is very remarkable.

"Well, I reckon that from his teeth to his toe-nail there's not a human of a more conquering nature than General Jackson."

One *gentleman* said to me: "I wish I had all hell boiled down to a pint, just to pour down your throat."

It is a great pity that the Americans have not adhered more to the Indian names, which are euphonious, and very often musical; but, so far from it, they appear to have had a pleasure in dismissing them altogether. There is a river running into Lake Champlain, near Burlington, formerly called by the Indians the Einooski; but this name has been superseded by the settlers, who, by way of improvement, have designated it the Onion River. The Americans have ransacked scripture, and ancient and modern history, to supply themselves with names, yet, notwithstanding, there appears to be a strange lack of taste in their selection. On the route to Lake Ontario you pass towns with such names as Manlius, Sempronius, Titus, Cato, and then you come to *Butternuts.* Looking over the catalogue of cities, towns, villages, rivers, and creeks in the different states in the Union, I find the following repetitions:

Of towns, etc., named after distinguished individuals, there are:

Washingtons	43	Carrolls	16
Jacksons	41	Adamses	18
Jeffersons	32	Bolivars	8
Franklins	41	Clintons	19
Madisons	26	Waynes	14
Monroes	25	Casses	6
Perrys	22	Clays	4
Fayettes	14	Fultons	17
Hamiltons	13		

Of other towns, etc., there are:

Columbias	27	Libertys	14
Centre Villes	14	Salems	24
Fairfields	17	Onions	28
Athenses	10	Muds	8
Romes	4	Little Muds	1

Crookeds	22	Muddies	11
Littles	20	Sandys	39
Longs	18		

In colours they have:

Clears	13	Greens	16
Blacks	33	Whites	15
Blues	8	Yellows	10
Vermilions	14		

Named after trees:

Cedars	25	Laurels	14
Cypresses	12	Pines	18

After animals:

Beavers	23	Foxes	12
Buffaloes	21	Otters	13
Bulls	9	Racoons	11
Deers	13	Wolfs	16
Dogs	9	Bears	12
Elks	11	Bear's Rump	1

After birds, etc.:

Gooses	10	Fishes	7
Ducks	8	Turkeys	12
Eagles	8	Swans	15
Pigeons	10	Pikes	20

The consequence of these repetitions is that if you do not put the name of the state, and often of the county in the state in which the town you refer to may be, your letter may journey all over the Union, and perhaps, after all, never arrive at its place of destination.

The states have already accommodated each other with nicknames, as per example:

Illinois people are termed .... Suckers
Missouri .... Pukes

Michigan	Wolverines
Indiana	Hoosiers
Kentucky	Corn Crackers
Ohio	Buckeyes, etc.

The names of persons are also very strange; and some of them are, at all events, obsolete in England, even if they ever existed there. Many of them are said to be French or Dutch names Americanized. But they appear still more odd to us from the high-sounding Christian names prefixed to them, as, for instance: Philo Doolittle, Populorum Hightower, Preserved Fish, Asa Peabody, Alonzo Lilly, Alceus Wolf, etc. I was told by a gentleman that Doolittle was originally from the French Dr. l'Hôtel; Peabody from Pibaudière; Bunker from Bon Coeur; that Mr. Ezekiel Bumpus is a desendant of Monsieur Bou Pas, etc., all which is very possible.

Everyone who is acquainted with Washington Irving must know that, being very sensitive himself, he is one of the last men in the world to do anything to annoy another. In his selection of names for his writings, he was cautious in avoiding such as might be known; so that, when he called his old schoolmaster Ichabod Crane, he thought himself safe from the risk of giving offence. Shortly afterwards a friend of his called upon him, accompanied by a stranger, whom he introduced as Major Crane; Irving started at the name; "Major Ichabod Crane," continued his friend, much to the horror of Washington Irving.

I was told that a merchant went down to New Orleans with one Christian name and came back, after a lapse of years, with another. His name was John Flint. The French at New Orleans translated his surname and called him Pierre Fusée; on his return the Pierre stuck to him, and rendered into English as Peter, and he was called Peter Flint ever afterwards. People may change their names in the United States by application to Congress. They have a story hardly worth relating, although considered a good one in America, having been told me by a member of Congress. A Mr. Whitepimple, having risen in the world, was persuaded by his wife to change his name, and applied for permission accordingly. The clerk of the office inquired of him what other name he would have, and he, being very indifferent about it himself, replied carelessly as he walked away, "Oh, anything"; whereupon the clerk enrolled him as Mr. *Thing.* Time passed on, and he had a numerous family, who found the new name not much more agreeable than the old one, for there was Miss Sally Thing, Miss Dolly Thing, the old Things, and all the little Things; and worst of all, the eldest son, being christened Robert, went by the name of Thingum Bob.

There were, and I believe still are, two lawyers in partnership in New York with the peculiarly happy names of Catchem and Chetum. People laughed at seeing these two names in juxtaposition over the door; so the lawyers thought it advisable to separate them by the insertion of their Christian names. Mr. Catchem's Christian name was Isaac, Mr. Chetum's Uriah. A new board was ordered, but when sent to the painter, it was found to be too short to admit the Christian names at full length. The painter, therefore, put in only the initials before the surnames, which made the matter still worse than before, for there now appeared—

"I. Catchem and U. Chetum."

I cannot conclude this chapter without adverting to one or two points peculiar to the Americans. They wish, in everything, to improve upon the Old Country, as they call us, and affect to be excessively refined in their language and ideas; but they forget that very often in the covering, and the covering only, consists the indecency, and that, to use the old aphorism—"Very nice people are people with very nasty ideas."

They object to everything nude in statuary. When I was at the house of Governor Everett,[2] at Boston, I observed

---

[2] Edward Everett (1794–1865), American orator and statesman, was born in Massachusetts. He graduated from Harvard in

a fine cast of the Apollo Belvidere; but, in compliance with general opinion, it was hung with drapery, although Governor Everett himself is a gentleman of refined mind and high classical attainments, and quite above such ridiculous sensitiveness. In language it is the same thing. There are certain words which are never used in America, but an absurd substitute is employed. I cannot particularize them after this preface, lest I should be accused of indelicacy myself. I may, however, state one little circumstance which will fully prove the correctness of what I say.

When at Niagara Falls I was escorting a young lady with whom I was on friendly terms. She had been standing on a piece of rock, the better to view the scene, when she slipped down, and was evidently hurt by the fall; she had, in fact, grazed her shin. As she limped a little in walking home, I said: "Did you hurt your leg much?" She turned from me, evidently much shocked, or much offended; and not being aware that I had committed any very heinous offence, I begged to know what was the reason of her displeasure. After some hesitation she said that, as she knew me well, she would tell me that the word *leg* was never mentioned before ladies. I apologized for my want of refinement, which was attributable to having been accustomed only to *English* society; and added, that as such articles must occasionally be referred to, even in the most polite circles in America, perhaps she would inform me by what name I might mention them without shocking the company. Her reply was that the word *limb* was used; "Nay," continued she, "I am not so particular as some peo-

---

1811, becoming a Unitarian minister two years later, but in 1815 he joined the Harvard faculty as Eliot professor of Greek. Everett was also editor of the *North American Review*. He was a strong Whig and in the 1830's served as governor of Massachusetts. An intimate of Daniel Webster, he was ap-

pointed Minister to Great Britain. Edward Everett is also remembered for having presented the major oration at the dedication of the National Cemetery at Gettysburg on November 19, 1863, after which Lincoln gave his considerably shorter Gettysburg Address.

ple are, for I know those who always say limb of a table, or limb of a pianoforte."

There the conversation dropped; but a few months afterwards I was obliged to acknowledge that the young lady was correct when she asserted that some people were more particular than even she was.

I was requested by a lady to escort her to a seminary for young ladies, and on being ushered into the reception-room, conceive my astonishment at beholding a square pianoforte with four *limbs*. However, that the ladies who visited their daughters might feel in its full force the extreme delicacy of the mistress of the establishment, and her care to preserve in their utmost purity the ideas of the young ladies under her charge, she had dressed all these four limbs in modest little trousers, with frills at the bottom of them!

CHAPTER XXXV

Slavery

It had always appeared to me as singular that the Americans, at the time of their Declaration of Independence, took no measures for the gradual, if not immediate, extinction of slavery; that at the very time they were offering up thanks for having successfully struggled for their own emancipation from what they considered foreign bondage, their gratitude for their liberation did not induce them to break the chains of those whom they themselves held in captivity. It is useless for them to exclaim, as they now do, that it was England who left them slavery as a curse and reproach us as having originally introduced the system among them. Admitting, as is the fact, that slavery did commence when the colonies were subject to the mother country, admitting that the petitions for its discontinuance were disregarded, still there was nothing to prevent immediate manumission at the time of the acknowledgment of their independence by Great Britain. They had then everything to recommence; they had to select a new form of government and to decide upon new laws; they pronounced, in their declaration, that "all men were equal"; and yet, in the face of this declaration, and their solemn invocation to the Deity, the Negroes, in *their* fetters, pleaded to them in vain.

I had always thought that this sad omission, which has left such an anomaly in the Declaration of Independence as to have made it the taunt and reproach of the Americans by the whole civilized world, did really arise from forgetfulness; that, as is but too often the case, when we are ourselves made happy, the Americans in their joy at their own deliverance from a foreign yoke, and the repossessing themselves of their own rights, had been too much engrossed to occupy themselves with the undeniable claims of others. But I was mistaken; such was not the case, as I shall presently show.

In the course of one of my sojourns in Philadelphia, Mr. Vaughan, of the Athenæum of that city, stated to me that he had found the *original draft* of the Declaration of Independence, in the hand-writing of Mr. Jefferson, and that it was curious to remark the alterations which had been made previous to the adoption of the manifesto which was afterwards promulgated. It was to Jefferson, Adams, and Franklin that was entrusted the primary drawing up of this important document, which was then submitted to others, and ultimately to the Convention, for approval; and it appears that the question of slavery had NOT been overlooked when the document was first framed, as the following clause, inserted in the original draft by Mr. Jefferson (but *expunged* when it was laid before the Convention), will sufficiently prove. After enumerating the grounds upon which they threw off their allegiance to the king of England, the declaration continued in Jefferson's nervous style:

> He [the king] has waged cruel war against human nature itself, violating its most sacred rights of *life and liberty*, in the person of a distant people who never offended him; captivating and carrying them into slavery, in another hemisphere, or to incur miserable death in their transportation thither. This piratical warfare, the approbrium of infidel powers, is the warfare of the Christian king of Great Britain, determined to keep open a market where men should be bought and sold;

he has prostituted his negative for suppressing every legislative attempt to prohibit or restrain this execrable commerce; and that this assemblage of horrors might want no fact of distinguished dye, he is now exciting these very people to rise in arms among us, and to purchase that liberty of which he has deprived them, by murdering the people upon whom he also obtruded them; thus paying off former crimes committed against the liberties of one people, with crimes which he urges them to commit against the lives of another." [1]

Such was the paragraph which had been inserted by Jefferson, in the virulence of his democracy and his desire to hold up to detestation the king of Great Britain. Such was at that time, unfortunately, the truth; and had the paragraph remained, and at the same time emancipation been given to the slaves, it would have been a lasting stigma upon George the Third. But the paragraph was expunged; and why? Because they could not hold up to public indignation the sovereign whom they had abjured without reminding the world that slavery still existed in a community which had declared that "all men were equal"; and that if, in a monarch, they had stigmatized it as "violating the most sacred rights of life and liberty" and "waging cruel war against human nature," they could not have afterwards been so barefaced and unblushing as to continue a system which was at variance with every principle which they professed.

It does, however, satisfactorily prove that the question of slavery was not *overlooked;* on the contrary, their determination to take advantage of the system was deliberate,

---

[1] Marryat is quite correct here. In the first draft of the Declaration of Independence there were these very strong words against slavery. See Carl L. Becker, *The Declaration of Independence* (New York: Vintage Books; 1958), pp. 180–81. The series of statements on slavery were the last of the charges against King George III. Both John Adams and Thomas Jefferson thought the passage excellent, but apparently their colleagues did not, for the words were deleted by Congress in the final version. Becker, *op. cit.*, p. 213.

and, there can be no doubt, well considered—the very omission of the paragraph proves it. I mention these facts to show that the Americans have no right to revile us on being the cause of slavery in America. They had the means, and were bound, as honourable men, to act up to their declaration; but they entered into the question, they decided otherwise, and decided that they would retain their ill-acquired property at the expense of their principles.

The degrees of slavery in America are as various in their intensity as are the communities composing the Union. They may, however, be divided with great propriety under two general heads—eastern and western slavery. By eastern slavery, I refer to that in the slave states bordering on the Atlantic, and those slave states on the other side of the Allegheny mountains, which may be more directly considered as their colonies, *viz.* in the first instance, Maryland, Delaware, Virginia, North and South Carolina, and, secondly, Kentucky and Tennessee. We have been accustomed lately to class the slaves as non-predial and predial—that is, those who are domestic, and those who work on the plantations. This classification is not correct, if it is intended to distinguish between those who are well and those who are badly treated. The true line to be drawn is between those who work separately and those who are worked in a gang and superintended by an overseer. This is fully exemplified in the United States, where it will be found that in all states where they are worked in gangs the slaves are harshly treated, while in the others their labour is light.

Now, with the exception of the rice grounds in South Carolina, the eastern states are growers of corn, hemp, and tobacco; but their chief staple is the breeding of horses, mules, horned cattle, and other stock. The largest portion of these states remain in wild luxuriant pasture, more especially in Virginia, Kentucky, and Tennessee, either of which states is larger than the other four mentioned.

The proportion of slaves required for the cultivation of the purely agricultural and chiefly grazing farms or plantations in these states is small, fifteen or twenty being sufficient for a farm of two hundred or three hundred acres; and their labour, which is mostly confined to tending stock, is not only very light, but of the quality most agreeable to the Negro. Half the day you will see him on horseback with his legs idly swinging as he goes along, or seated on a shaft-horse driving his wagons. He is quite in his glory; nothing delights a Negro so much as riding or driving, particularly when he has a whole team under his control. He takes his wagon for a load of corn to feed the hogs, sits on the edge of the shaft as he tosses the cobs to the grunting multitude, whom he addresses in the most intimate terms; in short, everything is done leisurely, after his own fashion.

In these grazing states, as they may very properly be called, the Negroes are well fed; they refuse beef and mutton and will have nothing but pork, and are, without exception, the fattest and most saucy fellows I ever met with in a state of bondage; and such may be said generally to be the case with all the Negroes in the eastern states which I have mentioned. The rice grounds in South Carolina are unhealthy, but the slaves are very kindly treated. But the facts speak for themselves. When the Negro works in a gang with the whip over him, he may be overworked and ill-treated; but when he is not regularly watched, he will take very good care that the work he performs shall not injure his constitution.

It has been asserted, and generally credited, that in the eastern states Negroes are regularly bred up like the cattle for the western market. That the Virginians, and the inhabitants of the other eastern slave states, do sell Negroes which are taken to the west, there is no doubt; but that the Negroes are bred expressly for that purpose is, as regards the majority of the proprietors, far from the fact; it is the effect of circumstances, over which they have had no control. Virginia, when first settled, was one of the richest states, but, by continually cropping the land without manuring it, and that for nearly two hundred years, the

major portion of many valuable estates has become barren, and the land is no longer under cultivation; in consequence of this, the Negroes (increasing so rapidly as they
do in that country), so far from being profitable, have become a serious task upon their masters, who have to rear
and maintain, without having any employment to give
them. The small portion of the estates under cultivation
will subsist only a certain portion of the Negroes; the remainder must, therefore, be disposed of, or they would
eat their master out of his home. That the slaves are not
willingly disposed of by many of the proprietors I am certain, particularly when it is known that they are purchased
for the west. I know of many instances of this, and was informed of others; and by wills, especially, slaves have been
directed to be sold for *two thirds* of the price which they
would fetch for the western market, on condition that
they were not to leave the state. These facts establish two
points, *viz.* that the slaves in the eastern states [are] well
treated, and that in the western states slavery still exists
with all its horrors. The common threat to, and ultimate
punishment of, a refractory and disobedient slave in the
east is to sell him for the western market. Many slave proprietors, whose estates have been worn out in the east, have
preferred migrating to the west with their slaves rather
than sell them, and thus is the severity of the western
treatment occasionally and partially mitigated.

But doing justice, as I always will, to those who have
been unjustly calumniated, at the same time I must admit
that there is a point connected with slavery in America
which renders it more odious than in other countries; I refer to the system of amalgamation which has, from promiscuous intercourse, been carried on to such an extent that
you very often meet with slaves whose skins are whiter than
their master's.

At Louisville, Kentucky, I saw a girl, about twelve
years old, carrying a child; and, aware that in a slave state
the circumstance of white people hiring themselves out to
service is almost unknown, I inquired of her if she were a

slave. To my astonishment, she replied in the affirmative. She was as fair as snow, and it was impossible to detect any admixture of blood from her appearance, which was that of a pretty English cottager's child. I afterwards spoke to the master, who stated when he had purchased her, and the sum which he had paid. . . .

It is a well-known fact [2] that a considerable portion of Mr. Jefferson's slaves were his own children. If any of them absconded, he would smile, thereby implying that he should not be very particular in looking after them; and yet this man, this great and GOOD man, as Miss Martineau calls him, this man who penned the paragraph I have quoted, as having been erased from the Declaration of Independence, who asserted that the slavery of the Negro was a violation of the most sacred rights of life and liberty, permitted these his slaves and his children, the issue of his own loins, to be sold at auction after his demise, not even emancipating them, as he might have done, before his death. And, but lately, a member of Congress for Georgia, whose name I shall not mention, brought up a fine family of children, his own issue by a female slave; for many years acknowledged them as his own children; permitted them to call him by the endearing title of *papa*, and eventually the whole of them were sold by public auction, and that, too, during his own lifetime!

But there is, I am sorry to say, a more horrible in-

---

[2] No reputable biographer gives any credence whatsoever to the story of Thomas Jefferson's supposed illegitimate children by a Negro slave woman. According to Donald Smalley in his introduction to Frances Trollope's *Domestic Manners of the Americans*, the story was probably the work of James Thomson Callender, "a British refugee who had fled to America to escape prosecution for libel in England." Smalley quotes a doggerel verse that was widely circulated.

"*Of all the damsels on the green,*
On mountain, or in valley,
A lass so luscious n'er was seen
As Monticellian Sally.
Yankee doodle, who's the noodle?
What wife was half so handy?
To breed a flock of slaves for stock,
A blackamoor's the dandy."
Jefferson did not stoop to issuing a denial of the canard.

stance on record and one well authenticated. A planter of good family (I shall not mention his name or the state in which it occurred, as he was not so much to blame as were the laws) connected himself with one of his own female slaves, who was nearly white; the fruits of this connexion were two daughters, very beautiful girls, who were sent to England to be educated.

They were both grown up when their father died. At his death his affairs were found in a state of great disorder; in fact, there was not sufficient left to pay his creditors. Having brought up and educated these two girls and introduced them as his daughters, it quite slipped his memory that, having been born of a slave, and not manumitted, they were in reality slaves themselves. This fact was established after his decease; they were torn away from the affluence and refinement to which they had been accustomed, sold and purchased as slaves, and with the avowed intention of the purchaser to reap his profits from their prostitution!!

It must not, however, be supposed that the planters of Virginia and the other eastern states encourage this intercourse; on the contrary, the young men who visit at the plantations cannot affront them more than to take notice of their slaves, particularly the lighter coloured, who are retained in the house and attend upon their wives and daughters. Independently of the moral feeling which really guides them (as they naturally do not wish that the attendants of their daughters should be degraded), it is against their interest in case they should wish to sell, as a mulatto or light male will not fetch so high a price as a full-blooded Negro; the cross between the European and Negro—especially the first cross, i.e., the mulatto—is of a sickly constitution, and quite unable to bear up against the fatigue of field labour in the west. As the race becomes whiter, the stamina is said to improve.

Examining into the question of emancipation in America, the first inquiry will be how far this consummation is likely to be effected by means of the abolitionists. Miss

Martineau, in her book, says: "The good work has begun, and will proceed." She is so far right; it has begun, and has been progressing very fast, as may be proved by the single fact of the abolitionists having decided the election in the state of Ohio in October last. But let not Miss Martineau exult; for the stronger the abolition party may become, the more danger is there to be apprehended of a disastrous conflict between the states.

The fact is that, by the Constitution of the United States, the federal government have not only no power to *interfere* or to *abolish* slavery, but they are bound to *maintain* it: the abolition of slavery is expressly *withheld*. The citizens of any state may abolish slavery in their own state; but the federal government cannot do so without an express violation of the federal compact. Should all the states in the Union abolish slavery, with the exception of one, and that one be Maryland (the smallest of the whole of the states), neither the federal government or the other states could interfere with her. The federal compact binds the general government, "first, not to *meddle* with the slavery of the states where it exists, and next, to *protect* it in the case of runaway slaves, and to *defend* it in case of *invasion* or *domestic violence* on account of it." [3]

It appears, therefore, that slavery can only be abolished by the slave state itself in which it exists; and it is not very probable that any class of people will voluntarily make themselves beggars by surrendering up their whole property to satisfy the clamour of a party. That this party is strong, and is daily becoming stronger, is very true; the stronger it becomes, the worse will be the prospects of the United States. In England the case was very different: the government had a right to make the sacrifice to public opinion by indemnification to the slave-holders; but in America

---

[3] Marryat is simply saying here that the federal Constitution guarantees the citizen's right to property. In those states where slavery existed as a result of state and municipal law, slaves were regarded as a form of property. I have not been able to determine the source for Marryat's quotation.

the government have not that power; and the efforts of the abolitionists will only have the effects of plunging the country into difficulties and disunion. As an American author truly observes: "The American abolitionists must trample on the constitution, and wade through the carnage of a civil war, before they can triumph."

Already the abolition party have done much mischief. . . . It is not, however, impossible that the abolition party in the eastern and northern states may be gradually checked by the citizens of those very states. Their zeal may be as warm as ever; but public opinion will compel them, at the risk of their lives, to hold their tongues. This possibility can, however, only arise from the northern and eastern states becoming manufacturing states, as they are most anxious to be. Should this happen, the raw cotton grown by slave labour will employ the looms of Massachusetts; and then, as the *Quarterly Review* very correctly observes: "By a cycle of commercial benefits, the northern and eastern states will feel that there is some material compensation for the moral turpitude of the system of slavery."

The slave proprietors in these states are as well aware as any political economist can be that slavery is a loss instead of a gain and that no state can arrive at that degree of prosperity under a state of slavery which it would under free labour. The case is simple. In free labour, where there is competition, you exact the greatest possible returns for the least possible expenditure; a man is worked as a machine; he is paid for what he produces, and nothing more. By slave labour, you receive the least possible return for the greatest possible expense, for the slave is better fed and clothed than the freeman and does as little work as he can. The slave-holders in the eastern states are well aware of this, and are as anxious to be rid of slavery as are the abolitionists; but the time is not yet come, nor will it come until the country shall have so filled up as to render white labour attainable. Such, indeed, are not the expectations expressed in the language of the representatives of their states when in Congress; but it must be remembered that this is a question which has convulsed the Union, and that, not only from a feeling of pride, added to indignation at the interference, but from a feeling of the necessity of not yielding up one tittle upon this question, the language of determined resistance is in Congress invariably resorted to. But these gentlemen have one opinion for Congress and another for their private table: in the first, they stand up unflinchingly for their slave rights; in the other, they reason calmly and admit what they could not admit in public. There is no labour in the eastern states, excepting that of the rice plantations in South Carolina, which cannot be performed by white men; indeed, a large proportion of the cotton in the Carolinas is now raised by a *free white* population. In the grazing portion of these states, white labour would be substituted advantageously, could white labour be procured at any reasonable price.

The time will come, and I do not think it very distant, say perhaps twenty or thirty years, when—provided America receives no check, and these states are not injudiciously interfered with—Virginia, Kentucky, Delaware, Maryland, North Carolina (and, eventually, but probably somewhat later, Tennessee and South Carolina) will, of their own accord, enrol themselves among the free states. . . .

In the western states, comprehending Missouri, Louisiana, Arkansas, Mississippi, Georgia, and Alabama, the Negroes are, with the exception perhaps of the two latter states, in a worse condition than they ever were in the West India islands. This may be easily imagined when the character of the white people who inhabit the larger portion of these states is considered—a class of people, the majority of whom are without feelings of honour, reckless in their habits, intemperate, unprincipled, and lawless, many of them having fled from the eastern states as fraudulent bankrupts, swindlers, or committers of other crimes, which have subjected them to the penitentiaries—miscreants defying the climate, so that they can defy the laws. Still, this representation of the character of the people inhabiting these states must, from the chaotic state of society in America, be received with many exceptions. In the city of New Orleans, for instance, and in Natchez and its vicinity, and also among the planters, there are many most honourable exceptions. I have said the majority, for we must look to the *mass*—the exceptions do but prove the rule. It is evident that slaves, under such masters, can have but little chance of good treatment, and stories are told of them at which humanity shudders.

It appears, then, that the slaves, with the rest of the population of America, are working *their way west,* and the question may now be asked—Allowing that slavery will be soon abolished in the eastern states, what prospect is there of its ultimate abolition and total extinction in America?

I can see no prospect of exchanging slave labour for free in the western states, as, with the exception of Missouri, I do not think it possible that white labour could be substituted, the extreme heat and unhealthiness of the climate being a bar to any such attempt. The cultivation of the land must be carried on by a Negro population, if it is to be carried on at all. The question, therefore, to be considered is whether these states are to be inhabited and cultivated by a free or a slave Negro population. It must be remembered that not one twentieth part of the land in the southern states is under cultivation; every year, as the slaves are brought in from the east, the number of acres taken into cultivation increases. Not double or triple the number of the slaves at present in America would be sufficient for the cultivation of the whole of these vast territories. Every year the cotton crops increase, and at the same time the price of cotton has not materially lowered; as an everywhere-increasing population takes off the whole supply, this will probably continue to be the case for many years, since it must be remembered that, independently of the increasing population increasing the demand, cotton, from its comparative cheapness, continually usurps the place of some other raw material; this, of course, adds to the consumption. In various manufactures, cotton has already taken the place of linen and fur; but there must eventually be a limit to consumption; and this is certain, that as soon as the supply is so great as to exceed the demand, the price will be lowered by the competition; and, as soon as the price, if by competition so lowered as to render the cost and keeping of the slave greater than the income returned by his labour, then, and not till then, is there any chance of slavery being abolished in the western states of America.

The probability of this consummation being brought about sooner is in the expectation that the Brazils, Mexico, and particularly the independent state of Texas will in a few years produce a crop of cotton which may considerably lower its price. At present, the United States grow nearly, if not more, than half of the cotton produced in the whole world. . . .

From circumstances, therefore, Texas, which but a few years since was hardly known as a country, becomes a state of the greatest importance to the civilized and moral world. . . . The fact is this: America (for the government looked on and offered no interruption) has seized upon Texas, with a view of extending the curse of slavery, and of finding a mart for the excess of her Negro population. If Texas is admitted into the Union, all chance of the abolition of slavery must be thrown forward to such an indefinite period as to be lost in the mist of futurity; if, on the contrary, Texas remains an independent province, or is restored to its legitimate owners, and in either case slavery is abolished, she then becomes, from the very circumstance of her fertility and aptitude for white labour, not only the great *check to slavery*, but eventually the means of its *abolition*. Never, therefore, was there a portion of the globe upon which the moral world must look with such interest.

England may if she acts promptly and wisely, make such terms with this young state as to raise it up as a barrier against the profligate ambition of America. Texas was a portion of Mexico, and Mexico abolished slavery; the Texans are bound (if they are *Texans* and not Americans) to adhere to what might be considered a treaty with the whole Christian world; if not, they can make no demand upon its sympathy or protection, and it *should be a sine qua non with England and all other European powers, previous to acknowledging or entering into commercial relations with Texas, that she should adhere to the law which was passed at the time that she was an integral portion of Mexico, and declare herself to be a Free State.* If she does not, unless the chains are broken by the Negro himself, the cause and hopes of *emancipation* are lost.

There certainly is one outlet for the slaves, which as they are removed farther and farther to the west will eventually be offered—that of escaping to the Indian tribes which are spread over the western frontier, and amalgamating with them; such indeed, I think, will some future day be the result, whether they gain their liberty by desertion, insurrection, or manumission.

Of insurrection there is at present but little fear. In the eastern slave states, the Negroes do not think of it, and if they did, the difficulty of combination and of procuring arms is so great that it would be attended with very partial success. The intervention of a foreign power might indeed bring it to pass, but it is to be hoped that England, at all events, will never be the party to foment a servile war. Let us not forget that for more than two centuries we have been *particeps criminis,* and should have been in as great a difficulty as the Americans now are had we had the Negro population on our own soil and not on distant islands which could be legislated for without affecting the condition of the mother country. Nay, at this very moment, by taking nearly the whole of the American cotton off their hands in exchange for our manufactures, we are ourselves virtually encouraging slavery by affording the Americans such a profitable mart for their slave labour.

There is one point to which I have not yet adverted, which is, Whether the question of emancipation is likely to produce a separation between the northern and southern states? The only reply that can be given is that it entirely depends upon whether the abolition party can be held in check by the federal government. That the federal government will do its utmost there can be no doubt, but the federal government is not so powerful as many of the societies formed in America, and especially the Abolition Society, which every day adds to its members. The interests of the north are certainly at variance with the measures of the society, yet still it gains strength. . . .

In England people have no idea of the fanaticism displayed and excitement created in these societies, which are a peculiar feature in the states, and arising from the nature of their institutions. Their strength and perseverance are such that they bear down all before them, and, regardless of all consequences, they may eventually control the government. As to the question, which portion of the states will be the losers by a separation, I myself think that it will be the northern states which will suffer. . . .

CHAPTER XXXVI

Religion in America

In theory nothing appears more rational than that everyone should worship the Deity according to his own ideas—form his own opinion as to His attributes and draw his own conclusions as to hereafter. An established church *appears* to be a species of coercion, not that you are obliged to believe in or follow that form of worship, but that, if you do not, you lose your portion of certain advantages attending that form of religion which has been accepted by the majority and adopted by the government. In religion, to think for yourself wears the semblance of a luxury, and like other luxuries, it is proportionably taxed.

And yet it would appear as if it never were intended that the mass should think for themselves, as everything goes on so quietly when other people think for them, and everything goes so wrong when they do think for themselves: in the first instance, where a portion of the people think for the mass, all are of one opinion; whereas in the second, they divide and split into many molecules, that they resemble the globules of water when expanded by heat, and like them are in a state of restlessness and excitement.

That the partiality shown to an established church creates some bitterness of feeling is most true, but being established by law, is it not the partiality shown for the legitimate over the illegitimate? All who choose may enter into its portals, and if the people will remain out of doors of their own accord, ought they to complain that they have no house over their heads? They certainly have a right to remain out of doors if they please, but whether they are justified in complaining afterwards is another question. Perhaps the unreasonableness of the demands of the dissenters in our own country will be better brought home to them by my pointing out the effects of the voluntary system in the United States.

In America everyone worships the Deity after his own fashion; not only the mode of worship, but even the Deity itself, varies. Some worship God, some Mammon; some admit, some deny, Christ; some deny both God and Christ; some are saved by living prophets only; some go to heaven by water, while some dance their way upwards. Numerous as are the sects, still are the sects much subdivided. Unitarians are not in unity as to the portion of divinity they shall admit to our Saviour; Baptists, as to the precise quantity of water necessary to salvation; even the Quakers have split into controversy, and the men of peace are at open war in Philadelphia, the city of brotherly love. . . .

Religion may, as to its consequences, be considered under two heads: as it affects the future welfare of the individual when he is summoned to the presence of the Deity, and as it affects society in general, by acting upon the moral character of the community. Now, admitting the right of every individual to decide whether he will follow the usual beaten track or select for himself a by-path for his journey upwards, it must be acknowledged that the results of this free-will are, in a moral point of view, as far as society is concerned, anything but satisfactory.

It would appear as if the majority were much too frail and weak to go alone upon their heavenly journey; as if they required the support, the assistance, the encouragement, the leaning upon others who are journeying with them, to enable them successfully to gain the goal. The effects of an established church are to cement the mass, cement society and communities, and increase the force of those natural ties by which families and relations are bound together. There is an attraction of cohesion in a uniform religious worship, acting favourably upon the morals of the mass, and binding still more closely those already united. Now, the voluntary system in America has produced the very opposite effects; it has broken one of the strongest links between man and man, for each goeth his own way; as a nation, there is no national feeling to be acted upon; in society, there is something wanting, and you ask yourself what is it? and in families it often creates disunion: I know one among many others who, instead of going together to the same house of prayer, disperse as soon as they are out of the door—one daughter to a Unitarian chapel, another to a Baptist, the parents to the Episcopal, the sons, anywhere or nowhere. But worse effects are produced than even these: where anyone is allowed to have his own peculiar way of thinking, his own peculiar creed, there neither is a watch nor a right to watch over each other; there is no mutual communication, no encouragement, no parental control; and the consequence is that by the majority, especially the young, religion becomes wholly and utterly disregarded.

Another great evil, arising from the peculiarity of the voluntary system, is that in many of the principal sects the power has been wrested from the clergy and assumed by the laity, who exercise an inquisition most injurious to the cause of religion; and to such an excess of tyranny is this power exercised that it depends upon the *laity,* and not upon the *clergy,* whether any individual shall or shall not be admitted as a *communicant* at the table of our Lord. . . .

I believe that in no other country is there more zeal shown by its various ministers, zeal even to the sacrifice of life; that no country sends out more zealous missionaries; that no country has more societies for the diffusion of the gospel; and that in no other country in the world are larger sums subscribed for the furtherance of those praiseworthy objects as in the eastern states of America. I admit all this, and admit it with pleasure, for I know it to be a fact; I only regret to add that in no other country are such strenuous exertions so incessantly required to stem the torrent of atheism and infidelity, which so universally exists in this. Indeed this very zeal, so ardent on the part of the ministers, and so aided by the well-disposed of the laity, proves that what I have just now asserted is, unfortunately, but too true.

It is not my intention to comment upon the numerous sects and the varieties of worship practised in the United States. The Episcopal church is small in proportion to the others, and as far as I can ascertain, although it may increase its members with the increase of population, it is not likely to make any vigorous or successful stand against the other sects. The two churches most congenial to the American feelings and institutions are the Presbyterian and Congregationalist. They may, indeed, in opposition to the hierarchy of the Episcopal, be considered as Republican churches; and admitting that many errors have crept into the established church from its too intimate union with the state, I think it will be proved that, in rejecting its errors and the domination of the mitre, the seceders have fallen into still greater evils, and have, for the latter, substituted a despotism to which everything, even religion itself, must in America succumb.

In a republic, or democracy, the people will rule in everything: in the Congregational church they rule as deacons; in the Presbyterian as elders. Affairs are litigated and decided in committees and councils, and thus is the pastoral office deprived of its primitive and legitimate influence, and the ministers are tyrannized over by the laity, in the most absurd and unjustifiable manner. If the minister does not submit to their decisions, if he asserts his right as a minister to preach the word according to his reading of it, he is arraigned and dismissed. In short, although sent for to instruct the people, he must consent to be instructed by them or surrender up his trust. Thus do the ministers lose all their dignity and become the slaves of the congregation, who give them their choice, either to read the Scriptures according to *their* reading or to go and starve. I was once canvassing this question with an American, who pronounced that the laity were quite right and that it was the duty of the minister to preach as his congregation wished. His argument was this: "If I send to Manchester for any article to be manufactured, I expect it to be made exactly after the pattern given; if not, I will not take it. So it is with the minister: he must find goods exactly suited to his customers, or expect them to be left on his hands!" . . .

The interference, I may say the tyranny, of the laity over the ministers of these democratic churches is, however, of still more serious consequences to those who accept such arduous and repulsive duty. It is a well-known fact that there is a species of *bronchitis,* or affection of the lungs, peculiar to the ministers in the United States, arising from their excessive labours in their vocation. I have already observed that the zeal of the minister is even unto death. . . .

It is no matter of surprise, then, that I heard the ministers at the camp meeting complain of the excess of their labours, and the difficulty of obtaining young men to enter the church; who, indeed, unless actuated by a holy zeal, would submit to such a life of degradation? What man of intellect and education could submit to be schooled by shoemakers and mechanics, to live poor, and at the mercy of tyrants, and drop down dead like the jaded and overladen beast from excess of fatigue and exertion? . . .

The fact is that there is little or no healthy religion in their most numerous and influential churches; it is all excitement. Twenty or thirty years back, the Methodists were considered as extravagantly frantic, but the Congregationalists and Presbyterians in the United States have gone far ahead of them; and the Methodist church in America has become to a degree Episcopal, and softened down into, perhaps, the most pure, most mild, and most simple of all the creeds professed.

I have said that in these two churches the religious

feeling was that of excitement: I believe it to be more or less the case in *all* religion in America; for the Americans are a people who are prone to excitement, not only from their climate, but constitutionally, and it is the *caviare* of their existence. If it were not so, why is it necessary that revivals should be so continually called forth?—a species of stimulus common, I believe, to almost every sect and creed, promoted and practised in all their colleges, and considered as most important and salutary in their results. Let it not be supposed that I am deprecating that which is to be understood by a revival, in the true sense of the word; not those revivals which were formerly held for the benefit of all and for the salvation of many. I am raising my voice against the modern system, which has been so universally substituted for the reality. . . .

And yet these revivals are looked up to and supported as the strong arm of religion. It is not only the ignorant or the foolish, but the enlightened and the educated also, who support and encourage them, either from a consideration of their utility or from that fear, so universal in the United States, of expressing an opinion contrary to the majority. How otherwise could they be introduced once or twice a year into all the colleges—the professors of which are surely most of them men of education and strong mind? Yet such is the fact. It is announced that some minister, peculiarly gifted to work in revivals, is to come on a certain day. Books are thrown on one side, study is abandoned, and ten days perhaps are spent in religious exercises of the most violent and exciting character. It is a scene of strange confusion, some praying, some pretending to pray, some scoffing. Day after day is it carried on, until the excitement is at its height, as the exhortations and the denunciations of the preacher are poured into their ears. A young American who was at one of the colleges, and gave me a full detail of what had occurred, told me that on one occasion a poor lad, frightened out of his senses, and anxious to pray, as the vengeance and wrath of the Almighty was poured out by the minister, sunk down upon his knees and

commenced his prayer with "Almighty and *diabolical* God!"
No misnomer, if what the preacher had thundered out was
the *truth*.

As an example of the interference of the laity, and
of the description of people who may be so authorized, the
same gentleman told me that at one revival a deacon said
to him previous to the meeting: "Now, Mr.——, if you
don't take advantage of this here revival and lay up a little
salvation for your soul, all I can say is, that you ought to
have your (something) confoundedly well kicked."

What I have already said on this subject will, I think,
establish two points: first, that the voluntary system does
not work well for society; and secondly, that the ministers
of the churches are treated with such tyranny and
contumely as to warrant the assertion that in a country, like
the United States, where a man may, in any other profession, become independent in a few years, the number of
those who enter into the ministry must decrease at the very
time that the population and demand for them will increase.

We have now another question to be examined, and
a very important one, which is—Are those who worship
under the voluntary system supplied at a cheaper rate than
those of the established churches in this kingdom?

I say this is an important question, as there is no
doubt that one of the principal causes of dissenting has
been the taxes upon religion in this country and the wish, if
it were attainable, of worshipping at free cost. In entering
into this question there is no occasion to refer to any
particular sect, as the system is much the same with them
all, and is nearly as follows:

Some pious and well-disposed people of a certain persuasion, we will say, imagine that another church might,
if it were built, be well filled with those of their own sect,
and that, if it is not built, the consequences will be that
many of their own persuasion will, from the habit of attending other churches, depart from those tenets which they
are anxious should not only be retained by those who have
embraced them, but as much as possible promulgated, so

as to gather strength and make converts—for it should be borne in mind that the sectarian spirit is one great cause of the rapid church-building in America.* One is of Paul, another of Apollos. They meet, and become the future deacons and elders, in all probability, to whom the minister has to bow; they agree to build a church at their own risk; they are not speculators, but religious people, who have not the least wish to make money, but who are prepared, if necessary, to lose it.

Say then that a handsome church (I am referring to the cities) of brick or stone is raised in a certain quarter of the city, and that it costs $75,000. When the interior is complete, and the pews are all built, they divide the whole cost of the church upon the pews, more or less value being put upon them according to their situations. Allowing that there are two hundred pews, the one hundred most eligible being valued at $500 each, and the other one hundred inferior at $250, these prices would pay the $75,000, the whole expense of the church building.

The pews are then put up to auction; some of the most eligible will fetch higher prices than the valuation, while some are sold below the valuation. If all are not sold, the residue remains upon the hands of the parties who built the church, and who may for a time be out of pocket. They have, however, to aid them the extra price paid for the best pews, and the sale of the vaults for burial in the church-yard.

Most of the pews being sold, the church is partly paid for. The next point is to select a minister, and, after due trial, one is chosen. If he be a man of eloquence and talent, and his doctrines acceptable to the many, the church fills, the remainder of the pews are sold, and so far the expenses of building the church are defrayed; but they have still to pay the salary of the minister, the heating and lighting of the church, the organist, and the vocalists. This

---

* Churches are also built upon speculation as they sometimes are in England.

is done by an assessment upon the pews, each pew being assessed according to the sum which it fetched when sold by auction.

I will now give the exact expenses of an American gentleman in Boston, who has his pew in one of the largest churches.

He purchased his pew at auction for $750, it being one of the best in the church. The salaries of the most popular ministers vary from $1,500 to $3,000 or $4,000. The organist receives about $500; the vocalists from $200 to $300 each. To meet his share of these and the other expenses, the assessment of this gentleman is $63 per annum. Now, the interest of $750 in America is $45, and the assessment being $63—$108 per annum . . . for his yearly expenses under the voluntary system. This, of course, does not include the offerings of the plate, charity sermons, etc., all of which are to be added. . . .

It does not appear by the above calculations that the voluntary system has cheapness to recommend it, when people worship in a respectable manner, as you might hire a house and farm of fifty acres in that state for the same rent which this gentleman pays for going to church; but it must also be recollected that it is quite optional and that those who do not go to church need not pay at all.

It was not, however, until late years that such was the case. In Massachusetts, and in most of the eastern states, the system was not voluntary, and it is to this cause that may be ascribed the superior morality and reverence for religion still existing, although decaying, in these states. By former enactments in Massachusetts, landowners in the country were compelled to contribute to the support of the church.[1]

---

[1] Separation of church and state in the United States did not automatically occur after the Revolution. "The Massachusetts Bill of Rights of 1780 declared it the duty of the legislature to re- quire the support of Protestant worship, and continued to it [the legislature] authority to compel attendance thereon where con- scientious scruples did not pre- vent the individual citizen." Wil-

Pews in cities or towns are mentioned in all deeds and wills as *personal* property; but in the country, before the late act, they were considered as *real* estate.[2]

A pew was allotted each farm, and whether the proprietor occupied it or not, he was obliged to pay for it; but by an act of the Massachusetts' state legislature, passed

---

liston Walker, *A History of the Congregational Churches in the United States* (New York: Christian Literature Co.; 1894), p. 236. Connecticut as well as Massachusetts "still maintained the principle that all persons should be taxed for the support of religious institutions, . . . But this system came to an end in Connecticut by the adoption of the present constitution in 1818, by which all religious bodies were made equal before the law and all connection between church and state were severed; and a similar disestablishment took place in Massachusetts in 1834." Walker, *op. cit.*, p. 236. For a very complete account of the problem, see Jacob C. Meyer, *Church and State in Massachusetts from 1740 to 1833* (Cleveland, Ohio: Western Reserve University Press; 1930).

[2] Marryat here is only partly correct and the real facts are as follows: "In the absence of any statutory provisions declaring them personal, pews are considered to be real estate. In Massachusetts the matter is governed by statute. Massachusetts Statutes, 1795, c. 53, s. 1, declares pews to be real estate. In Massachusetts Statutes, 1798, c. 42, the General Court provided that *in the City of Boston, alone, pews should be regarded as personal property*. This was done to permit the inhabitants of that City to revert to their "way and practice." The explanation lies in the fact that, historically, Boston has trod an ecclesiastical path separate from the remainder of the Commonwealth. Because of the rapid expansion, it could not be considered as a single parish governed by the general law, as was the case in all other towns. More than one religious society was needed within its limits; and, accordingly, no attempt was ever made to organize it into parishes. The provincial act of 1693 exempted its inhabitants from the general law regulating the choice and maintenance of ministers. They were accorded special means of raising revenue and could not be compelled to pay taxes for the support of public worship. They regarded their pews as personal property. The church structure itself was owned by a unique form of quasi corporation made up of pew proprietors. In any event, the General Court destroyed this nicety by passing the Massachusetts Statutes, 1855, c. 122, which provided that pews in all houses of public worship were to be personal property."—from Philip M. Isaacson, LL.B., to the editor, February 16, 1961.

within these few years, it was decided that no man should
be compelled to pay for religion. The consequence has
been that the farmers now refuse to pay for their pews, the
churches are empty, and a portion of the clergy have been
reduced to the greatest distress. An intinerant ranter, who
will preach in the open air and send his hat round for
cents, suits the farmers much better as it is much cheaper.
Certainly this does not argue much for the progressive
advancement of religion, even in the moral state of Massachusetts.

In other points the cause of morality has, till lately,
been upheld in these eastern states. It was but the other
day that a man was discharged from prison, who had been
confined for disseminating atheistical doctrines. It was,
however, said at the time that that was the last attempt
that would ever be made by the authorities to imprison a
man for liberty of conscience; and I believe that such will
be the case. . . .

It is, however, worthy of remark that those states that
have *enforced* religion, and morality, and have punished
infidelity, are now the most virtuous, the most refined,
and the most intellectual, and are quoted as such by
American authors. . . .

It is my opinion that the voluntary system will never
work well under any form of government, and still less so
under a democracy.

Those who live under a democracy have but one
pursuit, but one object to gain, which is wealth. No one can
serve God and Mammon. To suppose that a man who has
been in such ardent pursuit of wealth, as is the American
for six days in the week, can recall his attention and
thoughts to serious points on the seventh, is absurd; you
might as well expect him to forget his tobacco on Sunday.

Under a democracy, therefore, you must look for
religion among the women, not among the men, and such
is found to be the case in the United States. As Sam Slick
very truly says: "It's only women who attend meeting; the
men folks have their politics and trade to talk over and

haven't *time.*" [3] Even an established church would not make people as religious under a democratic form of government as it would under any other.

I have yet to point out how slander and defamation flourish under a democracy. Now, this voluntary system, from the interference of the laity, who judge not only the minister, but the congregation, gives what appears to be a legitimate sanction to this tyrannical surveillance over the conduct and behaviour of others. I really believe that the majority of men who go to church in America do so not from zeal towards God, but from fear of their neighbours; and this very tyranny in the more established persuasions is the cause of thousands turning away to other sects which are not subjected to scrutiny. The Unitarian is in this point the most convenient, and is therefore fast gaining ground. . . .

In the United States the variety of sects, the continual splitting and breaking up of those sects, and their occasional violent altercations have all proved most injurious to society and to the cause of religion itself. Indeed, religion in the states may be said to have been a source of continual discord and the unhingeing of society, instead of that peace and good-will inculcated by our divine Legislator. It is the division of the Protestant church which has occasioned its weakness in this country, and will probably eventually occasion, if not its total subversion, at all events its subversion in the western hemisphere of America.

The subjugation of the ministry to the tyranny of their congregations is another most serious evil; for either they

---

[3] This is a quotation from *The Clockmaker, or Sayings and Doings of Sam Slick of Slickville* (1837) written by Thomas Chandler Haliburton (1796–1865), the son of a loyalist who had emigrated to Nova Scotia after the Revolution. After a successful career as a lawyer, Thomas Chandler Haliburton was appointed Chief Justice of Nova Scotia. His fame rests not on his public life but on his humorous writings. His best-known books are those in *The Clockmaker* series, in which the sayings and doings of Sam Slick, a typical "down-Easter," are recorded.

must surrender up their consciences or their bread. In too many instances it is the same here in religion as in politics: before the people will permit anyone to serve them in any office, he must first prove his unfitness, by submitting to what no man of honesty or conscientious rectitude would subscribe to. This must of course, in both cases, be taken with exceptions, but it is but too often the fact. And hence has arisen another evil, which is that there are hundreds of self-constituted ministers, who wander over the western country, using the word of God as a cloak, working upon the feelings of the women to obtain money, and rendering religion a by-word among the men, who will, in all probability, some day rise up and lynch some dozen of them, as a hint for the rest to *clear out*.

It would appear as if Locofoco-ism [4] and infidelity had formed an union, and were fighting under the same banner. They have recently celebrated the birth-day of Tom Paine, in Cincinnati, New York, and Boston. In Cincinnati, Frances Wright Darusmont,[5] better known as Fanny Wright, was present, and made a violent politico-atheistical speech on the occasion, in which she denounced banking and almost

---

[4] Locofocoism was the name given to the movement dominated by the radical Jacksonians in New York and Massachusetts. The name originated in 1835 when the conservative Democrats, during a meeting at Tammany Hall, attempted to break up the assembly of radicals by extinguishing the lights. The radicals, forewarned, struck safety matches (a safety match at that time was called a locofoco), lighted fifty candles, and continued the meeting. For an extended discussion of the movement, see A. M. Schlesinger, Jr., *The Age of Jackson*, pp. 190–209.

[5] Fanny Wright (1795–1852), reformer and free-thinker, was born in Scotland. She first visited America in 1818 and, like many other travelers of that time, wrote a book giving an account of her experiences. The book, entitled *Views of Society and Manners in America*, appeared in 1821 and was notable for its very pro-American attitude. Fanny Wright returned to the United States in 1824 and became actively involved in schemes for the emancipation of the Negro. She was also associated with Robert Owen and his colony at New Harmony. She became an ardent spokesman for women's rights and her support of these views made her unpopular in conservative circles.

every other established institution of the country. The nature of the celebration in Boston will be understood from the following toast, giving on the occasion:

By George Chapman: *"Christianity* and the *banks,* tottering on their last legs: May their *downfall* be speedy," etc., etc. . . .

But there is another very strong objection, and most important one, to the voluntary system, which I have delayed to bring forward: which is, that there is *no provision for the poor* in the American voluntary church system. Thus only those who are rich and able to afford religion can obtain it. At present it is true that the majority of the people in America have means sufficient to pay for seats in churches, if they choose to expend the money; but as America increases her population, so will she increase the number of her poor; and what will be the consequence hereafter, if this evil is to continue? . . .

Two other remarks . . . are equally correct: first, that the voluntary system tends to the multiplication of sects without end; and next, that the voluntary system is a mendicant system, and involves one of the worst features of the church of Rome, which is, that it tends to the production of pious frauds. . . .

At present Massachusetts, and the smaller eastern states, are the strong-hold of religion and morality; as you proceed from them farther south or west, so does the influence of the clergy decrease, until it is totally lost in the wild states of Missouri and Arkansas. With the exception of certain cases to be found in Western Virginia, Kentucky, and Ohio, the whole of the states to the westward of the Allegheny mountains, comprising more than two thirds of America, may be said to be either in a state of neglect and darkness or professing the Catholic religion.

Although Virginia is a slave state, I think there is more religion there than in some of the more northern free states; but it must be recollected that Virginia has been long settled, and the non-*predial* state of the slaves is not attended with demoralizing effects; and I may here observe that the *black* population of America is decidedly the most religious, and sets an example to the white, particularly in the free states.

It may be fairly inquired, can this be true? Not fifty years back, at the time of the Declaration of Independence, was not the American community one of the most virtuous in existence? Such was indeed the case, as it is now equally certain that they are one of the most demoralized. The question is, then, what can have created such a change in the short period of fifty years?

The only reply that can be given is that, as the Americans, in their eagerness to possess new lands, pushed away into the west, so did they leave civilization behind and return to ignorance and barbarism; they scattered their population, and the word of God was not to be heard in the wilderness.

That as she increased her slave states, so did she give employment, land, and power to those who were indifferent to all law, human or divine. And as, since the formation of the Union, the people have yearly gained advantages over the *government* until they now control it, so have they controlled and fettered *religion* until it produces no good fruits.

Add to this the demoralizing effects of a democracy which turns the thoughts of all to Mammon, and it will be acknowledged that this rapid fall is not so very surprising.

But, if the Protestant cause is growing weaker every day, from disunions and indifference, there is one creed which is as rapidly gaining strength; I refer to the Catholic church, which is silently but surely advancing.* Its great

---

* Although it is not forty years since the first Roman Catholic see was created, there is now in the United States a Catholic population of 800,000 souls under the government of the Pope, or Archbishop, 12 Bishops, and 433 priests. The number of churches is 401; mass houses, about 300; colleges, 10; seminaries for young men, 9; theological seminaries, 5; novitiates for Jesuits, monasteries, and convents, with academies attached, 31; seminaries for young ladies, 30; schools of the Sisters of Charity, 29; an academy for coloured girls at Baltimore; a fe-

field is in the west where, in some states, almost all are Catholics or, from neglect and ignorance, altogether indifferent as to religion. The Catholic priests are diligent, and make a large number of converts every year, and the Catholic population is added to by the number of Irish and German emigrants to the west, who are almost all of them of the Catholic persuasion. . . .

It is true, as Mr. Tocqueville [6] observes, that the Catholic church reduces all the human race to the same standard, and confounds all distinctions—not, however, upon the principle of equality or democracy, but because it will ever equally exert its power over the high and the low, assuming its right to compel princes and kings to obedience, and their dominions to its subjection. The equality professed by the Catholic church is like the equality of death, all must fall before its power; whether it be to excommunicate an individual or an empire is to it indifferent; it assumes the power of the God-head, giving and taking away, and its members stand trembling before it, as they shall hereafter do in the presence of the Deity. . . .

At present Catholicism is, comparatively speaking, weak in America and the object of that church is to become strong; they do not, therefore, frighten or alarm their

---

male infant school; and 7 Catholic newspapers.

[6] Count Alexis de Tocqueville (1805–59), French statesman and political theorist, visited the United States in 1831 to study the penal systems of the country. His report, *Du Système Pénitentiare aux États-Unis et de son Application en France* (Paris, 1833), was highly praised and the Académie Française awarded it the Prix Monthyon. De Tocqueville is best remembered for his masterpiece, *Democracy in America* (1835), and for this book he was made a member of the Académie des Sciences Morales et Politiques. De Tocqueville was a member of the Chamber of Deputies before and shortly after the 1848 revolution; in 1849 he was, for a few months, Minister of Foreign Affairs. He was outspoken in his opposition to Louis Napoleon, and his political career was brought to a sudden end by the latter's successful coup d'état in 1851. His many writings include *Quinze Jours au Désert, L'Ancien Régime et la Révolution,* and *Souvenirs.*

converts by any present show of the invariable results, but
are content to bide their time, until they shall find themselves strong enough to exert their power with triumphant
success. The Protestant cause in America is weak, from the
evil effects of the voluntary system, particularly from its
division into so many sects. A house divided against itself
cannot long stand; and every year it will be found that the
Catholic church will increase its power; and it is a question
whether a hierarchy may not eventually be raised which,
so far from *advocating the principles of equality,* may serve
as a *check* to the spirit of democracy becoming more
powerful than the government, curbing public opinion, and
reducing to better order the present chaotic state of society.

Judge Haliburton asserts that all America will be a
Catholic country. That all America west of the Alleghenies
will eventually be a Catholic country, I have no doubt, as
the Catholics are already in the majority, and there is
nothing, as Mr. Cooper observes, to prevent any state from
establishing that, or any other religion, as the *Religion of
the State;* and this is one of the dark clouds which hang
over the destiny of the western hemisphere. . . .

I think that the author of *Sam Slick* may not be
wrong in his assertion that *all* America will be a Catholic
country. I myself never prophesy; but, I cannot help remarking that even in the most anti-Catholic persuasions in
America there is a strong Papistical *feeling;* that is, there
is a vying with each other, not only to obtain the best
preachers, but to have the best organs and the best
singers. It is the system of excitement which, without their
being aware of it, they carry into their devotion. It proves
that to them there is a weariness in the church service, a
tedium in prayer, which requires to be relieved by the
stimulus of good music and sweet voices. Indeed, what
with their *anxious seats,* their *revivals,* their *music* and
their *singing,* every class and sect in the states have even
now so far fallen into Catholicism that religion has become
more of an appeal to the *senses* than to the calm and
sober judgment.

CHAPTER XXXVII

Societies and Associations

Although in a democracy the highest stations and pre-ferments are open to all, more directly than they may be under any other form of government, still these prizes are but few and insufficient compared with the number of total blanks which must be drawn by the ambitious multi-tude. It is, indeed, a stimulus to ambition (and a matter of justice, when all men are pronounced equal) that they all should have an equal chance of raising themselves by their talents and perseverance; but, when so many competitors are permitted to enter the field, few can arrive at the goal, and the mass are doomed to disappointment. However fair, therefore, it may be to admit all to the compe-tition, certain it is that the competition cannot add to the happiness of a people, when we consider the feelings of bitterness and ill-will naturally engendered among the dis-appointed multitude.

In monarchical and aristocratical institutions, the middling and lower classes, whose chances of advancement are so small that they seldom lift their eyes or thoughts above their own sphere, are therefore much happier and, it may be added, much more virtuous than those who struggle continually for preferment in the tumultuous sea of democracy. Wealth can give some importance, but wealth in a democracy gives an importance which is so common to many that it loses much of its value; and when it has been acquired, it is not sufficient for the restless ambition of the American temperament, which will always spurn wealth for power. The effects, therefore, of a democracy are, first to raise an inordinate ambition among the people, and then to cramp the very ambition which it has raised; and, as I may comment upon hereafter, it appears as if this ambition of the people, *individually* checked by the nature of their institutions, becomes, as it were, concentrated and collected into a focus in upholding and contemplating the success and increase of power in the federal government. Thus has been produced a species of demoralizing reaction, the disappointed *units* to a certain degree satisfying themselves with any advance in the power and importance of the whole Union, wholly regardless of the means by which such increase may have been obtained.

But this unsatisfied ambition has found another vent in the formation of many powerful religious and other associations. In a country where there will ever be an attempt of the people to tyrannize over everybody and everything, power they will have; and if they cannot obtain it in the various departments of the state governments, they will have it in opposition to the government; for all these societies and associations connect themselves directly with politics. It is of little consequence by what description of tie "these sticks in the fable" are bound up together; once bound together, they are not to be broken. In America religion severs the community, but these societies are the bonds which to a certain degree reunite it.

To enumerate the whole of these societies actually existing, or which have been in existence, would be difficult. The following are the most prominent:

LIST OF BENEVOLENT SOCIETIES, WITH THEIR RECEIPTS
IN THE YEAR 1834

American Board of Commissioners for Foreign Missions $155,002.24

American Baptist Board of Foreign Missions	63,000.00
Western Foreign Mission Society at Pittsburgh, Pennsylvania	16,296.46
Methodist Episcopal Missionary Society	35,700.15
Protestant Episcopal Foreign and Domestic Missionary Society	26,007.97
American Home Missionary Society	78,911.24
Baptist Home Missionary Society	11,448.28
Board of Missions of the Reformed Dutch Church (Domestic)	5,572.97
Board of Missions of the General Assembly of the Presbyterian Church (Domestic) estimated	40,000.00
American Education Society	57,122.20
Board of Education of the General Assembly of the Presbyterian Churches	38,000.00
Northern Baptist Education Society	4,681.11
Board of Education of the Reformed Dutch Church	1,270.20
American Bible Society	88,600.82
American Sunday School Union	136,855.58
General Protestant Episcopal Sunday School Union	6,641.00
Baptist General Tract Society	6,126.97
American Tract Society	66,485.83
American Colonization Society	48,939.17
Prison Discipline Society	2,364.00
American Seamen's Friend Society	16,064.00
American Temperance Society	5,871.12
	$8,910,961.31

Many of these societies had not been established more than ten years at the date given; they must have increased very much since that period. Of course many of them are very useful and very well conducted. There are many others: New England Non-resistance Society, Sabbath Observance Society, etc.; in fact, the Americans are society mad. I do not intend to speak with the least disrespect of the societies, but the zeal or fanaticism, if I may use the term, with which many, if not all, of them are carried on, is too remarkable a feature in the American character to be passed over without comment. Many of these societies have done much good, particularly the religious societies; but many others, from being pushed too far, have done great mischief, and have very much assisted to demoralize the community. I remember once hearing a story of an ostler who confessed to a Catholic priest; he enumerated a long catalogue of enormities peculiar to his profession, and when he had finished, the priest inquired of him "whether he had ever greased horses' teeth to prevent their eating their corn," this peculiar offence not having been mentioned in his confession. The ostler declared that he never had; absolution was given, and he departed. About six months afterwards, the ostler went again to unload his conscience; the former crimes and peccadilloes were enumerated, but added to them were several acknowledgments of having at various times *"greased horses' teeth"* to prevent their eating their corn. "Ho—Ho!" cried the priest, "why, if I recollect aright, according to your former confession you had never been guilty of this practice. How comes it that you have added this crime to your many others?" "May it please you, father," replied the ostler, "I had *never heard of it,* until you told me."

Now this story is very *apropos* to the conduct pursued by many of these societies in America: they must display to the public their statistics of immorality and vice; they must prove their usefulness by informing those who were quite ignorant, and therefore innocent, that there are crimes of which they had no idea; and thus, in their fanatic wish to improve, they demoralize. Such have been the consequences among this excitable yet well-meaning people. . . .

I cannot help inquiring how is it, if the Americans are, as they assert, both orally and in their printed public documents, a *very moral nation,* that they find it necessary to resort to all these societies for the improvement of their brother citizens; and how is it that their reports are full of such unexampled atrocities, as are printed and circulated in evidence of the necessity of their stemming the current of vice? The Americans were constantly twitting me about the occasional cases of adultery and divorce which appear in our newspapers, assuring me, at the same time, that there was hardly ever such a thing heard of in their own moral community. Now, it appears that this subject has not only been taken up by the clergy (for Dr. Dwight,[1] late president of Yale College, preached a sermon on the seventh commandment, which an American author asserts "was heard with pain and confusion of face, and which never can be read in a promiscuous circle without exciting the same feelings") but by one of their societies also; and, although they have not assumed the name of the *Patent Anti-Adultery Society,* they are positively doing the work of such a one, and the details are entered into in promiscuous assemblies without the least reservation.

The author before mentioned says: [2]

> The common feeling on the subject has been declared false delicacy; and, in order to break ground against its sway, females have been forced into the van of this enterprise; and persuaded to act as agents, not only among their own sex, but in circumstances where they must necessarily agitate the subject with men,— not wives with husbands, which would be bad enough,

---

[1] Timothy William Dwight (1752–1817), American clergyman and educator, graduated from Yale College in 1769 and was a member of the faculty there from 1771 to 1777. During the Revolution he was an army chaplain; later he had churches in Northampton and Greenfield Hill. In 1795 he was appointed president of Yale. He was widely read and possessed an immense breadth of mind and interest. His own works, such as *Theology Explained and Defended* (1819) in five volumes, were immensely popular, and his *Travels in New England and New York* (1821–22) is most entertaining.

[2] This is a quotation from *A Voice from America to England* by An American Gentleman. The pseudonym was used by Calvin Colton (1789–1857), born in Massachusetts and graduated from Yale in 1812. For a time he lived in England where he served as a newspaper correspondent. Upon his return to the United States he joined the faculty of Trinity College in Hartford as a professor of political economy. He was well known for his many writings, which were published in England and in the United States; his best-known work was his *Life and Times of Henry Clay,* which appeared in 1844.

but *young and single women* with *young and single men!* And we have been credibly informed, that attempts have been made to form associations among *wives* to regulate the privileges, and so attain the end of temperance, in the *conjugal relation.* The next step, of course, will be tee-totalism in this particular; and, as a consequence, the extinction of the human race, unless peradventure the failure of the main enterprise of the Moral Reform Society should keep it up by progeny not to be honoured.

Let it be remembered that this is not a statement of my own, but it is an *American* who makes the assertion, which I could prove to be true, might I publish what I must not.

From the infirmity of our natures, and our proneness to evil, there is nothing so corrupting as the statistics of vice. Can young females remain pure in their ideas who read with indifference details of the grossest nature? Can the youth of a nation remain uncontaminated who are continually poring over pages describing sensuality; and will they not, in their desire of "something new," as the prophet says, run into the very vices of the existence of which they were before unconscious? It is this dangerous running into extremes which has occasioned so many of these societies to have been productive of much evil. A Boston editor remarks:

> The tendency of the leaders of the moral and benevolent reforms of the day to run into fanaticism, threatens to destroy the really beneficial effects of all associations for these objects. The spirit of propagandism, when it becomes over zealous, is next of kin to the spirit of persecution. The benevolent associations of the day are on the brink of a danger that will be fatal to their farther usefulness if not checked.

Of the Abolition Society and its tendency, I have already spoken in the chapter on slavery. I must not, however, pass over another which at present is rapidly extending its sway over the whole Union, and it is difficult to say whether it does most harm or most good—I refer to the Temperance Society.

The Reverend Mr. Reed [3] says:

> In the short space of its existence, upwards of seven thousand Temperance Societies have been formed, embracing more than one million two hundred and fifty thousand members. More than three thousand distilleries have been stopped, and more than seven thousand persons who dealt in spirits have declined the trade. Upwards of one thousand vessels have abandoned their use. And, most marvellous of all! it is said that above ten thousand drunkards have been reclaimed from intoxication.

And he adds—"I really know of no one circumstance in the history of this people, or of any people, so exhilarating as this. It discovers that power of self-government, which is the leading element of all national greatness, in an unexampled degree." Now here is a remarkable instance of a traveller taking for granted that what is reported to him is the truth. The worthy clergyman, himself, evidently without guile, fully believed a statement which was absurd, from the simple fact that only one side of the balance sheet had been presented.

That 7,000 Temperance Societies have been formed is true. That 3,000 distilleries have stopped from principle

---

[3] Andrew Reed (1787–1862), an Englishman, was the minister of Wycliffe Chapel, Mile End Road, London. He was ordained in 1811 and was extremely successful as a preacher. He was noted for his charitable activities, especially with respect to the creation and construction of orphanages. He wrote many theological works and also two novels. Marryat quotes extensively from Reed's *Visit to the American* *Churches by the Deputation from the Congregational Union of England,* which he wrote with James Matheson after the two men had visited the United States. For a life of Andrew Reed see A. Reed and C. Reed, *Memoirs of the life and Philanthropic Labours of Andrew Reed D.D.* (London, 1867), and also Emnia R. Pitman, *George Muller and Andrew Reed* (London, 1885).

may also be true; but the Temperance Society reports take no notice of the many which have been *set up in their stead* by those who felt no compunction at selling spirits. Equally true it may be that 7,000 dealers in spirits have ceased to sell them; but if they have declined the trade, *others have taken it up.* That the crews of many vessels have abandoned the use of spiritous liquors is also the fact, and that is the greatest benefit which has resulted from the efforts of the Temperance Society; but I believe the number to be greatly magnified. That 10,000 drunkards have been reclaimed—that is, that they have signed papers and taken the oath—may be true; but how many have fallen away from their good resolutions and become more intemperate than before is not recorded, nor how many who, previously careless of liquor, have, out of pure opposition, and in defiance of the society, actually become drunkards, is also unknown. In this society, as in the Abolition Society, they have canvassed for legislative enactments and have succeeded in obtaining them. The legislature of Massachusetts, which state is the stronghold of the society, passed an act last year by which it prohibited the selling of spirits in a smaller quantity than fifteen gallons, intending thereby to do away with the means of dram-drinking at the groceries, as they are termed; a clause, however, permitted apothecaries to retail smaller quantities, and the consequence was that all the grog-shops commenced taking out apothecaries' licences. That being stopped, the *striped pig* was resorted to: that is to say, a man charged people the value of a glass of liquor to see a *striped pig,* which peculiarity was exhibited as a sight, and, when in the house, the visitors were offered a glass of spirits for nothing. But this act of the legislature has given great offence, and the state of Massachusetts is now divided into two very strange political parties, to wit, the *topers* and the *teetotalers.* It is asserted that, in the political contest which is to take place, the topers will be victorious; and if so, it will be satisfactorily proved that, in the very enlightened and moral state of

Massachusetts, the pattern of the Union, there are more intemperate than sober men.

In this dispute between sobriety and inebriety the clergy have not been idle: some denouncing alcohol from the pulpit; some, on the other hand, denouncing the Temperance Societies as not being Christians. Among the latter the Bishop of Vermont has led the van. In one of his works, *The Primitive Church,* he asserts that—

"The Temperance Society is not based upon religious, but worldly principles.

"That it opposes vice and attempts to establish virtue in a manner which is not in accordance with the word of God," etc., etc.

His argument is briefly this: The Scriptures forbid drunkenness. If the people will not do right in obedience to the word of God, but only from the fear of public opinion, they show more respect to man than God.

The counter argument is: The Bible prohibits many other crimes, such as murder, theft, etc.; but if there were not punishments for these offences agreed upon by society, the fear of God would not prevent these crimes from being committed.

That in the United States public opinion has more influence than religion I believe to be the case; and that in all countries present punishment is more to be considered than future is, I fear, equally true. But I do not pretend to decide the question, which has occasioned great animosities, and on some occasions, I am informed, the dismissal of clergymen from their churches.

The teetotalers have carried their tenets to a length which threatens to invade the rites of the church, for a portion of them, calling themselves the Total Abstinence Society, will not use any wine which has alcohol in it in taking the sacrament, and as there is no wine without a portion of alcohol, they have invented a harmless mixture which they call wine. Unfortunately, many of these Temperance Societies, in their zeal, will admit of no medium party—you must either abstain altogether or be put down as a toper.

It is astonishing how obstinate some people are, and how great is the diversity of opinion. I have heard many anecdotes relative to this question. A man who indulged freely was recommended to join the society. "Now," said the minister, "you must allow that there is nothing so good, so valuable to man as water. What is the first thing you call for in sickness but water? What else can cool your parched tongue like water? What did the rich man ask for when in fiery torments? What does the wretch ask for when on the rack? You cannot always drink spirits, but water you can. Water costs nothing, and you save your money. Water never intoxicates, or prevents you from going to your work. There is nothing like water. Come, now, Peter, let me hear your opinion."

"Well, then, sir, I think water is very good, very excellent indeed—for navigation."

An old Dutchman, who kept an inn at Hoboken, had long resisted the attacks of the Temperance Societies, until one night he happened to get so very drunk that he actually signed the paper and took the oath. The next morning he was made acquainted with what he had unconsciously done, and, much to the surprise of his friends, he replied: "Well, if I have signed and have sworn, as you tell me I have, I must keep to my word," and from that hour the old fellow abstained altogether from his favourite schnapps. But the leaving off a habit which had become necessary had the usual result. The old man took to his bed, and at last became seriously ill. A medical man was called in, and when he was informed of what had occurred, perceived the necessity of some stimulus, and ordered that his patient should take one ounce of French brandy every day.

"An ounce of French brandy," said the old Dutchman, looking at the prescription. "Well, dat is goot; but how much is an ounce?" Nobody who was present could inform him. "I know what a quart, a pint, or a gill of brandy is," said the Dutchman, "but I never yet have had a customer call for an ounce. Well, my son, go to the schoolmaster; he is a learned man, and tell him I wish to know how much is one ounce."

The message was carried. The schoolmaster, occupied with his pupils and not liking the interruption, hastily, and without further inquiries of the messenger, turned over his Bonnycastle,[4] and arriving at the table of avoirdupois weight, replied: "Tell your father that *sixteen drams* make an *ounce.*"

The boy took back the message correctly, and when the old Dutchman heard it, his countenance brightened up. "A goot physician, a clever man. I only have drank twelve drams a day, and he tells me to take sixteen. I have taken one oath, when I was drunk, and I keep it; now dat I am sober I take anoder, which is, I will be very sick for de remainder of my days, and never throw my physic out of window."

There was a *cold water* celebration at Boston, on which occasion the hilarity of the evening was increased by the singing of the following ode. Nobody will venture to assert that there is any spirit in the composition, and, judging from what I have seen of American manners and customs, I am afraid that the sentiments of the last four lines will not be responded to throughout the Union.

ODE.

In Eden's green retreats
A water-brook that played
Between soft, and mossy seats
Beneath a plane-tree's shade,
Whose rustling leaves
Danced o'er its brink,

---

[4] John Bonnycastle (1750?–1821), English mathematician and schoolmaster, was private tutor to the sons of the Earl of Pomfret. He later became professor of mathematics at the Royal Military School at Woolwich. His works include: *The Scholar's First Guide to Arithmetic, Introduction to Algebra, Introduction to Mensuration and Practical Geometry.*

Was Adam's drink,
And also Eve's.

Beside the parent spring
　Of that young brook, the pair
Their morning chaunt would sing;
　And Eve, to dress her hair,
　　Kneel on the grass
　That fringed its side,
　And made its tide
　　Her looking-glass.

And when the man of God
　From Egypt led his flock,
They thirsted, and his rod
　Smote the Arabian rock,
　　And forth a rill
　Of water gushed,
　And on they rushed,
　　And drank their fill.

Would Eden thus have smil'd
　Had *wine* to Eden come?
Would Horeb's parching wild
　Have been refreshed with *rum?*
　　And had Eve's hair
　Been dressed in *gin,*
　Would she have been
　　Reflected fair?

Had Moses built a still
　And dealt out to that host,
To every man his gill,
　And pledged him in a toast,
　　How large a band
　Of Israel's sons
　Had laid their bones
　　In Canaan's land?

Sweet fields, beyond Death's flood,
Stand dressed in living green,
For, from the throne of God,
To freshen all the scene,
A river rolls,
Where all who will
May come and fill
Their crystal bowls.

If Eden's strength and bloom
Cold water thus hath given—
If e'en beyond the tomb,
It is the drink of heaven—
Are not *good wells*,
And *crystal springs*,
The very things
For our hotels?

CHAPTER XXXVIII

Law

The lawyers are the real aristocracy of America; they comprehend nearly the whole of the gentility, talent, and liberal information of the Union. Anyone who has had the pleasure of being at one of their meetings, such as the Kent Club at New York,[1] would be satisfied that there is no want of gentlemen with enlightened, liberal ideas in the United States; but it is to the law, the navy, and the army that you must chiefly look for this class of people. Such

[1] The Kent Club was a small intimate club presided over by Chancellor Kent. Philip Hone, a member of the club, describes it in this fashion: "The club consists of judges and lawyers, who meet and sup at each other's houses on Saturday evenings in succession; distinguished strangers are invited, and a few laymen . . . The evening is usually divided equally between wisdom and joviality. Until ten o'clock they talk law and science and philosophy, and then the scene changes to the supper-table, where Blackstone gives place to Heidsick, reports of champagne bottles are preferred to law reports, and the merits of oyster *pâtés* and *charlotte-russe* are alone summed up." —from Bayard Tuckerman, ed., *The Diary of Philip Hone,* Vol. I, p. 360. Among the members were Samuel Jones, John Duer, John Anthon, Ogden Hoffman, Peter A. Jay, Charles O'Conor, Francis B. Cutting, Edward Curtis, and J. Prescott Hall. These men were the legal luminaries of their day. See James Wilson, *The Memorial History of the City of New York* (New York: New York History Company; 1893), Vol. III, p. 373, and Francis Gerry Fairfield, *The Clubs of New York . . .* (New York: Hinton; 1873), pp. 7–8.

must ever be the case in a democracy, where the mass are to be led, the knowledge of the laws of the country and the habit of public speaking being essential to those who would reside at the helm or assist in the evolutions, the consequence has been that in every era of the Union, the lawyers have always been the most prominent actors; and it may be added that they ever will play the most distinguished parts. Clay and Webster of the present day are, and all leading men of the former generation were, lawyers.[2] Their Presidents have almost all been lawyers, and any deviation from this custom has been attended with evil results; witness the elevation of General Jackson to the Presidency, and the heavy price which the Americans have paid for their phantom glory. The names of Judge Marshall [3] and of Chancellor Kent [4] are well known in this country, and most deservedly so; indeed, I am informed it has latterly been the custom in our own law courts to cite as cases the decisions of many of the superior American

---

[2] The lawyer in America, like the country gentleman in England, tended to dominate the political scene. Of all of the Presidents from the founding of the national government to Van Buren, only Washington was not a lawyer.

[3] John Marshall (1755–1835), a Virginian and a Federalist, was a member of Congress in 1799 and a member of John Adams's Cabinet from late 1800 to early 1801. He was almost one of Adams's midnight appointments, in that he became Chief Justice very near Adams's retirement from the Presidency. Marshall was a very great judicial figure and did much to enlarge the powers of the central government by his court decisions. He advocated broad interpretations of the Constitution and was op-

posed to the more limiting views held by the Jeffersonians. For the definitive biography of John Marshall, see Albert J. Beveridge, *Life of John Marshall* (Boston, 1916–19), 4 volumes.

[4] James Kent (1763–1847), jurist and legal commentator, was born in New York and graduated from Yale in 1781. In 1793 Kent became the first professor of law at Columbia University. Five years later he resigned his post and became a judge, becoming ultimately in 1814 Chancellor of the New York Court of Chancery. Upon his retirement from the bench he again joined the faculty of Columbia University. He is best remembered for his great work, *Commentaries on American Law* (1826–30), and he may well be the American Blackstone.

judges—a just tribute to their discrimination and their worth.

The general arrangement of that part of the American Constitution relating to the judicature is extremely good, perhaps the best of all their legislative arrangements, yet it contains some great errors; one of which is that of district and inferior judges being *elected,* as it leaves the judge at the mercy of an excitable and overbearing people, who will attempt to dictate to him as they do to their spiritual teacher. Occasionally he must choose whether he will decide as they wish, or lose his situation on the ensuing election. Justice as well as religion will be interfered with by the despotism of the democracy.

The Americans are fond of law in one respect, that is, they are fond of going to law. It is excitement to them, and not so expensive as in this country. It is a pleasure which they can afford, and for which they cheerfully pay.

But, on the other hand, the very first object of the Americans, after a law has been passed, is to find out how they can evade it; this exercises their ingenuity, and it is very amusing to observe how cleverly they sometimes manage it. Every state enactment to uphold the morals, or for the better regulation of society, is immediately opposed by the sovereign people.

An act was passed to prohibit the playing of *nine-pins,* (a very foolish act, as the Americans have so few amusements); as soon as the law was put in force, it was notified everywhere: "*Ten* pins played here," and they have been played everywhere, ever since.

Another act was passed to put down billiard-tables, and in this instance every precaution was taken by an accurate description of the billiard-table, that the law might be enforced. Whereupon an extra *pocket* was added to the billiard-table, and thus the law was evaded.

When I was at Louisville, a bill which had been brought in by Congress, to prevent the numerous accidents which occurred in steam-navigation, came into force. Inspectors were appointed to see that the steamboats complied with the regulations; and those boats which were not provided according to law did not receive the certificate from the inspectors, and were liable to a fine of five hundred dollars if they navigated without it. A steamboat was ready to start; the passengers clubbed together and subscribed half the sum (two hundred and fifty dollars), and, as the informer was to have half the penalty, the captain of the boat went and informed against himself and received the other half; and thus was the fine paid.

At Baltimore, in consequence of the prevalence of hydrophobia, the civic authorities passed a law that all dogs should be muzzled or, rather, the terms were "that all dogs should wear a muzzle," or the owner of a dog not wearing a muzzle should be brought up and fined; and the regulation farther stated that anybody convicted of having "removed the muzzle from off a dog should also be severely fined." A man, therefore, tied a muzzle to his dog's tail (the act not stating where the muzzle was to be placed). One of the city officers, perceiving this dog with his muzzle at the wrong end, took possession of the dog and brought it to the town-hall; its master, being well known, was summoned and appeared. He proved that he had complied with the act in having fixed a muzzle on the dog; and, farther, the city officer having taken the *muzzle off* the dog's tail, he insisted that he should be fined five dollars for so doing. . . .

The mass of the citizens of the United States have certainly a very great dislike to all law except their own, i.e., the decision of the majority; and it must be acknowledged that it is not only the principle of equality, but the parties who are elected as district judges that, by their own conduct, contribute much to that want of respect with which they are treated in their courts. When a judge on his bench sits half asleep, with his hat on and his coat and shoes off, his heels kicking upon the railing or table which is as high or higher than his head, his toes peeping through a pair of old worsted stockings, and with a huge quid of tobacco in his cheek, you cannot expect that much respect will be paid to him. Yet such is even now the practice in the interior of the western states. I was much amused at reading an English critique upon a work by Judge Hall (a district judge), in which the writer says: "We can imagine his honour in all the solemnity of his flowing wig," etc., etc. The last time I saw his *honour* he was cashier to a bank at Cincinnati, thumbing American bank-notes—dirtier work than is ever practised in the lowest grade of the law, as anyone would say if he had ever had any American bank-notes in his possession.

As may be supposed, in a new country like America many odd scenes take place. In the towns in the interior, a lawyer's office is generally a small wooden house, of one room, twelve feet square, built of clap-boards, and with the door wide open; and the little domicile with its tenant used to remind me of a spider in its web waiting for flies.

Not forty years back, on the other side of the Allegeny mountains, deer-skins at forty cents per pound and the furs of other animals at a settled price were *legal* tender and received both by judges and lawyers as fees. The lawyers in the towns on the banks of the Susquehannah, where it appears the people (notwithstanding Campbell's beautiful description) were extremely litigious, used to receive all their fees in kind, such as skins, corn, whiskey, etc., etc., and, as soon as they had sufficient to load a raft, were to be seen gliding down the river to dispose of their cargo at the first favourable mart for produce. Had they worn the wigs and gown of our own legal profession, the effect would have been more picturesque.

There is a record of a very curious trial which occurred in the state of New York. A man had lent a large iron kettle, or boiler, to another, and it being returned *cracked,* an action was brought against the borrower for the value of the kettle. After the plaintiff's case had been heard, the counsel for the defendant rose and said: "Mister Judge, we defend this action upon three counts, all of which we shall most satisfactorily prove to you.

"In the first place, we will prove, by undoubted evidence, that the kettle was cracked when we borrowed it;

"In the second, that the kettle, when we returned it was whole and sound;

"And in the third, we will prove that we never borrowed the kettle at all."

There is such a thing as proving too much, but one thing is pretty fairly proved in this case, which is, that the defendant's counsel must have originally descended from the Milesian stock.

I have heard many amusing stories of the peculiar eloquence of the lawyers in the newly settled western states, where metaphor is so abundant. One lawyer was so extremely metaphorical upon an occasion when the stealing of a pig was the case in point that at last he got to "coruscating rays." The judge (who appeared equally metaphorical himself) thought proper to pull him up by saying— "Mr. ——, I wish you would take the feathers from the wings of your imagination and put them into the tail of your judgment."

Extract from an American paper:

Scene.— A Court-house not fifty miles from the city of Louisville — Judge presiding with great dignity — A noise is heard before the door — He looks up, fired with indignation.— "Mr. Sheriff, sir, bring them men in here; this is the temple of liberty—this is the sanctuary of justice, and it shall not be profaned by the cracking of nuts and the eating of gingerbread."—*Marblehead Register.*

I have already observed that there is a great error in the office of the inferior and district judges being elective, but there are others equally serious. In the first place the judges are not sufficiently paid. Captain Hamilton [5] remarks—

---

[5] Thomas Hamilton (1789–1842), an army officer, partici- pated in the Peninsular Campaign during the Napoleonic

The low salaries of the judges constitute matter of general complaint among the members of the bar, both at Philadelphia and New York. These are so inadequate, when compared with the income of a well-employed barrister, that the state is deprived of the advantage of having the highest legal talent on the bench. Men from the lower walks of the profession, therefore, are generally promoted to the office; and for the sake of a wretched saving of a few thousand dollars, the public are content to submit their lives and properties to the decision of men of inferior intelligence and learning.

In one respect, I am told, the very excess of democracy defeats itself. In some states the judges are so inordinately underpaid, that no lawyer who does not possess a considerable private fortune can afford to accept the office. From this circumstance, something of aristocratic distinction has become connected with it, and a seat on the bench is now more greedily coveted than it would be were the salary more commensurate with the duties of the situation.

The next error is that political questions are permitted to interfere with the ends of justice. It is a well-known fact that, not long ago, an Irishman, who had murdered his wife, was brought to trial upon the eve of an election; and, although his guilt was undoubted, he was acquitted, because the Irish party, which were so influential as to be able to turn the election, had declared that, if their countryman was convicted, they would vote on the other side.

But worst of all is the difficulty of finding an *honest* jury—a fact generally acknowledged. Politics, private animosities, bribery, all have their influence to defeat the ends of justice, and it argues strongly against the moral standard of a nation that such should be the case; but that it is so is undoubted. The truth is that the juries have no respect for the judges, however respectable they may be, and as

Wars. He contributed regularly to *Blackwoods Magazine* from 1818 onwards. He visited the United States and published his *Men and Manners in America* in 1833; the book had a wide sale and was extremely popular—but not with Americans.

many of them really are. The feeling "I'm as good as he" operates everywhere. There is no shutting up a jury and starving them out as with us; no citizen, "free and enlightened, aged twenty-one, white," would submit to such an invasion of his rights. Captain Hamilton observes—

> It was not without astonishment, I confess, that I remarked that three-fourths of the jury-men were engaged in eating bread and cheese, and that the foreman actually announced the verdict with his mouth full, ejecting the disjointed syllables during the intervals of mastication! In truth, an American seems to look on a judge exactly as he does on a carpenter or coppersmith; and it never occurs to him, that an administrator of justice is entitled to greater respect than a constructor of brass knockers, or the sheather of a ship's bottom. The judge and the brazier are paid equally for their work; and Jonathan firmly believes that, while he has money in his pocket, there is no risk of suffering from the want either of law or warming pans.

One most notorious case of bribery I can vouch for, as I am acquainted with the two parties, one of whom purchased the snuff-box in which the other enclosed the notes and presented to the jurymen. A gentleman at New York, of the name of Stoughton, had a quarrel with another, of the name of Goodwin; the latter followed the former down the street and murdered him in open day by passing a small sword through his body. The case was as clear as a case could be, but there is a great dislike to capital punishment in America, and particularly was there in this instance, as the criminal was of good family and extensive connections. It was ascertained that all the jury except two intended to acquit the prisoner upon some pretended want of evidence, but that these two had determined that the law should take its course, and were quite inexorable. Before the jury retired to consult upon the verdict, it was determined by the friends of the prisoner that an attempt should be made by bribery to soften down the resolution of these two men. As they were retiring, a snuff-box was put into the hands of one of them by a gentleman, with the observation that he and his friend would probably find a pinch of snuff agreeable after so long a trial. The snuff-box contained bank notes to the amount of $2,500 (£500). The snuff-box and its contents were not returned, and the prisoner was acquitted.

The unwillingness to take away life is a very remarkable feature in America, and were it not carried to such an extreme length, would be a very commendable one. An instance of this occurred just before my arrival at New York. A young man by the name of Robinson, who was a clerk in an importing house, had formed a connection with a young woman on the town, of the name of Ellen Jewitt. Not having the means to meet her demands upon his purse, he had for many months embezzled from the store goods to a very large amount, which she had sold to supply her wants or wishes. At last Robinson, probably no longer caring for the girl, and aware that he was in her power, determined upon murdering her. Such accumulated crime can hardly be conceived! He went to sleep with her, made her drunk with champagne before they retired to bed, and then as she lay in bed murdered her with an axe, which he had brought with him from his master's store. The house of ill-fame in which he visited her was at that time full of other people of both sexes, who had retired to rest—it is said nearly one hundred were there on that night, thoughtless of the danger to which they were exposed. Fearful that the murder of the young woman would be discovered and brought home to him, the miscreant resolved to set fire to the house, and by thus sending unprepared into the next world so many of his fellow creatures, escape the punishment which he deserved. He set fire to the bed upon which his unfortunate victim laid, and having satisfied himself that his work was securely done, locked the door of the room and quitted the premises. A merciful Providence, however, directed otherwise; the fire was discovered, and the flames extinguished, and his crime made manifest. The evidence in an English court would have been more than sufficient to convict him; but in America, such is the feeling against taking life that, strange to say, Robinson was acquitted, and permitted to leave for Texas, where it is said, he still lives under a false name. I have heard this subject canvassed over and over again in New York; and, although some, with a view of extenuating to a foreigner such a disgraceful disregard to security of life, have endeavoured to show that the evidence was not quite satisfactory, there really was not a shadow of doubt in the whole case.

But leniency towards crime is the grand characteristic of American legislation. Whether it proceeds (as I much suspect it does) from the national vanity being unwilling to admit that such things can take place among "a very moral people," or from a more praiseworthy feeling, I am not justified in asserting. . . .

I have been very much amused with the reports of the sentences given by my excellent friend the recorder [6] of New York. He is said to be one of the soundest lawyers in the Union, and a very worthy man; but I must say that, as recorder, he does not add to the dignity of the bench by his facetious remarks, and the peculiar lenity he occasionally shows to the culprits.

I will given an extract from the newspapers of some of

---

[6] Richard Riker (1773–1842), active politician and ardent supporter of Van Buren, was from 1802 to 1804 District Attorney of New York. He was elected Recorder of New York in 1815 and held the post until 1819, when he was removed in a party hassle. He was a "Bucktail" or Van Burenite and thus ran afoul of the Clintonians. Riker was reappointed in 1820 but was again removed in 1823; in 1824 he assumed the post once more and remained in it until 1838. He was considered to be a clever lawyer and was an extremely competent judge with a reputation for severity. He was immortalized in a poem entitled "The Recorder." For further details on Riker's career, see John S. Jenkins, *History of Political Parties in the State of New York* (Auburn, N.Y.: Alden and Parsons; 1849); DeAlva S. Alexander, *A Political History of New York* (New York: Henry Holt; 1906); and Jabez D. Hammond, *The History of Political Parties of the State of New York* (Buffalo: Phinney; 1850).

the proceedings in his court, as they will, I am convinced,
be as amusing to the reader as they have been to me.

　　The Recorder then called out— "Mr. Crier, make
the usual proclamation"; "Mr. Clerk, call out the prisoners, and let us proceed to sentencing them!"
　　Clerk. Put Stephen Schofield to the bar.
　　It was done.
　　Clerk. Prisoner, you may remember you have here-
tofore been indicted for a certain crime by you comit-
ted; upon your indictment you were arraigned; upon
your arraignment you pleaded guilty, and threw yourself upon the mercy of the court. What have you now to
say, why judgment should not be passed upon you according to law?
　　The prisoner, who was a bad-looking mulatto, was
silent.
　　Recorder. Schofield, you have been convicted of a
very bad crime; you attempted to take liberties with a
young white girl—a most serious offence. This is getting to be a very bad crime, and practised, I am sorry to
say, to a great extent in this community: it must be put
a stop to. Had you been convicted of the whole crime,
we should have sent you to the state-prison for life. As
it is, we sentence you to hard labour in the state-prison
at Sing Sing for five years; and that's the judgment of
the court; and when you come out, take no more liberties with white girls.
　　Prisoner. Thank your honour it ain't no worse.
　　Clerk. Bring out Mary Burns.
　　It was done.
　　Clerk. Prisoner, you may remember, etc., etc.,
upon your arraignment you pleaded not guilty, and put
yourself on your country for trial; which country hath
found you guilty. What have you now to say why judgment should not be pronounced upon you according to
law?
　　(Silent.)
　　Recorder. Mary Burns, Mrs. Forgay gave you her
chemise to wash.

Prisoner. No, she didn't give it to me.

Recorder. But you got it somehow, and you stole the money. Now, you see, our respectable fellow-citizens, the ladies, must have their chemises washed, and, to do so, they must put confidence in their servants; and they have a right to sew their money up in their chemise if they think proper, and servants must not steal it from them. As you're a young woman, and not married, it would not be right to deprive you of the opportunity to get a husband for five years; so we shall only send you to Sing Sing for two years and six months; the keeper will work you in whatever way he may think proper.— Go to the next.

Charles Liston was brought out and arraigned, *pro forma*. He was a dark Negro.

Clerk. Liston, what have you to say why judgment, etc.?

Prisoner. All I got to say to his honour de honourable court is, dat I see de error of my ways, and I hope dey may soon see de error of deirs. I broke de law of my free country, and I must lose my liberty, and go to Sing Sing. But I trow myself on de mercy of de Recorder; and all I got to say to his honour, de honourable Richard Riker, is, dat I hope he'll live to be de next mayor of New York till I come out of Sing Sing.

Recorder (laughing). A very good speech! But, Liston, whether I'm mayor or not, you must suffer some. This stealing from entries is a most pernicious crime, and one against which our respectable fellow-citizens can scarcely guard. Two-thirds of our citizens hang their hats and coats in entries, and we must protect their hats and coats. We, therefore, sentence you to Sing Sing for five years.— Go to the next.

John McDonald and Godfrey Crawluck were put to the bar.

Recorder. McDonald and Crawluck, you stole two beeves. Now, however much I like beef, I'd be very hungry before I'd steal any beef. You are on the high road to ruin. You went up the road to Harlem, and down the road to Yorkville, and you'll soon go to destruction.

We shall send you to Sing Sing for two years each; and when you come out, take your mother's maiden name, and lead a good life, and don't eat any more beef—I mean, don't steal any more beeves.—Go to the next.

Luke Staken was arraigned.

Recorder.— Staken, you slept in a room with Lahay, and stole all his gold (1000 dollars). This sleeping in rooms with other people, and stealing their things, is a serious offence, and practised to a great extent in this city; and what makes the matter worse, you stole one thousand dollars in specie, when specie is so scarce. We send you to Sing Sing for five years.

Jacob Williams was arraigned. He looked as if he had not many days to live, though a young man.

Recorder. Williams, you stole a lot of kerseymere [7] from a store, and ran off with it—a most pernicious crime! But, as your health is not good, we shall only send you to Sing Sing for three years and six months.

John H. Murray was arraigned.

Recorder. Murray, you're a deep fellow. You got a Green Mountain boy [8] into an alley, and played at "shuffle and burn," and you burned him out of a hundred dollars. You must go to Sing Sing for five years; and we hope the reputable reporters attending for the respectable public press will warn our respectable country friends, when they come into New York, not to go into Orange street, and play at "shuffle and burn" among bad girls and bad men, or they'll very likely get burnt, like this Green Mountain boy.— Go to the next.

William Shay, charged with shying glasses at the head of a tavern-keeper. Guilty.

Recorder. This rioting is a very bad crime, Shay, and deserves heavy punishment; but as we understand

---

[7] Kerseymere is a kind of cloth which is usually coarse and ribbed.

[8] A "Green Mountain Boy" is the term applied to a Vermonter. The Vermont mountains are referred to as the Green Mountains in contradistinction to the White Mountains of New Hampshire. In the case alluded to by Marryat, the "Green Mountain Boy" would be a Vermont yokel who was taken advantage of by a New York criminal.

you have a wife and sundry little Shays, we'll let you off, provided you give your solemn promise never to do so any more.

Shay. I gives it—wery solemnonly.

Recorder. Then we discharge you.

Shay. Thank your honour—your honour's a capital judge.

John Bowen, charged with stealing a basket. Guilty.

Recorder. Now, John, we've convicted you; and you'll have to get out stone for three months on Blackwell's island—that's the judgment of the court.

William Buckley and Charles Rogers, charged with loafing, sleeping in the park, and leaving the gate open—were discharged, with a caution to take care how they interfered with corporation rights in future, or they would get their corporation into trouble.

Ann Boyle, charged with being too *lively* in the street. Let off on condition of being quiet for the time to come.

Thomas Dixon, charged with petty larceny. Guilty.

Dixon. I wish to have judgment suspended.

Recorder. It's a bad time to talk about suspension; why do you request this?

Dixon. I've an uncle I want to see, and other relations.

Recorder. In that case we'll send you to Blackwell's island for six months, you'll be sure to find them all there. Sentence accordingly.

Charles Enroff, charged with petty larceny—coming Paddy over an Irish shoemaker, and thereby cheating him out of a pair of shoes.—Guilty.

Sentenced to the penitentiary, Blackwell's island, for six months, to get out stone.

Charles Thorn, charged with assaulting Miss Rachael Prigmore.

Recorder. Miss Prigmore, how came this man to strike you?

Rachael. Because I wouldn't have him. (A laugh.) He was always a teazing me, and spouting poetry about roses and thorns; so when I told him to be off he struck me.

Prisoner (theatrically). Me strike you! Oh, Rachael—

"Perhaps it was right to dissemble your love,
But why did you kick me down stairs?"

Prisoner's Counsel. That's it, your honour. Why did she kick him down stairs?

This the fair Rachael indignantly denied, and the prisoner was found guilty.

Recorder. This striking of women is a very bad crime, you must get out stone for two months.

Prisoner. She'll repent, your honour. She loves me —I know she does.

"On the cold flinty rock, when I'm busy at work,
Oh, Rachael, I'll think of thee."

Thomas Ward, charged with petty larceny. Guilty. Ward had nothing to offer to *ward* off his sentence, therefore he was sent to the island for six months.

Maria Brandon, charged with petty larceny. Guilty. Sentenced to pick oakum for six months.

Maria. Well, I've friends, that's comfort, they'll sing—

"Oh, come to this bower, my own stricken deer"

Recorder. You're right, Maria, it's an *oakum* bower you're going to.

The court then adjourned. . . .

Mr. Carey, in his publication on *Wealth,* asserts, that security of property and of person are greater in the United States than in England. How far he is correct I shall now proceed to examine. . . .

The question is, the comparative security of person and property in Great Britain and the United States. I acknowledge that, if Ireland were taken into the account, it would very much reduce our proportional numbers; but, then, there crime is *fomented* by traitors and demagogues—a circumstance which must not be overlooked.

Still, the whole of Ireland would offer nothing equal in atrocity to what I can prove relative to one small town in America: that of Augusta, in Georgia, containing only a population of three thousand, in which, in one year, there were *fifty-nine assassinations* committed in open day, without any notice being taken of them by the authorities.

This, alone, will exceed all Ireland, and I therefore do not hesitate to assert that if every crime committed in the United States were followed up by conviction, as it would be in Great Britain, the result would fully substantiate the fact that, in security of person and property, the advantage is considerably in favour of my own country.

Englishmen express their surprise that in a moral community such a monstrosity as lynch law [9] should exist; but although the present system, which has been derived from the original lynch law, cannot be too severely condemned, it must, in justice to the Americans, be considered that the original custom of lynch law was forced upon them by circumstances. Why the term of lynch law has been made use of, I do not know; but in its origin the practice was no more blamable than were the laws established by the pilgrim fathers on their first landing at Plymouth, or any law enacted amongst a community left to themselves, their own resources, and their own guidance and government. Lynch law, as at first constituted, was nothing more than punishment awarded to offenders by a community who had been injured, and who had no law to refer to, and could have no redress if they did not take the law into

---

[9] The origin of this term is ascribed variously to the following: James Lynch FitzStevens, mayor of Galway, tried his son for murder in 1493, and, when prevented from publicly executing him, hanged him from the window of his own house; or Charles Lynch (1736–96), planter and justice of the peace in Virginia, who employed extralegal methods of trial and punishment.

their own hands; the *present* system of lynch law is, on
the contrary, an illegal exercise of the power of the majority in opposition to and defiance of the laws of the country and the measure of justice administered and awarded
by those laws.

It must be remembered that fifty years ago there were
but a few white men to the westward of the Allegheny
mountains; that the states of Kentucky and Tennessee were
at that time as scanty in population as even now are the
districts of Ioway and Columbia; that by the institutions of
the Union a district required a certain number of inhabitants before it could be acknowledged as even a district;
and that previous to such acknowledgment, the people who
had *squatted* on the land had no claim to protection or law.
It must also be borne in mind that these distant territories
offered an asylum to many who fled from the vengeance of
the laws, men without principle, thieves, rogues, and vaga-
bonds, who, escaping there, would often interfere with the
happiness and peace of some small yet well-conducted
community, which had migrated and settled on these fertile
regions. These communities had no appeal against personal
violence, no protection from rapacity and injustice. They
were not yet within the pale of the Union; indeed there
are many even now in this precise situation (that of the
Mississippi for instance), who have been necessitated to
make laws of government for themselves, and who acting
upon their own responsibilities, do very often condemn to
death, and execute. It was, therefore, to remedy the defect of there being no established law that lynch law, as it
is termed, was applied to; without it, all security, all social
happiness would have been in a state of abeyance. By degrees, all disturbers of the public peace, all offenders against
justice met with their deserts; and as it is a query, whether
on its first institution, any law from the bench was more
honestly and impartially administered than this very lynch
law, which has now had its name prostituted by the most
barbarous excesses and contemptuous violation of all law
whatever. The examples I am able to bring forward of lynch

law, in its primitive state, will be found to have been based upon necessity and a due regard to morals and to justice. For instance, the harmony of a well-conducted community would be interfered with by some worthless scoundrel, who would entice the young men to gaming or the young women to deviate from virtue. He becomes a nuisance to the community, and in consequence the heads or elders would meet and vote his expulsion. Their method was very simple and straight-forward; he was informed that his absence would be agreeable, and that if he did not "clear out" before a certain day, he would receive forty lashes with a cow-hide. If the party thought proper to defy this notice, as soon as the day arrived he received the punishment, with a due notification that, if found there again after a certain time, the dose would be repeated. By these means they rid the community of a bad subject, and the morals of the junior branches were not contaminated. Such was in its origin the practice of lynch law.

A circumstance occurred within these few years in which lynch law was duly administered. At Dubuque, in the Ioway district, a murder was committed. The people of Dubuque first applied to the authorities of the state of Michigan, but they discovered that the district of Ioway was not within the jurisdiction of that state; and, in fact, although on the opposite side of the river there was law and justice, they had neither to appeal to. They would not allow the murderer to escape; they consequently met, selected among themselves a judge and a jury, tried the man, and, upon their own responsibility, hanged him. . . .

I have collected these facts to show that lynch law has been forced upon the American settlers in the western states by *circumstances*, that it has been acted upon in support of morality and virtue, and that its awards have been regulated by strict justice. But I must now notice this practice with a view to show how dangerous it is that any law should be meted out by the majority, and that what was commenced from a sense of justice and necessity has now changed into a defiance of law, where law and justice can be readily obtained. The lynch law of the present day, as practised in the states of the west and south, may be divided into two different heads: the first is, the administration of it in cases in which the laws of the states are considered by the majority as not having awarded a punishment adequate, in their opinion, to the offence committed; and the other, when from excitement the majority will not wait for the law to act, but inflict the punishment with their own hands. . . .

At present it will be sufficient to say that, as towns rise in the south and west, they gradually become peopled with a better class; and that, as soon as this better class is sufficiently strong to accomplish their ends, a purification takes place much to the advantage of society. I hardly need observe that these better classes come from the eastward. New Orleans, Natchez, and Vicksburg are evidences of the truth of observations I have made. . . .

That the society in the towns on the banks of the Mississippi can only, like the atmosphere, "be purified by storm" is, I am afraid, but too true.

I have now entered fully, and I trust impartially, into the rise and progress of lynch law, and I must leave my readers to form their own conclusions. That it has occasionally been beneficial, in the peculiar state of the communities in which it has been practised, must be admitted; but it is equally certain that it is in itself indefensible, and that but too often, not only the punishment is much too severe for the offence, but what is still more to be deprecated, the innocent do occasionally suffer with the guilty.

CHAPTER XXXIX

Climate

I wish the remarks in this chapter to receive peculiar attention, as in commenting upon the character of the Americans, it is but justice to them to point out that many of what may be considered their errors arise from *circumstances* over which they have no control; and one which has no small weight in this scale is the peculiar climate of the country, for various as is the climate, in such an extensive region, certain it is that in one point, that of *excitement*, it has, in every portion of it, a very pernicious effect.

When I first arrived at New York, the effect of the climate upon me was immediate. On the 5th of May, the heat and closeness were oppressive. There was a sultriness in the air, even at that early period of the year, which to me seemed equal to that of Madras. Almost every day there were, instead of our mild refreshing showers, sharp storms of thunder and lightning; but the air did not appear to me to be cooled by them. And yet, strange to say, there were no incipient signs of vegetation: the trees waved their bare arms, and while I was throwing off every garment which I well could, the females were walking up and down Broadway wrapped up in warm shawls. It appeared as if it required twice the heat we have in our own country, either to create a free circulation in the blood of the people or to stimulate nature to rouse after the torpor of a protracted and severe winter. In a week from the period I have mentioned, the trees were in full foliage, the belles of Broadway walking about in summer dresses and thin satin shoes, the men calling for ice and rejoicing in the beauty of the weather, the heat of which to me was most oppressive. In one respect there appears to be very little difference throughout all the states of the Union, which is in the extreme heat of the summer months and the rapid changes of temperature which take place in the twenty-four hours. When I was on Lake Superior the thermometer stood between 90° and 100° during the day, and at night was nearly down to the freezing point. When at St. Peter's, which is nearly as far north, and farther west, the thermometer stood generally at 100° to 106° during the day, and I found it to be the case in all the northern states when the winter is most severe, as well as in the more southern. When on the Mississippi and Ohio Rivers, where the heat was most insufferable during the day, our navigation was almost every night suspended by the thick dank fogs, which covered not only the waters but the inland country, and which must be anything but healthy. In fact, in every portion of the states which I visited, and in those portions also which I did not visit, the extreme heat and rapid changes in the weather were (according to the information received from other persons) the same.

But I must proceed to particulars. I consider the climate on the seacoasts of the eastern states, from Maine to Baltimore, as the most unhealthy of all parts of America, as, added to the sudden changes, they have cold and damp easterly winds, which occasion a great deal of consumption. The inhabitants, more especially the women, shew this in their appearance, and it is by the inhabitants that the climate must be tested. The women are very delicate and very pretty; but they remind you of roses which have budded fairly, but which a check in the season has not permitted to blow. Up to sixteen or seventeen, they promise perfection; at that age their advance appears to be checked.

Mr. Sanderson,[1] in a very clever and amusing work, which I recommend to everyone, called *Sketches of Paris*, says:

Our climate is noted for three eminent qualities—extreme heat and cold, and extreme suddenness of change. If a lady has bad teeth, or a bad complexion, she lays them conveniently to the climate; if her beauty, like a tender flower, fades before noon, it is the climate; if she has a bad temper, or a snub nose; still it is the climate. But our climate is active and intellectual, especially in winter, and in all seasons more pure and transparent than the inking skies of Europe. It sustains the infancy of beauty—why not its maturity? It spares the bud—why not the opened blossom, or the ripened fruit? Our negroes are perfect in their teeth—why not the whites? The chief preservation of beauty in any country is health, and there is no place in which this great interest is so little attended to as in America. To be sensible of this, you must visit Europe—you must see the deep bosomed maids of England upon the Place Vendome and the Rue Castiglione.

I have quoted this passage, because I think Mr. Sanderson is not just in these slurs upon his fair countrywomen. I acknowledge that a bad temper does not directly proceed from climate, although sickness and suffering, occasioned by climate, may directly produce it. As for the snub nose, I agree with him that climate has not so much to do with that. Mr. Sanderson is right in saying that the chief preservative of beauty is health; but may I ask him, upon what does health depend but upon exercise? and if so, how many days are there in the American summer in which the heat will admit of exercise, or in the American winter in which it is possible for women to *walk* out?—for carriage driving is not exercise, and if it were, from the changes in the weather in America, it will always be dangerous. The

---

[1] John Sanderson (1783–1844), scholar and man of letters. His major literary work was the multi-volumed *Biography of the* *Signers of the Declaration of Independence* (ca. 1823). He was also the author of *Sketches of Paris* (1838), quoted by Marryat.

fact is that the climate will not admit of the exercise necessary for health, unless by running great risks, and very
often contracting cold and chills, which end in consumption
and death. To accuse his countrywomen of natural indolence is unfair; it is an indolence forced upon them. As for
the complexions of the females, I consider they are much
injured by the universal use of close stoves, so necessary
in the extremity of the winters. Mr. S.'s implication, that
because Negroes have perfect teeth, therefore so should the
whites, is another error. The Negroes were born for, and in,
a torrid clime, and there is some difference between their
strong ivory masticators and the transparent pearly teeth
which so rapidly decay in the eastern states, from no other
cause than the variability of the climate. Besides, do the
teeth of the women in the western states decay so fast?
Take a healthy situation, with an intermediate climate,
such as Cincinnati, and you will there find not only good
teeth, but as deep-bosomed maids as you will in England;
so you will in Virginia, Kentucky, Missouri, and Wisconsin,
which, with a portion of Ohio, are the most healthy states
in the Union. There is another proof, and a positive one,
that the women are affected by the *climate* and not through
any fault of their own, which is, that if you transplant a
delicate American girl to England, she will in a year or two
become so robust and healthy as not to be recognized upon
her return home; showing that the even temperature of our
damp climate is, from the capability of constant exercise,
more conducive to health than the sunny yet variable atmosphere of America.

The Americans are fond of their climate and consider
it, as they do everything in America, as the very best in the
world. They are, as I have said before, most happy in their
delusions. But if the climate be not a healthy one, it is certainly a beautiful climate to the eye; the sky is so clear, the
air so dry, the tints of the foliage so inexpressibly beautiful
in the autumn and early winter months, and at night the
stars are so brilliant, hundreds being visible with the naked
eye which are not to be seen by us, that I am not surprised

at the Americans praising the *beauty* of their climate. The sun is terrific in his heat, it is true, but still one cannot help feeling the want of it—when in England, he will disdain to shine for weeks. Since my return to this country, the English reader can hardly form an idea of how much I have longed for the sun. After having sojourned for nearly two years in America, the sight of it has to me almost amounted to a necessity, and I am not therefore at all astonished at an American finding fault with the climate of England; nevertheless, our climate, although unprepossessing to the eye, and depressive to the animal spirits, is much more healthy than the exciting and changeable atmosphere, although beautiful in appearance, which they breathe in the United States.

One of the first points to which I directed my attention on my arrival in America was to the diseases most prevalent. In the eastern states, as may be supposed, they have a great deal of consumption; in the western, the complaint is hardly known; but the general nature of the American diseases are *neuralgic,* or those which affect the nerves, and which are common to almost all the Union. Ophthalmia, particularly the disease of the opthalmic nerve, is very common in the eastern states. The medical men told me that there were annually more diseases of the eye in New York City alone than perhaps all over Europe. How far this may be correct I cannot say; but this I can assert, that I never had any complaint in my eyes until I arrived in America, and during a stay of eighteen months, I was three times very severely afflicted. The oculist who attended me asserted that he had *seven hundred* patients.

The *tic douloureux* [2] is another common complaint throughout America—indeed, so common it is that I should say that one out of ten suffers from it, more or less; the majority, however, are women.

I *saw* more cases of *delirium tremens* in America than I ever *heard* of before. In fact, the climate is one of *extreme*

---

[2] Spasmodic neuralgia of the face.

excitement. I had not been a week in the country before I discovered how impossible it was for a foreigner to drink as much wine or spirits as he could in England, and I believe that thousands of emigrants have been carried off by making no alteration in their habits upon their arrival.*

The winters in Wisconsin, Ioway, Missouri, and Upper Canada are dry and healthy, enabling the inhabitants to take any quantity of exercise, and I found that the people looked forward to their winters with pleasure, longing for the heat of the summer to abate.

Michigan, Indiana, Illinois, and a portion of Ohio are very unhealthy in the autumns from the want of drainage, the bilious congestive fever, ague, and dysentery carrying off large numbers. Virginia, Kentucky, North Carolina, and the eastern portions of Tennessee are comparatively healthy. South Carolina, and all the other southern states, are, as it is well known, visited by the yellow fever, and the people migrate every fall to the northward, not only to avoid the contagion, but to renovate their general health, which suffers from the continual demand upon their energies, the western and southern country being even more exciting than the east. There is a fiery disposition in the southerners which is very remarkable; they are much more easily excited than even the Spaniard or Italian, and their feelings are more violent and unrestrainable, as I shall hereafter show. That this is the effect of climate I shall now attempt to prove by one or two circumstances, out of the many which fell under my observation. It is impossible to imagine a greater difference in character than exists between the hot-blooded southerner and the cold calculating Yankee of the eastern states. I have already said that there is a continual stream of emigration from the eastern states to the southward and westward, the farmers of the eastern

---

* Vermont, New Hampshire, the interior portion of the state of New York, and all the portions of the other states which abut on the Great Lakes are healthy, owing to the dryness of the atmosphere being softened down by the proximity of such large bodies of water.

states leaving their comparatively barren lands to settle down upon the more grateful soils of the interior. Now, it is a singular yet a well-known fact that in a very few years the character of the eastern farmer is completely changed. He arrives there a hard-working, careful, and sober man; for the first two or three years his ground is well tilled, and his crops are abundant; but by degrees he becomes a different character: he neglects his farm, so that from rich soil he obtains no better crops than he formerly did upon his poor land in Massachusetts; he becomes indolent, reckless, and often intemperate. Before he has settled five years in the western country, the climate has changed him into a western man, with all the peculiar virtues and vices of the country.

A Boston friend of mine told me that he was once on board of a steamboat on the Mississippi and found that an old schoolfellow was first mate of the vessel. They ran upon a snag and were obliged to lay the vessel on shore until they could put the cargo on board of another steamboat and repair the damage. The passengers, as usual on such occasions, instead of grumbling at what could not be helped, as people do in England, made themselves merry; and because they could not proceed on their voyage, they very wisely resolved to drink champagne. They did so; a further supply being required, this first mate was sent down into the hold to procure it. My Boston friend happened to be at the hatchway when he went down with a flaring candle in his hand, and he observed the mate creep over several small barrels until he found the champagne cases and ordered them up.

"What is in those barrels?" inquired he of the mate when he came up again.

"Oh, *gunpowder!*" replied the mate.

"Good Heavens!" exclaimed the Bostonian. "Is it possible that you could be so careless? Why I should have thought better of you; you used to be a prudent man."

"Yes, and so I was, until I came into this part of the country," replied the mate, "but somehow or another, I don't care for things now which, when I was in my own state. would have frightened me out of my wits." Here was a good proof of the southern recklessness having been imbibed by a cautious Yankee.

I have adduced the above instances because I consider that the excitement so general throughout the Union, and forming so remarkable a feature in the American character, is occasioned much more by climate than by any other cause; that the peculiarity of their institutions affords constant aliment for this excitement to feed upon is true, and it is therefore seldom allowed to repose. I think, moreover, that their climate is the occasion of two bad habits to which the Americans are prone, namely, the use of tobacco and of spirituous liquors. An Englishman could not drink as the Americans do; it would destroy him here in a very short time, by the irritation it would produce upon his nerves. But the effect of tobacco is narcotic and anti-nervous; it allays that irritation and enables the American to indulge in stimulating habits without their being attended with such immediate ill consequences.

To the rapid changes of the climate, and to the extreme heat, must be also a great degree ascribed the excessive use of spirituous liquors, the system being depressed by the sudden changes demanding stimulus to equalize the pulse. The extraordinary heat during the summer is also another cause of it. . . . To drink pure water during this extreme heat is very dangerous: it must be qualified with some wine or spirit; and thus is an American led into a habit of drinking, from which it is not very easy, indeed hardly possible, for him to abstain, except during the winter, and the winters in America are too cold for a man to leave off *any* of his *habits*. Let it not be supposed that I wish to excuse intemperance: far from it; but I wish to be just in my remarks upon the Americans and show that if they are intemperate (which they certainly are), there is more excuse for them than there is for other nations, from their temptation arising out of circumstances.

There is but one other point to be considered in examining into the climate of America. It will be admitted that the American stock is the very best in the world, being originally English, with a favourable admixture of German, Irish, French, and other northern countries. It moreover has the great advantage of a continual importation of the same varieties of stock to cross and improve the breed. The question then is, have the American race improved or degenerated since the first settlement? If they have degenerated, the climate cannot be healthy.

I was very particular in examining into this point, and I have no hesitation in saying that the American people are not equal in strength or in form to the English. I may displease the Americans by this assertion, and they may bring forward their backwoodsmen and their Kentuckians, who live at the spurs of the Allegheny mountains, as evidence to the contrary; but although they are powerful and tall men, they are not well made, nor so well made as the Virginians, who are the finest race in the Union. There is one peculiar defect in the American figure common to both sexes, which is, *narrowness of the shoulders,* and it is a very great defect; there seems to be a check to the expansion of the chest in their climate, the physiological causes of which I leave to others. On the whole, they certainly are a taller race than the natives of Europe, but not with proportionate muscular strength. Their climate, therefore, I unhesitatingly pronounce to be bad, being injurious to them in the two important points, of healthy vigour in the body and healthy action of the mind, enervating the one and tending to demoralize the other.

CHAPTER XL

Education

M r. Carey,[1] in his statistical work, falls into the great
error of most American writers—that of lauding
his own country and countrymen, and inducing them to believe that they are superior to all nations under heaven. This
is very injudicious and highly injurious to the national
character: it upholds that self-conceit to which the Americans are already so prone, and checks that improvement so
necessary to place them on a level with the English nation.
The Americans have gained more by their faults having
been pointed out by travellers than they will choose to allow; and, from his moral courage in fearlessly pointing out
the truth, the best friend to America, among their own
countrymen, has been Dr. Channing. I certainly was under
the impression, previous to my visit to the United States,
that education was much more universal there than in
England; but every step I took, and every mile I travelled,
lowered my estimate on that point. . . .

To estimate the amount of education in England by
the number of *national schools*[2] must ever be wrong. In

---

[1] See earlier note on Carey in
Marryat's introduction, p. 10.
[2] The national schools first appeared in 1811 as a result of the
creation of an Anglican organization called the "National Society for the Education of the
Poor in Accordance with the

America, by so doing, a fair approximation may be arrived at, as the education of all classes is chiefly confined to them; but in England the case is different; not only the rich and those in the middling classes of life, but a large proportion of the poor, sending their children to private schools. . . . The small parish of Kensington and its vicinity has only two national schools, but it contains 292 * private establishments for education; and I might produce fifty others in which the proportion would be almost as remarkable. I have said that a large portion of the poorer classes in England send their children to private teachers. This arises from a feeling of pride; they prefer paying for the tuition of their children rather than having their children educated by the *parish,* as they term the national schools. The consequence is that in every town, or village, or hamlet, you will find that there are "dame schools," as they are termed, at which about one half of the children are educated.

The subject of national education has not been warmly taken up in England until within these last twenty-five years, and has made great progress during that period. . . .

The state of Massachusetts is a *school;* it may be said that all there are educated. . . . I consider Connecticut equal to Massachusetts; but as you leave these two states, you find that education gradually diminishes. New York is

---

Principles of the Established Church." The promoters of the society required that the Anglican catechism be taught and the general tradition was Tory in politics. The national schools used the "Bell system" of teaching, that is, teaching by "monitors"—elder students who took charge of the less-advanced pupils. It was very economical because it required really only one real teacher for a very large group of children. The aim of the national schools movement was to provide primary education for the poor. In the Gilbert and Sullivan operetta *Ruddigore* Sir Ruthven Murgatroyd and Mad Margaret become teachers in a national school after abandoning their wild and wicked lives—the implication being that this form of teaching required little academic competence and might well be a fitting penance for evil deeds.

* I believe this estimate is below the mark.

the next in rank, and thus the scale descends until you
arrive at absolute ignorance. . . .

In making a comparison of the degree of education in
the United States and in England, one point should not be
overlooked. In England children may be sent to school, but
they are taken away as soon as they are useful and have
little time to follow up their education afterwards. Worked
like machines, every hour is devoted to labour, and a large
portion forget, from disuse, what they have learnt when
young. In America they have the advantage not only of being educated, but of having plenty of time, if they choose,
to profit by their education in after life. The mass in
America ought, therefore, to be better educated than the
mass in England, where *circumstances* are against it. I
must now examine the nature of education given in the
United States.

It is admitted as an axiom in the United States that
the only chance they have of upholding their present institutions is by the education of the mass; that is to say, a
people who would govern themselves must be enlightened.
Convinced of this necessity, every pains have been taken by
the federal and state governments to provide the necessary
means of *education.* This is granted; but we now have to
inquire into the nature of the education, and the advantages derived from such education as is received in the
United States.

In the first place, what is education? Is teaching a boy
to read and write education? If so, a large proportion of
the American community may be said to be educated; but,
if you supply a man with a chest of tools, does he therefore
become a carpenter? You certainly give him the means of
working at the trade, but instead of learning it, he may only
cut his fingers. Reading and writing, without the further
assistance necessary to guide people aright, is nothing more
than a chest of tools.

Then, what is education? I consider that education
commences before a child can walk: the first principle of

education, the most important, and without which all subsequent are but as leather and prunella, is the lesson of *obedience*—of submitting to parental control—*"Honour thy father and thy mother!"*

Now, anyone who has been in the United States must have perceived that there is little or no parental control. This has been remarked by most of the writers who have visited the country; indeed, to an Englishman it is a most remarkable feature. How is it possible for a child to be brought up in the way that it should go, when he is not obedient to the will of his parents? I have often fallen into a melancholy sort of musing after witnessing such remarkable specimens of uncontrolled will in children; and as the father and mother both smiled at it, I have thought that they little knew what sorrow and vexation were probably in store for them, in consequence of their own injudicious treatment of their offspring. Imagine a child of three years old in England behaving thus:

"Johnny, my dear, come here," says his mama.

"I won't," cries Johnny.

"You must, my love, you are all wet, and you'll catch cold."

"I won't," replies Johnny.

"Come, my sweet, and I've something for you."

"I won't."

"Oh! Mr. ——, do, pray make Johnny come in."

"Come in, Johnny," says the father.

"I won't."

"I tell you, come in directly, sir—do you hear?"

"I won't," replies the urchin taking to his heels.

"A sturdy republican, sir," says his father to me, smiling at the boy's resolute disobedience.

Be it recollected that I give this as one instance of a thousand which I witnessed during my sojourn in the country.

It may be inquired how is it that such is the case at present, when the obedience to parents was so rigorously inculcated by the puritan fathers that, by the blue laws, the punishment of disobedience was *death*? Captain Hall [3] ascribed it to the democracy and the rights of equality therein acknowledged; but I think, allowing the spirit of their institutions to have some effect in producing this evil, that the principal cause of it is the total neglect of the children by the father, and his absence in his professional pursuits, and the natural weakness of most mothers when their children are left altogether to their care and guidance.

Mr. Sanderson, in his *Sketches of Paris,* observes— "The motherly virtues of our women, so eulogized by foreigners, is not entitled to unqualified praise. There is no country in which maternal care is so assiduous; but also there is none in which examples of injudicious tenderness are so frequent." This I believe to be true; not that the American women are really more injudicious than those of England, but because they are not supported as they should be by the authority of the father, of whom the child should always entertain a certain portion of fear mixed with affection, to counterbalance the indulgence accorded by natural yearnings of a mother's heart.

The self-will arising from this fundamental error manifests itself throughout the whole career of the American's existence, and, consequently, it is a self-willed nation *par excellence.*

At the age of six or seven you will hear both boys and girls contradicting their fathers and mothers, and advancing their own opinions with a firmness which is very striking.

At fourteen or fifteen the boys will seldom remain longer at school. At college, it is the same thing; and they learn precisely what they please and no more. Corporal

---

[3] Basil Hall (1788–1844), British naval officer and author of many books of personal experiences and voyages. He was a contemporary of Marryat in the navy, joining in 1802 and retiring in 1823. He, too, visited the United States and wrote of his experiences. This book, *Travels in North America* (1829), is quoted by Marryat. Hall was very critical of America and the Americans.

punishment is not permitted; indeed, if we are to judge from an extract I took from an American paper, the case is reversed.

The following "Rules" are posted up in a New Jersey school-house:

"No kissing girls in school-time; no *licking* the *master* during holy-days."

At fifteen or sixteen, if not at college, the boy assumes the man; he enters into business, as a clerk to some merchant, or in some store. His father's home is abandoned, except when it may suit his convenience, his salary being sufficient for most of his wants. He frequents the bar, calls for gin cocktails, chews tobacco, and talks politics. His theoretical education, whether he has profited much by it or not, is now superseded by a more practical one, in which he obtains a most rapid proficiency. I have no hesitation in asserting that there is more practical knowledge among the Americans than among any other people under the sun.

It is singular that in America, everything, whether it be of good or evil, appears to assist the country in *going ahead*. This very want of parental control, however it may affect the morals of the community, is certainly advantageous to America as far as her rapid advancement is concerned. Boys are working like men for years before they would be in England; time is money, and they assist to bring in the harvest.

But does this independence on the part of the youth of America end here? On the contrary, what at first was *independence* assumes next the form of *opposition,* and eventually that of *control.*

The young men, before they are qualified by age to claim their rights as citizens, have their societies, their book-clubs, their political meetings, their resolutions, all of which are promulgated in the newspapers; and very often the young men's societies are called upon by the newspapers to come forward with their opinions. Here is *opposition. . . .*

But what is more remarkable is the fact that society has

been usurped by the young people, and the married and old people have been, to a certain degree, excluded from it. A young lady will give a ball and ask none but young men and young women of her aquaintance; not a *chaperon* is permitted to enter, and her father and mother are requested to stay upstairs, that they may not interfere with the amusement. This is constantly the case in Philadelphia and Baltimore, and I have heard bitter complaints made by the married people concerning it. Here is *control.* . . .

However, retribution follows: in their turn they marry and are ejected; they have children and are disobeyed. The pangs which they have occasioned to their own parents are now suffered by them in return, through the conduct of their own children; and thus it goes on, and will go on, until the system is changed.

All this is undeniable; and thus it appears that the youth of America, being under no control, acquire just as much as they please, and no more, of what may be termed theoretical knowledge. This is the first great error in American education, for how many boys are there who will learn without coercion in proportion to the number who will not? Certainly not one in ten, and therefore it may be assumed that not one in ten is properly instructed.*

Now, that the education of the youth of America is much injured by this want of control on the part of the parents is easily established by the fact that in those states where the parental control is the greatest, as in Massachusetts, the education is proportionably superior. But this great error is followed by consequences even more lamentable: it is the first dissolving power of the kindred attraction, so manifest throughout all American society. Beyond the period of infancy there is no endearment between the parents and children; none of that sweet spirit of affection

---

* The master of a school could not manage the *gals*, they being exceedingly contumacious. Beat them, he dared not; so he hit upon an expedient. He made a very strong decoction of wormwood, and for a slight offence, poured one spoonful down their throats; for a more serious one, he made them take *two*.

between brother and sisters; none of those links which unite one family; of that mutual confidence; that rejoicing in each other's success; that refuge, when they are depressed or afflicted, in the bosoms of those who love us— the sweetest portion of human existence, which supports us under, and encourages us firmly to brave, the ills of life —nothing of this exists. In short, there is hardly such a thing in America as "Home, sweet home." That there are exceptions to this, I grant; but I speak of the great majority of cases, and the results upon the character of the nation. . . .

The next error of American education is that, in their anxiety to instil into the minds of youth a proper and ardent love of their own institutions, feelings and sentiments are fostered which ought to be most carefully checked. It matters little whether these feelings (in themselves vices) are directed against the institutions of other countries; the vice once engendered remains, and *hatred,* once implanted in the breast of youth, will not be confined in its action. Neither will national conceit remain, only *national* conceit, or *vanity* be confined to admiration of a form of government; in the present mode of educating the youth of America, all sight is lost of humility, good-will, and the other Christian virtues, which are necessary to constitute a good man, whether he be an American or of any other country.

Let us examine the manner in which a child is taught. Democracy, equality, the vastness of his own country, the glorious independence, the superiority of the Americans in all conflicts by sea or land, are impressed upon his mind before he can well read. All their elementary books contain garbled and false accounts of naval and land engagements, in which every credit is given to the Americans and equal vituperation and disgrace thrown upon their opponents. Monarchy is derided, the equal rights of man declared— all is invective, uncharitableness, and falsehood. . . .

And so it is; and as if this scholastic drilling were not sufficient, every year brings round the 4th of July, on which is read in every portion of the states the act of independence, in itself sufficiently vituperative, but invariably followed up by one speech (if not more) from some great personage of the village, hamlet, town, or city, as it may be, in which the more violent he is against monarchy and the English, and the more he flatters his own countrymen, the more is his speech applauded.

Every year is this drilled into the ears of the American boy, until he leaves school, when he takes a political part himself, connecting himself with young men's society, where he spouts about tyrants, crowned heads, shades of his forefathers, blood flowing like water, independence, and glory. . . .

I think, after what I have brought forward, the reader will agree with me that the education of the youth in the United States is immoral, and the evidence that it is so is in the demoralization which has taken place in the United States since the era of the Declaration of Independence, and which fact is freely admitted by so many American writers.

It is, however, a fact that education (such as I have shown it to be) is in the United States more equally diffused. They have very few citizens of the states (except a portion of those in the west) who may be considered as "hewers of wood and drawers of water," those duties being performed by the emigrant Irish and German, and the slave population. The education of the higher classes is not by any means equal to that of the old countries of Europe. You meet very rarely with a good classical scholar or a very highly educated man, although some there certainly are, especially in the legal profession. The Americans have not the leisure for such attainments: hereafter they may have; but at present they do right to look principally to Europe for literature, as they can obtain it thence cheaper and better. In every liberal profession you will find that the ordeal necessary to be gone through is not such as it is with us; if it were, the difficulty of retaining the young men at college would be much increased. . . .

If the men in America enter so early into life that they

have not time to obtain the acquirements supposed to be requisite with us, it is much the same thing with the females of the upper classes, who, from the precocious ripening by the climate and consequent early marriages, may be said to throw down their dolls that they may nurse their children.

The Americans are very justly proud of their women, and appear tacitly to acknowledge the want of theoretical education in their own sex by the care and attention which they pay to the instruction of the other. Their exertions are, however, to a certain degree checked by the circumstance that there is not sufficient time allowed previous to the marriage of the females to give that solidity to their knowledge which would ensure its permanency. They attempt too much for so short a space of time. Two or three years are usually the period during which the young women remain at the establishments, or colleges I may call them (for in reality they are female colleges). In the prospectus of the Albany Female Academy, I find that the classes run through the following branches: French, book-keeping, ancient history, ecclesiastical history, history of literature, composition, political economy, American Constitution, law, natural theology, mental philosophy, geometry, trigonometry, algebra, natural philosophy, astronomy, chemistry, botany, mineralogy, geology, natural history, and technology, besides drawing, penmanship, etc., etc.

It is almost impossible for the mind to retain, for any length of time, such a variety of knowledge, forced into it before a female has arrived to the age of sixteen or seventeen, at which age the study of these sciences, as is the case in England, should *commence*, not *finish*. I have already mentioned that the examinations which I attended were highly creditable both to preceptors and pupils; but the duties of an American woman, as I shall hereafter explain, soon find her other occupation, and the *ologies* are lost in the realities of life. Diplomas are given at most of these establishments, on the young ladies completing their course of studies. Indeed, it appears to be almost necessary that a young lady should produce this diploma as a certificate of being qualified to bring up young republicans. I observed to an American gentleman how youthful his wife appeared to be. "Yes," replied he, "I married her a month after she had *graduated.*". . .

The ambition of the Americans to be ahead of other nations in everything produces, however, injurious effects, so far as the education of the women is concerned. The Americans will not *"leave well alone,"* they must "gild refined gold," rather than not consider themselves in advance of other countries, particularly of England. They *alter* our language, and think that they have *improved* upon it; as in the same way they would raise the standard of morals higher than with us, and consequently fall much below us, appearances supplying the place of the reality. In these endeavours they sink into a sickly sentimentality, and, as I have observed before, attempts at refinement in language really excite improper ideas. . . .

An advertisement of Mr. Bonfil's Collegiate Institute for Young Ladies, after enumerating the various branches of literature to be taught, winds up with the following paragraph:

"And finally, it will be constantly inculcated, that their education will be completed when they have the power to extend unaided, a spirit of investigation, searching and appreciating truth, *without passing the bounds assigned to the human understanding.*". . .

CHAPTER XLI

Travelling

I believe that the remarks of a traveller in any country not his own, let his work be ever so trifling or badly written, will point out some peculiarity which will have escaped the notice of those who were born and reside in that country, unless they happen to be natives of that portion of it in which the circumstance alluded to was observed. It is a fact that no one knows his own country; from assuetude and, perhaps, from the feelings of regard which we naturally have for our native land, we pass over what nevertheless does not escape the eye of a foreigner. Indeed, from the consciousness that we can always see such and such objects of interest whenever we please, we very often procrastinate until we never see them at all. I knew an old gentleman who, having always resided in London, every year declared his intention of seeing the Tower of London with its curiosities. He renewed this declaration every year, put it off until the next, and has since left the world without having ever put his intention into execution.

That the Americans would cavil at portions of the first part of my work, I was fully convinced, and as there are many observations quite new to most of them, they are by them considered to be false; but the United States, as I have before observed, comprehend an immense extent of territory, with a population running from a state of refinement down to one of positive barbarism; and although the Americans travel much, they travel the well-beaten paths, in which that which is peculiar is not so likely to meet the eye or even the ear. It does not, therefore, follow that, because what I remark is new to many of them, therefore it is false. The inhabitants of the cities in the United States (and it is those who principally visit this country) know as little of what is passing in Arkansas and Alabama as a cockney does of the manners and customs of Guernsey, Jersey, and the Isle of Man.

The other day one American lady observed that "it was too bad of Captain Marryat to assert that ladies in America carried pigtail in their work-boxes to present to the gentlemen," adding, "I never heard or saw such a thing in all my life." Very possible; and had I stated that at New York, Philadelphia, Boston, or Charleston such was the practice, she then might have been justifiably indignant. But I have been very particular in my localities, both in justice to myself and the Americans, and if they will be content to confine their animadversions to the observations upon the state to which they belong, or my general observations upon the country and government, I shall then be content; if, on the contrary, their natural vanity will not allow any remarks to be made upon the peculiarities of one portion of society without considering them as a reflection upon the whole of the Union, all I can say is that they must and will be annoyed.

The answer made to the lady who was "wrathy" about the pigtail was: "Captain M. has stated it to be a custom in one state. Have you ever been in that state?"

"No, I have not," replied the lady, "but I have never heard of it." So then, on a vast continent, extending almost from the Poles to the Equator, because one individual, one mere mite of creation among the millions (who are but a fraction of the population which the country will support) has not heard of what passes thousands of miles from her abode, therefore it cannot be true? Instead of cavilling, let the American read, mark, learn, and inwardly digest all that I have already said, and all that I intend to say in these volumes; and although the work was not written for them, but for my own countrymen, they will find that I have done them friendly service.

There is much comprehended in the simple word "travelling" which heads this chapter, and it is by no means an unimportant subject, as the degree of civilization of a country, and many important peculiarities, bearing strongly upon the state of society, are to be gathered from the high road, and the variety of entertainment for man and horse; and I think that my remarks on this subject will throw as much light upon American society as will be found in any chapter which I have written.

In a country abounding as America does with rivers and railroads, and where locomotion by steam, wherever it can be applied, supersedes every other means of conveyance, it is not to be expected that the roads will be remarkably good; they are, however, in consequence of the excellent arrangements of the townships and counties, in the eastern states, as good, and much better, than could be expected. The great objection to them is that they are not levelled, but follow the undulations of the country, so that you have a variety of short, steep ascents and descents which are very trying to the carriage-springs and very fatiguing to the traveller. Of course in a new country you must expect to fall in with the delightful varieties of Corduroy, etc., but wherever the country is settled and the population sufficient to pay the expense, the roads in America may be said to be as good as under circumstances could possibly be expected. There are one or two roads, I believe, not more, which are government roads; but, in general, the expense of the roads is defrayed by the states.

But, before I enter into any remarks upon the various modes of travelling in America, it may be as well to say a few words upon the horses, which are remarkably good in the United States; they appear to be more hardy, and have much better hoofs, than ours in England; throwing a

shoe therefore is not of the same consequence as it is with
us, for a horse will go twenty miles afterwards with little
injury. In Virginia and Kentucky the horses are almost all
thoroughbred, and from the best English stock. The dis-
tances run in racing are much longer than ours, and speed
without bottom is useless.

The Americans are very fond of fast trotting horses;
I do not refer to rackers, as they term horses that trot before and gallop behind, but fair trotters, and they certainly
have a description of horse that we could not easily match
in England. At New York, the Third Avenue, as they term
it, is the general rendezvous. I once went out there mounted
upon Paul Pry, who was once considered the fastest horse
in America; at his full speed he performed a mile in two
minutes and thirty seconds, equal to twenty-four miles per
hour. He took me at this devil of a pace as far as Hell Gate;
not wishing "to intrude," I pulled up there, and went home
again. A pair of horses in harness were pointed out to me
who could perform the mile in two minutes fifty seconds.
They use here light four-wheeled vehicles which they call
wagons, with a seat in the front for two persons and room
for your luggage behind; and in these wagons, with a pair
of horses, they think nothing of trotting them seventy or
eighty miles in a day, at the speed of twelve miles an hour;
I have seen the horses come in, and they did not appear
to suffer from the fatigue. You seldom see a horse bent
forward, but they are all daisy cutters.

The gentlemen of New York give very high prices for
fast horses; $1,000 is not by any means an uncommon
price. In a country where time is everything, they put a
proportionate value upon speed. Paul Pry is a tall grey
horse (now thirteen years old); to look at, he would not
fetch £10—the English omnibusses would refuse him.

Talking about omnibusses, those of New York, and
the other cities in America, are as good and as well regulated as those of Paris; the larger ones have four horses.
Not only their omnibusses, but their hackney coaches are
very superior to those in London; the latter are as clean as

private carriages; and with the former there is no swearing, no dislocating the arms of poor females, hauling them from one omnibus to the other—but civility without servility.

The American stagecoaches are such as experience has found out to be most suitable to the American roads, and you have not ridden in them five miles before you long for the delightful springing of four horses upon the level roads of England. They are something between an English stage and a French diligence, built with all the panels open, on account of the excessive heat of the summer months. In wet weather these panels are covered with leather aprons, which are fixed on with buttons, a very insufficient protection in the winter, as the wind blows through the intermediate spaces, whistling into your ears, and rendering it more piercing than if all was open. Moreover, they are no protection against the rain or snow, both of which find their way in to you. The coach has three seats, to receive nine passengers, those on the middle seat leaning back upon a strong and broad leather brace, which runs across. This is very disagreeable, as the centre passengers, when the panels are closed, deprive the others of the light and air from the windows. But the most disagreeable feeling arises from the body of the coach not being upon springs, but hung upon leather braces running under it and supporting it on each side; and when the roads are bad, or you ascend or rapidly descend the pitches (as they term short hills), the motion is very similar to that of being tossed in a blanket, often throwing you up to the top of the coach, so as to flatten your hat—if not your head.

The drivers are very skilful, although they are generally young men—indeed often mere boys—for they soon better themselves as they advance in life. Very often they drive six in hand; and if you are upset, it is generally more the fault of the road than of the driver. I was upset twice in one half hour when I was travelling in the winter time; but the snow was very deep at the time, and no one thinks anything of an upset in America. More serious accidents do, however, sometimes happen. When I was in New Hampshire, a neglected bridge broke down, and precipitated coach, horses, and passengers into a torrent which flowed into the Connecticut River. Some of the passengers were drowned. Those who were saved sued the township and recovered damages; but these mischances must be expected in a new country. The great annoyance of these public conveyances is that neither the proprietor or driver consider themselves the servants of the public; a stagecoach is a speculation by which as much money is to be made as possible by the proprietors; and as the driver never expects or demands a fee from the passengers, they or their comforts are no concern of his. The proprietors do not consider that they are bound to keep faith with the public, nor do they care about any complaints.

The stages which run from Cincinnati to the eastward are very much interfered with when the Ohio River is full of water, as the travellers prefer the steamboats; but the very moment that the water is so low on the Ohio that the steamboats cannot ascend the river up to Wheeling, double the price is demanded by the proprietors of the coaches. They are quite regardless as to the opinion or good-will of the public; they do not care for either, all they want is their money, and they are perfectly indifferent whether you break your neck or not. The great evil arising from this state of hostility, as you may almost call it, is the disregard of life which renders travelling so dangerous in America. You are completely at the mercy of the drivers, who are, generally speaking, very good-tempered, but sometimes quite the contrary; and I have often been amused with the scenes which have taken place between them and the passengers. As for myself, when the weather permitted it, I invariably went outside, which the Americans seldom do, and was always very good friends with the drivers. They are full of local information, and often very amusing. There is, however, a great difference in the behaviour of the drivers of the mails, and coaches which are *timed* by the post-office, and others which are not. If beyond his time, the driver is mulcted by the proprietors; and when dollars are in the question, there is an end to all urbanity and civility. . . .

I once myself was in a stagecoach, and found that the window glasses had been taken out; I mentioned this to the driver, as it rained in very fast. "Well, now," replied he, "I reckon you'd better ax the proprietors; my business is to drive the coach." And that was all the comfort I could procure. As for speaking to them about stopping, or driving slow, it is considered as an unwarrantable interference. . . .

As for stopping, they will stop to talk to anyone on the road about the price of the markets, the news, or anything else; and the same accommodation is cheerfully given to any passenger who has any business to transact on the way. The Americans are accustomed to it, and the passengers never raise any objections. There is a spirit of accommodation, arising from their natural good temper.*

I was once in a coach when the driver pulled up and entered a small house on the roadside; after he had been there some time, as it was not an inn, I expressed my wonder what he was about. "I guess I can tell you," said a man who was standing by the coach, and overheard me; "there's a pretty girl in that house, and he's doing a bit of courting, I expect." Such was the fact; the passengers laughed, and waited for him very patiently. He remained about three-quarters of an hour and then came out. The time was no doubt to him very short; but to us it appeared rather tedious. . . .

I have mentioned these little anecdotes, as they may amuse the reader; but it must be understood that, generally speaking, the drivers are very good-natured and obliging,

---

* This spirit of accommodation produces what would at first appear to be rudeness, but is not intended for it. When you travel, or indeed when walking the streets in the western country, if you have a cigar in your mouth, a man will come up—"Beg pardon, stranger," and whips your cigar out of your mouth, lights his own, and then returns yours. I thought it rather cool at first, but as I found it was the practice, I invariably did the same whenever I needed a light.

and the passengers very accommodating to each other, and submitting with a good grace to what cannot be ameliorated.

In making my observations upon the railroad and steamboat travelling in the United States, I shall point out some facts with which the reader must be made acquainted. The Americans are a restless, locomotive people: whether for business or pleasure, they are ever on the move in their own country, and they move in masses. There is but one conveyance, it may be said, for every class of people—the coach, railroad, or steamboat, as well as most of the hotels, being open to all; the consequence is that the society is very much mixed—the millionaire, the well-educated woman of the highest rank, the Senator, the member of Congress, the farmer, the emigrant, the swindler, and the pick-pocket are all liable to meet together in the same vehicle of conveyance. Some conventional rules were therefore necessary, and those rules have been made by public opinion—a power to which all must submit in America. The one most important, and without which it would be impossible to travel in such a gregarious way, is a universal deference and civility shown to the women, who may in consequence travel without protection all over the United States without the least chance of annoyance or insult. This deference paid to the sex is highly creditable to the Americans; it exists from one end of the Union to the other; indeed, in the southern and more lawless states, it is even more chivalric than in the more settled. Let a female be ever so indifferently clad, whatever her appearance may be, still it is sufficient that she is a female; she has the first accommodation, and until she has it, no man will think of himself. But this deference is not only shewn in travelling, but in every instance. An English lady told me that, wishing to be present at the inauguration of Mr. Van Buren, by some mistake, she and her daughters alighted from the carriage at the wrong entrance, and in attempting to force their way through a dense crowd were nearly crushed to death. This was perceived, and the word was given— "Make room for the ladies." The whole crowd, as if by one simultaneous effort, compressed itself to the right and left, locking themselves together to meet the enormous pressure, and made a wide lane, through which they passed with ease and comfort. "It reminded me of the Israelites passing through the Red Sea with the wall of waters on each side of them," observed the lady. "In any other country we must have been crushed to death."

When I was on board one of the steamboats, an American asked one of the ladies to what she would like to be helped. She replied, to some turkey, which was within reach, and off of which a passenger had just cut the wing and transferred it to his own plate. The American who had received the lady's wishes immediately pounced with his fork upon the wing of the turkey and carried it off to the young lady's plate; the only explanation given, *"For a lady, sir!"* was immediately admitted as sufficient.

The authority of the captain of a steamboat is never disputed; if it were, the offender would be landed on the beach. I was on board of a steamboat when, at tea time, a young man sat down with his hat on.

"You are in the company of ladies, sir," observed the captain very civilly, "and I must request you to take your hat off."

"Are you the captain of the boat?" observed the young man, in a sulky tone.

"Yes, sir, I am."

"Well, then, I suppose I must," growled the passenger, as he obeyed.

But if the stewards, who are men of colour, were to attempt to enforce the order, they would meet with such a rebuff as I have myself heard given.

"If it's the captain's orders, let the captain come and give them. I'm not going to obey a *nigger* like you."

Perhaps it is owing to this deference to the sex that you will observe that the Americans almost invariably put on their best clothes when they travel; such is the case whatever may be the cause; and the ladies in America, travelling or not, are always well, if not expensively dressed. They don't all swap bonnets as the two young ladies did in the stagecoach in Vermont.

But, notwithstanding the decorum so well preserved as I have mentioned, there are some annoyances to be met with from gregarious travelling. One is that occasionally a family of interesting young citizens who are suffering from the whooping-cough, small-pox, or any other complaint are brought on board, in consequence of the medical gentlemen having recommended change of air. Of course the other children, or even adults, may take the infection, but they are not refused admittance upon such trifling grounds; the profits of the steamboat must not be interfered with.

Of all travelling, I think that by railroad the most fatiguing, especially in America. After a certain time the constant coughing of the locomotive, the dazzling of the vision from the rapidity with which objects are passed, the sparks and ashes which fly in your face and on your clothes become very annoying; your only consolation is the speed with which you are passing over the ground.

The railroads in America are not so well made as in England, and are therefore more dangerous; but it must be remembered that at present nothing is made in America but to last a certain time; they go to the exact expense considered necessary and no further; they know that in twenty years they will be better able to spend twenty dollars than one now. The great object is to obtain quick returns for the outlay, and, except in few instances, durability or permanency is not thought of. One great cause of disasters is that the railroads are not fenced on the sides, so as to keep the cattle off them, and it appears as if the cattle who range the woods are very partial to take their naps on the roads, probably from their being drier than the other portions of the soil. It is impossible to say how many cows have been cut into atoms by the trains in America, but the frequent accidents arising from these causes have occasioned the Americans to invent a sort of shovel, attached to the front of the locomotive, which takes up a cow, tossing her off right or left. At every fifteen miles of the railroads there are refreshment rooms; the cars stop, all the doors are thrown open, and out rush the passengers like boys out of school, and crowd round the tables to solace themselves with pies, patties, cakes, hard-boiled eggs, ham, custards, and a variety of railroad luxuries, too numerous to mention. The bell rings for departure, in they all hurry with their hands and mouths full, and off they go again, until the next stopping place induces them to relieve the monotony of the journey by masticating without being hungry.

The Utica railroad is the best in the United States. The general average of speed is from fourteen to sixteen miles an hour; but on the Utica they go much faster. A gentleman narrated to me a singular specimen of the ruling passion which he witnessed on an occasion when the rail-cars were thrown off the road, and nearly one hundred people killed, or injured in a greater or less degree.

On the side of the road lay a man with his leg so severely fractured that the bone had been forced through the skin and projected outside his trousers. Over him hung his wife, with the utmost solicitude, the blood running down from a severe cut received on her head, and kneeling by his side was his sister, who was also much injured. The poor women were lamenting over him, and thinking nothing of their own hurts; and he, it appears, was also thinking nothing about his injury, but only lamenting the delay which would be occasioned by it.

"Oh! my dear, dear Isaac, what can be done with your leg?" exclaimed the wife in the deepest distress.

"What will become of my leg!" cried the man. "What's to become of my business, I should like to know?"

"Oh! dear brother," said the other female, "don't think about your business now; think of getting cured."

"Think of getting cured—I must think how the bills are to be met, and I not there to take them up. They will be presented as sure as I lie here."

"Oh! never mind the bills, dear husband—think of your precious leg."

"Not mind the bills! but I must mind the bills—my credit will be ruined."

"Not when they know what has happened, brother. Oh! dear, dear—that leg, that leg."

"D——n the leg; what's to become of my business?" groaned the man, falling on his back from excess of pain.

Now this was a specimen of true commercial spirit. If this man had not been nailed to the desk, he might have been a hero. . . .

The most general, the most rapid, the most agreeable, and, at the same time, the most dangerous of American travelling is by steamboats. . . .

Many of the largest of these rivers are at present running through deserts—others possess but a scanty population on their banks; but, as the west fills up, they will be teeming with life, and the harvest of industry will freight many more hundreds of vessels than those which at present disturb their waters.

The Americans have an idea that they are very far ahead of us in steam-navigation, a great error which I could not persuade them of. In the first place, their machinery is not by any means equal to ours; in the next, they have no sea-going steam vessels, which after all is the great desideratum of steam-navigation. Even in the number and tonnage of their mercantile steam vessels they are not equal to us, . . . nor have they yet arrived to that security in steam-navigation which we have. . . .

In consequence of their isolation, and having no means of comparison with other countries, the Americans see only their own progress, and seem to have forgotten that other nations advance as well as themselves. They appear to imagine that while they are going ahead all others are standing still, forgetting that England with her immense resources is much more likely to surpass them than to be left behind. . . .

The American steamboats are very different from ours in appearance, in consequence of the engines being invariably on deck. The decks also are carried out many feet wider on each side than the hull of the vessel, to give space; these additions to the deck are called guards. The engine being on the first deck, there is a second deck for the passengers, state-rooms, and saloons; and above this deck there is another, covered with a white awning. They have something the appearance of two-deckers, and when filled with company, the variety of colours worn by the ladies have a very novel and pleasing effect. The boats which run from New York to Boston, and up the Hudson River to Albany, are very splendid vessels; they have low-pressure engines, are well commanded, and I never heard of any accident of any importance taking place; their engines are also very superior—one on board of the *Narragansett*, with a horizontal stroke, was one of the finest I ever saw. On the Mississippi, Ohio, and their tributary rivers, the high-pressure engine is invariably used; they have tried the low-pressure, but have found that it will not answer, in consequence of the great quantity of mud contained in solution on the waters of the Mississippi, which destroys all the valves and leathers; and this is the principal cause of the many accidents which take place. At the same time it must be remembered that there is a recklessness—an indifference to life—shown throughout all America, which is rather a singular feature, inasmuch as it extends east as well as west. It can only be accounted for by the insatiate pursuit of gain among a people who consider that time is money, and who are blinded by their eagerness in the race for it, added to that venturous spirit so naturally imbibed in a new country at the commencement of its occupation. It is communicated to the other sex, who appear equally indifferent. The *Moselle* had not been blown up two hours before the other steamboats were crowded with women, who followed their relations on business or pleasure, up and down the river. "Go ahead" is the motto of the country; both sexes join in the cry; and they do go ahead—*that's a fact!* * . . .

---

* When the water in the rivers is low, the large steam vessels very often run aground, and are obliged to discharge their cargoes and passengers. At these times, the smaller steamboats

The attention of the American legislature has at length been directed to the want of security in steam navigation; and in July 1838 an act was passed to provide for the better security of the passengers. Many of the clauses are judicious, especially as far as the inspecting of them is regulated; . . .

It is to be hoped that some good effects will be produced by this act of the legislature. At present, it certainly is more dangerous to travel one week in America than to cross the Atlantic a dozen times. The number of lives lost in one year by accidents in steamboats, railroads, and coaches was estimated, in a periodical which I read in America, at *one thousand seven hundred and fifty!*

ply up and down the rivers to take advantage of these misfortunes by picking up passengers and making most exhorbitant charges for taking them or the goods out, because you *must* pay them or remain where you are. This species of cruising they themselves designate as *"going a-pirating."* I will say this for the Americans, that, if a person, who *considers* that he is not doing wrong, does *not* do wrong, they are a very honest people.

CHAPTER XLII

Hostelry and Gastronomy

To one who has been accustomed to the extortion of the inns and hotels in England, and the old continent, nothing at first is more remarkable than to find that there are more remains of the former American purity of manners and primitive simplicity to be observed in their establishments for the entertainment of man and horse than in any portion of public or private life. Such is the case, and the causes of the anomaly are to be explained.

I presume that the origin of hotels and inns has been much the same in all countries. At first the solitary traveller is received, welcomed, and hospitably entertained; but as the wayfarers multiply, what was at first a pleasure becomes a tax. For instance, let us take Western Virginia, through which the first irruption to the far west may be said to have taken place. At first everyone was received and accommodated by those who had settled there; but as this gradually became inconvenient, not only from interfering with their domestic privacy, but from their not being prepared to meet the wants of the travellers, the inhabitants of any small settlement met together and agreed upon one of them keeping the house of reception; this was not done with a view of profit, the travellers being only charged the actual value of the articles consumed. Such is still the case in many places in the far west; a friend of mine told me that he put up at the house of a widow woman; he supped, slept, had his breakfast, and his horse was also well supplied. When he was leaving, he inquired what he had to pay? The woman replied— "Well, if I don't charge something, I suppose you will be affronted. Give me a shilling" —a sum not sufficient to pay for the horse's corn.

The American innkeeper, therefore, is still looked upon in the light of your host; he and his wife sit at the head of the *table-d'hôte* at meal times; when you arrive he greets you with a welcome, shaking your hand; if you arrive in company with those who know him, you are introduced to him; he is considered on a level with you; you meet him in the most respectable companies, and it is but justice to say that, in most instances, they are a very respectable portion of society. Of course, his authority, like that of the captains of the steamboats, is undisputed; indeed, the captains of these boats may be partly considered as classed under the same head.

This is one of the most pleasing features in American society, and I think it is likely to last longer than most others in this land of change, because it is upheld by public opinion, which is so despotic. The mania for travelling, among the people of the United States, renders it most important that everything connected with locomotion should be well arranged; society demands it, public opinion enforces it, and therefore, with few exceptions, it is so. The respect shown to the master of a hotel induces people of the highest character to embark in the profession; the continual stream of travellers which pours through the country gives sufficient support by moderate profits to enable the innkeeper to abstain from excessive charges; the price of everything is known by all, and no more is charged to the President of the United States than to other people. Everyone knows his expenses; there is no surcharge, and fees to waiters are voluntary, and never asked for. At first I used to examine the bill when presented, but latterly I looked

only at the sum total at the bottom and paid it at once, reserving the examination of it for my leisure, and I never in
one instance found that I had been imposed upon. This is
very remarkable, and shows the force of public opinion in
America; for it can produce, when required, a very scarce
article all over the world, and still more scarce in the profession referred to—Honesty. Of course there will be exceptions, but they are very few, and chiefly confined to the
cities. I shall refer to them afterwards, and at the same time
to some peculiarities, which I must not omit to point out,
as they affect society. Let me first describe the interior arrangements of a first-rate American hotel.

The building is very spacious, as may be imagined
when I state that in the busy times, from one hundred and
fifty to two or even three hundred generally sit down at
the dinner-table. The upper stories contain an immense
number of bed-rooms, with their doors opening upon long
corridors, with little variety in their furniture and arrangement, except that some are provided with large beds for
married people and others with single beds. The basement
of the building contains the dinner-room, of ample dimen-
sions, to receive the guests, who at the sound of a gong rush
in, and in a few minutes have finished their repast. The
same room is appropriated to breakfast and supper. In
most hotels there is but one dining-room, to which ladies
and gentlemen both repair, but in the more considerable,
there is a smaller dining-room for the ladies and their con-
nexions who escort them. The ladies have also a large par-
lour to retire to; the gentlemen have the reading-room, containing some of the principal newspapers, and the *Bar,* of
which hereafter. If a gentleman wants to give a dinner to a
private party in any of these large hotels, he can do it; or if
a certain number of families join together, they may also
eat in a separate room (this is frequently done at Washington); but if a traveller wishes to seclude himself *à l'Anglaise,*
and dine in his own room, he must make up his mind to
fare very badly, and, moreover, if he is a foreigner, he will

give great offence and be pointed out as an aristocrat—almost as serious a charge with the majority in the United States as it was in France during the Revolution.

The largest hotels in the United States are Astor House, New York; Tremont House, Boston; Mansion House, Philadelphia; the hotels at West Point and at Buffalo; but it is unnecessary to enumerate them all. The two pleasantest are the one at West Point, which was kept by Mr. Cozens, and that belonging to Mr. Head, the Mansion House at Philadelphia; but the latter can scarcely be considered as a hotel, not only because Mr. Head is, and always was, a gentleman with whom it is a pleasure to associate, but because he is very particular in whom he receives, and only gentlemen are admitted. It is more like a private club than anything else I can compare it to, and I passed some of my pleasantest time in America at his establishment, and never bid farewell to him or his sons, or the company, without regret. There are some hotels in New York upon the English system: the Globe is the best, and I always frequented it; * and there is an excellent French restaurateur's (Delmonico's).[1]

---

* The Americans are apt to boast that they have not to pay for civility, as we do in England, by feeing waiters, coachmen, etc. In some respects this is true, but in the cities the custom has become very prevalent. A man who attends a large dinner-table will of course pay more attention to those who give him something than to those who do not; one gives him something, and another, if he wishes for attention and civility, is obliged to do the same thing. In some of the hotels at New York, and in the principal cities, you not only must fee, but you must fee much higher than you do in England, if you want to be comfortable.

[1] Delmonico's, a celebrated restaurant in New York City in the nineteenth century, was founded by John Delmonico (1788–1842), a former Swiss sea captain who had settled in America in 1825 as the owner of a wine-shop. In 1827 John Delmonico and his brother, Peter Delmonico, opened a café and confectionary shop, and this gradually was expanded into a regular restaurant. After the great New York fire of 1835 the Delmonico brothers opened a new and more splendid establishment which was situated at 2 South William Street, and it is this restaurant, officially opened in 1837, to which Marryat refers. For a further account of Delmonico's, see "This Was New York, Delmonico," in *The New Yorker*, November 10, 1956, pp. 189–210.

Of course, where the population and traffic are great, and the travellers who pass through numerous, the hotels are large and good; where, on the contrary, the road is less and less frequented, so do they decrease in importance, size, and respectability, until you arrive at the farm-house entertainment of Virginia and Kentucky; the grocery, or mere grog-shop, or the log-house of the far west. The wayside inns are remarkable for their uniformity; the furniture of the bar-room is invariably the same: a wooden clock, map of the United States, map of the state, the Declaration of Independence, a looking-glass, with a hair-brush and comb hanging to it by strings, *pro bono publico;* * sometimes with the extra embellishment of one or two miserable pictures, such as General Jackson scrambling upon a horse, with fire or steam coming out of his nostrils, going to the battle of New Orleans, etc., etc.

He who is of the silver-fork school will not find much comfort out of the American cities and large towns. There are no neat, quiet little inns, as in England. It is all the "rough and tumble" system, and when you stop at humble inns you must expect to eat peas with a two-pronged fork and to sit down to meals with people whose exterior is anything but agreeable, to attend upon yourself, and to sleep in a room in which there are three or four other beds (I have slept in one with nearly twenty), most of them carry-

---

* If I am rightly informed, there are very unpleasant cutaneous diseases to which the Americans are subject, from the continual use of the same brush and comb, and from sleeping together, etc., but it is a general custom. At Philadelphia, a large ball was given (called, I think, the Fireman's Ball), and at which about 1,500 people were present, all the fashion of Philadelphia; yet even here there were six combs and six brushes, placed in a room with six looking-glasses for the use of *all* the gentlemen. An American has come into my room in New York, and *sans ceremonie* taken up my hairbrush, and amused himself with brushing his head. They are certainly very unrefined in the toilet as yet. When I was travelling, on my arrival at a city I opened my dressing case, and a man passing by my room when the door was open, attracted by the glitter, I presume, came in and looked at the apparatus which is usually contained in such articles— "Pray, sir," said he, "are you a *dentist?*"

ing double, even if you do not have a companion in your own.

A New York friend of mine travelling in an Extra [2] with his family, told me that at a western inn he had particularly requested that he might not have a bed-fellow, and was promised that he should not. On his retiring, he found his bed already occupied, and he went down to the landlady, and expostulated. "Well," replied she, "it's only your *own driver;* I thought you wouldn't mind him!"

Another gentleman told me that, having arrived at a place called Snake's Hollow, on the Mississippi, the bed was made on the kitchen-floor, and the whole family and travellers, amounting in all to seventeen, of all ages and both sexes, turned into the same bed altogether. Of course this must be expected in a new country, and is a source of amusement, rather than of annoyance.

I must now enter into a very important question, which is that of eating and drinking. Mr. Cooper, in his remarks upon his own countrymen, says, very ill-naturedly:

> The Americans are the grossest feeders of any civilized nation known. As a nation, their food is heavy, coarse, and indigestible, while it is taken in the least artificial forms that cookery will allow. The predominance of grease in the American kitchen, coupled with the habits of hearty eating, and of constant expectoration, are the causes of the diseases of the stomach which are so common in America.

This is not correct. The cookery in the United States is exactly what it is and must be everywhere else—in a ratio with the degree of refinement of the population. In the principal cities you will meet with as good cookery in private houses as you will in London, or even Paris; indeed, considering the great difficulty which the Americans have

---

[2] An "Extra" in this case is a private carriage or coach. The traveler arranged for an "extra" if he did not choose to ride in a public stagecoach. The privilege of privacy cost an extra rate of fare.

to contend with, from the almost impossibility of obtaining good servants, I have often been surprised that it is so good as it is. At Delmonico's, and the Globe Hotel at New York, where you dine from the Carte, you have excellent French cookery; so you have at Astor House, particularly at private parties; and, generally speaking, the cooking at all the large hotels may be said to be good; indeed, when it is considered that the American table-d'hôte has to provide for so many people, it is quite surprising how well it is done. The daily dinner, at these large hotels, is infinitely superior to any I have ever sat down to at the *public* entertainments given at the Free-Masons' Tavern, and others in London, and the company is usually more numerous. The bill of fare of the table-d'hôte of the Astor House is *printed every day.* I have one with me which I shall here insert, to prove that the eating is not so bad in America as described by Mr. Cooper.

ASTOR HOUSE, *Wednesday, March 21, 1838.*
Table-d'Hôte.

Vermicelli Soup	Salade de Volaille
Boiled Cod Fish and Oysters	Ballon de Mouton au Tomato
" Corn'd Beef	Tête de Veau en Marinade
" Ham	Casserolle de Pomme de Terre
" Tongue	garnie
" Turkey and Oysters	Compote de Pigeon
" Chickens and Pork	Rolleau de Veau a la
" Leg of Mutton	Jardinière
Oyster Pie	Cotellettes de Veau Sauté
Cuisse de Poulet Sauce	Filet de Mouton Pique aux
Tomato	Ognons
Poitrine de Veau au Blanc	Ronde de Boeuf
Fricandeau de Veau aux	Roast Chickens
Epinards	" Wild Ducks
Cotelettes de Mouton Panée	" Wild Goose
Macaroni au Parmesan	" Guinea Fowl
Roast Beef	Roast Brandt
" Pig	Queen Pudding
" Veal	Mince Pie

Roast Leg of Mutton   Cream Puffs
  " Goose   Dessert.
  " Turkey

Of course, as you advance into the country, and population recedes, you run through all the scale of cookery until you come to the *"corn bread and common doings"* (i.e., bread made of Indian meal, and fat pork) in the far west. In a new country, pork is more easily raised than any other meat, and the Americans eat a great deal of pork, which renders the cooking in the small taverns very greasy—with the exception of the Virginian farm taverns, where they fry chickens without grease in a way which would be admired by Ude himself; but this is a state recipe, handed down from generation to generation, and called *chicken fixings.* The meat in America is equal to the best in England, . . . The American markets in the cities are well supplied. I have been in the game market, at New York, and seen at one time nearly three hundred head of deer, with quantities of bear, racoons, wild turkeys, geese, ducks, and every variety of bird in countless profusion. Bear I abominate; racoon is pretty good. The wild turkey is excellent; but the great delicacies in America are the terrapin, and the canvasback ducks. To like the first I consider as rather an acquired taste. I decidedly prefer the turtle, which are to be had in plenty, all the year round; but the canvasback duck is certainly well worthy of its reputation. Fish is well supplied. They have the sheep's head, shad, and one or two others, which we have not. Their salmon is not equal to ours, and they have no turbot. Pineapples, and almost all the tropical fruits, are hawked about in carts in the eastern cities; but I consider the fruit of the temperate zone, such as grapes, peaches, etc., inferior to the English. Oysters are very plentiful, very large, and, to an English palate, rather insipid. As the Americans assert that the English and French oysters taste of copper, and that therefore they cannot eat them, I presume they do; and that's the reason why we do not like the American oysters, copper being better than no flavour at all.

I think, after this statement, that the English will agree with me that there are plenty of good things for the table in America; but the old proverb says: "God sends meat, and the devil sends cooks"; and such is and unfortunately must be the case for a long while, in most of the houses in America, owing to the difficulty of obtaining or keeping servants. But I must quit the subject of eating for one of much more importance in America, which is that of drinking.

I always did consider that the English and the Swiss were the two nations who most indulged in potations; but on my arrival in the United States, I found that our descendants, in this point most assuredly, as they fain would be thought to do in all others, surpassed us altogether.

Impartiality compels me to acknowledge the truth: we must, in this instance, submit to a national defeat. There are many causes for this: first, the heat of the climate; next, the coldness of the climate; then, the changeableness of the climate; add to these, the cheapness of liquor in general, the early disfranchisement of the youth from all parental control, the temptation arising from the bar and association, and, lastly, the pleasantness, amenity, and variety of the potations.

Reasons, therefore, are as plentiful as blackberries, and habit becomes second nature.

To run up the whole catalogue of the indigenous compounds in America, from "iced water" to a "stone fence," or "streak of lightning," would fill a volume; I shall first speak of foreign importations.

The port in America is seldom good; the climate appears not to agree with the wine. The quantity of champagne drunk is enormous, and would absorb all the vintage of France, were it not that many hundred thousand bottles are consumed more than are imported.

The small state of New Jersey has the credit of supplying the *American* champagne, which is said to be concocted out of turnip juice, mixed with brandy and honey.[3] It is a pleasant and harmless drink, a very good imitation, and may be purchased at six or seven dollars a dozen. I do not know what we shall do when America fills up, if the demand for champagne should increase in proportion to the population; we had better drink all we can now.

Claret, and the other French wines, do very well in America, but where the Americans beat us out of the field is in their Madeira, which certainly is of a quality which we cannot procure in England. This is owing to the extreme heat and cold of the climate, which ripens this wine; indeed, I may almost say that I never tasted good Madeira until I arrived in the United States. The price of wines, generally speaking, is very high, considering what a trifling duty is paid, but the price of good Madeira is surprising. There are certain brands which, if exposed to public auction, will be certain to fetch from twelve to twenty, and I have been told even forty dollars a bottle. I insert a list of the wines at Astor House, to prove that there is no exaggeration in what I have asserted. Even in this list of a tavern, the reader will find that the best Madeira is as high as twelve dollars a bottle, and the list is curious from the variety which it offers.

List of Wines, Astor House

MOSELLE

Oberemmel	$1.50

---

[3] The making of pseudo-champagnes and the like seems to have been not at all unusual in the nineteenth century. In the Great Exhibition of 1851 in London, among the exhibits were wines made from rather peculiar things "alcoholic drinks . . . derived from unusual sources," there are bottles of champagne made from rhubarb, bottles of "champagne sparkling hock" made from a mixture of raisins, sugar candy and honey, bottles of Madeira made from malt and sugar extract, and bottles of Frontignac flavoured with the "evil smelling flower of the elder."—from Christopher Hobhouse, *1851 and the Crystal Palace* (London: Transatlantic Arts; 1950), pp. 71–72.

SAUTERNE

Morton's Y. Chem	$2.00
Lynch's	2.00

HOCK

Steinberger, 1811	2.00
Marcobronner, 1825	2.00
Rüdesheimer, 1822	2.50
Rüdesheimer Hinterhausen, 1834	2.50
Wormser Leibfraumilch	2.50
Johannisberger, 1831	3.00
Steinberger, (box bottles)	3.00
Assmanshauser, 1825	3.00
Ausbruck Cabinet Rothenberg of 1831	3.00
Ausbruck Marcobronner, 1831	3.00
Ausbruck Cabinet Graffenberg, 1831	4.00
Ausbruck Cabinet Rothenberg, 1822	4.00
Cabinet Claus Johannisberger, 1822	5.00
Prince Metternich, celebrated Castle bottled, gold seal Johannisberger, vintage, 1822	8.00

HERMITAGE

Red Roche	2.00
White, 1815	2.00

CHAMPAGNE

Beaver Sillery	2.00
Napoleon	2.00
Duc de Montebello	2.00
Cliquot	2.00
Forrest & Co.	2.00
Renwick's J. C. (Rilley)	2.00
Bever Sillery Baun, (Amber) very dry	2.50
Pints of many of the above brands	1.00
Sparkling Hock	3.00
" (pints)	1.50

CLARET

Violett & Co., Bordeaux, ws vc	1.00
Leoville, Bordeaux	1.00

Château de Crock			$1.50
St. Pierre		Morton's	1.50
LaRose, Violette & Co.			1.75
St. Julien	1828,	"	2.00
Leoville	1828,	"	2.00
Braun Mouton	1831,	"	2.00
Rauzan Margeaux	1828, Morton's		2.50
De Vivens　　"	1828,	"	2.50
Gruaud Larose	1827,	"	2.50
Pichon Longueville	1827,	"	2.50
Pontet Canet	1828,	"	2.50
Château Latour	1828,	"	2.50
Cos Destournel	1827,	"	3.00
Château Lafitte	1828,	"	2.50
Château Margeaux, Palmer's			
"　　　　"	1831, Lynch's		3.00

PORT

Old London, imported in glass	2.00
Bees Wing	2.00
Port, bottled in London	2.50
Black Seal, old	2.50
Pure Juice, bottled 1828, J.	2.50
White Port	3.00

BURGUNDY

Chambertin, 1827	2.50
Corton	2.50
Romanee	3.00

SHERRY

Robert's Pale	2.00
Lobo, Pale, C.S. old dry	2.00
Tower Amber	2.00
Tower Brown	2.00
S.L.M. Pale Sherry	2.00
Yriarte, Gold G.	2.25
Sorelia, Brown, 1805, B.X.	2.50
Harmony's Gold H.	2.50
Ravini's Pale Gold, superior	2.50
Lobo, Brown, FO, long bottled	3.00

Romano, Brown, very old	$3.00
Sorelia, Pale, 1805, X.	3.00
Romano, Pale, very old	3.00
Lobo, Pale, M.L., delicate	3.00
Ne Plus Ultra	4.00

MADEIRA

Sea Bird	2.00
Halaway	2.00
Bobby Lennox	2.50
Howard, March and Co.'s Madeira, imported for the Astor House, F.	2.00
Dunn & Co., imported 1833, E.	2.00
" " " O.	2.50
Newton, Gordon, and Murdock's (NGM.)	2.50
Phelps, Phelps, and Laurie, vintage 1811, via East Indies	2.50
Yellow Seal, old, bottled, East India	3.00
Vaughan, two voyages to East Indies, vintage 1811 (yellow seal)	3.00 / 3.00
Monterio, 1825, MT.	3.00
Old West India, WI.	3.00
Murdock, Yuille & Woodrope, MYW.	3.00
Nabob	3.00
Brahmin, A.	3.50
Mary Elizabeth, Jr.	3.50
Red Seal, old, bottled, East India	4.00
Monterio, 6 years in East Indies, Metior	4.00
Old racked East India Leacock Madeira, EIL (black seal)	4.00
Boston (Dr. Robbins)	4.00
Davis' Sercial	4.50
Old Calcutta, bottled in Calcutta, 1814, imported 1824	4.50
Rapid, imported 1818	
Stark's Madeira, bottled in Calcutta, imported 1825	5.00
Edward Tuckerman, Esq., Boston, Madeira March's Wine—went to East Indies in 1818, bottled 1820, E.I.M.	5.00
Edward Tuckerman, Esq., Scott, Laughnan,	

Penfold, and Co.'s, imported 1820, P.M.	$ 5.00
Gov. Philips, Page, Phelps, and Co.'s Sercial, imported 1820	5.00
Gratz (yellow seal) 1806	5.00
" (green seal) "	5.00
" (black seal) "	5.00
" (red seal) bottled 1806	5.00
Robert Oliver's 25 years in bottle	5.00
Old Baltimore (Oliver's own)	5.00
Wanton (exceedingly delicate) 30 years in wood, W.	5.00
Sercial, 20 years in bottle, saved from the great conflagration	5.00
John A. Gordon's Madeira, imported into Philadelphia, 1798	5.00
Everett, 25 years in bottle	5.00
Gordon, Duff, Ingliss, Co.'s imported by H. G. Otis and Edward Tuckerman, Esqrs., 1811, G.	6.00
Essex, Jr., imported 1819	6.00
Smith and Huggins (Dyker's white top) bottled 1800, in St. Eustatia	7.00
Wedding Wine	8.00
Gov. Phillips'	9.00
Gov. Kirby's original bottles, OO.	12.00

But the Americans do not confine themselves to foreign wines or liquors; they have every variety at home, in the shape of compounds, such as mint-julep and its varieties; slings in all their varieties; cocktails. But I really cannot remember, or if I could, it would occupy too much time to mention the whole battle array against one's brains. I must, however, descant a little upon the mint-julep, as it is, with the thermometer at 100°, one of the most delightful and insinuating potations that ever was invented, and may be drunk with equal satisfaction when the thermometer is as low as 70°. There are many varieties, such as those composed of Claret, Madeira, etc.; but the ingredients of the real mint-julep are as follows. I learnt how to make them, and succeeded pretty well. Put into a tumbler about

a dozen sprigs of the tender shoots of mint, upon them put
a spoonful of white sugar, and equal proportions of peach
and common brandy, so as to fill it up one third, or perhaps
a little less. Then take rasped or pounded ice, and fill
up the tumbler. Epicures rub the lips of the tumbler with a
piece of fresh pineapple, and the tumbler itself is very often
incrusted outside with stalactites of ice. As the ice melts,
you drink. I once overheard two ladies talking in the next
room to me, and one of them said: "Well, if I have a weakness for any one thing, it is for a mint-julep"—a very
amiable weakness, and proving her good sense and good
taste. They are, in fact, like the American ladies, irresistible.

The Virginians claim the merit of having invented this
superb compound, but I must dispute it for my own country, although it has been forgotten of late. In the times of
Charles I and II it must have been known, for Milton expressly refers to it in his *Comus:*

> Behold the cordial *julep* here
> Which flames and dances in its crystal bounds
> With spirits of *balm* and fragrant *syrups* mixed.
> Not that Nepenthes, which the wife of Thone
> In Egypt gave to Jove-born Helena
> Is of such power to stir up joy like this,
> To life so friendly, or so *cool to thirst.*

If that don't mean mint-julep, I don't know the English language. . . .

I have mentioned the principal causes to which must
be assigned the propensity to drink, so universal in America. This is an undeniable fact, asserted by every other
writer, acknowledged by the Americans themselves in print,
and proved by the labours of their Temperance Societies. It
is not confined to the lower classes, but pervades the whole
mass; of course, where there is most refinement, there is
less intoxication, and in the southern and western states it
is that the custom of drinking is most prevalent.

I have said that in the American hotels there is a par-lour for the ladies to retire to; there is not one for the gentlemen, who have only the reading-room, where they stand and read the papers, which are laid out on desks, or the bar.

The bar of an American hotel is generally a very large room on the basement, fitted up very much like our gin palaces in London, not so elegant in its decorations indeed, but on the same system. A long counter runs across it, behind which stand two or three bar-keepers to wait upon the customers, and distribute the various potations, compounded from the contents of several rows of bottles behind them. Here the eye reposes on masses of pure crystal ice, large bunches of mint, decanters of every sort of wine, every variety of spirits, lemons, sugar, bitters, cigars and tobacco; it really makes one feel thirsty, even the going into a bar. Here you meet everybody and everybody meets you. Here the Senator, the member of Congress, the merchant, the store-keeper, travellers from the far west and every other part of the country, who have come to purchase goods, all congregate.

Most of them have a cigar in their mouth, some are transacting business, others conversing, some sitting down together whispering confidentially. Here you obtain all the news, all the scandal, all the politics, and all the fun; it is this dangerous propinquity, which occasions so much intemperance. Mr. Head has no bar at the Mansion-House in Philadelphia, and the consequence is that there is no drinking, except wine at dinner; but in all the other hotels, it would appear as if they purposely allowed the frequenters no room to retire to, so that they must be driven to the bar, which is by far the most profitable part of the concern.

The consequence of the bar being the place of general resort is that there is an unceasing pouring out and amalgamation of alcohol and other compounds, from morning to late at night. To drink with a friend when you meet him is good fellowship, to drink with a stranger is politeness, and a proof of wishing to be better acquainted. . . .

They say that the English cannot settle anything properly without a dinner. I am sure the Americans can fix nothing without a drink. If you meet, you drink; if you part, you drink; if you make acquaintance, you drink; if you close a bargain, you drink; they quarrel in their drink, and they make it up with a drink. They drink because it is hot; they drink because it is cold. If successful in elections, they drink and rejoice; if not, they drink and swear; they begin to drink early in the morning, they leave off late at night; they commence it early in life, and they continue it, until they soon drop into the grave. To use their expression, the way they drink, is "quite a caution." * As for water, what the man said, when asked to belong to the Temperance Society, appears to be the general opinion: "It's very good for navigation."

So much has it become the habit to cement all friendship, and commence acquaintance by drinking, that it is a cause of serious offence to refuse, especially in a foreigner, as the Americans like to call the English. I was always willing to accommodate the Americans in this particular, as far as I could (there, at least, they will do me justice); that at times I drank much more than I wished is certain, yet still I gave most serious offence, especially in the west, because I would not drink early in the morning, or before dinner, which is a general custom in the states, although much more prevalent in the south and west, where it is literally: "Stranger, will you drink or fight?" This refusal on my part, or rather excusing myself from drinking with all those who were introduced to me, was eventually the occasion of much disturbance and of great animosity towards me—certainly, most unreasonably, as I was introduced to at least twenty every forenoon; and had I drunk with them all, I should have been in the same state as many of them were—that is, not really sober for three or four weeks at a time.

That the constitutions of the Americans must suffer

---

* It was not a bad idea of a man who, generally speaking, was very low-spirited, on being asked the cause, replied that he did not know, but he thought "that he had been born with *three drinks too little* in him."

from this habit is certain; they do not, however, appear to suffer so much as we should. They say that you may always know the grave of a Virginian as, from the quantity of juleps he has drunk, mint invariably springs up where he has been buried. . . .

I did not see it myself, but I was told that somewhere in Missouri, or thereabouts, west of the Mississippi, all the bars have what they term a *kicking-board,* it being the custom with the people who live there, instead of touching glasses when they drink together, to kick sharply with the side of the foot against the board, and that after this ceremony you are sworn friends. I have had it mentioned to me by more than one person, therefore I presume it is the case. What the origin of it is I know not, unless it intends to imply, "I'm yours to the *last kick.*" *

Before I finish this article on hotels, I may as well observe here that there is a custom in the United States, which I consider very demoralizing to the women, which is that of taking up permanent residence in large hotels.

There are several reasons for this: one is, that people marry so very early that they cannot afford to take a house with the attendant expenses, for in America it is cheaper to

---

* In a chapter which follows this, I have said that the women of America are physically superior to the men. This may appear contradictory, as of course they could not be born so; nor are they, for I have often remarked how very fine the American male children are, especially those lads who have grown up to the age of fourteen or sixteen. One could hardly believe it possible that the men are the same youths advanced in life. How is this to be accounted for? I can only suppose that it is from their plunging too early into life as men, having thrown off parental control, and commencing the usual excesses of young men in every country at too tender an age. The constant stimulus of drink must, of course, be another powerful cause; not that the Americans often become intoxicated, on the contrary, you will see many more in this condition every day in this country than you will in America. But occasional intoxication is not so injurious to the constitution as that continual application of spirits, which must enfeeble the stomach, and, with the assistance of tobacco, destroy its energies. The Americans are a *drinking* but not a *drunken* nation, and, as I have before observed, the climate operates upon them very powerfully.

live in a large hotel than to keep a house of your own; another is the difficulty of obtaining servants and, perhaps, the unwillingness of the women to have the fatigue and annoyance which is really occasioned by an establishment in that country—added to which is the want of society, arising from their husbands being from morning to night plodding at their various avocations. At some of the principal hotels you will find the apartments of the lodgers so permanently taken that the plate with their name engraved on it is fixed on the door. I could almost tell whether a lady in America kept her own establishment or lived at a hotel, the difference of manners was so marked; and, what is worse, it is chiefly the young married couples who are to be found there. . . .

In the hotels, the private apartments of the boarders seldom consist of more than a large bed-room, and although company are admitted into it, still it is natural that the major portion of the women's time should be passed down below in the general receiving room. In the evening, especially in the large western cities, they have balls almost every night; indeed, it is a life of idleness and vacuity of outward pretence, but of no real good feeling.

Scandal rages—everyone is busy with watching her neighbour's affairs; those who have boarded there longest take the lead, and every newcomer or stranger is canvassed with the most severe scrutiny; their histories are ascertained, and they are very often sent to Coventry, for little better reason than the will of those who, as residents, lay down the law.

Indeed, I never witnessed a more ridiculous compound of pretended modesty, and real want of delicacy, than is to be found with this class of sojourners on the highway. Should any of their own sex arrive, of whom some little scandal has been afloat, they are up in arms and down they plump in their rocking-chairs; and although the hotel may cover nearly an acre of ground, so afraid are they of contamination, that they declare they will not go down to dinner, or eat another meal in the hotel, until the obnoxious parties "clear out." The proprietors are summoned, husbands are bullied, and, rather than indignant virtue should starve in her rocking-chair, a committee is formed, and the libelled parties, guilty or not guilty, are requested to leave the hotel. As soon as this purification is announced, virtue, appeased, recovers her appetite, and they all eat, drink, talk scandal, flirt, and sing without invitation as before. . . .

CHAPTER XLIII

Emigration & Migration

In this chapter I shall confine myself to the emigration to the United States. . . . In discussing this question I have no statistics to refer to and must, therefore, confine myself to general observations.

What the amount of emigration from the old continent to the United States may be at present I do not think the Americans themselves can tell, as many who arrive at New York go on to the Canadas. The emigrants are, however, principally English, Irish, and German; latterly, the emigration to New South Wales, New Zealand, and particularly Texas has reduced the influx of emigrants to the United States.

It ought to be pointed out that among the emigrants are to be found the portion of the people in the United States the most disaffected and the most violent against England and its monarchical institutions, and who assist very much to keep up the feelings of dislike and ill-will which exist towards us. Nor is this to be wondered at; the happy and the wealthy do not go into exile; they are mostly disappointed and unhappy men, who attribute their misfortunes, often occasioned by their own imprudence, to any cause but the true one, and hate their own country and its institutions because they have been unfortunate in it. They

393

form Utopian ideas of liberty and prosperity to be obtained by emigration; they discover that they have been deceived, and would willingly, if possible, return to the country they have abjured and the friends they have left behind. This produces an increase of irritation and ill-will, and they become the more violently vituperative in proportion as they feel the change.

I have had many conversations with English emigrants in the United States, and I never yet found one at all respectable who did not confess to me that he repented of emigration. One great cause of this is honourable to them: they feel that in common plain-dealing they are no match for the keen-witted, and I must add unprincipled, portion of the population with which they are thrown in contact. They must either sacrifice their principle or not succeed.

Many have used the same expression to me. "It is no use, sir, you must either turn regular Yankee and do as they do, or you have no chance of getting on in this country."

These people are much to be pitied; I used to listen to them with feelings of deep compassion. Having torn themselves away from old associations, and broken the links which should have bound them to their native soil, with the expectation of finding liberty, equality, and competence in a new country, they have discovered when too late that they have not a fraction of the liberty which is enjoyed in the country which they have left; that they have severed themselves from their friends to live amongst those with whom they do not like to associate; that they must now labour with their own hands, instead of employing others; and that the competence they expected, if it is to be obtained, must be so by a sacrifice of those principles of honesty and fair-dealing imbibed in their youth, adhered to in their manhood, but which, now that they have transplanted themselves, are gradually, although unwillingly, yielded up to the circumstances of their position.

I was once conversing with an Irishman; he was not very well pleased with his change; I laughed at him and said: "But here you are free, Paddy." — "Free!" replied he, "and pray who the devil was to buy or sell me when I was in Ireland? Free! och! that's all talk; you're free to work as hard as a horse, and get but little for so doing."

The German emigrants are by far the most contented and well-behaved. They trouble themselves less about politics, associate with one another as much as possible, and when they take a farm, always, if they possibly can, get it in the neighbourhood of their own countrymen.

The emigrants most troublesome but, at the same time, the most valuable to the United States are the Irish. Without this class of people the Americans would not have been able to complete the canals and railroads and many other important works. They are, in fact, the principal labourers of the country, for the poor Germans who come out prefer being employed in any other way than in agriculture, until they amass sufficient to obtain farms of their own. As for the Irish, there are not many of them who possess land in the United States; the major portion of them remain labourers and die very little better off than when they went out. Some of them set up groceries (these are the most calculating and intelligent) and by allowing their countrymen to run in debt for liquor, etc., they obtain control over them, and make contracts with the government agents or other speculators (very advantageous to themselves) to supply so many men for public works; by these means a few acquire a great deal of money, while the many remain in comparative indigence.

We have been accustomed to ascribe the turbulence of the Irish lower classes to ill-treatment and a sense of their wrongs, but this disposition appears to follow them everywhere. It would be supposed that, having emigrated to America and obtained the rights of citizens, they would have amalgamated and fraternized to a certain degree with the people; but such is not the case; they hold themselves completely apart and distinct, living with their families in the same quarter of the city and adhering to their own manners and customs. They are just as little pleased with the institutions of the United States as they are with the government at home; the fact is that they would prefer no government at all, if (as Paddy himself would say) they knew where to find it. They are the leaders in all the political rows and commotions, and very powerful as a party in all elections, not only on account of their numbers (if I recollect rightly, they muster forty thousand at New York), but by their violence preventing other people from coming to the poll, and, further, by multiplying themselves, so as greatly to increase their force, by voting several times over, which they do by going from one ward to another. I was told by one of them that, on the last election, he had voted *seven* times.

An American once said to me that the lower Irish ruled the United States, and he attempted to prove his assertion as follows: The New York election is carried by the Irish; now the New York election has great influence upon the other elections and often carries the state. The state of New York has great influence upon the elections of other states, and therefore the Irish of New York govern the country.—Q.E.D.

The Irish, in one point, appear to improve in the United States—they become much more provident, and many of them hoard their money. They put it into the Savings Banks, and when they have put in the sum allowed by law to one person, they deposit in other names.

A captain of one of the steamboats told me an anecdote or two relative to the Irish emigrants, by which it would appear that they are more saving of their money than is quite consistent with honesty.

He constantly received them on board, and said that sometimes, if they were very few, they would declare at the end of the trip that they had no money, although when detained they never failed to produce it; if they were very numerous they would attempt to fight their way without paying. In one instance, an Irishman declared that he had no money, when the captain, to punish him, seized his old jacket and insisted upon retaining it for payment. The Irishman suffered it to be taken off, expecting, it is to be presumed, that it would be returned to him as valueless, when the captain jerked it overboard. "Oh! murder! Captain, drop the boat," cried Paddy; "pick my jacket up, or I'm a ruined man. *All my money's* in it." The jacket was fortunately picked up before it sank, and, on ripping it up, it was found to contain, sewed up in it, upwards of fifty sovereigns and gold eagles. The same captain narrated to me the particulars of one instance in which about one hundred Irish were on board who, when asked for payment, commenced an attack upon the captain and crew with their bludgeons; but, having before experienced such attempts, he was prepared for them, and receiving assistance from the shore, the Irishmen were worsted, and then every man paid his fare. The truth is that they are very turbulent, and the lower orders of the Americans are very much enraged against them. On the 4th of July there were several bodies of Americans, who were out on the look-out for the Irish, after dark, and many of the latter were severely beaten, if not murdered; the Irish, however, have to thank themselves for it.

The spirit of the institutions of the states is so opposed to servitude that it is chiefly from the emigrants that the Americans obtain their supply of domestics; the men servants in the private houses may be said to be, with few exceptions, either emigrants or free people of colour. Amongst other points upon which the Americans are to be pitied, and for which the most perfect of theoretical governments could never compensate, is the misery and annoyance to which they are exposed from their domestics. They are absolutely slaves to them, especially in the western free states; there are no regulations to control them. At any fancied affront they leave the house without a moment's warning, putting on their hats or bonnets, and walking out of the street-door, leaving their masters and mistresses to get on how they can. I remember when I was staying with a gentleman in the west that, on the first day of my arrival, he apologized to me for not having a man servant, the fellow having then been drunk for a week; a woman had been hired to help for a portion of the day, but most of the labour fell upon his wife, whom I found one morning cleaning my room. The fellow remained ten days drunk, and then (all his money being spent) sent to his master to say that he would come back on condition that he would give him a little more liquor. To this proposition the gentleman was compelled to assent, and the man returned as if he had conferred a favour. The next day, at dinner, there being no porter up, the lady said to her husband: "Don't send —— for it, but *go yourself,* my dear; he is so very cross again that I fear he will leave the house." A lady of my acquaintance in New York told her coachman that she should give him warning; the reply from the box was— "I reckon I have been too long in the woods to be scared with an owl." Had she noticed this insolence, he would probably have got down from the box and have left her to drive her own cattle. The coloured servants are, generally speaking, the most civil; after them the Germans; the Irish and English are very bad. At the hotels, etc., you very often find Americans in subordinate situations, and it is remarkable that when they are so, they are much more civil than the imported servants. Few of the American servants, even in the large cities, understand their business, but it must be remembered that few of them have ever learnt it, and, moreover, they are expected to do three times as much as a servant would do in an English house. The American houses are much too large for the number of servants employed, which is another cause for service being so much disliked.

It is singular that I have not found in any one book, written by English, French, or German travellers, any remarks made upon a custom which the Americans have of almost entirely living, I may say, in the basement of their houses, and which is occasioned by their difficulties in housekeeping with their insufficient domestic establishments. I say custom of the Americans, as it is the case in nine houses out of ten, only the more wealthy travelled and refined portion of the community in their cities deviating from the general practice.

I have before observed that, from the wish of display,

the American houses are generally speaking too large for the proprietors and for the domestics which are employed. Vying with each other in appearance, their receiving rooms are splendidly furnished, but they do not live in them. The basement in the front area, which with us is usually appropriated to the housekeeper's room and offices, is in most of their houses fitted up as a dining-room—by no means a bad plan, as it is cool in summer, warm in winter, and saves much trouble to the servants. The dinner is served up in it, direct from the kitchen, with which it communicates. The master of the house, unless he dines late, which is seldom the case in American cities, does not often come home to dinner, and the preparations for the family are of course not very troublesome. But although they go on very well in their daily routine, to give a dinner is to the majority of the Americans really an effort, not from the disinclination to give one, but from the indifference and ignorance of the servants; and they may be excused without being taxed with want of hospitality. It is a very common custom, therefore, for the Americans to invite you to come and "take wine" with them, that is, to come after dinner, when you will find cakes, ices, wine, and company, already prepared. But there is something unpleasant in this arrangement; it is too much like the bar of the tavern in the west, with— "Stranger, will you drink?" It must, however, be recollected that there are many exceptions to what I have above stated as the general practice. There are houses in the principal cities of the states where you will sit down to as well-arranged and elegant a dinner as you will find in the best circles of London and Paris; but the proprietors are men of wealth, who have in all probability been on the old continent and have imbibed a taste for luxury and refinement generally unknown and unfelt in the new hemisphere.

I once had an instance of what has been repeatedly observed by other travellers of the dislike to be considered as servants in this land of equality.

I was on board of a steamboat from Detroit to Buffalo and entered into conversation with a young woman who was leaning over the taffrail. She had been in service and was returning home.

"You say you lived with Mr. W."

"No, I didn't," replied she, rather tartly. "I said I lived with *Mrs.* W."

"Oh! I understand. In what situation did you live?"

"I lived in the house."

"Of course you did, but what as?"

"What as? As a *gal* should live."

"I mean what did you do?"

"I helped Mrs. W."

"And now you are tired of helping others?"

"Guess I am."

"Who is your father?"

"He's a doctor."

"A doctor! And he allows you to go out?"

"He said I might please myself."

"Will he be pleased at your coming home again?"

"I went out to please myself, and I come home to please myself. Cost him nothing for four months; that's more than all gals can say."

"And now you're going home to spend your money?"

"Don't want to go home for that; it's all gone."

I have been much amused with the awkwardness and nonchalant manners of the servants in America. Two American ladies who had just returned from Europe told me that, shortly after their arrival at Boston, a young man had been sent to them from Vermont to do the duty of footman. He had been a day or two in the house when they rang the bell and ordered him to bring up two glasses of lemonade. He made his appearance with the lemonade, which had been prepared and given to him on a tray by a female servant, but the ladies, who were sitting one at each end of a sofa and conversing, not being ready for it just then, said to him— "We'll take it presently, John." — "Guess I can wait," replied the man, deliberately taking his seat on the sofa between them and placing the tray on his knees.

When I was at Tremont House, I was very intimate

with a family who were staying there. One morning we had been pasting something, and the bell was rung by one of the daughters, a very fair girl with flaxen hair, who wanted some water to wash her hands. An Irish waiter answered the bell. "Did you ring, ma'am?" — "Yes, Peter, I want a little warm water." "Is it to *shave with,* miss?" inquired Paddy, very gravely.

But the emigration from the old continent is of little importance compared to the migration which takes place in the country itself.

As I have before observed, all America is working west. In the north, the emigration by the lakes is calculated at one hundred thousand per annum, of which about thirty thousand are foreigners; the others are the natives of New England and the other eastern states, who are exchanging from a sterile soil to one "flowing with milk and honey." But those who migrate are not all of them agriculturalists; the western states are supplied from the north-eastern with their merchants, doctors, schoolmasters, lawyers, and, I may add, with their members of Congress, Senators, and governors. New England is a *school,* a sort of manufactory of various professions, fitted for all purposes—a talent bazaar, where you have everything at choice; in fact, what Mr. Tocqueville says is very true, and the states fully deserve the compliment:

"The civilization of New England has been like a beacon lit upon a hill, which, after it has diffused its warmth around, tinges the distant horizon with its glory."

From the great extent of this emigration to the west, it is said that the female population in the New England states is greater than the male. In the last returns of Massachusetts the total population was given, but males and females were not given separately, an omission which induces one to believe that such was the truth. But it is not only from the above states that the migration takes place; the fondness for "shifting right away," the eagerness for speculation, and the by no means exaggerated reports of the richness of the western country induce many who are really well settled in the states of New York, Pennsylvania, and other fertile states to sell all and turn to the west. The state of Ohio alone is supposed to have added many more than a million to her population since the last census. An extensive migration of white population takes place from North and South Carolina and the adjacent states, while from the eastern slave states there is one continual stream of black population pouring in, frequently the cavalcade headed by the masters of their families.

As the numerous tributary streams pour their waters into the Mississippi, so do rivers of men from every direction continually and unceasingly flow into the west. It is indeed the promised land, and that the whites should have been detained in the eastern states so long without a knowledge of the fertile soil beyond the Alleghenies reminds you of the tarrying of the Jewish nation in the wilderness before they were permitted to take possession of their inheritance.

Here there is matter for deep reflection. I have already given my opinion upon the chances of the separation of the northern and southern states upon the question of slavery; but it appears to me that, while the eyes of their legislators have been directed with so much interest to the prospects arising from the above question, their backs have been turned to a danger much more imminent, and which may be attended by no less consequences than a convulsion of the whole Union.

The southern and northern states may separate on the question of slavery, and yet be in reality better friends than they were before; but what will be the consequence when the western states become, as they assuredly will, so populous and powerful as to control the Union? For not only population, but *power* and wealth, are fast working their way to the west. New Orleans will be the first maritime port in the universe, and Cincinnati will not only be the Queen of the West, but Queen of the Western *World*. Then will come the real clashing of interests, and the eastern states must be content to succumb and resign their present power, or the western will throw them off, as a useless appendage to her might. This may at present appear chimerical to some, and would be considered by many others as too far distant; but be it remembered that ten years in America is as a century; and even allowing the prosperity of the United States to be checked, as very probably it may soon be, by any quarrel with a foreign nation, the western states will not be those who will suffer. Far removed from strife, the population hardly interfered with, when the eastern resources are draining, *they* will continue to advance in population and to increase in wealth. I refer not to the slave states bordering on the Mississippi, although I consider that they would suffer little from a war, as neither England, nor any other nation, will ever be so unwise in future as to attack in a quarter where she would have extended the olive branch, even if it were not immediately accepted. Whether America is engaged in war, therefore, or remains in peace, the western states must, and will soon be, the arbiters and dictate as they please to the eastern.

At present, they may be considered as infants, not yet of age, and the eastern states are their guardians; the profits of their produce are divided between them and the merchants of the eastern cities, who receive at least thirty per cent as their share. This must be the case at present, when the advances of the eastern capitalists are required by the cotton growers, who are precisely in the same position with the eastern states as the West India planters used to be with the merchants of London and Liverpool, to whom they consigned their cargoes for advances received. But the western states (to follow up the metaphor) will soon be of age and no longer under control; even last year, vessels were freighted direct from England to Vicksburg, on the Mississippi; in a few years there will be large importing houses in the far west, who will have their goods direct from England at one half the price which they now pay for them, when forwarded from New York, by canal, and other conveyances. Indeed, a very little inquiry will prove that the prosperity of the eastern free states depends in a great measure upon the western and southern. The eastern states are the receivers and transporters of goods and the carriers of most of the produce of the Union. They advance money on the crops and charge high interest, commissions, etc. The transport and travelling between the eastern, southern, and western states are one great source of this prosperity, from the employment on the canals, railroads, and steamboats.

All these are heavy charges to the western states, and can be avoided by shipping direct from, and sending their produce direct to, the old continent. As the western states advance in wealth, so will they advance in power, and in proportion as they so do, will the eastern states recede, until they will be left in a small minority, and will eventually have little voice in the Union.

Here, then, is a risk of convulsion; for the clashing of interests, next to a war, is the greatest danger to which a democracy can be exposed. In a democracy, everyone legislates, and everyone legislates for his own interests. The eastern states will still be wealthy and formidable, from their population; but the commerce of the principal eastern cities will decrease, and they will have little or no stable produce to return to England or elsewhere; whereas the western states can produce everything that the heart of man can desire, and can be wholly independent of them. They have, in the west, every variety of coal and mineral, to a boundless extent; a rich alluvial soil, hardly to be exhausted by bad cultivation, and wonderful facilities of transport; independent of the staple produce of cotton, they might supply the whole world with grain; sugar they already cultivate; the olive flourishes; wine is already produced on the banks of the Ohio, and the prospect of raising silk is beyond calculation. In a few days, the manufactures of the Old World can find their way from the mouth of the Mississippi by its thousand tributary streams, which run like veins through every portion of the country, to the confines of Arkansas and Missouri, to the head of navigation at St. Peter's, on again to Wisconsin, Michigan, and to the northern lakes, at a *much cheaper rate* than they are supplied at present.

One really is lost in admiration when one surveys this great and glorious western country and contemplates the splendour and riches to which it must ultimately arrive.

As soon as the eastern states are no longer permitted to remain the factors of the western, they must be content to become manufacturing states, and probably will compete with England. The western states, providentially, I may say, are not likely to be manufacturers to any great extent, for they have not *water* powers; the valley of the Mississippi is an alluvial flat, and although the Missouri and Mississippi are swift streams, in general the rivers are sluggish, and at all events, they have not the precipitate falls of water necessary for machinery, and which abound in the northeastern states; indeed, if the western states were to attempt to manufacture, as well as to produce, they would spoil the market for their own produce. Whatever may be the result, whether the eastern states submit quietly to be shorn of their greatness (a change which must take place) or to contest the point until it ends in a separation, this is certain, that the focus of American wealth and power will eventually be firmly established in the free states on the other side of the Allegheny mountains.

CHAPTER XLIV

Newspaper Press

M r. Tocqueville observes "that not a single individual of the twelve millions who inhabit the territory of the United States has as yet dared to propose any restrictions upon the liberty of the press." This is true, and all the respectable Americans acknowledge that this liberty has degenerated into a licentiousness which threatens the most alarming results, as it has assumed a power which awes not only individuals, but the government itself. A due liberty allowed to the press may force a government to do right, but a licentiousness may compel it into error. . . . The press in the United States is licentious to the highest possible degree, and defies control; my object is to point out the effect of this despotism upon society, and to show how injurious it is in every way to the cause of morality and virtue.

Of course, the newspaper press is the most mischievous, in consequence of its daily circulation, the violence of political animosity, and the want of respectability in a large proportion of the editors. The number of papers published and circulated in Great Britain, among a population of twenty-six millions, is calculated at about three hundred and seventy. The number published in the United States, among thirteen millions, are supposed to vary between *nine and ten thousand*. Now the value of newspapers may be fairly calculated by the capital expended upon them; and not only is not one-quarter of the sum expended in England, upon three hundred and seventy newspapers, expended upon the nine or ten thousand in America; but I really believe that the expense of the *Times* newspaper alone, is equal to at least *five thousand* of the *minor* papers in the United States, which are edited by people of no literary pretension and at an expense so trifling as would appear to us not only ridiculous, but impossible. . . .

I can also assert that there are many very highly respectable and clever editors in the United States. The New York papers are most of them very well conducted and very well written. The New York *Courier and Enquirer,* by Colonel Webb; the *Evening Star,* by Noah; the *Albion,* by Doctor Bartlett; *Spirit of the Times,* and many others, which are too numerous to quote, are equal to many of the English newspapers. The best-written paper in the states, and the happiest in its sarcasm and wit, is the *Louisville Gazette,* conducted by Mr. Prentice of Kentucky; indeed, the western papers are, generally speaking, more amusing and witty than the eastern; the *New Orleans Picayune,* by Kendall, is perhaps, after Prentice's, the most amusing; but there are many more, which are too numerous to mention, which do great credit to American talent. Still, the majority are disgraceful not only from their vulgarity, but from their odious personalities and disregard to truth. The bombast and ignorance shown in some of these is very amusing. Here is an extract or two from the small newspapers published in the less populous countries. An editor down east, speaking of his own merits, thus concludes—

I'm a real catastrophe—a small creation; Mount Vesuvius at the top, with red hot lava pouring out of the crater, and routing nations—my fists are rocky mountains—arms, Whig liberty poles, with iron springs. Every step I take is an earthquake—every blow I strike is a clap of thunder—and every breath I breathe is a tornado. My disposition is Dupont's best, and goes off at a flash—when I blast there'll be nothing left but a hole three feet in circumference and no end to its depth.

Another writes the account of a storm as follows:

On Monday afternoon, while the haymakers were all out gathering in the hay, in anticipation of a shower from the small cloud that was seen hanging over the hilly regions towards the south-east, a tremendous storm suddenly burst upon them, and forced them to seek shelter from its violence. The wind whistled outrageously through the old elms, scattering the beautiful foliage, and then going down into the meadow, where the men had just abruptly left their work unfinished, and overturning the half-made ricks, whisked them into the air, and filled the *whole afternoon* full of hay.

I copied the following from a western paper:

Yes, my countrymen, a dawn begins to open upon us; the crepusculous rays of returning republicanism are fast extending over the darkness of our political horizon, and before their brightness, those myrmidons shall slink away to the abode of the demons who have generated them, in the hollow caves of darkness.

Again—

Many who have acquired great fame and celebrity in the world, began their career as printers. Sir William Blackstone, the learned English commentator of laws, was a printer by trade, *King Charles III* was a printer, and not unfrequently worked at the trade after he ascended the throne of England.

Who Charles III of England was I do not know, as he is not yet mentioned in any of our histories.

The most remarkable newspaper for its obscenity and total disregard for all decency and truth in its personal attacks is the *Morning Herald* of New York, published by a person of the name of Bennett, and being published in so large a city, it affords a convincing proof with what impunity the most licentious attacks upon private characters are permitted. But Mr. Bennett [1] is *sui generis* and demands particular notice. He is indeed a remarkable man, a species of philosopher, who acts up to his tenets with a moral courage not often to be met with in the United States. His maxim appears to be this—"Money will find me everything in this world, and money I will have, at any risk, except that of my life, as, if I lost that, the money would be useless." Acting upon this creed, he has lent his paper to the basest and most malignant purposes, to the hatred of all that is respectable and good, defaming and inventing lies against every honest man, attacking the peace and happiness of private families by the most injurious and base calumny. As may be supposed, he has been horse-whipped, kicked, trodden under foot, and spat upon, and degraded in every possible way; but all this he courts, because it brings money. Horse-whip him, and he will bend his back to the lash, and thank you, as every blow is worth so many dollars. Kick him, and he will remove his coattails, that you may have a better mark, and he courts the application of the toe, while he counts the total of the damages which he may obtain. Spit upon him, and he prizes it as precious ointment, for it brings him the sovereign remedy for his disease, a fever for specie.

The day after the punishment, he publishes a full and particular account of how many kicks, tweaks of the nose, or lashes he may have received. He prostitutes his pen, his

---

[1] James Gordon Bennett (1795–1872), American newspaper editor, was born in Scotland and emigrated to the United States in 1819. Bennett, who is considered by many authorities to be the father of "yellow journalism" in America, tried to reach all classes in his paper, the *Herald*, which was founded in 1835. For the businessman, he provided accounts of Wall Street, for the socially minded he created the "Society page," and for the common man he provided scandal and sensationalism. His paper was run on modern lines and he used pictures, reporters, and "scoops." Although tolerant of slavery and considered "copperhead" in sympathy during the Civil War, his reporting of news from the front was of the highest calibre.

talent, everything for money. His glory is that he has passed
the rubicon of shame; and all he regrets is that the public
is at last coming to the unanimous opinion that he is too
contemptible, too degraded, to be even touched. The other
and more respectable editors of newspapers avoid him, on
account of the filth which he pours forth; like a pole-cat, he
may be hunted down; but no dog will ever attempt to
worry him, as soon as he pours out the contents of his fetid
bag.

It is a convincing proof of the ardent love of defamation
in this country that this modern Thersites, who throws the
former of that name so immeasurably into the background,
has still great sway over men in office; everyone almost
who has a character is afraid of him and will purchase his
silence, if they cannot his good-will.

During the crash at New York, when even the suspicion of insolvency was fatal, this miscreant published
some of the most respectable persons of New York as bankrupts, and yet received no punishment. His paper is clever,
that is certain; but I very much doubt if Bennett is the clever
man—and my reason is this, Bennett was for some time in
England, and during that time the paper, so far from falling off, was better written than before. I myself, before I
had been six weeks in the country, was attacked by this
wretch, and, at the same time, the paper was sent to me
with this small note on the margin: "Send twenty dollars,
and it shall be stopped." — "I only wish you may get it,"
said I to myself. . . .

It must be remembered that newspapers are vended
at a very low price throughout the states, and that the support of the major portion of them is derived from the ignorant and lower classes. Every man in America reads his
newspaper, and hardly anything else; and while he considers that he is assisting to govern the nation, he is, in
fact, the dupe of those who pull the strings in secret, and
by flattering his vanity, and exciting his worst feelings, make
him a poor tool in their hands. People are too apt to imagine
that the newspapers echo their own feelings; when the fact

is that by taking in a paper, which upholds certain opinions, the readers are, by daily repetition, become so impressed with these opinions that they have become slaves to them. I have before observed that learning to read and write is not education, and but too often is the occasion of the demoralization of those who might have been more virtuous and more happy in their ignorance. The other day when I was in a steam vessel, going down to Gravesend, I observed a foot-boy sitting on one of the benches—he was probably ten or eleven years old, and was deeply engaged in reading a cheap periodical, mostly confined to the lower orders of this country, called the *Penny Paul Pry.* Surely it had been a blessing to the lad if he had never learnt to read or write, if he confined his studies, as probably too many do, from want of further leisure, to such an immoral and disgusting publication.

In a country where every man is a politican, and flatters himself that he is assisting to govern the country, political animosities must of course be carried to the greatest lengths, and the press is the vehicle for party violence; . . .

But let me add the authority of Americans. Mr. Webster, in his celebrated speech on the public lands, observes in that powerful and nervous language for which he is so celebrated:

> It is one of the thousand calumnies with which the press teemed, during an excited political canvass. It was a charge, of which there was not only no proof or probability, but which was, in itself, wholly impossible to be true. No man of common information ever believed a syllable of it. Yet it was of that class of falsehoods, which by continued repetition, through all the organs of detraction and abuse, are capable of misleading those who are already far misled, and of farther fanning passion, already kindled into flame. Doubtless, it served in its day, and, in greater or less degree, the end designed by it. Having done that, it has sunk into the general mass of stale and loathed calumnies. It is the very cast-off slough of a *polluted* and *shameless* press.

And Mr. Cooper [2] observes— "Every honest man appears to admit that the press in America is fast getting to be
intolerable. In escaping from the tyranny of foreign aristo-
crats, we have created in our bosoms a *tyranny of a character so insuportable,* that a change of some sort is getting
indispensable to peace."

Indeed, the spirit of defamation, so rife in America, is
so intimately connected with its principal channel, the
press, that it is impossible to mention one without the other,
and I shall, therefore, at once enter into the question.

Defamation is the greatest curse in the United States,
and its effects upon society I shall presently point out. It
appears to be inseparable from a democratic form of
government, and must continue to flourish in it, until it
pleases the Supreme to change the hearts of men. When
Aristides inquired of the countryman, who requested him to
write down his own name on the oyster-shell, what cause
of complaint he had against Aristides, the reply given was:
"I have none; except, that I do not like to hear him always
called the *Just."* So it is with the free and enlightened citizens of America. Let any man rise above his fellows by superior talent, let him hold a consistent, honest career, and
he is exalted only into a pillory, to be pelted at and be de-
filed with ordure. False accusations, the basest insinuations,
are industriously circulated, his public and private character are equally aspersed, truth is wholly disregarded; even
those who have assisted to raise him to his pedestal, as
soon as they perceive that he has risen too high above them,
are equally industrious and eager to drag him down again.
Defamation exists all over the world, but it is incredible to
what an extent this vice is carried in America. It is a disease which pervades the land; which renders every man
suspicious and cautious of his neighbour, creates eye-
service and hypocrisy, fosters the bitterest and most malignant passions, and unceasingly irritates the morbid sen-

---

[2] See earlier note on Cooper, in Marryat's Introduction, p. 10.

sibility, so remarkable among all classes of the American people. . . .

That the political animosities, arising from a free and enlightened people governing themselves, have principally engendered and fostered this vice, is most certain; and it would be some satisfaction if, after the hostile feelings had subsided, the hydra also sank to repose.

But this cannot be the case. A vice, like detraction, so congenial to our imperfect natures, is not to be confined to one channel and only resorted to, as a political weapon, when required. It is a vice which, when once called into action and unchecked by the fear of punishment or shame, must exist and be fed. It becomes a confirmed habit, and the effect upon society is dreadful. If it cannot aim its shafts at those who are in high places, if there is no noble quarry for its weapons, it will seek its food amongst smaller game, for it never tires. The consequence is that it pervades and feeds upon society—private life is embittered; and, as Mr. Cooper most justly observes, *"rendering men indifferent to character, and indeed rendering character of little avail."*

Indeed, from the prevalence of this vice, society in America appears to be in a state of constant warfare—Indian warfare, as everyone is crouched, concealed, watching for an opportunity to scalp the reputation of his neighbour! They exist in fear and trembling, afraid to speak, afraid to act, or follow their own will, for in America there is no free will. When I have asked why they do not this or that, the reply has invariably been, that they dare not. In fact, to keep their station in society, they must be slaves—not merely slaves, for we are all so far slaves that if we do that which is not right, we must be expelled from it; but abject and cowardly slaves, who dare not do that which is innocent, lest they should be misrepresented. This is the cause why there is such an attention to the *outward* forms of religion in the United States, and which has induced some travellers to suppose them a religious people, as if it were possible that any real religion could exist where morality is at so low an ebb. When I first went to Boston, I did not go to church on the following day. An elderly gentleman called upon and pointed out to me that I had omitted this duty; "but," continued he, "I have had it put into one of the newspapers that you attended divine service at such a church, so all is right." All was right; yes, all was right, according to the American's ideas of "all was right." But I thought at the time that my sin of omission was much more venial than his of commission.

When at Detroit, I was attacked in the papers because I returned a few calls on a Sunday. I mention this, not because I was justified in so doing, but because I wish to show the censorship exercised in this very moral country.

The prevalence of this evil acts most unfortunately upon society in other ways. It is the occasion of your hardly ever knowing whom you may or whom you may not be on terms of intimacy with, and of the introduction of many people into society who ought to be wholly excluded. Where slander is so general, when in the space of five minutes you will be informed by one party that Mr. So and So is an excellent person, and by another that he is a great scoundrel, just as he may happen to be on their side or the opposite, in politics, or from any other cause, it is certain that you must be embarrassed as to the person's real character; and as a really good man may be vituperated, so the reports against one who is unworthy are as little credited—the fact is, you never know whom you are in company with.

Almost all the duels which are so frequent in America, and I may add all the assassinations in the western country, arise principally from defamation. The law gives no redress, and there is no other way of checking slander than calling the parties to account for it. Every man is therefore ready and armed against his fellow.

Inadvertently affront any party, wound his self-love, and he will immediately coin some malignant report, which is sure to be industriously circulated. You are at the mercy of the meanest wretch in the country; for although praise is received with due caution, slander is everywhere welcomed.

An instance occurred with respect to myself. I was at Lexington, and received great kindness and civility from Mr. Clay. One day I dined at his table; there was a large party, and at the further end, at a distance where he could not possibly have heard what passed between Mr. Clay and me, there sat a young man, whose name is not worth mentioning. When he returned to Louisville, he spread a report that I had grossly insulted Mr. Clay at his own table. Now the catalogue of enormities circulated against me was already so extensive that I was not in very good odour; but Mr. Clay is so deservedly the idol of this state, and indeed of almost the whole Union, that there could not be a more serious charge against me—even those who were most friendly avoided me, saying they could forgive me what I had formerly done, but to insult Mr. Clay was too bad. So high was the feeling, and so industriously was the calumny circulated, that at last I was compelled to write to Mr. Clay on the subject, and I received in return a most handsome letter, acquitting me of the malicious charge. This I showed to some, and they were satisfied; and they advised me to print it, that it might be better known. This was a compliment I did not choose to pay them; and the impression of the majority still is that I insulted Mr. Clay. The affair being one of the many connected with myself, I should not have mentioned it except to prove how lightly such a practice is estimated.

Whatever society permits, people will do and, moreover, will not think that they are wrong in so doing. In England, had a person been guilty of a deliberate and odious lie, he would have been scouted from society, his best friends would have cut him; but how was this person treated for his conduct? When I showed Mr. Clay's letter, one said: "Well now, that was very wrong of A." — Another, "I did not believe that A. would have done so" — A third, "that A. ought to be ashamed of himself"; but they did not one of them, on account of this falsehood, think it necessary to avoid him. On the contrary, he was walking arm-in-arm with the men, dancing and flirting with the women just as before, although his slander, and the refutation of it, were both well known.

The reader will now perceive the great moral evil arising from this vice, which is that it habituates people to falsehood. The lie of slander is the basest of all lies; and the practice of it, the most demoralizing to the human heart. Those who will descend to such deliberate and malignant falsehood will not scruple at any other description. The consequence is that what the Americans have been so often taxed with is but too prevalent, "a disregard to *truth.*"

To what must we ascribe the great prevalence of this demoralizing habit in the United States? That the licentiousness of the press feeds it, it is true; but I am rather inclined to imagine that the real source of it is to be found in the peculiarity of their institutions. Under a democracy, there are but two means by which a man can rise above his fellows—wealth and character; and when all are equal, and each is struggling to rise above the other, it is to the principle that, if you cannot rise above another by your own merit, you can at least so far equalize your condition by pulling him down to your own level, that this inordinate appetite for defamation must be ascribed. It is a state of ungenerous warfare, arising from there being no gradation, no scale, no discipline, if I may use the term, in society. Everyone asserts his equality and at the same time wishes to rise above his fellows; and society is in a state of perpetual and disgraceful scuffle. . . .

In politics, especially, character becomes of much more importance than wealth, and if a man in public life can once be rendered odious, or be made suspected, he loses his supporters, and there is one antagonist removed in the race for pre-eminence. Such is one of the lamentable defects arising from a democratical form of government. How different from England, and the settled nations of the Old World, where it may be said that everything and everybody is comparatively speaking in his place!

Although many will, and may justifiably, attempt to rise beyond his circumstances and birth, still there is order and regularity; each party knows the precise round in the ladder on which he stands, and the majority are content with their position.

It is lamentable to observe how many bad feelings, how many evil passions, are constantly in a state of activity from this unfortunate chaotical want of gradation and discipline, where all would be first, and everyone considers himself as good as his neighbour. . . .

In a moral sense, this is also true, the nobler virtues which are chiefly produced in the fertile field of aristocracy do occasionally appear; but the whole surface is covered with a layer of democracy which, like the lava which the volcano continually belches forth, has gradually poured down and reduced the country round it to barrenness and sterility. . . . The press of America, as I have described it, is all-powerful; but still it must be borne in mind that it is but the slave of the majority, which, in its turn, it dare not oppose.

Such is its tyranny that it is the dread of the whole community. No one can—no one dare oppose it; whosoever falls under its displeasure, be he as innocent and as pure as man can be, his doom is sealed. But this power is only delegated by the will of the majority, for let any author in America oppose that will, and he is denounced. You must drink, you must write, not according to your own opinions, or your own thoughts, but as the majority will.

Mr. Tocqueville observes: "I know no country in which there is so little true independence of mind, and freedom of discussion, as in America."

CHAPTER XLV

Society: Women

The women of America are unquestionably, physically, as far as beauty is concerned, and morally, of a higher standard than the men; nevertheless they have not that influence which they ought to possess. In my former remarks upon the women of America I have said that they are the prettiest in the world, and I have put the word *prettiest* in italics, as I considered it a term peculiarly appropriate to the American women. In many points the Americans have, to a certain degree, arrived at that equality which they profess to covet, and in no one, perhaps, more than in the fair distribution of good looks among the women. This is easily accounted for: there is not to be found, on the one hand, that squalid wretchedness, that half-starved growing up, that disease and misery, nor on the other, that hereditary refinement, that inoculation of the beautiful, from the constant association with the fine arts, that careful nurture, and constant attention to health and exercise, which exist in the dense population of the cities of the Old World and occasion those variations from extreme plainness to the perfection of beauty which are to be seen, particularly in the metropolis of England. In the United States, where neither the excess of misery nor of luxury and refinement are known, you have, therefore, a more equal distribution of good looks, and, although you often meet with beautiful women, it is but rarely that you find one that may be termed ill-favoured. The *coup-d'oeil* is, therefore, more pleasing in America—enter society and turn your eyes in any direction, you will everywhere find cause for pleasure, although seldom any of annoyance. The climate is not, however, favourable to beauty, which, compared to the English, is very transitory, especially in the eastern states; and when a female arrives at the age of thirty, its reign is, generally speaking, over.

The climate of the western states appears, however, more favourable to it, and I think I saw more handsome women at Cincinnati than in any other city of the Union; their figures were more perfect, and they were finer grown, not receiving the sudden checks to which the eastern women are exposed.

Generally speaking, but a small interval elapses between the period of American girls leaving school and their entering upon their duties as wives; but during that period, whatever it may be, they are allowed more liberty than the young people in our country, walking out without *chaperons* and visiting their friends as they please. There is a reason for this: the matrons are compelled, from the insufficiency of their domestics, to attend personally to all the various duties of housekeeping; their fathers and brothers are all employed in their respective money-making transactions, and a servant cannot be spared from American establishments; if, therefore, they are to walk out and take exercise, it must be alone, and this can be done in the United States with more security than elsewhere, from the circumstance of everybody being actively employed, and there being no people at leisure who are strolling or idling about. I think that the portion of time which elapses between the period of a young girl leaving school and being married is the happiest of her existence. I have already remarked upon the attention and gallantry shown by the Americans to the women, especially to the unmarried. This is carried to an extent which, in England, would be considered by our young women as no compliment; to a certain degree it pervades every class, and even the sable damsels have no reason to complain of not being treated with the excess of politeness; but in my opinion (and I believe the majority of the American women will admit the correctness of it) they do not consider themselves flattered by a species of homage which is paying no compliment to their good sense, and after which the usual attentions of an Englishman to the sex are by some considered as amounting to hauteur and neglect.

Be it as it may, the American women are not spoiled by this universal adulation which they receive previous to their marriage. It is not that one is selected for her wealth or extreme beauty to the exception of all others; in such a case it might prove dangerous; but it is a flattery paid to the whole sex, given to all, and received as a matter of course by all, and therefore it does no mischief. It does, however, prove what I have said at the commencement of this chapter, which is, that the women have not that influence which they are entitled to, and which, for the sake of morality, it is to be lamented that they have not; when men *respect* women they do not attempt to make fools of them, but treat them as rational and immortal beings, and this general adulation is cheating them with the shadow, while they withhold from them the substance.

I have said that the period between her emancipation from school and her marriage is the happiest portion of an American woman's existence; indeed, it has reminded me of the fêtes and amusements given in a Catholic country to a young girl previous to her taking the veil and being immured from the world; for the duties of a wife in America are from circumstances very onerous, and I consider her existence after that period as but one of negative enjoyment. And yet she appears anxious to abridge even this small portion of freedom and happiness, for marriage is considered almost as a business or, I should say, a duty, an idea probably handed down by the first settlers, to whom an increase of population was of such vital importance.* However much the Americans may wish to deny it, I am inclined to think that there are more marriages of *convenance* in the United States than in most other countries. The men begin to calculate long before they are of an age to marry, and it is not very likely that they could calculate so well upon all other points and not upon the value of a dowry; moreover, the old people "calculate some," and the girls accept an offer without their hearts being seriously compromised. Of course there are exceptions; but I do not think that there are many *love* matches made in America, and one reason for my holding this opinion is my having discovered how quietly matches are broken off and new engagements entered into; and it is, perhaps, from a knowledge of this fact, arising from the calculating spirit of the gentlemen, who are apt to consider $20,000 as preferable to $10,000, that the American girls are not too hasty in surrendering their hearts.

I knew a young lady who was engaged to an acquaintance of mine; on my return to their city a short time afterwards, I found that the match was broken off and that she was engaged to another, and nothing was thought of it. I do not argue from this simple instance, but because I found, on talking about it, that it was a very common circumstance, and because, where scandal is so rife, no remarks were made. If a young lady behaves in a way so as to give offence to the gentleman she is engaged to, and sufficiently indecorous to warrant his breaking off the match, he is gallant to the very last, for he writes to her, and begs that she will dismiss *him*. This I knew to be done by a party I was acquainted with; he told me that it was considered *good taste*,

---

* Bigamy is not uncommon in the United States from the women being in too great a hurry to marry, and not obtaining sufficient information relative to their suitors. The punishment is chipping stone in Sing Sing for a few years. It must, however, be admitted, that when a foreigner is the party, it is rather difficult to ascertain whether the gentleman has or has not left an old wife or two in the Old World.

and I agreed with him. On the whole, I hold it very fortunate that in American marriages there is, generally speaking, more prudence than love on both sides, for from the peculiar habits and customs of the country, a woman who loved without prudence would not feel very happy as a wife.

Let us enter into an examination of the married life in the United States.

All the men in America are busy; their whole time is engrossed by their accumulation of money; they breakfast early and repair to their stores or counting-houses; the majority of them do not go home to dinner, but eat at the nearest tavern or oyster-cellar, for they generally live at a considerable distance from the business part of the town, and time is too precious to be thrown away. It would be supposed that they would be home to an early tea; many are, but the majority are not. After fagging, they require recreation, and the recreations of most Americans are politics and news, besides the chance of doing a little more business, all of which, with drink, are to be obtained at the bars of the principal commercial hotels in the city. The consequence is that the major portion of them come home late, tired, and go to bed; early the next morning they are off to their business again. Here it is evident that the women do not have much of their husband's society; nor do I consider this arising from any want of inclination on the part of the husbands, as there is an absolute necessity that they should work as hard as others if they wish to do well, and what one does, the other must do. Even frequenting the bar is almost a necessity, for it is there that they obtain all the information of the day. But the result is that the married women are left alone; their husbands are not their companions, and if they could be, still the majority of the husbands would not be suitable companions for the following reasons. An American starts into life at so early an age that what he has gained at school, with the exception of that portion brought into use from his business, is lost. He has no time for reading, except the newspaper; he becomes perfect in that, acquires a great deal of practical knowledge useful for making money, but for little else. This he must do if he would succeed, and the major portion confine themselves to such knowledge alone. But with the women it is different; their education is much more extended than that of the men, because they are more docile and easier to control in their youth; and when they are married, although their duties are much more onerous than with us, still, during the long days and evenings, during which they wait for the return of their husbands, they have time to finish, I may say, their own educations and improve their minds by reading. The consequence of this, with other adjuncts, is that their minds become, and really are, much more cultivated and refined than those of their husbands; and when the universal practice of using tobacco and drinking among the latter is borne in mind, it will be readily admitted that they are also much more refined in their persons.

These are the causes why the American women are so universally admired by the English and other nations, while they do not consider the men as equal to them either in manners or personal appearance. Let it be borne in mind that I am now speaking of the majority, and that the exceptions are very numerous; for instance, you may except one whole profession, that of the lawyers, among whom you will find no want of gentlemen or men of highly cultivated minds; indeed, the same may be said with respect to most of the liberal professions, but only so because their profession allows that time for improving' themselves which the American in general, in his struggle on the race for wealth, cannot afford to spare.

As I have before observed, the ambition of the American is from circumstances mostly directed to but one object— that of rapidly raising himself above his fellows by the accumulation of a fortune; to this one great desideratum all his energies are directed, all his thoughts are bent, and by it all his ideas are engrossed. When I first arrived in America, as I walked down Broadway, it appeared strange to me that there should be such a remarkable family likeness among the people. Every man I met seemed to me by his features to be a brother or a connection of the last man who had passed me; I could not at first comprehend this, but the mystery was soon revealed. It was that they were all intent and engrossed with the same object; all were, as they passed, calculating and reflecting; this produced a similar contraction of the brow, knitting of the eyebrows, and compression of the lips—a similarity of feeling had produced a similarity of expression, from the same muscles being called into action. Even their hurried walk assisted the error; it is a saying in the United States "that a New York merchant always walks as if he had a good dinner before him, and a bailiff behind him," and the metaphor is not inapt.

Now, a man so wholly engrossed in business cannot be a very good companion if he were at home; his thoughts would be elsewhere, and therefore perhaps it is better that things should remain as they are. But the great evil arising from this is that the children are left wholly to the management of their mothers, and the want of paternal control I have already commented upon. The Americans have reason to be proud of their women, for they are really good wives—much *too good* for them; I have no hesitation in asserting this, and should there be any unfortunate difference between any married couple in America, all the lady has to say is: "The fact is, sir, I'm much too good for you, and Captain Marryat says so." (I flatter myself there's a little mischief in that last sentence.)

It appears, then, that the American woman has little of her husband's society, and that in education and refinement she is much his superior, notwithstanding which she is a domestic slave. For this the Americans are not to blame, as it is the effect of circumstances over which they cannot be said to have any control. But the Americans are to blame in one point, which is that they do not properly appreciate or value their wives, who have not half the influence which wives have in England, or one quarter that legitimate influence to which they are entitled. That they are proud of them, flatter them, and are kind to them after their own fashion, I grant, but female influence extends no farther.

Some authors have said that by the morals of the women you can judge of the morals of a country; generally speaking, this is true, but America is an exception, for the women are more moral, more educated, and more refined than the men, and yet have at present no influence whatever in society.

What is the cause of this? It can only be ascribed to the one great ruling passion which is so strong that it will admit of no check or obstacles being thrown in its way, and will listen to no argument or entreaty, and because, in a country when everything is decided by public opinion, the women are as great slaves to it as the men. Their position at present appears to be that the men will not raise themselves to the standard of the women, and the women will not lower themselves to the standard of the men; they apparently move in different spheres, although they repose on the same bed.

It is, therefore, as I have before observed, fortunate that the marriages in America are more decided by prudence than by affection; for nothing could be more mortifying to a woman of sense and feeling than to awake from her dream of love and discover that the object upon which she has bestowed her affection is indifferent to the sacrifice which she has made.

If the American women had their due influence, it would be fortunate; they might save their country by checking the tide of vice and immorality, and raising the men to their own standard. Whether they ever will effect this, or whether they will continue as at present, to keep up the line of demarcation, or gradually sink down to the level of the other sex, is a question which remains to be solved.

That the American women have their peculiarities, and in some respects they might be improved, is certain. Their principal fault in society is that they do not sufficiently modulate their voices. Those faults arising from association, and to which both sexes are equally prone, are a total indifference to or rather a love of change, "shifting right away," without the least regret, from one portion of the Union to another; a remarkable apathy as to the sufferings of others, an indifference to loss of life, a fondness for politics, all of which are unfeminine; and lastly, a passion for dress carried to too great an extent; but this latter is easily accounted for, and is inseparable from a society where all would be equal. But, on the other hand, the American women have a virtue which the men have not, which is moral courage, and one also which is not common with the sex, physical courage. The independence and spirit of an American woman, if left a widow without resources, is immediately shown; she does not sit and lament but applies herself to some employment, so that she may maintain herself and her children, and seldom fails in so doing. Here are faults and virtues, both proceeding from the same origin. . . .

The remarks of Miss Martineau upon the women of America are all very ungracious, and some of them very unjust. That she met with affectation and folly in America is very probable—where do you not? There is no occasion to go to the United States to witness it. As for the charge of carrying in their hands seventy-dollar pocket-handkerchiefs, I am afraid it is but too true; but when there is little distinction, except by dress, ladies will be very expensive. I do not know why, but the American ladies have a custom of carrying their pocket-handkerchiefs in their hands, either in a room, or walking out, or travelling; and moreover, they have a custom of marking their names in the corner, at full length, and when in a steamboat or rail-car, I have, by a little watching, obtained the names of ladies sitting near me, in consequence of this custom, which of course will be ascribed by Miss Martineau to a wish to give information to strangers.

The remark upon the Washington belles * I am afraid is too true, as I have already pointed out that the indifference

---

* A Washington belle related to me the sad story of the death of a young man who fell from a small boat into the Potomac in the night—it is supposed in his sleep. She told me where and how his body was found, and what relation he had left, and finished with "he will be much missed at parties."

to human life in America extends to the softer sex; and I perfectly well remember, upon my coming into a room at New York with the first intelligence of the wreck of the *Home,* and the dreadful loss of life attending it, that my news was received with a "dear me!" from two or three of the ladies, and there the matter dropped. . . .

There is, however, one remark of Miss Martineau's which I cannot pass over without expressing indignation; I will quote the passage.

"It is no secret on the spot, that the habit of intemperance is not unfrequent among women of station and education in the most enlightened parts of the country." . . .

Miss Martineau is a lady; and, therefore, it is difficult to use the language which I would, if a man had made such an assertion. I shall only state that it is one of the greatest libels that ever was put into print, for Miss Martineau implies that it is general habit among the American women; so far from it, the American women are so abstemious that they do not drink sufficient for their health. They can take very little exercise, and did they take a little more wine, they would not suffer from *dyspepsia,* as they now do, as wine would assist their digestion. The origin of this slander I know well, and the only ground for it is that there are two or three ladies of a certain city who, having been worked upon by some of the Evangelical Revival Ministers, have had their minds crushed by the continual excitement to which they have been subjected. The mind affects the body, and they have required, and have applied to, stimulus, and if you will inquire into the moral state of any woman among the higher classes, either in America or England, who has fallen into the vice alluded to, nine times out of ten you will find that it has been brought about by religious excitement. Fanaticism and gin are remarkably good friends all over the world. It is surprising to me that, when Miss Martineau claims for her sex the same privilege as ours, she should have overlooked one simple fact which ought to convince *her* that they are the weaker vessels. I refer to what she acknowledges to be true, which is that the evangelical preachers invariably apply to women for proselytes instead of men, not only in America but everywhere else, and that, for one male, they may reckon at least twenty females among their flocks. . . .

In the United States divorces are obtained without expense and without it being necessary to commit crime, as in England. The party pleads in *forma pauperis*, to the state legislature, and a divorce is granted upon any grounds which may be considered as just and reasonable. . . .

I was myself told of an instance in which a divorce was granted upon the plea of the husband being such an *"awful swearer";* and really, if anyone heard the swearing in some parts of the western country, he would not be surprised at a religious woman requesting to be separated. I was once on board of a steamboat on the Mississippi when a man let off such a volley of execrations that it was quite painful to hear him. An American who stood by me, as soon as the man had finished, observed: "Well, I'm glad that fellow has nothing to do with the engines; I reckon he'd burst the *biler.*"

Miss Martineau observes: "In no country I believe are the marriage laws so iniquitous as in England, and the conjugal relation, in consequence, so impaired." . . . I am afraid that these remarks are but too true; and it is the more singular, as not only in the United States, but in every other Protestant community that I have ever heard of, divorce can be obtained upon what are considered just and legitimate grounds. It has been supposed that, should the marriage tie be loosened, divorces without number would take place.

It was considered so, and so argued, at the time that Zurich (the only Protestant canton in Switzerland that did not permit divorce, except for adultery alone) passed laws similar to those of the other cantons; but so far from such being the case, only one divorce took place, within a year after the laws were amended. What is the reason of this? It can, in my opinion, only be ascribed to the chain being worn more lightly when you know that, if it oppresses you, it may be removed. Men are naturally tyrants, and they bear down upon the woman who cannot escape from their thraldom; but, with the knowledge that she can appeal against them, they soften their rigor. On the other hand, the woman, when unable to escape, frets with the feeling that she must submit and that there is no help or hope in prospect; but once aware that she has her rights, and an appeal, she bears with more and feels less than otherwise she would. You may bind, and from assuetude and time (putting the better feelings out of the question) the ties are worn without complaint, but if you bind too tight, you cut into the flesh, and after a time the pain becomes insupportable. In Switzerland, Germany, and, I believe, all the Protestant communities of the Old World, the grounds upon which divorce is admissible are as follows: adultery, condemnation of either party to punishment considered as infamous, madness, contagious chronic diseases, desertion, and incompatibility of temper.

The last will be considered by most people as no ground for divorce. Whether it is or not, I shall not pretend to decide, but this is certain, that it is the cause of the most unhappiness and, ultimately, of the most crime.

All the great errors, all the various schisms in the Christian church, have arisen from not taking the holy writings as a great moral code (as I should imagine they were intended to be) which legislates upon broad principles, but selecting particular passages from them upon which to pin your faith. And it certainly appears to me to be reasonable to suppose that those laws which tended to diminish the aggregate of crime must be more acceptable to our Divine Master than any which, however they might be in spirit more rigidly conformable to His precepts, were found in their working not to succeed. And here I cannot help observing that the heads of the Church of England appear not to have duly weighed this matter, when an attempt was lately made to legislate upon it. Do the English bishops mean to assert that they know better than the heads of all the other Protestant communities in the world—that they are more accurate expounders of the gospel, and have a more intimate knowledge of God's will? Did it never occur to them, when so many good and virtuous ecclesiastics of the same persuasion in other countries have decided upon the propriety of divorce, so as to leave them in a very small minority, that it might be possible that they might be wrong, or do they intend to set up and claim the infallibility of the papistical hierarchy?

Any legislation to prevent crime, which produces more crime, must be bad and unsound, whatever may be its basis: witness the bastardy clause in the New Poor Law Bill. That the former arrangements were defective is undeniable, for by them there was a premium for illegitimate children. This required amendment; but the remedy has proved infinitely worse than the disease. For what has been the result? That there have been many thousands fewer illegitimate children *born*, it is true; but has the progress of immorality been checked? On the contrary, crime has increased, for to the former crime has been added one much greater, that of infanticide, or producing abortion. Such has been the effect of attempting to legislate for the affections; for in most cases a woman falls a sacrifice to her better feelings, not to her appetite.

In every point connected with marriage has this injurious plan been persevered in; the marriage ceremony is a remarkable instance of this, for, beautiful as it is as a service, it is certainly liable to this objection—that of making people vow before God that which it is not in human nature to control. The woman vows to love, and to honor, and to cherish; the man to love and cherish until death doth them part.

Is it right that this vow should be made? A man deserts his wife for another, treats her cruelly, separates her from her children. Can a woman love, or honor, or cherish such a man? Nevertheless, she has vowed before God that she will. Take the reverse of the picture when the fault is on the woman's side, and the evil is the same; can either party control their affections? Surely not, and therefore it would be better that such vows should not be demanded.

There is another evil arising from one crime being the only allowable cause of divorce, which is that the possession of one negative virtue on the part of the woman is occasionally made an excuse for the practice of vice, and a total disregard of her duties as a wife. I say negative virtue, for chastity very often proceeds from temperament, and as often from not being tempted.

A woman may neglect her duties of every kind—but she is chaste; she may make her husband miserable by indulgence of her ill-temper—but she is chaste; she may squander his money, ruin him by expense—but she is chaste; she may, in short, drive him to drunkenness and suicide—but still she is chaste; and chastity, like charity, covers the whole multitude of sins, and is the scapegoat for every other crime, and violation of the marriage vow.

It must, however, be admitted that although the faults may occasionally be found on the side of the women, in nine times out of ten it is the reverse; and that the defects of our marriage laws have rendered English women liable to treatment which ought not to be shown towards the veriest slaves in existence. . . .

The Americans claim excessive purity for their women, and taunt us with the *exposés* occasionally made in our newspapers. In the first place—which shows the highest regard for morality, a country where any deviation from virtue is immediately made known and held up to public indignation? or one which, from national vanity, and a wish that all should *appear* to be correct, instead of publishing, conceals the facts and permits the guilty parties to escape without censure, for what they consider the honor of the nation?

To suppose there is no conjugal infidelity in the United States is to suppose that human nature is not the same everywhere. That it never, to my knowledge, was made public, but invariably hushed up when discovered, I believe; so is suicide. But *one* instance came to my knowledge, during the time that I was in the states, which will give a very fair idea of American feeling on this subject. It was supposed that an intrigue had been discovered or it had actually been discovered, I cannot say which, between a foreigner and the wife of an English gentleman. It was immediately seized upon with ecstasy, circulated in all the papers with every American embellishment, and was really the subject of congratulation among them, as if they had gained some victory over this country. It so happened that an American called upon the lady, and among other questions put to her, inquired in what part of England she was born? She replied "that she was not an English-woman, but was born in the states, and brought up in an American city."

It is impossible to imagine how this mere trifling fact affected the Americans. She was then an American—they were aghast—and I am convinced that they would have made any sacrifice to have been able to have recalled all that they had done and have hushed up the matter.

The fact is that human nature *is* the same everywhere, and I cannot help observing that if their community is so much more moral, as they pretend that it is, why is it that they have considered it necessary to form societies on such an extensive scale, for the prevention of a crime from which they declare themselves (comparatively with us and other nations) to be exempt? . . .

Miss Martineau says that "the girls have too much pride for domestic service" and, therefore, argues that they will not be immoral; now, the two great causes of women falling off from virtue are poverty and false pride. What difference there is between receiving money for watching a spinning-jenny and doing household work, I do not see; in either case it is servitude, although the former may be preferred, as being less under control, and leaving more time at your own disposal. I consider the pride, therefore, which Miss Martineau upholds, to be *false* pride, which will actuate them in other points; and when we find the factory girls vying with each other in silks and laces, it becomes a query whether the passion for dress, so universal in America, may not have its effect there as well as elsewhere. I must confess that I went to Lowell doubting all I had heard—it was so contrary to human nature that five hundred girls should live among a population of fifteen hundred, or more, all pure and virtuous, and all dressed in silks and satin. When I went to Lowell I travelled with an American gentleman who will, I have no doubt, corroborate my statement, and I must say that, however pure Lowell may have been at the time when the encomiums were passed upon it, I have every reason to believe, from American authority as well as my own observation, that a great alteration has taken place, and that the manufactories have retrograded with the whole mass of American society. In the first place, I never heard a more accomplished swearer, east of the Alleghenies, than one young lady who addressed me and my American friend, and as it was the *only instance* of swearing on the part of a female that I ever met with in the United States, it was the more remarkable. I shall only observe that two days at Lowell convinced me that "human nature was the same everywhere," and thus I dismiss the subject. . . .

Public opinion acts as *law* in America; appearances are there substituted for the reality, and provided appearances are kept up, whether it be in religion or morality, it is sufficient; but should an exposure take place, there is no mercy for the offender. As those who have really the least virtue in themselves are always the loudest to cry out at any lapse which may be discovered in others, so does society in America pour out its anathemas in the inverse ratio of its real purity. Now, although the authority I speak from is undoubted, at the same time I wish to say as little as possible. That there are fewer illegitimate children *born* in the United States is very true. But why so? Because public opinion there acts as the bastardy clause in the New **Poor** Law Bill has done in this country; . . .

CHAPTER XLVI

Public Opinion, or the Majority

The majority are always in the *right*. . . . The great question is, what is a majority? must it be a whole nation, or a portion of a nation, or a portion of the population of a city, or, in fact, any *plus* against any *minus*, be they small or be they large? For instance, two against one are a majority, and, if so, any two scoundrels may murder an honest man and be in the right; or it may be the majority in any city, as in Baltimore, where they rose and murdered an unfortunate minority; * or it may be a majority on the Canada frontier, when a set of miscreants defied their own

---

* A striking instance of the excesses which may be occasioned by the despotism of the majority occurred at Baltimore in 1812. At that time the war was very popular in Baltimore. A journal, which had taken the other side of the question, excited the indignation of the inhabitants by its opposition. The populace assembled, broke the printing-presses, and attacked the houses of the newspaper editors. The militia was called out, but no one obeyed the call, and the only means of saving the poor wretches, who were threatened by the frenzy of the mob, were to throw them into prison as common malefactors. But even this precaution was ineffectual; the mob collected again during the night, the magistrates again made a vain attempt to call out the militia, the prison was forced, one of the newspaper editors was killed upon the spot, and the others were left for dead; when the guilty parties were brought to trial, they were *acquitted* by the jury.

government, and invaded the colony of a nation with whom they were at peace—all of which is of course right.

I have before observed that Washington left America a republic, and that in the short space of fifty years it has sunk into a democracy.

The barrier intended to be raised against the encroachments of the people has been swept away—the Senate (which was intended, by the arrangements for its election, to have served as the aristocracy of the legislature, as a deliberative check to the impetus of the majority, like our House of Lords), having latterly become virtually nothing more than a second Congress, receiving instructions, and submissive to them, like a pledged representative. This is what Washington did not foresee.

Washington was himself an aristocrat; he showed it in every way. He was difficult of access, except to the higher classes. He carried state in his outward show, always wearing his uniform as general of the forces and attended by a guard of honour. Indeed, one letter of Washington's proves that he was rather doubtful as to the working of the new government shortly after it had been constituted. He says—

> Among men of reflection few will be found, I believe, who are not *beginning* to think that our system is better in *theory* than in *practice*, and that notwithstanding the *boasted virtue* of America, it is more than probable we shall exhibit the *last melancholy proof*, that mankind are incompetent to their own government without *the means of coercion in the sovereign.**

This is a pretty fair admission from such high authority; and fifty years has proved the wisdom and foresight of the observation. Gradually as the aristocracy of the country wore out (for there was an aristocracy at that time in America) and the people became less and less enlightened, so did they encroach upon the Constitution. President after President gradually laid down the insignia

---

* Washington's letter to Chief Justice Jay, 10th March, 1787.

and outward appearance of rank, the Senate became less and less respectable, and the people more and more authoritative. . . .

It was not, however, until the Presidency of General Jackson that the democratic party may be said to have made any serious inroads upon the Constitution. Their previous advances were indeed sure, but they were, comparatively speaking, slow; but raised as he was to the office of President by the mob, the demagogues who led the mob obtained the offices under government, to the total exclusion of the aristocratic party, whose doom was then sealed. Within the last ten years the advance of the people has been like a torrent, sweeping and levelling all before it, and the will of the majority has become not only absolute with the government, but it defies the government itself, which is too weak to oppose it.

Is it not strange, and even ridiculous, that under a government established little more than fifty years, a government which was to be a *lesson* to the whole world, we should find political writers making use of language such as this: "We are for *reform, sound progressive reform,* not subversion and destruction." Yet such is an extract from one of the best-written American periodicals of the day. This is the language that may be expected to be used in a country like England, which still legislates under a government of eight hundred years old; but what a failure must that government be which in fifty years calls forth even from its advocates such an admission!! . . .

My object in this chapter is to inquire what effect has been produced upon the morals of the American people by this acknowledged dominion of the majority?

1st. As to the mass of the people themselves. It is clear, if the people not only legislate, but, when in a state of irritation or excitement, they defy even legislation, that they are not to be compared to *restricted* sovereigns but to despots, whose will and caprice are law. The vices of the court of a despot are, therefore, practised upon the people; for the people become, as it were, the court, to whom those in authority, or those who would be in authority, submissively bend the knee. A despot is not likely ever to hear the truth, for moral courage fails where there is no law to protect it and where honest advice may be rewarded by summary punishment. The people, therefore, like the despot are never told the truth; on the contrary, they receive and expect the most abject submission from their courtiers, to wit, those in office, or expectants.

Now, the President of the United States may be considered the Prime Minister of an enlightened public, who govern themselves, and his communication with them is in his annual message.

Let us examine what Mr. Van Buren says in his last message.

First, he humbly acknowledges their power.

"A national bank," he tells them, "would impair the rightful *supremacy* of the popular *will*."

And this he follows up with that most delicate species of flattery, that of praising them for the very virtue which they are most deficient in; telling them they are "A people to whom the *truth*, however unpromising, can *always* be told with *safety*."

At the very time when they were defying all law and all government, he says: "It was reserved for the American Union to test the advantage of a government entirely dependent on the continual exercise of the popular will, and our experience has shown that it is as *beneficent* in *practice*, as well as it is just in *theory*." . . .

This is quite enough; Mr. Van Buren's motives are to be re-elected as President. That is very natural on his part; but how can you expect a people to improve who *never hear the truth?* . . .

The same system is pursued by all those who would arrive at or remain in place and power; and what must be the consequence? That the straight-forward, honorable upright man is rejected by the people, while the parasite, the adulator, the demagogue, who flatters their opinion, asserts their supremacy, and yields to their arbitrary demands, is the one selected by them for place and power. Thus do they demoralize each other; and it is not until a man has, by his abject submission to their will, in contradiction to his own judgment and knowledge, proved that he is unworthy of the selection which he courts, that he is permitted to obtain it. Thus it is that the most able and conscientious men in the states are almost unanimously rejected. . . .

Indeed, no high-minded consistent man will now offer himself, and this is one cause among many why Englishmen and foreigners have not done real justice to the people of the United States. The scum is uppermost, and they do not see below it. The prudent, the enlightened, the wise, and the good have all retired into the shade, preferring to pass a life of quiet retirement, rather than submit to the insolence and dictation of a mob. . . .

It appears, then, that the more respectable portion of its citizens have retired, leaving the arena open to those who are least worthy: that the majority dictate, and scarcely anyone ventures to oppose them; if anyone does, he is immediately sacrificed; the press, obedient to its masters, pours out its virulence, and it is incredible how rapidly a man, unless he be of a superior mind, falls into nothingness in the United States, when once he has dared to oppose the popular will. He is morally bemired, bespattered, and trod under foot, until he remains a lifeless carcass. He falls, never to rise again, unhonored and unremembered. . . .

To be popular with the majority in America, to be a favourite with the people, you must first divest yourself of all freedom of opinion; you must throw off all dignity; you must shake hands and drink with every man you meet; you must be, in fact, slovenly and dirty in your appearance or you will be put down as an aristocrat. I recollect once an American candidate asked me if I would walk out with him? I agreed; but he requested leave to change his coat, which was a decent one, for one very shabby, "for," says he, "I intend to look in upon some of my constituents, and if they

ever saw me in that other coat, I should lose my election."
This cannot but remind the reader of the custom of candi-
dates in former democracies—standing up in the market-
place as suppliants in tattered garments, to solicit the
"voices" of the people.

That the morals of the nation have retrograded from
the total destruction of the aristocracy, both in the government and in society, which has taken place within the last
ten years, is most certain. . . .

The tyranny of the majority has completely destroyed
the moral courage of the American people, and without
moral courage what chance is there of any fixed standard of
morality? . . .

There are a few exceptions—Clay and Webster are men
of such power as to be able, to a certain degree, to hold
their independence. Dr. Channing has proved himself an
honour to his country and to the world. Mr. Cooper has also
great merit in this point; and no man has certainly shown
more moral courage, let his case be good or not, than Garrison, the leader of the abolition party.

But with these few and remarkable exceptions, moral
courage is almost prostrate in the United States. The most
decided specimen I met with to the contrary was at Cincinnati, when a large portion of the principal inhabitants
ventured to express their opinion, contrary to the will of
the majority, in my defence, and boldly proclaimed their
opinions by inviting me to a public dinner. I told them my
opinion of their behaviour, and I gave them my thanks. I
repeat my opinion and my thanks now; they had much to
contend with; but they resisted boldly; and not only from
that remarkable instance of daring to oppose public opinion
when all others quailed, but from many other circumstances, I have an idea that Cincinnati will one day take an
important lead, as much from the spirit and courage of her
citizens, as from her peculiarly fortunate position. I had a
striking instance to the contrary at St. Louis, when they
paraded me in effigy through the streets. Certain young

Bostonians, who would have been glad enough to have seized my hand when in the eastern states, before I had happened to affront the majority, kept aloof, or shuffled away, so as not to be obliged to recognize me. Such have been the demoralizing effects of the tyranny of public opinion in the short space of fifty years, . . .

CHAPTER XLVII

Patriotism

This is a word of very doubtful meaning; and until we have the power to analyze the secret springs of action, it is impossible to say who is or who is not a patriot. . . . I consider that if, in most cases, in all countries, the word egotism were substituted it would be more correct, and particularly so in America. . . .

The fact is that the American is aware that what affects the general prosperity must affect the individual, and he therefore is anxious for the general prosperity; he also considers that he assists to legislate for the country, and is therefore equally interested in such legislature being prosperous; if, therefore, you attack his country, you attack him personally—you wound his vanity and self-love.

In America, it is not our rulers who have done wrong or right; it is we (or rather I) who have done wrong or right, and the consequence is that the American is *rather* irritable on the subject, as every attack is taken as personal. It is quite ridiculous to observe how some of the very best of the Americans are tickled when you praise their country and institutions; how they will wince at any qualification in your praise, and actually writhe under any positive disparagement. They *will* put questions, even if they anticipate an unfavourable answer; they cannot help it. What is the reason of this? Simply their better sense wrestling with the errors of education and long-cherished fallacies. They feel that their institutions do not work as they would wish, that the theory is not borne out by the practice, and they want support against their own convictions. They cannot bear to eradicate deep-rooted prejudices, which have been from their earliest days a source of pride and vain-glory, and to acknowledge that what they have considered as most perfect, what they have boasted of as a *lesson* to other nations, what they have suffered so much to uphold, in surrendering their liberty of speech, of action, and of opinion, has after all proved to be a miserable failure, and instead of a lesson to other nations—a warning.

Yet such are the doubts, the misgivings which fluctuate in and irritate the minds of a very large proportion of the Americans; and such is the decided conviction of a portion who retire into obscurity and are silent; and every year adds to the number of both these parties. They remind one of a husband who, having married for love, and supposed his wife to be perfection, gradually finds out she is full of faults, and renders him anything but happy; but his pride will not allow him to acknowledge that he has committed an error in his choice, and he continues before the world to descant upon her virtues and to conceal her errors, while he feels that his home is miserable.

It is because it is more egotistical that the patriotism of the American is more easily roused and more easily affronted. He has been educated to despise all other countries and to look upon his own as the first in the world; he has been taught that all other nations are slaves to despots and that the American citizen only is free, and this is never contradicted. For although thousands may in their own hearts feel the falsehood of their assertions, there is not one who will venture to express his opinion. The government sets the example, the press follows it, and the people receive the incense of flattery, which in other countries is offered to the court alone, and if it were not for the occasional compunctions and doubts, which his real good sense will sometimes visit him with, the more enlightened American would be happy in his own delusions, as the majority most certainly may be said to be. . . .

There are, however, other causes which assist this delusion on the part of the majority of the Americans, the principal of which is the want of comparison. The Americans are too far removed from the old continent and are too much occupied, even if they were not, to have time to visit it and make the comparison between the settled countries and their own. America is so vast that, if they travel in it, their ideas of their own importance become magnified. The only comparisons they are able to make are only as to the quantity of square acres in each country, which, of course, is vastly in their favour. . . .

After all, is there not a happiness in this delusion on the part of the American majority, and is not the feeling of admiration of their own country borrowed from ourselves? The feeling may be more strong with the Americans, because it is more egotistical; but it certainly is the *English* feeling transplanted, and growing in a ranker soil. We may accuse the Americans of conceit, of wilful blindness, of obstinacy; but there is after all a great good in being contented with yourself and yours. The English show it differently; but the English are not so good-tempered as the Americans. They grumble at everything; they know the faults of their institutions, but at the same time they will allow of no interference. Grumbling is a luxury so great that an Englishman will permit it only to himself. The Englishman grumbles at his government, under which he enjoys more rational liberty than the individual of any other nation in the world. The American, ruled by the despotism of the majority, and without liberty of opinion or speech, praises his institutions to the skies. The Englishman grumbles at his climate, which, if we were to judge from the vigour and perfection of the inhabitants, is, notwithstanding its humidity, one of the best in the world. The American vaunts his above all others, and even thinks it necessary to apologize for a bad day, although the climate, from its sudden extremes, withers up beauty and destroys the nervous system. In everything connected with and relating to America, the American has the same feeling. Calculating, wholly matter-of-fact and utilitarian in his ideas, without a poetic sense of his own, he is annoyed if a stranger does not express that rapture at their rivers, waterfalls, and woodland scenery which he himself does not feel. As far as America is concerned, everything is for the best in this best of all possible countries. It is laughable, yet praiseworthy, to observe how the whole nation will stoop down to fan the slightest spark which is elicited of native genius—like the London cit[izen], who is enraptured with his own stunted cucumbers, which he has raised at ten times the expense which would have purchased fine ones in the market. It were almost a pity that the American should be awakened from his dream, if it were not that the arrogance and conceit arising from it may eventually plunge him into difficulty.

But let us be fair: America is the country of enthusiasm and hope, and we must not be too severe upon what from a virgin soil has sprung up too luxuriantly. It is but the English *amor patriae* carried to too great an excess. The Americans are great boasters; but are we far behind them? . . . Nor is it altogether wrong to encourage these feelings; although arrogance is a fault in an individual, in a national point of view it often becomes the incentive to great actions and, if not excessive, insures the success inspired by confidence. As by giving people credit for a virtue which they have not, you very often produce that virtue in them, I think it not unwise to implant this feeling in the hearts of the lower classes, who, if they firmly believe that they can beat three Frenchmen, will at all events attempt to do it. That too great success is dangerous, and that the feeling of arrogance produced by it may lead us into the error of despising our enemy, we ourselves showed an example of in our first contest with America during the last war. In that point America and England have now changed positions, and from false education, want of comparison, and unexpected success in their struggle with us, they are now much more arrogant than we were when most flushed with victory. They are blind to their own faults and to the merits of others, and while they are so, it is clear that they will offend strangers and never improve themselves. I have often laughed at the false estimate held by the majority in America as to England. One told me, with a patronizing air, that "in a short time, England would only be known as having been the mother of America.". . .

This national vanity is fed in every possible way. At one of the museums I asked the subject of a picture representing a naval engagement; the man (supposing I was an American, I presume) replied, "that ship there," pointing to one twice as big as the other, "is the *Macedonian* English frigate, and that other frigate," pointing to the small one, "is the *Constitution* American frigate, which captured her in less than five minutes." Indeed, so great has this feeling become from indulgence that they will not allow anything to stand in its way and will sacrifice anybody or anything to support it. It was not until I arrived in the United States that I was informed by several people that Captain Lawrence,[1] who commanded the *Chesapeake,* was drunk when he went into action. Speaking of the action, one man shook his head, and said: "Pity poor Lawrence had his failing; he was otherwise a good officer." I was often told the same thing, and a greater libel was never uttered; but thus was a gallant officer's character sacrificed to soothe the national vanity. I hardly need observe that the American naval

---

[1] This is a reference to the battle between the U.S.S. *Chesapeake* and the H.M.S. *Shannon* in June 1813. The *Shannon,* smaller in size but in better fighting trim, demolished the *Chesapeake,* which had an inexperienced crew. The entire engagement lasted but fifteen minutes. Lawrence, the commander of the American ship, was mortally wounded and died a prisoner. It was this battle which gave the American navy the traditional cry: "Don't give up the ship!" Marryat's allusion to Lawrence's drunkenness is not borne out by any reputable historian. The natural implication, of course, assumed by the Americans of Marryat's day was that if Lawrence had been sober he would have won easily. The actual facts do not bear out such a chauvinistic interpretation of events. For a full account, see C. S. Forester, *The Age of Fighting Sail,* pp. 161–66.

officers are as much disgusted with the assertion as I was myself. That Lawrence fought under disadvantages—that many of his ship's company, hastily collected together from leave, were not sober, and that there was a want of organization from just coming out of harbor—is true, and quite sufficient to account for his defeat; but I have the evidence of those who walked with him down to his boat that he was perfectly sober, cool, and collected, as he always had proved himself to be. But there is no gratitude in a democracy, and to be unfortunate is to be guilty.

There is a great deal of patriotism of one sort or the other in the American women. I recollect once, when conversing with a highly cultivated and beautiful American woman, I inquired if she knew a lady who had been sometime in England and who was a great favourite of mine. She replied, "Yes." "Don't you like her?" "To confess the truth, I do not," replied she; "she is *too English* for me." "That is to say, she likes England and the English." "That is what I mean." I replied, that had she been in England, she would probably have become *too English* also, for, with her cultivated and elegant ideas, she must naturally have been pleased with the refinement, luxury, and established grades in society, which it had taken eight hundred years to produce. "If that is to be the case, I hope I may never go to England."

Now, this was *true* patriotism, and there is much true patriotism among the higher classes of the American women; with them there is no alloy of egotism.

Indeed, all the women in America are very *patriotic;* but I do not give them all the same credit. In the first place, they are controlled by public opinion as much as the men are; and without assumed patriotism they would have no chance of getting husbands. As you descend in the scale, so are they the more noisy and, I imagine, for that very reason the less sincere.

Among what may be termed the middling classes, I have been very much amused with the compound of vanity and ignorance which I have met with. Among this class they can read and write, but almost all their knowledge is confined to their own country, especially in geography, which I soon discovered. It was hard to beat them on American ground, but as soon as you got them off that, they were defeated. I wish the reader to understand particularly that I am not speaking now of the well-bred Americans, but of that portion which would with us be considered as on a par with the middle class of shop-keepers; for I had a very extensive acquaintance. My amusement was to make some comparison between the two countries, which I knew would immediately bring on the conflict I desired, and not without danger, for I sometimes expected, in the ardor of their patriotism, to meet with the fate of Orpheus.

I soon found that, the more I granted, the more they demanded, and that the best way was never to grant anything. I was once in a room full of the softer sex, chiefly girls, of all ages, when the mama of a portion of them, who was sitting on the sofa, as we mentioned steam, said: "Well, now, Captain, you will allow that we are ahead of you there."

"No," replied I, "quite the contrary. Our steamboats go all over the world—yours are afraid to leave the rivers."

"Well now, Captain, I suppose you'll allow America is a bit bigger country than England?"

"It's rather broader—but, if I recollect right, it's not quite so long."

"Why, Captain!"

"Well, only look at the map."

"Why, isn't the Mississippi a bigger river than you have in England?"

"Bigger? Pooh! Haven't we got the Thames?"

"The Thames? Why that's no river at all."

"Isn't it? Just look at the map and measure them."

"Well now, Captain, I tell you what, you call your Britain the mistress of the seas, yet we whipped you well, and you know that."

"Oh! yes. You refer to the *Shannon* and *Chesapeake*, don't you?"

"No! Not that time, because Lawrence was drunk, they say; but didn't we *whip* you well at New Orleans?"

"No, you didn't."

"No? Oh, Captain!"

"I say you did not. If your people had come out from behind their cotton bales and sugar casks, we'd have knocked you all into a cocked hat; but they wouldn't come, so we walked away in disgust."

"Now, Captain, that's romancing—that won't do." Here the little ones joined in the cry, "We did beat you, and you know it." And hauling me into the centre of the room, they joined hands in a circle, and danced round me, singing:

> Yankee doodle is a tune,
> Which is nation handy,
> All the British ran away
> At Yankee doodle dandy.

I shall conclude by stating that this feeling, call it patriotism or what you please, is so strongly implanted in the bosom of the American by education and association that wherever, or whenever, the national honour or character is called into question, there is no sacrifice which they will not make to keep up appearances. It is this which induces them to acquit murderers, to hush up suicides, or any other offence which may reflect upon their asserted morality. I would put no confidence even in an official document from the government, for I have already ascertained how they will invariably be twisted, so as to give no offence to the majority; and the base adulation of the government to the people is such that it dare not tell them the truth or publish anything which might wound its self-esteem.

I shall conclude with two extracts from a work of Mr. Cooper, the American:

> We are almost entirely wanting in national pride, though abundantly supplied with an *irritable vanity,* which might rise to pride had we greater confidence in our facts. . . .

We have the sensitiveness of provincials, increased by the consciousness of having our spurs to earn on all matters of glory and renown, and *our jealousy extends even to the reputations of the cats and dogs.* . . .

This feeling becomes stronger every day. They want to *whip* the whole world. The wise and prudent perceive the folly of this, and try all they can to produce a better feeling; but the majority are now irresistible, and their fiat will decide upon war or peace. The government is powerless in opposition to it; all it can do is to give a legal appearance to any act of violence.

This idea of their own prowess will be one cause of danger to their institutions, for war must ever be fatal to democracy. In this country, during peace, we become more and more democratic; but whenever we are again forced into war, the reins will be again tightened from necessity, and thus war must ever interfere with free institutions. A convincing proof of the idea the Americans have of their own prowess was when General Jackson made the claim for compensation from the French. Through the intermediation of England the claim was adjusted and peace preserved; and the Americans are little aware what a debt of gratitude they owe to this country for its interference. They were totally ignorant of the power and resources of France. They had an idea, and I was told so fifty times, that France paid the money from *fear,* and that if she had not, they would have *"whipped* her into the little end of nothing."* . . .

There are many reasons why the Americans have an inveterate dislike [of England]. In the first place, they are educated to dislike us and our monarchical institutions; their short history points out to them that we have been their only oppressor in the first instance, and their opponent ever since. Their annual celebration of the independence is an opportunity for vituperation of this country which is never lost sight of. Their national vanity is hurt by feeling what they would fain believe, that they are not the "greatest nation on earth"; that they are indebted to us, and the credit we give them, for their prosperity and rapid advance; that they must still look to us for their literature and the fine arts; and that, in short, they are still dependent upon England. I have before observed that this hostile spirit against us is fanned by discontented emigrants, and by those authors who, to become popular with the majority, laud their own country and defame England; but the great cause of this increase of hostility against us is the democratic party having come into power, and who consider it necessary to excite animosity against this country. Whenever it is requisite to throw a tub to the whale, the press is immediately full of abuse; everything is attributed to England and the machinations of England; she is, by their accounts, here, there, and everywhere, plotting mischief and injury, from the Gulf of Florida to the Rocky Mountains. If we are to believe the democratic press, England is the cause of everything offensive to the majority: if money is scarce, it is England that has occasioned it; if credit is bad, it is England; if eggs are not fresh or beef is tough, it is, it must be, England. . . .

How, then, is it possible that the lower classes in the United States (and the lower and unenlightened principally compose the majority) can have other than feelings of ill-will towards this country? And of what avail is it to us that the high-minded and sensible portion think otherwise, when they are in such a trifling minority and afraid to express their sentiments? When we talk about a nation, we look to the mass, and that the mass are hostile, and inveterately hostile to this country, is a most undeniable fact.

There is another cause of hostility which I have not adverted to, the remarks upon them by travellers in their country, such as I am now making; but as the Americans never hear the truth from their own countrymen, it is only from foreigners that they can. Of course, after having been accustomed to flattery from their earliest days, the truth, when it does come, falls more heavily, and the injury and insult which they consider they have received are never forgotten. . . .

That there should be a hostile feeling when Englishmen go over to America to compete with them in business or in any profession, is natural; it would be the same everywhere; this feeling, however, in the United States is usually shown by an attack upon the character of the party, so as to influence the public against him. There was an American practising phrenology, when a phrenologist arrived from England. As this opposition was not agreeable, the American immediately circulated a report that the English phrenologist had asserted that he had examined the skulls of many Americans and that he had never fallen in with such *thick-headed fellows* in his life. This was quite sufficient—the English operator was obliged to *clear out* as fast as he could and try his fortune elsewhere. . . .

CHAPTER XLVIII

Society: General Characteristics

The character of the Americans is that of a restless, un-easy people—they cannot sit still, they cannot listen attentively, unless the theme be politics or dollars, they must do something, and, like children, if they cannot do anything else, they will do mischief—their curiosity is unbounded, and they are very capricious. Acting upon impulse, they are very generous at one moment and without a spark of charity the next. They are good-tempered and possess great energy, ingenuity, bravery, and presence of mind. Such is the estimate I have formed of their general character, independent of the demoralizing effects of their institutions, which renders it so anomalous. . . .

The Americans have few amusements; they are too busy. Athletic sports they are indifferent to; they look only to those entertainments which feed their passion for excitement. The theatre is almost their only resort, and even that is not so well attended as it might be, considering their means. There are some very good and well-conducted theatres in America: the best are the Park and National at New York, the Tremont at Boston, and the Chestnut Street Theatre at Philadelphia. The American *stock* actors, as they term those who are not considered as *stars,* are better than our own; but were the theatres to depend upon stock actors they would be deserted—the love of novelty is the chief inducement of the Americans to frequent the theatre, and they look for importations of star actors from this country as regularly as they do for our manufactured goods or the fashions from Paris. In most of the large cities they have two theatres, one for legitimate drama and the other for melodrama, etc.—as the Bowery Theatre at New York and the Walnut Street Theatre in Philadelphia; these latter are seldom visited by the aristocratical portion of the citizens.

The National Theatre at New York was originally built as an opera house, and the company procured from the Havannah; but the opera, from want of support, was a failure.[1] It has since been taken by Mr. James Wallack,[2] in opposition to the Park Theatre. The first two seasons its success was indifferent, the Park having the advantage in situation as well as of a long-standing reputation. But lat-

---

[1] The first opera house in New York City was built in 1833 at the cost of $150,000 and was situated on the southwest corner of Church and Leonard Streets. The first production in the new structure took place on November 18, 1833, when Rossini's opera, *La Gazza Ladra,* was performed. The management continued to present Italian operas until July 1834. Unfortunately, the cost of such productions being $81,155.98 and the receipts $51,780.89, it was found impossible to continue. The theatre was then leased for the next season to other managers, but opera continued to be unprofitable. At the end of the second season the house was rented to Henry Willard and Thomas Flynn, who ran it as a legitimate theatre. It was named The National Theatre and the first production under the new management was *The Merchant of Venice.* Arthur Hornblow, *A History of the*

Theatre in America (Philadelphia: J. B. Lippincott; 1919), Vol. II, pp. 104–105.

[2] James Wallack (1794–1864), an English actor who first appeared in New York in 1818, was one of the leading actor-managers of his day. Wallack appeared in theatrical productions all over the United States, but his chief endeavours were in New York. In 1852 he opened his own theatre in the city and gave a series of superb productions. He managed the theatre and appeared in many plays himself. For an account of Wallack's career and influence on the American theatre, see Glenn Hughes, *A History of the American Theatre 1700–1950* (New York: S. French; 1951). Hughes does not confirm Marryat's statements that Wallack assumed the management of the National Theatre in opposition to the Park Theatre.

terly, from the well-known talent and superior management of Mr. Wallack, and from his unwearied exertions in providing novelties for the American public, it has been very successful; so much so, that it is said this last year to have decidedly obtained the superiority over its rival. I have seen some splendid representations in the National Theatre, with a propriety in scenery and costume which is seldom exceeded even in our great theatres.

Indeed, in three seasons, Mr. Wallack has done much to improve the national taste; and from his exertions, the theatres in general in America may be said to have been much benefitted. But there is one objection to this rivalry between the Park and National; which is, that the *stars* go out too fast, and they will soon be all expended. Formerly things went on very regularly; Mr. Price [3] sent out to Mr. Simpson,[4] duly invoiced, a certain portion of talent for every season; and Mr. Simpson, who is a very clever manager, first worked it up at New York, and then despatched it to Boston, Philadelphia, and the other theatres in the Union. But now, if Mr. Simpson has two stars sent to him, James Wallack comes home and takes out three; whereupon, Mr. Price sends out a bigger star; and so they go on, working up the stars so fast that the supply will never equal the demand. There are not more than two or three actors of eminence in England who have not already made their appearance on the American boards; and next season will probably use them up. It is true that some actors can return there again and again: as Power,[5] who is most de-

---

[3] Stephen Price (1782–1840) joined Thomas Abthorpe Cooper as co-manager of the Park Theatre in 1808. Price was not an actor himself but a businessman and brought to the Park Theatre sound financing and promotional talent. He was famous for hiring foreign—especially English—actors and actresses.

[4] Edmund Shaw Simpson (1784–1848) was an English actor who had joined the Park Theatre company in 1809. He was associated with Price in the recruitment of British actors, one of the most notable of whom was James Wallack.

[5] See earlier note on Power in Marryat's Introduction, p. 9.

servedly a favourite with them, and Ellen Tree,[6] who is equally so. Celeste [7] has realized a large fortune. Mrs. Wood [8] and the Keeleys [9] were also very great favourites; but there are not many actors who can venture there a second time—at least not until a certain interval has elapsed for the Americans to forget them. When there are no longer any stars, the theatres will not be so well attended—as, indeed, is the case everywhere. To prove how fond the Americans are of anything that excites them, I will mention a representation which I one day went to see— that of the "Infernal Regions." There were two or three of these shown in the different cities in the states. I saw the remnants of another myself; but, as the museum-keeper very appropriately observed to me, "It was a fine thing once, but now it had all gone to h–ll." You entered a dark room where, railed off with iron railings, you beheld a long perspective of caverns in the interior of the earth and a molten lake in the distance. In the foreground were the most horrible monsters that could be invented—bears with men's heads, growling—snakes darting in and out hissing—here a man lying murdered, with a knife in his heart; there a suicide, hanging by the neck—skeletons lying about in all directions, and some walking up and down in muslin

---

[6] Ellen Tree (1805–80), Shakespearian actress and wife of the great actor, Charles Kean. She popularized the song "Home Sweet Home" in America.
[7] Celine Celeste (1814–82), French actress, who first appeared in the United States in 1827. As she then knew no English, she was a pantomimist. She returned to Europe, learned English, and reappeared in New York in 1834, where for the next decade she had great popularity. After 1844 she resided chiefly in England but made several trips to the United States.

[8] Mary Ann Wood (1802–64), English opera singer, appeared first in America in 1833 in Rossini's opera *La Cenerentola*. She had a magnificent voice and her début was a sensational success. In fact, she was as widely acclaimed as Jenny Lind a couple of decades later. Mary Ann Wood and her husband, Joseph Wood, made several tours in the United States.
[9] Robert Keeley (1793–1869) and Mary Ann Keeley (1805?–99), an English theatrical couple, acted in many plays in both the United States and England.

shrouds. The machinery was very perfect. At one side was the figure of a man sitting down, with a horrible face, boar's tusks protruding from his mouth, his eyes rolling, and horns on his head; I thought it was mechanism as well as the rest, and was not a little surprised when it addressed me in a hollow voice: "We've been waiting some time for you, Captain." As I found he had a tongue, I entered into conversation with him. The representation wound up with showers of fire, rattling of bones, thunder, screams, and a regular cascade of the d——d, pouring into the molten lake. When it was first shown, they had an electric battery communicating with the iron railing; and whoever put his hand on it, or went too near, received a smart electric shock. But the alarm created by this addition was found to be attended with serious consequences, and it had been discontinued.

The love of excitement must of course produce a love of gambling, which may be considered as one of the American amusements; it is, however, carried on very quietly in the cities. In the south, and on the Mississippi, it is as open as the noon day; and the gamblers may be said to have there become a professional people. I have already mentioned them, and the attempts which have been made to get rid of them. Indeed, they are not only gamesters who practise on the unwary, but they combine with gambling the professions of forgery, and uttering of base money. If they lose, they only lose forged notes. There is no part of the world where forgery is carried on to such an extent as it is in the United States, chiefly in the western country. The American banks are particularly careful to guard against this evil, but the ingenuity of these miscreants is surprising, and they will imitate so closely as almost to escape detection at the banks themselves. Bank-note engraving is certainly carried to the highest state of perfection in the United States, but almost in vain. I have myself read a notice, posted up at Boston, which may appear strange to us: "Bank-notes made here to any pattern." But the eastern banks are seldom forged upon. Counterfeit money is also very plentiful. When

I was in the west, I had occasion to pay a few dollars to a friend; when I saw him a day or two afterwards, he said to me: "Do you know that three dollars you gave me were counterfeits?" I apologized and offered to replace them. "Oh! no," replied he, "it's of no consequence. I gave them in payment to my people, who told me that they *were* counterfeit; but they said it was of no consequence, as they could easily pass them." In some of the states lotteries have been abolished; in others they are still permitted. They are upon the French principle and are very popular.

There is one very remarkable point in the American character, which is that they constantly change their professions. I know not whether it proceeds simply from their love of change or from their embracing professions at so early a period that they have not discovered the line in which from natural talents they are best calculated to succeed. I have heard it said that it is seldom that an American succeeds in the profession which he had first taken up at the commencement of his career. An American will set up as a lawyer, quit, and go to sea for a year or two; come back, set up in another profession; get tired again, go as clerk or steward in a steamboat, merely because he wishes to travel; then apply himself to something else and begin to amass money. It is of very little consequence what he does; the American is really a jack of all trades and master of any to which he feels at last inclined to apply himself.

In Mrs. Butler's clever journal there is one remark which really surprised me. She says: "The absolute absence of imagination is of course the absolute absence of humor. An American can no more understand a fanciful jest than a poetical idea; and in society and conversation the *strictest matter of fact* prevails," etc.

If there was nothing but *"matter of fact"* in society and conversation in America or elsewhere, I imagine that there would not be many words used, but I refer to the passage, because she says that the Americans are not imaginative, whereas I think that there is not a more imaginative people existing. It is true that they prefer broad humor and delight in the hyperbole, but this is to be expected in a young nation, especially as their education is, generally speaking, not of a kind to make them sensible to very refined wit, which, I acknowledge, is thrown away upon the majority. What is termed the undercurrent of humor, as delicate raillery, for instance, is certainly not understood. . . .

The hyperbole is their principal forte, but what is lying but imagination? and why do you find that a child of promising talent is so prone to lying? Because it is the first effort of a strong imagination. Wit requires refinement, which the Americans have not, but they have excessive humor, although it is, generally speaking, coarse.

An American, talking of an ugly woman with a very large mouth, said to me: "Why, sir, when she yawns, you can see right down to her garters"; and another, speaking of his being very seasick, declared that he "threw everything up, down to his knee-pans."

If there required any proof of the dishonest feeling so prevalent in the United States, arising from the desire of gain, it would be in the fact that almost every good story which you hear of an American is an instance of great ingenuity and very little principle. So many have been told already that I hesitate to illustrate my observation, from fear of being accused of uttering stale jokes. Nevertheless, I will venture upon one or two.

"An American (down East, of course), when his father died, found his patrimony to consist of several hundred dozen of boxes of ointment for the cure of a certain complaint, said (by us) to be more common in the north than in England. He made up his pack, and took a round of nearly one hundred miles, going from town to town and from village to village, offering his remedy for sale. But unfortunately for him, no one was afflicted with the complaint, and they would not purchase on the chance of any future occasion for it. He returned back to his inn, and having reflected a little, he went out, inquired where he could find the disease, and having succeeded, inoculated himself with it. When he was convinced that he had it with sufficient.

virulence, he again set forth, making the same round, and taking advantage of the American custom, which is so prevalent, he shook hands with everybody whom he had spoken to on his former visit, declaring he was ' 'tarnal glad to see them again.' Thus he went on till his circuit was completed, when he repaired to the first town again and found that his ointment, as he expected, was now in great request; and he continued his route as before, selling every box that he possessed."

There is a story of a Yankee clock-maker's ingenuity that I have not seen in print. He also "made a circuit, having a hundred clocks when he started; they were all very bad, which he well knew; but by 'soft sawder and human natur,' as Sam Slick says, he contrived to sell ninety-nine of them and reserve the last for his intended *'ruse.'* He went to the house where he had sold the first clock and said: 'Well, now, how does your clock go? Very well, I guess.' The answer was as he anticipated: 'No, very bad.' 'Indeed! Well, now, I've found it out at last. You see, I had one clock which was I know a bad one, and I said to my boy: 'You'll put that clock aside, for it won't do to sell such an article.' Well, the boy didn't mind, and left the clock with the others; and I found out afterwards that it had been sold somewhere. Mighty mad I was, I can tell you, for I'm not a little particular about my credit; so I have asked here and there, everywhere almost, how my clocks went, and they all said that 'they actually regulated the sun.' But I was determined to find out who had the bad clock, and I am most particular glad that I have done it at last. Now, you see I have but one clock left, a very superior article, worth a matter of ten dollars more than the others, and I must give it you in change, and I'll only charge you five dollars difference, as you have been annoyed with the bad article.' The man who had the bad clock thought it better to pay five dollars more to have a good one; so the exchange was made, and then the Yankee, proceeding with the clock, returned to the next house. 'Well, now, how does your clock go? Very well, I guess.' The same answer—the same story repeated

—and another five dollars received in exchange. And thus did he go round, exchanging clock for clock, until he had received an extra five dollars for every one which he had sold."

Logic.—"A Yankee went into the bar of an inn in a country town: 'Pray what's the price of a pint of shrub?' 'Half a dollar,' was the reply of the man at the bar. 'Well, then, give it me.' The shrub was poured out, when the bell rang for dinner. 'Is that your dinner-bell?' 'Yes.' 'What may you charge for dinner?' 'Half a dollar.' 'Well, then, I think I had better not take the shrub, but have some dinner instead.' This was consented to. The Yankee went in, sat down to his dinner, and when it was over, was going out of the door without paying. 'Massa,' said the Negro waiter, 'you not paid for your dinner.' 'I know that; I took the dinner instead of the shrub.' 'But, massa, you not pay for the shrub.' 'Well, I did not have the shrub, did I, you nigger?' said the Yankee, walking away. The Negro scratched his head; he knew that something was wrong, as he had got no money; but he could not make it out till the Yankee was out of sight."

I do not think that *democracy* is marked upon the features of the lower classes in the United States; there is no arrogant bearing in them, as might be supposed from the despotism of the majority; on the contrary, I should say that their lower classes are much more civil than our own. I had a *slap* of equality on my first landing at New York: I had hired a truckman to take up my luggage from the wharf; I went ahead, and missed him when I came to the corner of the street where I had engaged apartments, and was looking round for him in one direction when I was saluted with a slap on the shoulder, which was certainly given with good-will. I turned and beheld my carman, who had taken the liberty to draw my attention in this forcible manner. He was a man of few words; he pointed to his truck where it stood with the baggage, and then went on.

This civil bearing is peculiar, as when they are excited by politics, or other causes, they are most insolent and overbearing. In his usual demeanour, the citizen born is quiet and obliging. The insolence you meet with is chiefly from the emigrant classes. I have before observed that the Americans are a good-tempered people; and to this good temper I ascribe their civil bearing. But why are they good-tempered? It appears to me to be one of the few virtues springing from democracy. When the grades of society are distinct, as they are in the older institutions, when difference of rank is acknowledged and submitted to without murmur, it is evident that if people are obliged to control their tempers in presence of their superiors or equals, they can also yield to them with their inferiors; and it is this yielding to our tempers which enables them to master us. But under institutions where all are equal, where no one admits the superiority of another, even if he really be so, where the man with the spade in his hand will beard the millionaire, and where you are compelled to submit to the caprice and insolence of a domestic or lose his services, it is evident that every man must from boyhood have learnt to control his temper, as no ebullition will be submitted to, or unfollowed by its consequences. I consider that it is this habitual control, forced upon the Americans by the nature of their institutions, which occasions them to be so good-tempered, when not in a state of excitement. The Americans are in one point, as a mob, very much like the English: make them laugh, and they forget all their animosity immediately.

One of the most singular points about the lower classes in America is that they will call themselves ladies and gentlemen and yet refuse their titles to their superiors. . . . I bought one of the small newspapers just as I was setting off in a steamboat from New York to Albany. The boy had no change and went to fetch it. He did not come back himself, but another party made his appearance. "Are you the *man* who bought the newspaper?" "Yes," replied I. "The young *gentleman* who sold it to you has sent me to pay you four cents."

A gentleman was travelling with his wife, they had stopped at an inn, and during the gentleman's momentary absence the lady was taken ill. The lady, wishing for her husband, a man very good-naturedly went to find him, and when he had succeeded, he addressed him: "I say, Mister, your *woman* wants you; but I told the *young lady of the house* to fetch her a glass of water."

There was no insolence intended in this; it is a peculiarity to be accounted for by their love of title and distinction.

It is singular to observe human nature peeping out in the Americans, and how tacitly they acknowledge by their conduct how uncomfortable a feeling there is in perfect equality. The respect they pay to a title is much greater than that which is paid to it in England, and naturally so; we set a higher value upon that which we *cannot* obtain. I have been often amused at the variance on this point between their words and their feelings, which is shown in their eagerness for rank of some sort among themselves. Every man who has served in the militia carries his title until the day of his death. There is no end to generals, and colonels, and judges; they keep taverns and grog shops, especially in the western states; indeed, there are very few who have not brevet rank of some kind; and I, being only a captain, was looked upon as a very small personage, so far as rank went. An Englishman, who was living in the state of New York, had sent to have the chimney of his house raised. The morning afterwards he saw a labourer mixing mortar before the door. "Well," said the Englishman, "when is the chimney to be finished?" "I'm sure I don't know; you had better ask the colonel." "The colonel? What colonel?" "Why, I reckon that's the colonel upon the top of the house, working away at the chimney."

After all, this fondness for rank, even in a democracy, is very natural, and the Americans have a precedent for it. His Satanic Majesty was the first democrat in heaven, but as soon as he was dismissed to his abode below, if Milton be correct, he assumed his title. . . .

The Americans possess courage, presence of mind, perseverance, and energy, but these may be considered rather as endowments than as virtues. They are propelling powers which will advance them as a people and, were they regulated and tempered by religious and moral feeling, would make them great and good, but without these adjuncts they can only become great and vicious.

I have observed in my preface that the virtues and vices of a nation are to be traced to the form of government, the climate, and circumstances, and it will be easy to show that to the above may be ascribed much of the merit as well as the demerits of the people of the United States.

In the first place, I consider the example set by the government as most injurious: as I shall hereafter prove, it is insatiable in its ambition, regardless of its faith, and corrupt to the highest degree. This example I consider as the first cause of the demoralization of the Americans. The errors incident to the voluntary system of religion are the second: the power of the clergy is destroyed, and the tyranny of the laity has produced the effect of the outward form having been substituted for the real feeling, and hypocrisy has been but too often substituted for religion.

To the evil of bad example from the government is super-added the natural tendency of a democratic form of government to excite ambition without having the power to gratify it morally or virtuously; and the debasing influence of the pursuit of gain is everywhere apparent. It shows itself in the fact that money is in America everything, and everything else nothing; it is the only sure possession, for character can at any time be taken from you, and therefore becomes less valuable than in other countries, except so far as mercantile transactions are concerned. . . .

I have before observed that whatever society permits, men will do and not consider to be wrong, and if the government considers a breach of trust towards it as not of any importance, and defaulters are permitted to escape, it will of course become no crime in the eyes of the majority. . . .

Such is unfortunately the case at present; it may be said to have commenced with the Jackson dynasty, and it is but a few years since this dreadful demoralization has become so apparent and so shamelessly avowed. . . .

It may indeed be fairly said that nothing is disgraceful with the majority in America, which the law cannot lay hold of. You are either in or out of the penitentiary; if once in, you are lost forever, but keep out and you are as good as your neighbour. Now one thing is certain, that where honesty is absolutely necessary, honesty is to be found, as, for example, among the New York merchants, who are, as a body, highly honourable men. When, therefore, the Americans will have moral courage sufficient to drive away vice and not allow virtue to be in bondage, as she at present is, the morals of society will be instantly restored—and how and when will this be effected? I have said that the people of the United States, at the time of the Declaration of Independence, were perhaps the most moral people existing, and I now assert that they are the least so; to what cause can this change be ascribed? Certainly not wholly to the spirit of gain, for it exists everywhere, although perhaps nowhere so strongly developed as it is under a form of government which admits of no other claim to superiority. I consider that it arises from the total extinction, or if not extinction, absolute bondage, of the aristocracy of the country, both politically as well as socially. There was an aristocracy at the time of the independence—not an aristocracy of title, but a much superior one: an aristocracy of great, powerful, and leading men, who were looked up to and imitated; there was, politically speaking, an aristocracy in the Senate, which was elected by those who were then independent of the popular will; but although a portion of it remains, it may be said to have been almost altogether smothered, and in society it no longer exists. It is the want of this aristocracy that has so lowered the standard of morals in America, and it is the revival of it that must restore to the people of the United States the morality they have lost. The loss of the aristocracy has sunk the republic into a democracy; the renewal of it will again restore them to their former condition. Let not the Americans start at this idea. An aristocracy is not only not incompatible, but absolutely necessary for the duration of a democratic form of government. It is the third estate, so necessary to preserve the balance of power between the executive and the people, and which has unfortunately disappeared. An aristocracy is as necessary for the morals as for the government of a nation. Society must have a head to lead it, and without that head there will be no fixed standard of morality, and things must remain in the chaotic state in which they are at present.

Some author has described the English nation as resembling their own beer—froth at the top, dregs at the bottom, and in the middle excellent. There is point in this observation, and it has been received without criticism and quoted without contradiction, but it is in itself false; it may be said that the facts are directly the reverse, there being more morality among the lower class than in the middling, and still more in the higher than in the lower. We have been designated as a nation of shopkeepers, a term certainly more applicable to the Americans, where all are engaged in commerce and the pursuit of gain, and who have no distinctions or hereditary titles. Trade demoralizes; there are so many petty arts and frauds necessary to be resorted to by every class in trade, to enable them to compete with each other; so many lies told, as a matter of business, to tempt a purchaser, that almost insensibly and by degrees the shopkeeper becomes dishonest. These demoralizing practices must be resorted to, even by those who would fain avoid them, or they have no chance of competing with their rivals in business. It is not the honest tradesman who makes a rapid fortune; indeed, it is doubtful whether he could carry on his business; and yet, from assuetude and not being taxed with dishonesty, the shopkeeper scarcely ever feels that he is dishonest. Now, this is the worst state of demoralization, where you are blind to your errors and conscience is never awakened, and in this state may be considered, with few exceptions, every class of traders, whether in England, America, or elsewhere.

Among the lower classes, the morals of the manufacturing districts and of the frequenters of cities will naturally be at a low ebb, for men when closely packed demoralize each other; but if we examine the agricultural classes, which are by far the most numerous, we shall find that there is much virtue and goodness in the humble cottage; we shall there find a piety and resignation, honesty, industry, and content more universal than would be imagined, and the Bible pored over, instead of the day-book or ledger. . . .

When you allow *your* aristocracy to take the reins, you will be better governed, and your morals will improve by example. What is the situation of America at present? The aristocracy of the country are either in retirement or have migrated, and if the power of the majority should continue as it now does its despotic rule, you will have still further emigration. At present there are many hundreds of Americans who have retired to the old continent, that they may receive that return for their wealth which they cannot in their own country; and if not flattered, they are at least not insulted and degraded. . . .

This is the fact; and the wealth of America increases every day, so will those who possess it swarm off as fast as they can to other countries, if there is not a change in the present society and a return to something like order and rank. Who would remain in a country where there is no freedom of thought or action, and where you cannot even spend your money as you please? Mr. Butler the other day built a house at Philadelphia with a *porte-cochère*, and the consequence was that they called him an aristocrat and would not vote for him. In short, will enlightened and refined people live to be dictated to by a savage and ignorant majority, who will neither allow your character nor your domestic privacy to be safe!

The Americans, in their fear of their institutions giving way, and their careful guard against any encroachments upon the liberty of the people, have fallen into the error of sacrificing the most virtuous portion of the community and driving a large portion of them out of the country. This will eventually be found to be a serious evil; absenteeism will daily increase, and will be as sorely felt as it is in Ireland at the present hour. The Americans used to tell me with exultation that they never could have an aristocracy in their country, from the law of entail having been abolished. They often asserted, and with some truth, that in that country property never accumulated beyond two generations and that the grandson of a *millionaire* was *invariably* a pauper. This they ascribe to the working of their institutions, and argue that it will *always* be impossible for any family to be raised above the mass by a descent of property. Now the very circumstance of this having been invariably the case induces me to look for the real cause of it, as there is none to be found in their institutions why all the grandsons of *millionaires* should be paupers. It is not owing to their institutions, but to moral causes, which, although they have existed until now, will not exist forever. In the principal and wealthiest cities in the Union, it is difficult to spend more than twelve or fifteen thousand dollars per annum, as with such an expenditure you are on a par with the highest, and you can be no more. What is the consequence? A young American succeeds to fifty or sixty thousand dollars a year, the surplus is useless to him; there is no one to vie with—no one who can reciprocate—he must stand alone. He naturally feels careless about what he finds to be of no use to him. Again, all his friends and acquaintances are actively employed during the whole of the day in their several occupations; he is a man of leisure and must either remain alone or associate with other men of leisure; and who are the majority of men of leisure in the towns of the United States? Blacklegs of genteel exterior and fashionable appearance, with whom he associates, into whose snares he falls, and to whom he eventually loses property about which he is indifferent. To be an idle man when everybody else is busy is not only a great unhappiness, but a situation of great peril. Had the sons of *millionaires,* who remained in the states and left their children paupers, come over to the old continent, as many have done, they would have stood a better chance of retaining their property.

All I can say is that if they cannot have an aristocracy, the worse for them; I am not of the opinion that they will not have one, . . . I grant that no single people has by its own free will created an aristocracy, but circumstances will make one in spite of the people; and if there is no aristocracy who have a power to check, a despotism may be the evil arising from the want of it. At present America is thinly peopled, but let them look forward to the time when the population shall become denser; what will then be the effect? Why, a division between the rich and the poor will naturally take place; and what is that but the foundation if not the formation of an aristocracy? An American cannot entail his estate, but he can leave the whole of it to his eldest son if he pleases; and, in a few years, the lands which have been purchased for a trifle will become the foundation of noble fortunes. . . .

There is, therefore, no want of preparation for an aristocracy in America, and, although at present the rich are so much in the minority that they cannot coalesce, such will not be the case, perhaps, in twenty or thirty years; they have but to rally and make a stand when they become more numerous and powerful, and they have every chance of success. The fact is that an aristocracy is absolutely necessary for America, both politically and morally, if the Americans wish their institutions to hold together, for if some stop is not put to the rapidly advancing power of the people, anarchy must be the result. I do not mean an aristocracy of title; I mean such an aristocracy of talent and power which wealth will give—an aristocracy which shall lead society and purify it. How is this to be obtained in a democracy?—simply by purchase. In a country where the suffrage is confined to certain classes, as in England, such purchase is not to be obtained, as the people who have the right of suffrage are not poor enough to be bought; but in a country like America, where the suffrage is universal, the people will eventually sell their birth-right; and if by such means an aristocratical government is elected, it will be able to amend the Constitution and pass what laws it pleases. This may appear visionary, but it has been proved already that it can be done, and if it can be done now, how much more easily will it be accomplished when the population has quadrupled and the division commences between the rich and the poor. I say it has been done already, for it was done at the last New York election. The democratic party made sure of success: but a large sum of money was brought into play, and the whole of the *committees* of the democratic party were bought over, and the Whigs carried the day.

The greatest security for the duration of the present institutions of the United States is the establishment of an aristocracy. It is the third power which was intended to act, but which has been destroyed and is now wanting. Let the Senate be aristocratical—let the Congress be partially so; and then what would be the American government of President, Senate, and Congress but *mutato nomine,* kings, Lords, and Commons? . . .

The Americans are more ambitious of birth and aristocracy than any other nation, which is very natural, if it were only from the simple fact that we always most desire what is out of our reach. Since the Americans have come over in such numbers to this country, our Herald's Office has actually been *besieged* by them, in their anxiety to take out the arms and achievements of their presumed forefathers; this is also very natural and proper, although it may be at variance with their institutions. The determination to have an aristocracy in America gains head every day; a conflict must ensue when the increase of wealth in the country adds sufficiently to the strength of the party. . . .

CHAPTER XLIX

Government

I t is not my intention to enter into a lengthened examination of the American form of government. I have said that, as a government, "with all its imperfections, it is the best suited to *the present condition of America, in so far as* it is the one under which the country has made, and will continue to make, the most rapid strides"; but I have not said that it was a better form of government than others. Its very weakness is favourable to the advance of the country; it may be compared to a vessel which, from her masts not being wedged, and her timbers being loose, sails faster than one more securely fastened. Considered merely as governments for the preservation of order and the equalization of pressure upon the people, I believe that few governments are bad, as there are always some correcting influences, moral or otherwise, which strengthen those portions which are the weakest. . . .

It is so far complicated that a variety of wheels are at work; but it is not complicated, from the circumstance that the *same principle* prevails throughout, from the Township to the Federal Head, and that it is put in motion by one great and universal propelling power. It may be compared to a cotton-thread manufactory, in which thousands and thousands of reels and spindles are all at work, the labour of so many smaller reels turned over to larger, which in their turn yield up their produce, until the whole is collected into one mass. The principle of the American government is good; the power that puts it in motion is enormous, and therefore, like the complicated machinery I have compared it to, it requires constant attention, and proper regulation of the propelling power, that it may not become out of order. The propelling power is the sovereignty of the people, otherwise the will of the majority. The motion of all propelling powers must be regulated by a fly-wheel, or corrective check; if not, the motion will gradually accelerate, until the machinery is destroyed by the increase of friction. But there are other causes by which the machinery may be deranged, as, although the smaller portions of the machine, if defective, may at any time be taken out and repaired without its being necessary for the machinery to stop, yet if the larger wheels are by chance thrown out of their equilibrium, the machinery may be destroyed just as it would be by a too rapid motion, occasioned by the excess of propelling power. Further, there are external causes which may endanger it; and the machine may be thrown out of its level by a convulsion, or shock, which will cause it to cease working, if even it does not break it into fragments.

Now, the dangers which *threaten* the United States are the Federal government being still weaker than it is at present, or its becoming, as it may from circumstances, too powerful.

The *present* situation of the American government is that the fly-wheel, or regulator of the propelling power (that is to say the aristocracy, or power of the Senate), has been nearly destroyed, and the consequences are that the motion is at this moment too much accelerated and threatens in a few years to increase its rapidity, at the risk of the destruction of the whole machinery.

But, although it will be necessary to point out the weakness of the Federal government, when opposed to the states or the majority, inasmuch as the morality of the people is seriously affected by this weakness, my object is not to enter into the merits of the government of the United States as a *working* government, but to enquire how far the Americans are correct in their boast of its being a model for other countries.

Let us consider what is the best form of government. Certainly that which most contributes to security of life and property, and renders those happy and moral who are submitted to it. This I believe will be generally acknowledged, and it is upon these grounds that the government of the United States must be tested. They abjured our monarchy, and left their country for a distant land, to obtain *freedom.* They railed at the vices and imperfections of continental rule, and proposed to themselves a government which should be perfect, under which every man should have his due weight in the representation, and prove to the world that a people could govern themselves. Disgusted with the immorality of the age and the disregard to religion, they anticipated an amendment in the state of society. This new, and supposed perfect, machinery has been working for upwards of sixty years, and let us now examine how far the theory has been supported and borne out by the practical result.

I must first remind the reader that I have already shewn the weakness of the Federal government upon one most important point, which is that there is not sufficient security for person and property. When such is the case, there cannot be that adequate punishment for vice so necessary to uphold the morals of a people. I will now proceed to prove the weakness of the Federal government whenever it has to combat with the several states, or with the will of the majority.

It will be perceived, by an examination into the Constitution of the United States, that the states have reserved for themselves all the real power, and that the Federal Union exists but upon their sufferance. Each state still insists upon its right to withdraw itself from the Union whenever it pleases, and the consequence of this right is that, in every conflict with a state, the Federal government has invariably to succumb. . . .

When the people are thus above the law, it is of very little consequence whether the law is more or less weak; at present the Federal government is a mere cypher when opposed by the majority. Have, then, the Americans improved upon us in this point? It is generally admitted that a strong and vigorous government, which can act when it is necessary to restrain the passions of men under excitement, is most favourable to social order and happiness; but, on the contrary, when the dormant power of the executive should be brought into action, all that the Federal government can do is to become a passive spectator or a disregarded suppliant.

The next question to be examined into is, has this government of the United States set an example of honour, good faith, and moral principle to those who are subjected to it? Has it, by so behaving, acted favourably upon the morals of the people and corrected the vices and errors of the monarchical institutions which the Americans hold up to such detestation?

The Americans may be said to have had, till within the last twenty years, little or no relation with other countries. They have had few treaties to make, and very little diplomatic arrangements with the old continent. But even if they had had, they must not be judged by them; a certain degree of national honour is necessary to every nation, if they would have the respect of others, and a dread of the consequences would always compel them to adhere to any treaty made with great and powerful countries. The question is, has the Federal government adhered to its treaties and promises made with and to those who have been too weak to defend themselves? Has it not repeatedly, in the short period of their existence as a nation, violated the national honour whenever without being in fear of retaliation or exposure it has been able to do so. Let this question be answered by an examination into their conduct towards the unhappy Indians, who, to use their own expression, are "now melting away like snow before the white men." We are not to estimate the morality of a government by its strict adherence to its compacts with the powerful, but by its strict moral sense of justice towards the weak and defenceless; and it should be borne in mind that one example of a breach of faith on the part of a democratic government is more injurious to the morals of the people under that government than a thousand instances of breach of faith which may occur in society; for a people who have no aristocracy to set the example must naturally look to the conduct of their rulers and to their decisions as a standard for their guidance. To enumerate the multiplied breaches of faith towards the Indians would swell out this work to an extra volume. . . .

Indeed, I have reason to believe that the major portion of the land obtained from the Indians has been ceded by parties who had no power to sell it, and the treaties with these parties have been enforced by the Federal government. . . .

The next instance which I shall bring forward to prove the want of principle of the Federal government is its permitting, and it may be said tacitly acquiescing, in the seizure of the province of Texas, and allowing it to be ravished from the Mexican government, with whom they were on terms of amity, but who was unfortunately too weak to help herself. In this instance the American government had no excuse, as it actually had an army on the frontier, and could have compelled the insurgents to go back; but no; it perceived that the Texas [*sic*], if in its hands, or if independent of Mexico, would become a mart for their extra slave population, that it was the finest country in the world for producing cotton, and that it would be an immense addition of valuable territory. . . .

Indeed, it may be boldly asserted that in every measure taken by the Federal government, the moral effect of that measure upon the people has never been thought worthy of a moment's consideration.

We must now examine into one or two other points.

The Americans consider that they are the only people on earth who govern themselves; they assert that *we* have not a free and perfect representation. We will not dispute that point; the question is not what the case in England may be, but what America may have gained. This is certain, that if they have not a free impartial representation, they do *not*, as they suppose, govern themselves. Have they, with universal suffrage, obtained a representation free from bribery and corruption? If they have, they certainly have gained their point; if they have not, they have sacrificed much, and have obtained nothing. . . .

It must be remembered that the struggle in America is for place, not for principle; for whichever party obtains power, their principle of acting is much the same. Occasionally a question of moment will come forward and nearly convulse the Union, but this is very rare; the general course of legislation is in a very narrow compass, and is seldom more than a mere routine of business. With the majority, who lead a party (particularly the one at present in power), the contest is not, therefore, for principle, but, it may almost be said, for bread; and this is one great cause of the virulence accompanying their election struggles. The election of the President is of course the most important. . . . The elections in the large cities are those which next occupy the public attention. I have before stated that at the last election in New York the committees of the opposite party were bought over by the Whigs, and that by this bribery the election was gained; . . .

When I was one day with one of the most influential of the Whig party at New York, he was talking about their success in the contest— "We beat them, sir, literally with their own weapons." "How so," replied I. "Why, sir, we bought over all their bludgeon men at so many dollars a head, and the very sticks intended to be used to keep us from the poll were employed upon the heads of the Locofocos!" So much for *purity of election.*

Another point which is worthy of inquiry is, how far is the government of the United States a cheap government;

that is, not as to the amount of money expended in that country as compared to the amount of money paid in England or France, but cheap as to the work done for the money paid? And, viewing it in this light, I rather think it will be found a very expensive one. It is true that the salaries are low, and the highest officers are the worst paid, but it should be recollected that everybody is paid. The expenses of the Federal government, shown up to the world as a proof of cheap government, is but a portion of the real expenses which are paid by the several states. Thus the government will promulgate to the world that they have a surplus revenue of so many millions, but at the same time it will be found that the states themselves are borrowing money and are deeply in debt. The money that disappears is enormous; I never could understand what has become of the boasted surplus revenue which was lodged in the pet banks, as they were termed. . . . To enter into any estimate of expense would be impossible; all I assert is that there is a much greater waste of public money in the United States than in other countries, and that for the work done they pay very dearly.

The Americans, and with justice, hold up Washington as one of the first of men; if so, why will they not pay attention to his opinions? Because the *first* of men must not interfere with their prejudices, or, if he does, he immediately in their eyes becomes the *last*. Nevertheless, Washington proved his ability when he made the following observation, in his letter to Chief Justice Jay, dated 10th of March, 1787; even at that early period he perceived that the institutions of America, although at the time much less democratical than at present, would not stand. Hear the words of Washington, for they were a *prophecy*—

> Among men of reflection, few will be found, I believe, who are not beginning to think that our system is better in *theory* than in *practice;* and that, notwithstanding the boasted virtue of America, it is more than probable that we shall exhibit the last melancholy proof,

that mankind are incompetent to their own government
without the means of coercion in the sovereign.

Now, if you were to put this extract into the hands of
an American, his admiration of Washington would immediately fall down below Zero, and in all probability he would
say, as they do of poor Captain Lawrence— "Why, sir,
Washington was a great man, but great men have their
failings. I guess he wrote that letter *after dinner*." . . .

I do not intend to deny the right of the people to claim
an extension of their privileges, in proportion as they rise
by education to the right of governing themselves; unfortunately these privileges have been given, or taken, previous
to their being qualified. A republic is certainly, in theory,
the most just form of government, but, up to the present
day, history has proved that no people have been prepared
to receive it.

That there is something very imposing in the present
rapid advance of the United States, I grant, but this grandeur is not ascribed by the Americans to its true source:
it is the magnificent and extended country, not their government and institutions, which has been the cause of their
prosperity. The Americans think otherwise, and, as I have
before observed, they are happy in their own delusions—
they do not make a distinction between what they have
gained by their country and what they have gained by their
institutions. Everything is on a vast and magnificent scale,
which at first startles you; but if you examine closely and
reflect, you are convinced that there is at present more
show than substance, and that the Americans are actually
existing (and until they have sufficient labourers to sow
and reap, and gather up the riches of the land, must continue to exist) upon the credit and capital of England.

The American republic was commenced very differently from any other, and with what were real advantages,
if she had not been too ambitious and too precipitate in
seizing upon them. A republic has generally been considered the most primitive form of rule; it is, on the contrary,

the very last pitch of refinement in government, and the cause of its failure up to the present has been that no people have as yet been sufficiently enlightened to govern themselves. Republics, generally speaking, have at their commencement been confined to small portions of territory having been formed by the extension of townships after the inhabitants had become wealthy and ambitious. In America, on the contrary, the republic commenced with unbounded territory—a vast field for ambition and enterprise that has acted as a safety-valve to carry off the excess of disappointed ambition, which, like steam, is continually generating under such a form of government. And, certainly, if ever a people were in a situation, as far as education, knowledge, precepts and lessons for guidance and purity of manners could enable them to govern themselves, those were so who first established the American independence.

Fifty years have passed away, and the present state of America I have already shown. From purity of manners, her moral code has sunk below that of most other nations. She has attempted to govern herself—she is dictated to by the worst of tyrannies. She has planted the tree of liberty; instead of its flourishing, she has neither freedom of speech nor of action. She has railed against the vices of monarchical forms of government, and every vice against which she has raised up her voice is still more prevalent under her own. She has cried out against corruption—she is still more corrupt; against bribery—her people are to be bought and sold; against tyranny—she is in fetters. She has proved to the world that, with every advantage on her side, the attempt at a republic has been a miserable failure, and that the time is not yet come when mankind can govern themselves. Will it ever come? In my opinion, never!

Although the horizon may be clear at present, yet I consider that the prospect of the United States is anything but cheering. It is true that for a time the states may hold together, that they may each year rapidly increase in prosperity and power, but each year will also add to their de-moralization and to their danger. It is impossible to say from what quarter of the compass the clouds may first rise, or which of the several dangers that threaten them they will have first to meet and oppose by their energies. At present, the people, or majority, have an undue power, which will yearly increase, and their despotism will be more severe in proportion. If they sell their birthright (which they will not do until the population is much increased, and the higher classes are sufficiently wealthy to purchase, although their freedom will be lost), they will have a better chance of happiness and social order. But a protracted war would be the most fatal to their institutions, as it would, in all probability, end in the dismemberment of the Union, and the wresting of their power from the people by the bayonets of a dictator.

The removal of the power and population to the west, the rapid increase of the coloured population, are other causes of alarms and dread; but, allowing that all these dangers are steered clear of, there is one (a more remote one indeed, but more certain) from which it has no escape —that is, the period when, from the increase of population, the division shall take place between the poor and the rich, which no law against entail will ever prevent, and which must be fatal to a democracy. . . .

I think I can show that the vices of the Americans are chiefly to be attributed to their present form of government.

The example of the Executive is most injurious. It is insatiable in its ambition, regardless of its faith, corrupt in the highest degree: never legislating for morality, but always for expediency. This is the first cause of the low stand-ard of morals; the second is the want of an aristocracy, to set an example and give the tone to society. These are followed by the errors incident to the voluntary system of religion and a democratical education. To these must be super-added the want of moral courage, arising from the dread of public opinion, and the natural tendency of a demo-

cratic form of government to excite the spirit of gain, as
the main-spring of action, and the *summum bonum* of existence. . . .

All the above evils may be traced to the nature of their
institutions; and I hold it as an axiom that the chief end
of government is the happiness, social order, and morality
of the people; that no government, however perfect in
theory, can be *good* which in practice *demoralizes those
who are subjected to it*. Never was there a nation which
commenced with brighter prospects; the experiment has
been made and it has failed; this is not their fault. They
still retain all the qualities to constitute a great nation, and
a great nation, or assemblage of nations, they will eventually
become. At present, all is hidden in a futurity much too
deep for any human eye to penetrate; they progress fast in
wealth and power, and as their weight increases, so will
their speed be accelerated, until their own rapid motion will
occasion them to split into fragments, each fragment sufficiently large to compose a nation of itself. What may be
the eventual result of this convulsion, what may be the destruction, the loss of life, the chaotic scenes of strife and
contention, before the portions may again be restored to
order under new institutions, it is as impossible to foresee
as it is to decide upon the period at which it may take place;
but one thing is certain, that come it will, and that every
hour of increase of greatness and prosperity only adds to
the more rapid approach of the danger, and to the important
lesson which the world will receive.

I have not written this book for the Americans; they
have hardly entered my thoughts during the whole time
that I have been employed upon it, and I am perfectly
indifferent either to their censure or their praise. I went
over to America well-inclined towards the people and anxious to ascertain the truth among so many conflicting opinions. I did expect to find them a people more virtuous and
moral than our own, but I confess on other points I had
formed no opinions; the results of my observations I have
now laid before the English public, for whom only they have

been written down. Within these last few years, that is, since the passing of the Reform Bill, we have made rapid strides towards democracy, and the cry of the multitude is still for more power, which our present rulers appear but too willing to give them. I consider that the people of England have already as much power as is consistent with their happiness and with true liberty, and that any increase of privilege would be detrimental to both. My object in writing these pages is to point out the effects of a democracy upon the morals, the happiness, and the due apportionment of liberty to all classes; to show that if, in the balance of rights and privileges, the scale should turn on one side or the other, as it invariably must in this world, how much safer it is, how much more equitable I may add, it is that it should preponderate in favour of the intelligent and enlightened portion of the nation. I wish that the contents of these pages may render those who are led away by generous feelings, and abstract ideas of right, to pause before they consent to grant to those below them what may appear to be a boon, but will in reality prove a source of misery and danger to all parties—that they may confirm the opinions of those who are wavering and support those who have true ideas as to the nature of government. If I have succeeded in the most trifling degree in effecting these ends, which I consider vitally important to the welfare of this country— if I have any way assisted the cause of Conservatism—I am content, and shall consider that my time and labour have not been thrown away.

Bibliography

Adair, James: *History of the American Indians*. London, 1775.

Alexander, De Alva S.: *A Political History of the State of New York (1774–1884)*. 3 vols. New York: Henry Holt; 1906–09.

Anonymous: "Transatlantic Travelling." *Dublin Review*, Vol. XIV (November 1839), pp. 399–429.

Bader, A. L.: "The Gallant Captain and Brother Jonathan." *The Colophon*, Vol. II, New Series (Autumn 1936).

Becker, Carl L.: *The Declaration of Independence*. New York: Vintage Books; 1958.

Boas, Franz, et al.: *General Anthropology*. New York: D. C. Heath and Co.; 1938.

Boudinot, Elias: *A Star in the West*. Trenton, N.J., 1816.

Buley, R. Carlyle: *The Old Northwest*. Bloomington, Ind.: Indiana University Press; 1951.

Butler, Frances Kemble: *Journal*. Philadelphia, 1835.

Carey, Henry Charles: *Essay on the Rate of Wages*. Philadelphia, 1835.

———: *Principles of Political Economy*. Philadelphia, 1837–40.

Collier, John: *Indians of the Americas*. New York: Mentor Books; 1947.

Colton, Calvin: *A Voice from America to England*. London, 1839.

Conrad, Joseph: *Notes on Life and Letters*. Garden City, N.Y.: Doubleday, Page and Co.; 1921.

Cooper, James Fenimore: *England, with Sketches of Society in the Metropolis*. London, 1837.

———: *Excursions in Switzerland*. London, 1836.

Decelles, Alfred D.: *Papineau.* Oxford: Oxford University Press; 1926.

————: *The "Patriotes" of '37.* Toronto: Glasgow, Brook and Co.; 1916.

Dewey, Davis Rich: *Financial History of the United States.* New York: Longmans, Green and Co.; 1903.

Dorfman, Joseph: *The Economic Mind in American Civilization, 1606–1865.* New York: Viking Press; 1946.

Dow, E. F.: "A Portrait of the Millennial Church of the Shakers." *University of Maine Studies,* Vol. XIX, Second Series (1931).

Fillmore, Millard: "Sketch of Joseph Clary," in the "Millard Fillmore Papers." *Publications of the Buffalo Historical Society,* Vol. XI (1907).

Forester, C. S.: *The Age of Fighting Sail.* New York: Doubleday and Co.; 1956.

Greenleaf, E. B.: *Ballads and Sea Songs of Newfoundland.* Cambridge, Mass.: Harvard University Press; 1933.

Haliburton, Thomas Chandler: *The Clockmaker; or the Sayings and Doings of Samuel Slick of Slicksville.* London, 1837–40.

Hall, Basil: *Travels in North America in the Years 1827 and 1828.* Philadelphia, 1829.

Hamilton, Thomas: *Men and Manners in America.* Endinburgh, 1833.

Hannay, David: *Life of Frederick Marryat.* London, 1889.

Hobhouse, Christopher: *1851 and the Crystal Palace.* London: Transatlantic Arts; 1950.

Hone, Philip: *The Diary of Philip Hone 1828–1851.* Edited by Bayard Tuckerman. New York: Dodd, Mead and Co.; 1889.

Hornblow, Arthur: *A History of the Theatre in America.* Philadelphia: J. B. Lippincott Co.; 1919.

Hughes, Glenn: *A History of the American Theatre, 1700–1950.* New York: Samuel French; 1951.

Ingelton, Geoffrey C.: *True Patriots All; or, News from Early Australia.* Sydney, Australia: Angus and Robertson; 1952.

Irving, Theodore: *The Conquest of Florida by Hernan de Soto.* Philadelphia, 1835.

Jackman, Sydney W.: *Galloping Head, a Biography of Sir Francis Bond Head.* London: Phoenix House; 1958.

Jenkins, John S.: *History of Political Parties in the State of New York.* Auburn, N.Y.: Alden and Parsons; 1849.

Johnson, Allen, Ed.: *Dictionary of American Biography.* New York: Charles Scribner's Sons; 1928.

Kilbourn, William: *The Firebrand: William Lyon Mackenzie and the Rebellion in Upper Canada.* Toronto: Clarke Irwin and Co.; 1956.

Leach, Douglas: *Flintlock and Tomahawk.* New York: Macmillan and Co.; 1958.

Lloyd, Christopher: *Captain Marryat and the Old Navy.* London: Longmans, Green and Co.; 1939.

Lower, A. R. M.: *Canadians in the Making.* Toronto: Longmans, Green and Co.; 1958.

Marry-it, Captain, *pseud.: Lie-ary on America! With Yarns on Its Institutions.* Boston, 1840.

Marryat, Florence: *Life and Letters of Captain Marryat.* London, 1872.

Marryat, Frederick: *A Diary in America, with Remarks on Its Institutions.* New York, 1839.

———: *Second Series of a Diary in America, with Remarks on Its Institutions.* Philadelphia, 1840.

———: *A Diary in America.* Edited by J. Zanger. Bloomington, Ind.: Indiana University Press; 1960.

———: *Complete Works.* Edited by W. L. Courtney. Boston: Little, Brown and Co.; 1904.

Martineau, Harriet: *Harriet Martineau's Autobiography.* Edited by M. W. Chapman. Boston: Houghton, Mifflin Co.; 1877.

Martineau, Harriet: *Retrospect of Western Travel.* London, 1838.

——: *Society in America.* London, 1837.

McInnis, Edgar: *Canada, a Political and Social History.* New York: Rinehart and Co.; 1959.

Meyer, Jacob C.: *Church and State in Massachusetts from 1740–1833.* Cleveland, Ohio; Western Reserve University Press; 1930.

Meyers, Marvin: *The Jacksonian Persuasion.* Stanford: Stanford University Press; 1957.

Munsell, J.: *Collections on the History of Albany.* Albany, 1867.

Odell, George: *Annals of the New York Stage.* New York: Columbia University Press; 1927–49.

Peckham, Howard H.: *Pontiac and the Indian Uprising.* Princeton: Princeton University Press; 1947.

Pierson, George W.: *Tocqueville and Beaumont in America.* New York: Oxford University Press; 1938.

Pitman, Emnia R.: *George Muller and Andrew Reed.* London, 1885.

Pontoppidon, Erik: *The Natural History of Norway.* London, 1755.

Potter, Commander E. B.: *The United States and World Sea Power.* Englewood Cliffs, N.J.: Prentice-Hall, Inc.; 1955.

Reed, Andrew: *Visit to the American Churches by the Deputation from the Congregational Union of England.* London, no date.

Reed, A., and Reed, Charles: *Memoirs of the Life and Philanthropic Labours of Andrew Reed, D.D.* London, 1867.

Reniers, Perceval: *The Springs of Virginia.* Chapel Hill, N.C.: University of North Carolina Press; 1941.

Rotundo, Joseph: "Eliphalet Nott." *New York History,* Vol. XIII, No. 2 (April 1932).

Sanderson, John: *Sketches of Paris: in Familiar Letters to His Friends.* Philadelphia, 1838.

Schlesinger, Arthur M., Jr.: *The Age of Jackson*. Boston: Little, Brown and Co.; 1946.

Scott, Walter: *The Pirate*. Boston: Dana, Estes and Co.; 1893.

Stephen, Leslie, Ed.: *Dictionary of National Biography*. London: Macmillan Co.; 1885.

Strong, George Templeton: *The Diary of George Templeton Strong*. Edited by Allan Nevins and Milton H. Thomas. New York: Macmillan Co.; 1952.

Thwaites, Reuben G.: "An English Officer's Description of Wisconsin in 1837." *Wisconsin Historical Collections*, Vol. XIV (1898).

Tocqueville, Alexis de: *Democracy in America*. London, 1835–40.

———: *Democracy in America*. New York: Vintage Books; 1954.

Trollope, Frances: *Domestic Manners of the Americans*. Edited by Donald Smalley. New York: Alfred A. Knopf; 1949.

Turner, A. J.: "The History of Fort Winnebago." *Wisconsin Historical Collections*, Vol. XIV (1898).

Walker, Williston: *A History of the Congregational Churches in the United States*. New York: Christian Literature Co.; 1894.

Wallace, Irving: *The Fabulous Showman*. New York: Alfred A. Knopf; 1959.

Wallace, W. S., Ed.: *Encyclopedia of Canada*. Toronto: University Associates of Canada; 1935.

Warner, Oliver: *Captain Marryat*. New York: Macmillan Co.; 1953.

Webb, Robert K.: *Harriet Martineau, a Radical Victorian*. New York: Columbia University Press; 1960.

Wish, Harvey: *Society and Thought in Early America*. New York: Longmans, Green and Co., 1950.

Woolf, Virginia: *The Captain's Death Bed and Other Essays*. New York: Harcourt, Brace and Co.; 1950.

Index

i

A NOTE ON THE TYPE

THE TEXT of this book was set on the Linotype in a new face called PRIMER, designed by RUDOLPH RUZICKA, earlier responsible for the design of Fairfield and Fairfield Medium, Linotype faces whose virtues have for some time now been accorded wide recognition. The complete range of sizes of Primer was first made available in 1954, although the pilot size of 12 point was ready as early as 1951. The design of the face makes general reference to Linotype Century (long a serviceable type, totally lacking in manner or frills of any kind) but brilliantly corrects the characterless quality of that face.

A NOTE ON THE TYPE

THE TEXT of this book was set on the Linotype in a new face called PRIMER, designed by RUDOLPH RUZICKA, earlier responsible for the design of Fairfield and Fairfield Medium, Linotype faces whose virtues have for some time now been accorded wide recognition. The complete range of sizes of Primer was first made available in 1954, although the pilot size of 12 point was ready as early as 1951. The design of the face makes general reference to Linotype Century (long a serviceable type, totally lacking in manner or frills of any kind) but brilliantly corrects the characterless quality of that face.